E
165   Sanford   66-3266
S25   Quest for America, 1810-
1964a   1824

JUL.   2000

Date Due

Quest for America, 1810–1824

DOCUMENTS IN AMERICAN CIVILIZATION SERIES

General Editors:
HENNIG COHEN AND JOHN WILLIAM WARD

QUEST FOR AMERICA
1810–1824

Edited with an Introduction by
Charles L. Sanford

New York University Press
1964

Grateful acknowledgment is made to the following for permission to use excerpts of copyrighted material:

THE BUSINESS HISTORY REVIEW. Jonathan T. Lincoln, "Beginnings of the Machine Age in New England: Documents Relating to the Introduction of the Power Loom," *Bulletin of the Business Historical Society*, XII, pp. 6–13 (October 1933). A letter of Francis C. Lowell to David Greenough, June 9, 1816, pp. 7–8. Reprinted by permission.

COLUMBIA UNIVERSITY PRESS. Benjamin H. B. Latrobe, *Impressions Respecting New Orleans*, edited by Samuel Wilson, Jr. H. M. Pierce Gallagher, *Robert Mills, Architect of the Washington Monument, 1781–1855*. Reprinted by permission.

HARVARD UNIVERSITY PRESS. Kenneth Wiggins Porter, *John Jacob Astor, Business Man*, Vol. I. Reprinted by permission.

THE HISTORICAL SOCIETY OF PENNSYLVANIA. Greville and Dorothy Bathe, *Oliver Evans: A Chronicle of Early American Engineering*. Reprinted by permission.

THE C. V. MOSBY COMPANY. J. S. Meyer, *Life and Letters of Dr. William Beaumont*. Reprinted by permission.

DR. ALLAN NEVINS. *The Diary of John Quincy Adams, 1794–1845*, edited by Allan Nevins. Reprinted by permission.

OXFORD UNIVERSITY PRESS and MRS. FERDINAND LATROBE. Talbot Hamlin, *Benjamin Henry Latrobe*. Reprinted by permission.

UNIVERSITY OF NORTH CAROLINA PRESS. Minnie C. Yarborough, editor, *Reminiscences of William C. Preston, 1794–1860*. Reprinted by permission.

VERMONT HISTORICAL SOCIETY. "The Travel Diary of James Guild," *Vermont Historical Society Proceedings*, new series, Vol. V (1937). Reprinted by permission.

YALE UNIVERSITY PRESS. Washington Irving, "Personalia," in *Tour in Scotland, 1817*, edited by Stanley T. Williams. Reprinted by permission.

This book was first published
in 1964 by Anchor Books.

Introduction

We are always "in transition." Every period of human culture is a formative period, consolidating or intensifying certain tendencies already in existence and releasing new forces which make the future uncertain and different.

Nevertheless, the period 1810–1824 has a special significance. The date 1815, according to a recent thesis, marks an important turning point in American civilization, when the simple, relatively homogeneous, unified and stable agrarian society began to break up and the old certitudes of some two hundred years began to be replaced by the restlessness and insecurity so familiar today.[1]

The documents in this volume, visual as well as verbal, would seem to support such an interpretation. They suggest that the bland, though sometimes bumptious nationalism of the so-called "Era of Good Feelings" masked a regrouping of forces and energies which began to explode toward the end of the period with a prophetic violence. By 1825, the age of competition was at hand; the Virginia dynasty was dead, its demise accompanied by charges of a "corrupt bargain" between Henry Clay and John Quincy Adams for the succession to leadership.

The documents chosen to represent this period are grouped into three main divisions. The first attempts to define the pattern and special quality of national life. The second section contains expressions of national feeling in war and peace, in art, science, political economy, foreign relations, education, and literature. The last section develops themes of dispersion, expansion, and change. A

[1] Rowland Berthoff, "The American Social Order: A Conservative Hypothesis," *American Historical Review*, LXV (1960), pp. 495–514.

unifying motif of the period is a pervasive though often muted sense of cultural conflict between older traditions and new modes of self-expression.

The search for native self-expression grew out of a wide-spread feeling that the American was a new man in a new world with a special destiny to fulfill. This volume, then, records the struggle to embody this feeling in practical achievements different from those of Europe. It also affords an opportunity to evaluate some of the results of this struggle, one of the more important of which was the development of what has been called the "vernacular tradition."

The word "vernacular" suggests, of course, a colloquial manner of speech, but cultural historians have extended its meaning to embrace all unself-conscious democratic folk art as the outward manifestation of what it feels like inwardly to be instinctively, indigenously *American*. Vernacular expression—whether in speech, architecture, household arts, agricultural artifacts, or industrial design—implies, then, an intimate relationship between Americans and their environment. It is distinguished by such qualities as adaptability, flexibility, naturalness, functionalism, and organic form, qualities requiring a sensitive adjustment of thought and feeling to practice by "plain people." Professor Kouwenhoven has attributed its development largely to the impact of machine technology and economy upon an unprecedented social structure. He would regard the Jethro Wood plow (see doc. 91), which utilizes the principle of standard, interchangeable parts, as a particularly fine example of vernacular art.

In this period, however, vernacular art expressed a total cultural struggle to free Americans from inherited European traditions in order to assert the superiority of a natural, relatively uncomplicated way of life over the supposedly effete, artificial civilization of Europe. At this time, at least, the vernacular tradition drew its main source of inspiration from *nature*, from the march of Americans toward the wilderness to establish a fancied

paradise of liberty, prosperity, and public virtue.[2] This
view of the American mission is expounded, for instance,
by a young South Carolinian named Hugh Swinton Legaré
in the first document of this volume, "The Idea of the
Nation."

This document also sums up the main assumptions and
inner contradictions of the period. In the first place, it
takes the form of a Fourth of July oration, though its
fusion of eloquence, learning, and close reasoning raises it
far above the level of that genre, making it perhaps the
most impressive early statement of the American Dream.
The Fourth of July oration—boastful, rhetorical, evangelical, historical, and communal—typified early American nationalism. It was stylistically akin to the revival meeting at
one extreme (doc. 15) and at the other to the "monumental" historical painting and architecture of the period,
as represented by Krimmel's painting of the Fourth of
July in Centre Square (doc. 34) or John Trumbull's national pictures for the Capitol rotunda (doc. 37).

Legaré's rhetoric belongs to the cultivated tradition,
whereas his central intention—to celebrate the uniqueness
of the American people—required perhaps a different style.
The problem may be seen more clearly by contrasting
Legaré's high style with the vernacular idiom of James
Guild (doc. 9), a self-educated Vermont peddler whose
sensibilities were more nearly on a level with most Americans who listened to Fourth of July orations. To be sure,
one spoke for the ideal; the other recorded practical experience without expecting to be heard. But the difference touches on a fundamental contradiction in American
life—or at least a fundamental source of confusion and
ambiguity—that is, a disjunction between the real and the
ideal.

[2] See my study of the American Edenic myth, *The Quest for
Paradise: Europe and the American Moral Imagination* (Ur-
bana: University of Illinois Press, 1961). The most important
study of the vernacular tradition is John A. Kouwenhoven,
Made in America: the Arts in Modern Civilization (Garden
City, N.Y.: Doubleday & Company, 1948).

This division was related to the polarization of American habits of thought and feeling by opposing ways of life. At one extreme was the rude pioneering existence at the edge of the forest, at the other the great cities of Europe, and between, a proud agricultural people who were unable to express their consciousness of self except in terms of the city or the forest, alternately attracted and repelled by both. Thus, Hugh Swinton Legaré, in his oration, simultaneously attacked European tyranny, invoked the spirit of the wilderness to explain America's superior virtues, compared these virtues to those of ancient Greece and Rome, and hailed the progess of civilization which was to despoil the wilderness.

Americans for the most part, however much committed to civilized progress, could not confront the disappearance of the wilderness without nostalgia, anguish, and even, at times, guilt. The troubled conscience of so many American writers from James Fenimore Cooper to William Faulkner has reflected their sense of being dispossessed from an earthly paradise. This source of tension became more acute with the opening up of the West to settlement and with the gradual advent of what we later came to call the Industrial Revolution. The completion of the Cumberland Road and the Erie Canal, breaching the Appalachian barrier, launched the westward movement of large populations, while new means of transportation, communication, and industrial production were being created which would subjugate and transform the entire continent. Within the span of less than a generation, a people accustomed to horseback and horse-drawn vehicles, living sedately in small rural communities, found their lives in some degree accelerated by steam power piped to boats, carriages, and factories.

The dramatic overtones of this transformation are suggested in the juxtaposition of four pictures (docs. 2–4), whose subject matter was vividly present to the consciousness of that generation. Weber's painting of Nootka Sound reminded them of the Lewis and Clark expedition, of Stephen Long's more recent explorations, of John Jacob

Astor's settlement at far Astoria, of a noble, primitive past
and a nobler future. But what they were to become was
already crowding fearfully upon them in the image of a
civilized outpost of Europe, as suggested by Milbert's view
of Boston (doc. 4). In an age of rapid, unprecedented
change, Washington Irving's "Rip Van Winkle" was a representative anecdote. John Quidor's portrayal of the return of Rip Van Winkle (doc. 107) thus evokes bewilderment and nostalgia for a vanishing way of life.

This sense of dislocation as the country moved westward, wrenched out of space-and-time, its old leaders dis-
placed by a cruder type, family ties constantly dissolving
and reforming, the measure and achievement of status becoming more uncertain—all this helps to account for the
great wave of religious revivals throughout this period
(docs. 15–16). Self-appointed prophets of the Lord such
as Lorenzo Dow roamed the countryside, interpreting current events to prove that either the Apocalypse or the
blessed Millennium was at hand and exhorting sinners to
reform before it was too late. Evangelical religion and nationalism reinforced each other in the belief that America
was a chosen country—"holy ground," Legaré said—set
apart from Europe by God for the redemption of mankind.

The connection between national feeling and evangelical religion is made clear in Lorenzo Dow's "Hints on the
Fulfillment of Prophecy" (doc. 16), typical of many such
tracts during the period. These tracts and sermons by
backwoods preachers added to the already well-established
idea of national mission a heightened sense of urgency and
expectation, as if the nation were rushing toward some
grand climax of history, every step along the way to which
must be examined for cosmic imports of good or evil. This
apocalyptic inheritance is largely responsible for a habitual tendency in many Americans, a tendency still evident
today, to live emotionally from crisis to crisis, anxiously
poised, as on tiptoe, to seize from the bright, winged moment some total, glorious fulfillment, but terribly fearful
of plunging, after all, to utter destruction.

Americans as diverse in outlook as Thomas Jefferson, Washington Irving, and Peter Cartwright saw an almost apocalyptic national significance in such "signs of the times" as the earthquake which accompanied the appearance of the first steamboat on the Mississippi in 1811 (docs. 18–19), the burning of the Richmond theatre soon afterward with the loss of the governor and many other notables of Virginia (doc. 21), the destruction of Washington by the British (doc. 25), the Panic of 1819 (doc. 23), and the Missouri Compromise (doc. 24). The emotional flavor of early nationalism contributed greatly to the causes of the War of 1812, established a strong anti-intellectual undercurrent which inhibited education and intellectual maturity, and discouraged a realistic solution of such problems as slavery. But it also speeded the completion of great national enterprises like the Erie Canal and, in general, made Americans perhaps the most vital, energetic, well-disposed people on earth.

The horrified response to the Richmond theatre fire expressed in doc. 21 belongs to patriotic rhetoric because it depicts a moment of national revelation, much as did the historical paintings and monuments of the period. The emotional intensity which they generated was felt as often in their composition as in their content. The surge of emotion in the Richmond fire scene declares itself through twisting lines of action, sharply contrasted color values, and especially the triangular upward thrust of its composition. These are essentially the organizing principles of other contemporary works which embodied moments of national revelation—for instance, Weber's painting of Nootka Sound (doc. 2) and Charles W. Peale's "Exhuming the First American Mastodon" (doc. 43). John Trumbull's famous picture of the Signing of the Declaration, particularly in its earlier, smaller version (doc. 37), gains dramatic effect in an otherwise static scene through its triangular composition.

These are traits common, of course, to much romantic art everywhere. American national feeling tended to be romantic. For the most part, however, it was a restrained, controlled romanticism. The towering obelisk of the Washington Monument, built in this period, has a classic purity and grace. The magnificent dome of the Capitol is balanced by restful horizontal masses. The strong feeling in Peale's painting of the mastodon excavation is controlled and disciplined by his commitment to historical fact. Even the lurid portrayal of the Richmond fire is a controlled work, not to say contrived: the stilted attitudes and melodramatic postures of the figures in this picture, its stylized treatment of the women victims, echo a sentimental convention which dates back at least to Samuel Richardson's English novels, *Pamela* and *Clarissa*.

The sentimental veneration of womanhood revealed in this picture, to be found also in contemporary British and French prints of a similar nature, has nevertheless a special significance for American culture. It was part of an inherited convention steeped in Puritanism, fortified by Southern ideas of gallantry and racial purity, and sanctified by the national obsession with an Edenic virtue—a special case of the division of popular sympathies between aspirations toward the ideal and sentiments of the real. An American Eve could not exist except as an abstraction, a moral idea, as evidenced by the outraged public response to John Vanderlyn's nude "Ariadne" (doc. 7), which he had brought back from Europe, or by the testimony of William Preston (doc. 6), Cooper's genteel portrayal of Elizabeth Templeton in *The Pioneers* (doc. 101), the careful supervision of women at Lowell factory town (doc. 74), and even by the preachments of school textbooks (docs. 51–52). In a symbolic sense, it may be said that the main goal of all American striving was the restoration of a sinless Eve and Adam, recently redeemed from the hellish Old World, to the garden of desire.

Symbolic of a final delivery from European bondage, the War of 1812 became one of the more important moments of national revelation in the period. As Henry Adams has written, it forced the United States into a nationality of character which the Revolution had failed to bring about. It exposed at first a deep sectional antago-

nism, but ended by banishing forever from influence at
the seat of government the disaffected Federalists and
Tertium Quids along the Eastern seaboard thought to
sympathize with Europe; it released energies for the creation of a national market and home industries, which in
turn created a new kind of leadership; above all, it produced Andrew Jackson, whose emergence as a national
hero signified a shift in the mysterious center of influence
from the South toward the North and West.

Docs. 25 and 26 may help to explain the rather short-
lived adulation of naval heroes like Oliver Perry and Stephen Decatur in contrast to the continuing fame of Jackson. A single brilliant land victory did more than a dozen
equally brilliant victories at sea to salvage the nation's
honor, in the name of which, ostensibly, the war was
fought. The western and southern Warhawks who urged
Madison into a declaration of war espoused, for the most
part, a code of honor which had much in common with
dueling and with Sir Walter Scott's evocations of courtly
conduct. Perhaps these hot-blooded patriots were not as interested in the British impressment of American sailors as
they claimed. Indeed, a letter from John Jacob Astor to
Thomas Jefferson (doc. 27) is included as a reminder that
national pride was not inconsistent with imperialistic
cupidity as a cause for war.

The code of the *duello* was an expression of sensitive
pride imported into the South from Europe. Like the
Greek and Roman Revival in architecture, it could not
long survive its transplantation into other parts of the
Union. It was too aristocratic. Also, people began to realize, since the death of Alexander Hamilton in 1804, that
it sanctioned murder. The naval hero Stephen Decatur
died in a much-publicized duel in 1820, another martyr
for the legal abolition of dueling. His death, for example,
inspired a number of tracts against dueling, among them
one by Mason Weems, the author of popular patriotic
biographies who invented the story of Washington and the
cherry tree. Two cartoons from his tract (doc. 29) associate the practice of dueling with the South and with

Weems' own anti-foreign prejudices. His appeal was to moralistic preconceptions about the national character rather than to reason.

The assumption of national virtue derived not only from the identification of morality with natural law, but also from agricultural pursuits and the agrarian belief that America was a land of nature as opposed to urbanized Europe. Throughout this period, most Southern leaders remained ardent exponents of Jefferson's agrarian nationalism and were listened to with respect in the rest of the Union. Their rather moderate views on slavery at this time, occasioned in part by the decline of tobacco culture through falling prices and soil exhaustion, are represented in the American colonization documents (doc. 71). Nevertheless, the Missouri Compromise was, as Jefferson believed, "a fire-bell in the night," and many Northerners already felt Southern society to be too stereotyped, too tinged with the feudal class ideas of old Europe, to be able to contribute creatively to the wave of the future.

Sectional feeling is chiefly represented in this volume by documents relating to internal improvements, a greater sectional issue at the time than either the tariff or slavery. Largely because of sectional rivalry in Congress, New York undertook alone the most ambitious national enterprise of the period: the construction of a 350-mile canal linking Atlantic civilization to dreams of destiny in the Far West, where already waved the New Yorker Astor's flag of empire. The Erie Canal, which, as a symbol of the future, fertilized the intellectual life of the whole state, became an engineering school for the nation. But it demonstrated, too, the need for professional training, and Amos Eaton, after conducting a geological survey along the canal, induced Stephen Van Rensselaer, one of the canal commissioners, to found Rensselaer Polytechnic Institute, the first purely scientific school in the English-speaking world. In the meanwhile, Emma Willard had been encouraged by New York's reputation for liberality to apply there for the support of her new female seminary.

Thomas Jefferson made use of New York's advances in

public education under Governor Clinton to prod his own
Virginian legislature into more generous support for the
University of Virginia. "Surely Governor Clinton's display . . . ," he wrote in 1820, "will stimulate the pride
as well as the patriotism of our legislature, to look to the
reputation and safety of their own country." After enu-
merating New York's educational achievements, he concluded, "What a pigmy to this is Virginia become, with a
population almost equal to that of New York! And whence
this difference? From the difference their rulers set on the
value of knowledge, and the prosperity it produces."[3] One
might also mention the fructifying influence of a far-flung
commerce extending from the Mississippi Valley via the
Erie Canal and Hudson to Europe and the Orient, making
New York City the leading seaport of the nation by the
end of this period.

Enterprising New Yorkers, under the able leadership of
De Witt Clinton, produced new images for the nation in
almost every field of endeavor, not the least of which was
social legislation. But the focal center of creativity was the
Hudson River valley, with its gateway to the West point-
ing like an arrow. John Jacob Astor, an early patron of the
writers Fitz-Greene Halleck and Washington Irving, became a prototype of the new capitalist leadership. Robert
Fulton and Robert Livingston gave Americans a new concept of transportation. The first notable body of literature
produced by Americans, that of Washington Irving, William Cullen Bryant, and James Fenimore Cooper, arose in
conjunction with the discovery of patriotic themes and romantic landscape along the pathways of empire. Thomas
Cole, another New Yorker, translated this interest in
American nature into poetic canvasses which established
the Hudson River School of native painting. It is not surprising, perhaps, that one of the earliest symbols of
Yankee enterprise, "Uncle Sam," a figure revered and also
much vilified from the start, as James Kirke Paulding's

[3] Thomas Jefferson, *Works*, Vol. XII, pp. 169–72. New York:
G. P. Putnam's Sons, 1904–5.

sectional allegory (doc. 66) shows, was born in the Hudson River valley during this period.

A key to understanding the period is *change*, and New York stood for constructive change as opposed to the more static arcadian republicanism of the South. Many documents in this volume therefore highlight such instruments of change as the factory, the steamboat, canals, and bridges—as well as public attitudes toward these developments, greeted with mixed feelings of anticipation and apprehension. Responsive to the public clamor for faster transportation, for instance, newspapers of the day were filled with advertisements for fast coaches. Yet people were horrified when their demand for greater speed resulted in serious steamboat explosions (see doc. 83). The fantastic rate of growth not only of the number of steam engines in use during this period, but also of their horsepower and boiler pressures, is one sure measure of the accelerated tempo and increasing complexity of people's lives. Bridges, on the other hand, are presented in this volume as a dominant symbol in an age of change of the desire to maintain an unbroken continuity with traditional values of the past.

The new inventions were often vernacular expressions of the American environment, different from their counterparts in England. Doc. 85, for example, demonstrates a distinct difference in styling between the early steamboats designed by Robert Fulton for Eastern waters and those which appeared on the Mississippi a few years later. Fulton's cumbersome Bolton and Watts low-pressure engine was concealed in the hull, which had a relatively deep draft like traditional sailing vessels. But the river traffic required a shallow draft and also more powerful engines in order to make headway upstream. Therefore, Captain Shreve in 1816 built a river steamboat with a flat hull like a keelboat, a high superstructure, and, housed on the deck, a compact, high-pressure engine which was hardly more than a piston attached directly to a single paddle-wheel in the stern (compare the drawings in doc. 84).

Many of Shreve's innovations were soon incorporated into the Eastern steamboats, although the Mississippi

boats reverted to side paddle-wheels as soon as the Fulton
patent monopoly was broken. An English engineer, David
Stevenson, considered American designs more advanced
than the English. The location of the machinery, he noted,
formed "one of the most prominent and striking parts of
an American steam-boat . . . , presenting, as may naturally be supposed, a strange effect in the eyes of those accustomed to see European steam-boats only, in which no
part of the machinery is visible even from the deck of the
vessel."[4] Other American designs of early steam-powered
vehicles exhibited similar differences, emphasizing a combination of crudeness and strength, greater simplicity and
flexibility, more power and speed. Compare, for example,
the picture of an English steam dredge with Oliver Evans'
Orukter Amphibolos (doc. 89), which used a system of
pulleys and shafts to adapt the strange monster to a variety
of functions.

A rather similar difference appears in the pictures of the
Stevens and Trevithick locomotives (doc. 87), which emphasize the crudity and functional directness of the American design, suggesting also that American designers were
more willing to sacrifice the old to the new. Indeed, the
Englishman Gurney conceived his steam carriage in the
image of the traditional coach for the upper-class gentry
(doc. 88). On the other hand, English scientists and inventors often enjoyed a great advantage over the Americans in the patronage of wealthy aristocrats. The contrast
between the thronging, urban area where Trevithick exhibited his locomotive and the unpeopled scenes in which
Stevens' locomotive and Oliver Evans' steam dredger appear may also suggest a readier soil for public interest and
support during the early experimental stages of invention.

America was more seriously hampered at this time by a
lack of trained mechanics, native or otherwise. The United
States Mint could not be staffed, for example, without
importing German and English technicians. The advantages enjoyed by the British in all these respects help to

[4] David Stevenson, *Sketch of the Civil Engineering of North
America,* pp. 130–31. London: 1838.

account for the fact that they were usually first with inventions which Americans adopted and modified for their
own use only later. The high-pressure steam engine was
known first in England, as were the power loom, the locomotive, and other important inventions of the period. The
use of standardized, interchangeable parts and assembly-
line techniques of production were introduced in France,
but did not survive. These developments were made available to the American people, for the most part, through
the efforts of a few highly skilled native technicians like
Paul Moody at Lowell, Oliver Evans in Philadelphia, and
Eli Whitney at New Haven. The great demand in an expanding America for power, speed, and labor-saving devices then favored their adoption on a wide scale.

The principle of standardized, interchangeable parts developed by Thomas Blanchard and Eli Whitney was
quickly adapted to the manufacture of guns, clocks, and
farm implements in this period. Theoretical science lagged
behind useful knowledge. Americans nevertheless succeeded, as documents in this volume show, in also making
significant contributions to science. They were conscious of
trying to stake out a national claim to eminence in science
and invention as in the arts, and they inevitably measured
American achievements, whether in geology, ornithology,
or bridge-building, by comparison with those of Europe.
The discovery and excavation of an American mastodon
was celebrated in patriotic paintings and school histories,
and the skeleton was exhibited in Europe. Cultural nationalism made the popular Peale Museum in Philadelphia (see doc. 42) an encyclopedic collection of achievements in both the arts and sciences.

Peale's mastodon was to American science what Andrew Jackson was to political life and Natty Bumppo to
literature—a testimonial to the grandeur and integrity of
the American earth in its influence upon character. Scientists themselves not only wrote poetic tributes to the
beauty of the landscape, but sometimes referred to the
natural setting as a stimulant to inquiry lacking in Europe.
Many of their most significant contributions during the

early 1800's came in connection with explorations of the plains and forest: Jedidiah Morse, father of the inventor, in geography; Dr. Daniel Drake of Cincinnati in the study of contagious disease in the Mississippi Valley; Dr. William Beaumont, a frontier doctor, in the chemistry of the stomach (doc. 45); William Maclure in geology (doc. 41); Alexander Wilson in ornithology (doc. 44); Thomas Say in entomology; Thomas Nuttall in botany; and John Heckewelder in Indian lore. So even science found its orientation and mission in the polarity of the New World and the Old, the city and the wilderness.

The mastodon, relic from primeval forests, reminded the American Adam of his own engagement with time. A major source of anxiety during the period was the fear that the advance of technology and civilization into the wilderness would destroy the moral fiber of the nation. This fear, encouraged by evangelical frontier religions, was the chief ingredient of the burgeoning reform movements which would soon flower into the crusade for Abolition. An early anti-slavery tract of the period, Jesse Torrey's *Portraiture of Domestic Slavery* (1817), suggests that slavery was less to be feared if it could be restricted to the old settled areas. Slavery was becoming a national problem only as plantation culture, revivified and vulgarized by Whitney's cotton gin, spread westward to sink deep its roots in the fabled Eden of interior America.

One consequence of the spread of cotton was a new domestic slave traffic which Torrey considered more inhuman than the African trade to which it succeeded. Two pictures from his tract (docs. 72 and 26) communicate its spirit: the first depicting a particularly brutal kidnapping, enacted against a backdrop of sunny skies and fertile fields, and the second a group of manacled slaves being led in front of the ruined buildings of the national Capitol. Torrey defined slavery as a national sin and was especially concerned for its moral effects upon the white population. He noted that many slave owners lived like vassal lords, often bankrupting themselves to maintain the magnificent style of living and the habits of amusement and sport which had been imposed upon them by their ancestors. But Torrey might also have pointed to extravagant social fashions in the North, where resorts like Saratoga Springs and the Union Race Track were becoming popular. A sensation of the 1823 racing season at the Union Course, incidentally, was the Eclipse-Henry match race, in which a sporting set from the North and the South wagered $20,000. The Yankee horse won this early sectional contest (see doc. 66).

The reformers of this period assailed extravagance of living for much the same reasons that they attacked dueling, drunkenness, and slavery—as sins upon the land. Social extravagance denoted the existence of class distinctions which democratic dogma denied. Yet the rapid growth of American industry and commerce inevitably widened the distance between the classes, as docs. 75 through 81 testify. Krimmel's pictures of the departure for boarding school and the return (doc. 59) satirize the influence of fashion upon a middle-class farming family. Note the affectations, the haughtiness, the dissatisfaction which the young lady has acquired—along with a piano—at the expense of her hard-working mother and father. Krimmel's vernacular treatment here of the theme of success-striving, emphasizing drama, action, and conflict, should be contrasted with the more finished style and greater, even respectful, detachment of Henry Sargent's *Tea Party* and *Dinner Party*, depicting the upper classes of Boston as if they were posing on a stage (docs. 80 and 81).

Class distinctions are also reflected, with perhaps less theatricality, in the social arrangements at the new Lowell factory village (see docs. 75 through 78), where the dwelling houses of the resident manager, foreman, skilled and unskilled mill operatives were set apart from each other invidiously. In another important sense, however, the founding of Lowell partook of the reform-mindedness of the period, polarized by the moral distance between Europe and the American frontier. The factory owners had to counter widespread fears, especially among the rural population, that manufacturing would depress the moral, religious, and social standards of workers as in Europe. In order, therefore, to attract "virtuous farm girls" to work in their mills, since other labor was scarce, the owners provided them with well-supervised dormitories, chaperones, churches, and schools.

Paternalistic factory communities were largely confined to the North. The orderly layout at Lowell (doc. 56) may be contrasted with the disorder and even slum-like squalor surrounding the Union Textile Mills in Maryland (doc. 79), an example of what Americans feared. On the other hand, the paternalistic rationalizing of the industrial community had much in common with the utopian impulse at Jefferson's University of Virginia, Fanny Wright's Nashoba community in Tennessee, and Robert Dale Owen's New Harmony in Indiana. A pictorial comparison of Lowell and the University of Virginia (docs. 55 and 56) thus shows a rather similar rectangular, self-contained unit of buildings dominated architecturally by the building most important functionally to each: the library and the mill. The greater symmetry of the University of Virginia is explained partly by a difference in the artists' perspectives and partly by the lack of a consistent statement of an ideal in the company town, the English Gothic church tower of the latter conflicting with the colonial cubes and both with the modified Grecian design of the outlying resident manager's home. The total impression of the University of Virginia is classic; of Lowell, feudal.

The truth is that America was searching for a style to express its sense of the great changes taking place. The search for style was a search for the deeper meaning of American life. But, for the time being, Americans could only express *conflict*, which, possibly, for them *was* the deeper meaning. Feeling themselves about to enter upon an era of unlimited progress for the human race, they celebrated their civilizing mission chiefly by a return to antiquity and to nature. Captain Basil Hall, a British visitor, captured the essence of this paradox in two etchings, one of a view from the Mt. Holyoke range in Massachusetts and the other a view of the Erie Canal, which he placed on the same page of his book "to show the contrast between a scene entirely artificial, and one where nature is left to her own course" (see doc. 69). But Americans frequently expressed this tension within a single work, as in "View of the Canal" (doc. 70). Here one senses a division of the artist's attention between his admiration for wild, disheveled, jagged nature and his respect for the man-made order which reduces it to geometric line. The small human figures in the foreground and on the aqueduct itself, however, foreshadow the popularity of landscape paintings in which the human figure is utterly dwarfed by romantically awesome forests and mountains. Such a treatment appears in Thomas Cole's "The Last of the Mohicans" (doc. 62), one of the earliest paintings of the Hudson River School. Critical of the civilizing mission and a lover of the wild, Cole helped to create the American religion of nature. Many years later, in a picture called "The Oxbow," he romanticized the view from Mt. Holyoke seen by Basil Hall.

The most direct, self-conscious confrontation during this early period of the problem of reconciling the actuality of American experience with the dream of nature was that of James Fenimore Cooper. The illustration from *The Pioneers* (doc. 101), the earliest known picture of Natty Bumppo, shows this rough-hewn man of the forest taking his leave of the Templetons, the genteel bearers of civilization. The picture has omitted a significant detail, Natty's deferential act of removing his hat. It was not a farewell between social equals. Cooper's attempt to resolve the dilemma by having Elizabeth Templeton marry the dandy of the picture, a nobleman of nature through a long forest tutelage under Natty as well as civilized gentleman, is not convincing.

In spite of his allegiance to the cultivated tradition, Cooper often succeeded in making his characters speak in the vernacular idiom of a pioneer settlement. This achievement offended many leaders of public taste whose cultural moorings, like their reading habits, were tied to Europe. Their reaction to Cooper's novel is exemplified in the letters of James Gates Percival (doc. 100), whose genteel poetry could not compete with the rising star of the West. The influence of the West on the national style can be seen also in pictures of the new heroes as well as in the design of steamboats or plows. Compare, for instance, the artistic conception of Natty Bumppo, undoubtedly based on Daniel Boone (doc. 102), with Gilbert Stuart's famous Lansdowne painting of George Washington (doc. 103). The difference is not merely a matter of skill, but of outlook. Stuart was a traditionalist whose style was moulded by Europe. The picture of Daniel Boone, on the other hand—the only authentic picture we have— was engraved from a painting by Chester Harding, a self-taught frontier artist. The picture of Boone, like that of Leatherstocking, emphasizes a functional harmony with environment, though Leatherstocking's dogs and long rifle are retired to the background.

In this period, bourgeois aspirations for respectability were making portraiture a popular genre, as the record of James Guild (doc. 9) testifies, but the great Stuart was languishing in his studio for want of commissions. These were going increasingly to vernacular painters like Chester Harding, who charged less for sittings. According to Harding (doc. 14), even Boston aristocrats accustomed to the high London style of Benjamin West, art teacher for early America, were beginning to patronize upstart native painters. Docs. 10 through 13 will help the reader to determine whether this change in taste represented a vulgarization of American art. The subjects of all four pictures are obviously people of means. The first two are by an unknown primitive painter, the third by Benjamin West himself, and the fourth by his pupil, Samuel F. B. Morse.

Changes in popular taste also presented the problem of choosing careers, best exemplified here, perhaps, in the works of Samuel Morse, Benjamin Latrobe, and Robert Fulton. Before the advent of the Industrial Revolution, one aspired to be a gentleman farmer, a doctor, lawyer, clergyman, or statesman—not even an established "man of letters" or an artist went without honor. But the new age elevated the practical man: the maker of "likenesses" (as portraits came to be called), the mechanic, inventor, engineer, carpenter-builder, manufacturer, and businessman. Thus, Robert Fulton launched a promising career in art, but shifted his interests to engineering and invention. Born in 1765, he nevertheless expressed to the end of his life the humanistic culture and broad mental horizons of the earlier age. His letter to Aaron Ogden (doc. 82), though concerned with steamboat litigation and patent rights, is a graceful literary production, studded with art allusions and poetic analogies. A comparison with the business letter of Francis C. Lowell (doc. 86), a representative of the younger promoters, may suggest a narrowing of mental horizons.

Benjamin Latrobe, a professional architect of rare sensitivity, integrity, and skill, who almost single-handedly created the Classical Revival in the United States, found so little respect for professionalism, even in the halls of Congress which he had been commissioned to rebuild, that he went bankrupt and was forced into building and promoting steamboats on the Mississippi. Doc. 98 contains his criticism of the carpenter-builder system which he held responsible for his plight.

Quite as pathetic was the situation of Samuel Morse, one of the most patriotic and self-sacrificing artists of the period. His painting of the Old House of Representatives, after a major effort requiring eighteen months and hundreds of dollars in its execution, according to James Gates Percival (doc. 100), cost him $110 to exhibit to a New York public. Attempting to please almost everybody in order to remain in the profession, he experimented with allegories and landscapes; he lent himself to sentimentality; he turned to patriotic subjects in the grand manner; he tried portraits of the rich and poor, an example of which appears in doc. 13. Little appreciated as an artist, he became a noted inventor. Henry David Thoreau was to question whether his invention of the telegraph was worthwhile in view of the uses to which it was put.

Morse's style with the brush was traditional rather

than experimental. The dilemma of artists and other shapers of culture, it has been argued, stemmed from a tendency to judge authentic American achievement by the false, inappropriate, cultivated standards of Europe. By this token, artists like Morse and Latrobe should have searched for the kind of native expression so modestly displayed in the long-barreled Kentucky rifle (doc. 102), Thomas Blanchard's wood-working lathe, the Western steamboat (doc. 85), bridges (docs. 93–97), and mass-production techniques. Indeed, there was considerable effort during the period, not always successful and sometimes absurd, to combine the best of both traditions: traditional design with structural innovations, aesthetic merit with practical function, idealistic feeling and common sense, elite standards and democratic values.

Vernacular expression was encouraged by an almost instinctive folk feeling for whatever was functional, useful, and natural as opposed to the artificial and sophisticated. But the inspiration of nature did not always yield the same result, for the organic view of nature made slow headway in this period against the dominant intellectual, religious commitment to nature as moral idea. The theme of the return to nature, insofar as it stressed moral imperatives and national ideals, and the companion theme of the return to antiquity with its springs in Europe, taken together, complicated matters considerably. They fostered the aesthetic virtue of simplicity, even austerity, but conflicted with the impulse to experimentation, change, and growth.

Benjamin Latrobe himself was by no means a slave to classical forms. He once disputed successfully with Thomas Jefferson in substituting lanterns for the latter's impractical skylights in the Capitol dome: "What shall I do when the condensed vapor showers down upon the heads of the members from 100 skylights?"[5] Yet his well-known corncob and tobacco capitals in the place of the traditional acanthus leaves for the columns of the Senate

[5] Cited in Talbot Hamlin, *Benjamin Henry Latrobe*, p. 274. New York: Oxford University Press, 1955.

Rotunda seem too artfully, consciously designed for folk art. Rather, they serve to weld the two themes of the return to nature and antiquity into a single statement of the national ideal. His Graeco-Roman temple for housing a steam pump and smokestack at Centre Square (docs. 34 and 35), on the other hand, seems to us merely ludicrous.

His pupils, Robert Mills and William Strickland, were more willing to experiment with new materials and structural changes in a way which was not simply eclectic or monstrous. Mills built the first fireproof building, the Grecian Public Record Office at Charleston, South Carolina. Elsewhere Strickland used iron reinforcing rods and interior columns. Mills had an almost unresolvable problem, however, in the Monumental Church (doc. 99), built to replace the Richmond theatre (doc. 21). As Latrobe once said, religion in America required a church wholly different from the Grecian temple. Fortunately, Mills' original design for the Monumental Church, combining a modified Tuscan block with a New England spire, was unacceptable to his church committee.

Greater cultural incongruities were to come in the next period, with Greenough's sculpture of General Washington in a Roman toga and P. T. Barnum's conversion of Peale's Museum into a gallery of waxworks and freaks. The fragmentation of Peale's original museum into specialized collections of art on the one hand and on the other the Smithsonian Institution of Science perhaps best illustrates the failure of encyclopedic philosophy to provide a durable unity in an age of technological change and expansion. The encyclopedic movement assumed a unity-in-multiplicity similar to that of great religions. It assumed explicitly the embodiment of universal archetypes in the particulars of American experience: the glory and the virtues of Hellenism reborn in America and discoverable through encyclopedic collections, allegorical art, historical paintings and monuments, and monumental public buildings. It assumed, that is to say, the existence of immutable natural laws and forms which urgent, practical, day-to-day necessity—that mother of novelty and new dreams—constantly subverted or ignored. It could not even assimilate the steam engine, product of Newtonian laws.

The failure of the encyclopedic movement can be traced in allegorical art. The problem which allegorical art posed is dealt with by John Quincy Adams (doc. 32), whose Puritan heritage inclined him to favor for the purpose of representing America Christian allegory over pagan, and by Benjamin Latrobe (doc. 31), who despised both. It was the old problem of fusing the ideal and the real, of fleshing the bones of allegory with a virtual presence. This problem is dramatized in the contrast between Madame Plantou's allegorical "Peace of Ghent" (doc. 5) and John Trumbull's more literal "The Declaration of Independence" (doc. 37). The same problem is felt in James Kirke Paulding's attempt to endow his fable of Uncle Sam (doc. 66) with vernacular speech in order to vivify political and sectional abstractions.

The only artist of the period who successfully wedded folk expression to allegory was the wood-carving genius, William Rush. His allegorical figure of the Schuylkill River (doc. 34), for which he used a live model, is, however, less convincing than his "Comedy" and "Tragedy" (doc. 108). These last two, among the most richly evocative works of the period, are more femininely alive in figure, gesture, and facial expression—even more daring— than Vanderlyn's famed "Ariadne" (doc. 7). The very lines of the gowns, the one emphasizing a brazen swell of breasts and thighs, the other gathered and knotted, as in pain, at the waist, contribute to the total impression. These two figures prove the possibility of redeeming any stylistic convention from triteness.

At the advent of the Industrial Revolution, Americans floundered between the two worlds of the disappearing frontier and civilized progress, powerless to be reborn quite as the myth of the American Adam required. In their patriotic posturing, in the contrasts, often ironic, between their illusions and their true conditions, lay materials for tragic awareness which remained unrecognized. They yearned for a simple transcendent unity, expressed in government by Daniel Raymond's definition of the national interest (doc. 48) or Jefferson's statement of the Monroe Doctrine (doc. 49); in the arts by the themes of the return to nature and antiquity; in religion by the vision of a new heaven and a new earth. Yet their society was becoming increasingly characterized by a multiplicity of competing self-interests and individualistic, materialistic success-striving of the kind associated with John Marshall's Supreme Court decisions defining the sanctity of contracts and private property, with the bourgeois aspirations of careerists like James Guild or John Jacob Astor, and above all with the new expansive energies of industrial enterprise.

In the important matter of style, by which the inward sense of these things was translated, vernacular expression was perhaps best suited to render the multiplicity of American experience. But it would be an exaggeration to say that it was altogether adequate as an alternative to cultivated modes of expression. The vernacular tradition has helped to make us as a people strong in the applied arts, weak in theoretical science; adept at technological innovation, but often at the expense of humanitarian values; energetic in individualistic enterprise, but without a strong sense of public interest; adaptive, resourceful, and manipulative in an open society, but lacking the inner discipline to conserve our human and natural resources.

The documents in this volume would seem to reinforce the view that some kind of reconciliation of traditional values and native self-expression is necessary if we are to save ourselves from ourselves. Theodore Burr's praiseworthy vernacular attempt without benefit of theory to throw a 360-foot span over the Susquehanna River in 1815 (doc. 97) did not save his bridge from collapsing. Today, even more than ever, we need to build strong bridges across the chasm between the old and new.

Charles L. Sanford

Acknowledgments

I wish to thank my colleague at Rensselaer Polytechnic Institute, Professor Isadore Traschen, for many helpful suggestions in matters of style and tone. Rensselaer Polytechnic Institute came to my rescue in the latter stages of the work, when my funds for completing it were exhausted. Of course, there would have been no volume at all without the generous permission from publishers, editors, and custodians of pictorial collections to reproduce many of the documents for it. I am grateful also to Mrs. Doris Nock and Mrs. Leo Bruns for secretarial assistance. Mrs. Rebecca Gould of the Rensselaer Polytechnic Institute library staff rendered invaluable service in locating titles and rare books. Through the generosity of Mr. Mason Tolman and Mrs. Ida M. Cohen, finally, the vast resources of the New York State Library were made available to me. I hope very much that all these people will be pleased with the results, for which I must be held responsible.

Contents

PART III: DISPERSION, EXPANSION, AND CHANGE

A. SECTIONALISM AND NATIONALISM

B. THE INDUSTRIAL REVOLUTION

         (PLATES 35, 36, 37 AND 38)
                            in group following page 322
     79. Mill and Mess   362
         (PLATE 39)   in group following page 322
80–81. High Life in Boston   363
         (PLATES 40 AND 41) in group following page 322
     82. The Fulton Monopoly   364
         Robert Fulton
     83. Steamboat Litigation and Explosions   371
         Oliver Evans
     84. Two Major Styles in Steam Engine Design   380
     85. Two Major Styles in Steamboat Design   382
         (PLATES 42 AND 43) in group following page 322
     86. Styles of Promotion in Technology and
         Industry   383
         Oliver Evans, John Stevens and
         Francis C. Lowell
     87. An American and English Locomotive on
         Exhibit   389
         (PLATES 44 AND 45) in group following page 322
     88. Gurney's Steam Carriage   390
     89. An American and English Steam Dredge   392
         (PLATES 46 AND 47) in group following page 322
     90. The Design of American and British
         Ploughs (Plows)   393
     91. Representative American Plows   399
     92. Representative English Ploughs   401

              C. CONFLICTING STYLES AND TRADITIONS

     93. The Flying Pendent Lever Bridge: A Poem   403
         Thomas Pope
     94. View of the Flying Pendent Lever Bridge   410
         (PLATE 48)   in group following page 322
     95. The Lattice-truss Wooden Bridge: A
         Treatise   411
         Ithiel Town
     96. View of the Lattice-truss Wooden Bridge   420
         (PLATE 49)   in group following page 322

Like half a Rainbow rising on yon shore

While its twin partner spans the semi o'er

And makes a perfect whole that need not part

Till time has furnish'd us a nobler art.

"Like Half a Rainbow Rising," from Thomas Pope, A TREATISE ON BRIDGE ARCHITECTURE, opp. p. 5 (New York: 1811). Photo by Burns Studio.

PART I

The Character of American Experience

Document 1

The Idea of the Nation

Hugh Swinton Legaré (1797–1843), lawyer, editor, man of letters, and statesman, delivered this stirring Fourth of July address in his native Charleston, South Carolina, in 1823, shortly after serving a term in the state legislature. Charleston, as the numerous references to it in this book will suggest, was then a leading cultural center of the South and the nation. Legaré's address was at once published and given a wide circulation. After reading it, one is not surprised to learn that he became a foe of Southern nullification or that he rose in the nation's councils shortly before his death to the position of Secretary of State. The nation was richer also for his having founded the *Southern Review,* one of the earliest Southern periodicals of distinction.

Two other significant statements of American nationalism in this period, Charles J. Ingersoll's *Discourse Concerning the Influence of America on the Mind* (Philadelphia, 1823) and John Quincy Adams' First Annual Message to Congress (1825), have both been reprinted elsewhere. Legaré's address is of particular value because it helps explain how the Classical Revival could exist on the scale that it did side by side with "modern progress" and the rising cult of nature. Legaré's address proceeds from a deeper level of thought and feeling.

SOURCE: Hugh Swinton Legaré, *Collected Writings,* Vol. I, pp. 257–69. Charleston, S.C.: 1845–46.

Cicero begins a celebrated oration by congratulating himself upon the felicity of his subject—in the discussion of which he thought that an orator, were he never so feeble or unpractised, could not fail to be more embarrassed with the *choice*, than the *invention* of his topics, and to carry along with him the entire sympathy of his audience. For the occasion required him to dwell upon the virtues and achievements of the great Pompey—a man, who had been, from his earliest youth, identified with the glory of his country—who had transcended and eclipsed the recorded honours of her Scipios and Metellus'—and, under whose auspices, "victory flew with her eagles" from Lusitania to Caucasus and the Euphrates. But what would not the genius of the Roman orator, who found so much scope for the amplifications of his unrivalled eloquence, in the events of a single life, and the glory of a few campaigns, have made of a subject—so interesting in itself—so peculiarly affecting, and so dear to his auditors—so fertile, so various, so inspiring—as that to which he who now addresses you will have been indebted, for whatever of interest, or of attention it may be his good fortune to awaken? What were the exploits of a single individual, to the efforts of a whole people—heated with all the enthusiasm of a mighty contest, and rushing into the battles of Liberty, under the impulses of a patriotism, the most heroic and self-devoting? What were the victories of Pompey—to the united achievements of our Washingtons and Montgomerys and Greens—our Franklins and Jeffersons and Adams' and Laurens'—of the Senate of Sages, whose wisdom conducted—of the band of warriors, whose valour accomplished—of the "noble army of martyrs", whose blood sealed and consecrated the Revolution of '76? What were the events of a few campaigns—however brilliant and successful—in the wars of Italy, or Spain, or Pontus—to by far the greatest era—excepting, perhaps, the Reformation—that has occurred in the political history of modern times—to an era that has fixed forever the destinies of a whole quarter of the globe, with the numbers without number that are soon to inhabit it—and has already had, as it will probably continue to have, a visible influence upon the condition of society in all the rest? Nay—shall I be accused of extravagance, if going still further I ask, what is there even in the most illustrious series of victories and conquests, that can justly be considered as affording, to a mind that dares to make a philosophic estimate of human affairs, a nobler and more interesting subject of contemplation and discourse, than the causes which led to the foundation of this mighty empire—than the wonderful and almost incredible history of what it has since done and is already grown to—than the scene of unmingled prosperity and happiness that is opening and spreading all around us—than the prospect as dazzling as it is vast, that lies before us—the uncircumscribed career of aggrandizement and improvement which we are beginning to run under such happy auspices and with the advantage of having *started* at a point where it were well for the species had it been the lot of many nations even to have *ended* theirs.

It is true, we shall not boast to day that the pomp of triumph has three hundred times ascended the steps of our capitol—or that the national temple upon its brow blazes in the spoils of a thousand cities. True, we do not send forth our prætors to plunder and devastate the most fertile and beautiful portions of the earth, in order that a haughty aristocracy may be enriched with booty, or a worthless populace be supplied with bread—nor in every region under the sun, from the foot of the Crampian hills, to the land of frankincense and myrrh, is the spirit of man broken and debased by us beneath the iron yoke of a military domination. No, my friends! This is, indeed, what the world calls *glory*—but let us be glad that we are not come here to boast of such things. *Our* triumphs are the triumphs of *reason*—of happiness—of human nature. Our rejoicings are greeted with the most cordial sympathy of the cosmopolite and the philanthrophist: and the good and the wise all round the globe give us back the echo of our acclamations. It is the singular fortune—or I should rather say—it is the proud distinction of Americans—it is what we are now met to return thanks for and to exult in —that in the race of moral improvement, which society has been every where running for some centuries past, we have outstripped every competitor and have carried our institutions, "in the sober certainty of waking bliss," to a higher pitch of perfection than ever warmed the dreams of enthusiasm or the speculations of the theorist. It is that a whole continent has been set apart, as if it were holy ground, for the cultivation of pure truth—for the pursuit of happiness upon rational principles, and, in the way that is most agreeable to nature—for the development of all the sensibilities, and capacities, and powers of the human mind, without any artificial restraint or bias, in the broad daylight of modern science and political liberty. It is that, over the whole extent of this gigantic empire—stretching as it does from the St. Croix to the Sabine, and from the waters of the Atlantic almost to those of the Pacific—wherever man is found, he is seen to walk abroad in all the dignity of his nature—with none to intimidate, or to insult, or to oppress him—with no superior upon this earth that does not deserve to be so—and that, in the proud consciousness of his privileges, his soul is filled with the most noble apprehensions, and his aspirations lifted up to the most exalted objects, and his efforts animated and encouraged in the pursuit of whatever has a tendency to bless and adorn his existence. *This* is the boast we make—*this* is the theme of the day we are celebrating—and do any of you envy the feelings of the man—who denies that the one is as rational and just, as the other is noble and transporting?

It has been usual on this occasion—as nothing, certainly, can be more appropriate and natural—to expatiate upon the events of the revolutionary contest, and to honour, in a suitable strain of panegyric, such of the founders of the Republic as were supposed to have rendered it the most important services, at a crisis so full of peril and glory. But as these topics, however interesting in themselves, and eminently well fitted for the purposes of popular declamation, are become so trite that it would be difficult, by any art of composition, to bestow upon them the graces of novelty, I have chosen rather to exhibit some of the *general features*—the great *leading characteristics*—by which, I conceive that memorable event to be distinguished from all others of a similar kind, that are recorded in the annals of empire.

The *first* of these peculiarities which I shall notice, is, that the Revolution was altogether the *work of principle*.

Whoever is anywise conversant with political history knows that such has always been the blind infatuation, the supine carelessness, or the abject servility of mankind, that not only have they submitted with patience to the grossest abuses and misrule, but that they have seldom been roused up to resistance, except by a long course of *positive suffering*—or by events that powerfully affect the *senses* and fill the bosom, even of the most indifferent spectator, with indignation and horror. The expulsion of the Tarquins—the overthrow of the Decemvirs—the repeated secessions of the people to the sacred mount—with many other incidents of a like kind, are familiar examples of this truth. A romantic tradition ascribes to a similar cause the origin of Helvetic liberty. The despotism of Philip II. would never have been resisted and shaken, nor Holland emerged, in the glory and greatness of freedom, out of that obscurity to which nature seemed so studiously to have condemned her, had it not been for the infernal atrocities of Alva, and the martyrdom of Egmont and Horn—and even the Revolution of '88, which seems, in this respect, to approach nearest to our own—not to mention that it grew out of the heats of religious and even a bigoted and fanatic zeal, rather than the love of civil liberty—was not effected until a whole century had passed away in strife, and persecution, and cruelty, and woe—until kindred hosts had been arrayed against each other in many a field of blood—until Algernon Sidney had died like a felon by the hands of the executioner; until, in short, the daring though feeble attempt of the second James had left his subjects no alternative, but to rid themselves at once of the predestinated and incurable perverseness of a race, that had neither learned nor forgotten any thing, even under the discipline of adversity and exile. But, in accounting for our declaration of independence, it is quite hyperbolical to speak—as it has been too common to do—of the tyranny of the mother country, and the evils under which the Colonies laboured, as too grievous to be endured. They were, indeed, intolerable—but only to such men as our fathers. There was, it must be confessed, good cause for resistance—but it may be affirmed with confidence that no other people upon earth would have rebelled for such a cause. There was nothing in their situation to excite the passions of vulgar men. There was none of the atrocities by which other nations have been goaded into the fury of civil war—no royal outrages—no patrician insolence—no religious persecution—no bloody proscription of the wise and the brave. Even the right of taxation against which they were contending was a prospective and contingent evil, rather than an actual grievance, and nothing can be more just than the quaint metaphor of Burke, that "they augured misgovernment at a distance, and snuffed tyranny in every tainted gale." The first intelligence of the stamp act, threw the whole country at the same instant into a flame: it was even then in a state of open rebellion. The encroachments of the ministry were resisted at the very threshold, and the moment the Colonies became *conscious* of the yoke, they shook it off. One spirit, one mind, pervaded and animated the whole mass. They argued—refined—distinguished—explained, with all the learned ingenuity of the schools. But if they reasoned about their rights with the subtlety of doctors—they were prepared to maintain them with the constancy of martyrs, and, for the first time in the history of civil society, a metaphysical dispute resulted in the creation of a great empire.

This fact, sufficiently remarkable for its singularity, assumes a still more important aspect, when viewed, as it ought to be in connection with the progress of society, with the causes that account for it, and with some inferences and anticipations which it seems naturally to suggest. Undoubtedly, the situation of the Colonies, at such an immense distance from the centre of the British Empire, must have weakened every sort of attraction by which they were held to it—and the peculiar character, too, of the first settlers will conduce very much to the solution of this curious problem. They were of all men the most sensitive and the best informed upon the subject of their rights and liberties. They were the devoted Huguenots, who, after having extorted by their valor in the field, with Bourbon and Coligni, with Rohan and Soubise, a short interval of repose from persecution, had at length abjured forever their beautiful native land—the soft and delicious banks of the Loire, where industry made them rich, virtuous, happy—not, as other adventurers constrained by poverty and embarrassments at home to seek their fortunes on a distant shore—not to search for gold and silver mines, nor to overrun vast regions and cement, with the blood of exterminated nations, the dominion of some potentate ambitious of reigning over a waste at the distance of five thousand miles from his capital—but to plunge into the depths of an untrodden wilderness, covered with swamps, breathing pestilence, yielding the bare necessaries of life only to the sweat of labor—because in its dreary solitudes they could commune with their God!—because, amidst its savage desolation, they could pour out the feelings of gratitude and adoration with which their hearts were filled and which they could not utter in the country of Fenelon and Pascal, without being hunted down like wild beasts! They were the austere and gloomy Puritans of England—the stern and fanatic followers of Pym and Hollis and Hampden—who had been republicans even in Europe, and had quitted Europe because it was unworthy of a Republic—those men to whom, according to the very probable opinion of the historian Hume, England herself is altogether indebted for what has made her, in these latter ages, the wonder of the world—the democratic part of her constitution. It was these heroes and tried champions of religious liberty—who looked upon the riches and honors of this world as dust and ashes in comparison of the principles upon which they built their steadfast faith—who not only loved liberty as something desirable in itself and essential to the dignity of human nature, but regarded it as a solemn *duty*, to free themselves from every species of restraint that was incompatible with the fullest rights of conscience—who, possessing all that devotedness and elevation of character, so natural to minds nursed in the habitual contemplation of such subjects and penetrated with their majesty and importance, had learned in the sublime language of Racine, "to fear God, and to know no other fear"—it was such men as these, together with the unfortunate, the persecuted, the adventurous, the bold, the aspiring of all climes and conditions, congregated and confounded in one vast asylum, and exercised, by the hardships incident to the colonization of a new country, with a sort of Spartan discipline—that laid the foundation of those flourishing commonwealths, whose first united efforts are the subject of this commemoration. Is it wonderful that a nation, composed of such elements and accustomed, too, to go on from one reform of abuses to another (for it is very important to observe that the whole history of the colonies is a history of successive revolutions in their municipal government and administration, and it is only by a figure of speech that we confine that term exclusively to the declaration of independence) should have shown themselves, at once, so sensitive and so determined, in a contest in which their rights were so seriously concerned?

But, although the situation of the country and the peculiar character of the people, go very far to explain the phenomenon I have noticed, it might be shewn—if either the limits to which I am confined, or the nature of this address, would permit me to enter into one of the most curious speculations in the history of the human mind— that it is not unconnected with causes of a more general nature—that a most surprising revolution has taken place in the whole structure of society—and that nothing, therefore, can be more superficial than to reason from what are called the analogies of former republics to the condition and prospects of our own. It is, of course, difficult to convey an adequate idea of so complicated a subject in a single hint—but I cannot refrain from observing, that the difference seems chiefly to consist in the habits of abstraction and reflection which have prevailed so much more for a century or two past, than they ever did at any former period, and in the consequent attachment to *principles* and *laws*, as if they were something tangible and personified—just as, in religion, the worship of images, of sensible representations of the Deity, which is of the very essence of the mythologies of early ages and the faith of simple minds, is utterly rejected by the more severe and spiritual, but not less rapturous devotion of a more philosophic era.

But *another* most fortunate and striking peculiarity of the Revolution we are celebrating is that it occurred in a New World.

The importance that ought to be attached to this circumstance will be obvious to every one who will reflect, for a moment, upon the miracles which are exhibiting in the settlement of this country and the increase of its population. Behold how the pomœrium of the republic advances in the wilderness of the West! See how empires are starting up into being, in periods of time, shorter even than the interval between infancy and manhood in the span allotted to the individuals that compose them! Contemplate the peaceful triumphs of industry—the rapid progress of cultivation—the diffusion of knowledge—the growth of populous cities, with all the arts that embellish life, and soften while they exalt the character of man—and think of the countless multitudes that are springing up to inherit these blessings! The three millions by whom our independence was achieved, less than half a century ago, are already grown to *ten*, which in the course of another half century will have swelled up to *fifty*; and so on, with a continually accelerated progress, until, at no distant day, the language of Milton shall be spoken from shore to shore, over the vastest portion of the earth's surface that was ever inhabited by a race worthy of speaking a language consecrated to Liberty.

Now—to feel how deep an interest this circumstance is fitted to throw into the story of the Revolution—let us imagine a spectator of the battle of Bunker's Hill—or let us rather suppose an *actor*, in that greatest and proudest of days, to have turned his thoughts upon the future, which we see present and realized. Would he not, think ye, have trembled at the awful responsibility of his situation? Would he not have been overwhelmed with the unbounded anticipation? It depends upon *his* courage and conduct, and upon the strength of *his* right arm, whether, not his descendants only—not some small tract of country about his own fireside—not Massachusetts alone—No! nor all that shall inherit it in the ages that are to come—shall be governed by satraps and viceroys, or as reason and nature dictate that they should be—but whether, a republic, embracing upwards of twenty distinct and great empires, shall exist or not—whether a host, worthy to combat and to conquer with Jackson, shall issue from the yet unviolated forests of Kentucky and Tennessee, to spurn from New-Orleans the very foe, whose vengeance he now dares, for the first time, to encounter in the field, when that foe shall be crowned with yet prouder laurels, and shall come in more terrible might—whether the banks of the great lakes shall echo to the accents of liberty, and the Missouri and the Mississippi roll through the inheritance of freemen!

But there is yet another point of view, in which the circumstance of the Revolution occurring in a new country cannot fail to strike you as peculiarly important. It gave our fathers, who were great reformers, an opportunity of purifying the fountains of society—of forming the character and controlling, in some degree, and directing the destinies of the infant commonwealth, by such principles as philosophy and experience had shewn to be best, although they had no where else been fully admitted in practice. They had no inveterate prejudices to encounter here—there was no inheritance of abuses come down from remote ages—they were no grievances established by custom—no corruptions sanctified by their antiquity. They were not afraid to correct a defect in one part, lest it should derange every thing that was connected with it—to administer a mild and salutary remedy, lest the constitution should sink under it—to remove a superfluous buttress, or unseemly scaffolding, lest the whole edifice should be loosened and convulsed to its foundation. In a word, they adopted amendments in their political institutions, just as they would have received improvements in agriculture and the mechanical arts—and while they made no change for the sake of change, and were remarkable for their entire exemption from that perverse enthusiasm, which has defeated more than one effort to do good, by aiming to do too much, they hesitated not to act upon many maxims of government which had been regarded, until then, as altogether visionary—to reduce to practice, as they have done with triumphant success, many projects of amelioration, that had been classed, by common consent, among the chimæras and imaginations of speculative minds. Thus, it had been taught, in almost every school of political philosophy, that democracy could exist only within a very narrow compass—and, but a few years before the Declaration of independence, an illustrious writer* expresses a doubt, whether a universal toleration of religions would ever become the standing policy of a great empire. Now, what would the simplest rustic in the United States say, if he were told that grave and wise men had pronounced the state of society, in which we have been living for fifty years, to be altogether imaginary and impossible.

Voltaire remarks of the discoveries of Columbus that all that was great and imposing in the eyes of men seemed to disappear before this species of new creation. The remark is striking, and might, I have sometimes thought, be applied to the equally bold and successful adventures of our fathers in the science of political society. The first voyage across the unexplored, and, as it was then thought, illimitable and shoreless deep, was scarcely further removed from the ignoble coasting of the Ægean Sea, than the formation of the constitution under which we live was from all that senates and lawgivers had before done in that kind—and it is, perhaps, not too fanciful to say,

* Adam Smith.

that the discovery of America has in this, as in some other respects, enlarged the boundaries of the moral world, as much as it did those of the natural world.

It is owing, then, to these circumstances that we find ourselves in a situation so novel and peculiar—so entirely unlike any of the antiquated and corrupt systems of the old world—so peaceful, so prosperous, so full of high hope, and unparalleled progression, and triumphant success. It looks almost like a special providence that this continent was not revealed to mankind until Europe was highly enlightened. It was then peopled, not by her outcasts (as the first settlers have been sometimes called) but by men who were in more respects than one, the elect of the earth—circumstances favoured them in their new abode— every germ of excellence and improvement was fully developed and expanded—all the vices and redundances and defects, produced, by accidental circumstances, in the institutions of older countries, were corrected and removed—the human race began a new career in a new universe, realizing the celebrated and prophetic lines of Virgil's *Pollio*—

Novus ab integro sœclorum nascitur ordo, &c.;

or, to borrow a most noble passage from one of the prose compositions of the first of poets and the first of *men*— the language in which Milton himself has uttered a vision, inspired by his own holy zeal for social improvement, and the liberties of mankind—"methinks I see in my mind—a noble and puissant nation, rousing herself like a strong man after sleep, and shaking her invincible locks—methinks I see her as an eagle, mewing her mighty youth and kindling her undazzled eyes at the full midday beam, purging and unscaling her long abused sight at the fountain itself of heavenly radiance—while the whole noise of timorous and flocking birds, with those also that love the twilight, flutter about amazed at what she means.

Such was that memorable epoch in the history of man, the Declaration of American Independence—such were the triumphs of the heroes and sages of '76—such were the principles upon which they acted—such was the in-heritage they bequeathed to us—such the example they set to the world. And, upon such an occasion—while we are celebrating so great a jubilee of national independence and happiness—should we—can we be indifferent about the progress of those principles, and the influence of that venerable example? Can we look, without the deepest concern, upon the extraordinary scene that is acting in Europe? Can we witness, without the strongest feelings of scorn and detestation, that conspiracy of a few insolent men against the liberties and improvement of the whole species, the Holy Alliance? And can we reflect, without shame and sorrow, that those who conquered at Lodi and Marengo, are cowering and submissive under such a yoke —and that the swords, which have so often flashed in the blaze of battle, where empires were at stake, and kings were pale with fear, now sleep in their inglorious scabbards—and that the bosoms which, but yesterday, beat high in the exultation of glory and conquest, are brooding with impotent anguish and "wordless ire" over wrongs that cannot awaken their courage—and oh! can we think, without, from the bottom of our hearts, imprecating discomfiture and utter ruin upon those audacious usurpers, that an army of Frenchmen has been marched over the Pyrennees—a slavish instrument of dishonor and ruin—to blast there the very best fruits which their own high example has yet produced—and that a spirit, worthy of the ancient freedom of Arragon and the hereditary pride of Castile—that the spirit of that noble people that dared to resist and to revenge, when these mighty men were happy to fawn, and proud if they were not trampled upon—that a spirit, of which the heroic elevation is equalled only by its innocence and honesty—should, in the age in which we live, be made the object of a crusade, a thousand times more hateful and pernicious, than ever disgraced the ignorance and fanaticism of the darkest times! And when is it that these conspirators against mankind are pouring their myrmidons into Spain? At the very moment when they are pursuing, with respect to Greece, a policy so totally— and, were it not an evidence of reckless consistency in an evil scheme, I should add, so astonishingly different—when they have been utterly deaf to the voice of patriotism and valour—of kindred sympathies, and a common religion, imploring their assistance from the heights that look over Thermopylæ—when they have renounced their connection with the land of Homer and Lycurgus and Sophocles and Plato—with the school to which modern genius is indebted, for the elements of every art and every science— with the GREAT MOTHER COUNTRY of all freedom and civilization—because, I suppose, she too is guilty of the inexpiable crime of rebellion!—that is to say, because she has, AT LENGTH, risen up as with the resuscitated might of Marathon and Salamis, against the brutal barbarism by which she has been, for so many ages, degraded and polluted and trodden under foot! But honour to the valour of the free! Honour and glory to those who dare to be MEN! Greece has again done wonders, and Europe will again be convulsed, until every throne in it, that is not supported by the love of the people, shall be shaken down and buried in the dust. They are greatly deceived—at least I fondly think so—who imagine that the revolutionary spirit, as it is called, has been quelled either by battle or strict league—either at Waterloo, or Vienna. Despotism is, indeed, mighty at present—mighty in its own resources—still more mighty, in what gives strength to all usurpers, the fears and divisions and weakness of the people. But it is at war with the eternal nature of things, and its triumph *cannot* be enduring. Let it revel in the drunkenness of its recent successes! Let it soothe itself with the calm that reigns for a moment! It will soon find that there is something ominous and fearful in it—that it is the pause of the elements, when they are gathering strength and fury for some sweeping desolation—the gloomy, portentous, appalling stillness, that is wont to precede the terrors of the earthquake!

> "Fond, impious men! think ye yon sanguine cloud
> Raised by your breath, hath quenched the orb of day?
> To-morrow he repairs his golden flood,
> And warms the nations with redoubled ray."

I have, already, trespassed so much upon your patience, that I find myself constrained to omit, entirely, a topic upon which I should otherwise have insisted with peculiar satisfaction—and which ought to be exhibited in the most striking lights to the youth of this country, and to be impressed upon their minds, and recommended to the enthusiasm of their hearts, by every variety of argument and illustration—I mean the fact that the name of RE-PUBLIC is inscribed upon the most imperishable monuments of the species, and the probability that it will continue to be associated, as it has been in all past ages, with whatever is heroic in character, and sublime in genius, and elegant and brilliant in the cultivation of arts and letters. It would not have been difficult to prove that the base hirelings who, in this age of legitimacy and downfall, have so industriously inculcated a contrary doctrine, have been compelled to falsify history and abuse reason. I might have "called up antiquity from the old schools of Greece" to shew that these apostles of despotism would have passed at Athens for barbarians and slaves. I might have asked triumphantly, what land had even been visited with the influences of liberty, that did not flourish like the Spring? What people had ever worshipped at her altars, without kindling with a loftier spirit and putting forth more noble energies? Where she had ever acted, that her deeds had not been heroic? Where she had ever spoken, that her eloquence had not been triumphant and sublime? It might have been demonstrated that a state of society in which nothing is obtained by patronage—nothing is yielded to the accidents of birth and fortune—where those who are already distinguished, must exert themselves lest they be speedily eclipsed by their inferiors, and these inferiors are, by every motive, stimulated to exert themselves that they may become distinguished—and where, the lists being open to the whole world, without any partiality or exclusion, the champion who bears off the prize, must have tasked his powers to the very uttermost, and proved himself the first of a thousand competitors—is necessarily more favourable to a bold, vigorous and manly way of thinking and acting, than any other. I should have asked with Longinus—who but a Republican could have spoken the philippics of Demosthenes? and what has the patronage of despotism ever done to be compared with the spontaneous productions of the Attic, the Roman and the Tuscan muse?

With respect to ourselves, who have been so systematically vilified by British critics—if any answer were expected to be given to their shallow and vulgar sophistry, and there was not a sufficient practical refutation of it, in the undoubted success of some of the artists and writers that are springing up in our own times—we should be perfectly safe, in resting, upon the operation of general causes and the whole analogy of history, our anticipation of the proudest success, in all the pursuits of a high and honorable ambition. That living, as we do, in the midst of a forest, we have been principally engaged in felling and improving it—and that those arts, which suppose wealth and leisure and a crowded population, are not yet so flourishing amongst us as they will be in the course of a century or two, is so much a matter of course, that instead of exciting wonder and disgust, one is only surprised how it should even have attracted notice—but the question, whether we are destitute of genius and sensibility and loftiness of character, and all the aspirings that prompt to illustrious achievements, and all the elements of national greatness and glory, is quite a distinct thing —and we may appeal, with confidence, to what we have done and to what we are, to the Revolution we are this day celebrating, to the career we have since run, to our recent exploits upon the flood and in the field, to the skill of our diplomacy, to the comprehensive views and undoubted abilities of our statesmen, to the virtues and prosperity of our people, to the exhibition on every occasion of all the talent called for by its exigencies and admitted by its nature—nay, to the very hatred—the vehement and irrepressible hatred, with which these revilers themselves have so abundantly honored us—to shew that nothing can be more preposterous than the *contempt*, with which they have sometimes *affected* to speak of us.

And, were there no *other* argument, as there are many, to prove that the character of the nation is altogether worthy of its high destinies, would it not be enough to say that we live under a form of government and in a state of society, to which the world has never yet exhibited a parallel? Is it then *nothing* to be *free?* How many nations, in the whole annals of human kind, have proved themselves worthy of being so? Is it nothing that we are Republicans? Were all men as enlightened, as brave, as *proud* as they ought to be, would they suffer themselves to be insulted with any other title? Is it nothing, that so many independent sovereignties should be held together in such a confederacy as ours? What does history teach us of the difficulty of instituting and maintaining such a polity, and of the glory that, of consequence, ought to be given to those who enjoy its advantages in so much perfection, and on so grand a scale? For, can any thing be more striking and sublime, than the idea of an Imperial Republic—spreading over an extent of territory, more immense than the empire of the Cæsars, in the accumulated conquests of a thousand years—without præfects or proconsuls or publicans—founded in the maxims of common sense—employing within itself no arms, but those of reason—and known to its subjects only by the blessings it bestows or perpetuates—yet, capable of directing, against a foreign foe, all the energies of a military despotism—a Republic, in which men are completely insignificant, and *principles* and *laws* exercise, throughout its vast dominion, a peaceful and irresistible sway—blending in one divine harmony such various habits and conflicting opinions —and mingling in our institutions the light of philosophy with all that is dazzling in the associations of heroic achievement and extended domination, and deep seated and formidable power!

To conclude: Our institutions have sprung up naturally in the progress of society. They will flourish and decay with those improvements of which they were the fruit —they will grow with the growth of knowledge—they will strengthen with the strength of reason—their influence will be extended by every advance of *true* civilization—every thing that has a tendency to make man wiser and better, will confirm and improve and adorn them. If humanity was not endowed, in vain, with such noble faculties, many ages of glory and freedom are before us—many nations shall learn, from our example, how to be free and great. The fortunes of the species, are thus, in some degree, identified with those of THE REPUBLIC—and if our experiment fail, there is no hope for man on this side of the grave.

And now, my friends! Let us be proud that we are free—let us exult in a distinction as singular as it is honorable. Our country exhibits the last specimen of that form of government, which has done so much for the dignity and happiness of man. It stands alone—it is surrounded with ruins. In the language of Byron—

> The name of Commonwealth, is past and gone
> O'er the three fractions of the groaning globe.

But, painful as is that reflection, we may be allowed to repeat, with honest triumph, the lines which follow—to proclaim to the world, that

> "Still one great clime,
> Whose vigorous offspring by dividing ocean
> Are kept apart, and nursed in the devotion
> Of freedom, which their fathers fought for and
> Bequeathed—a heritage of heart and hand,
> And proud distinction from each other land—
> Still ONE GREAT CLIME, in full and free defence
> Yet rears her crest—unconquered and sublime—
> Above the far Atlantic."

A Brave New World

Hugh Swinton Legaré associated the peculiar virtues and special destiny of the United States with the purifying, invigorating influence of the wilderness. The poet Bryant (see doc. 61) was deeply moved by the "continuous woods/ Where rolls the Oregon, and hears no sound . . ." "For a transitory enchanted moment," F. Scott Fitzgerald has written more recently, "man must have held his breath in the presence of this continent, compelled into an aesthetic contemplation he neither understood nor desired, face to face for the last time in history with something commensurate to his capacity for wonder."

Document 2, painted by a member of the expedition which in 1792 explored the mouth of the Columbia River in Oregon, communicates something of the spell which the West held for Americans in the early nineteenth century. The sense of brooding destiny and awe which pervades this picture, however, is only distantly related to the economic motives which led to the founding of Astoria in 1811 at the mouth of the Columbia (see doc. 27).

DOCUMENT 3

(PLATES 2 AND 3)

Pioneer's Progress

The two pictures in this document record the central
fact of American life during this period: the subjugation of the wilderness. Forty-five years are supposed to
have elapsed between the two pictures, between the
clearing of an opening in the woods for a wilderness
home and the prosperous rural landscape with its
tilled fields and a small village in the distance. Poetry,
wonder, and awe have vanished with the trees, which,
supposedly, have been replaced with an air of comfort,
a sense of well-being and content, which is more fiction than fact if we examine into the tensions of the
period revealed by other documents in this volume.
The only poetry which remains is suggested by the
title, "Pioneer's Progress," which associates the American's rise in life with John Bunyan's allegory of
Christian's laborious ascent to the celestial city. Such
allegory was more meaningful than poetry because it
was more in accord with popular utilitarian morality.

Document 4

(Plate 4)

Boston: "A City on the Hill"

The picture in this document could as well have
been Philadelphia, Charleston, South Carolina, or any
other fair-sized city of the period insofar as the American psyche was concerned. The first colonists, especially in the North but also in the South, were, if
we are to believe their leaders, intent upon founding
a second Jerusalem in the New World. They called
their symbolic city "a city on the hill" because it was
supposed to crown the Mount of Paradise. The artist
of this picture, though a Frenchman, has stressed the
same qualities of peace and quiet prosperity which pervade the second scene of "Pioneer's Progress"—qualities
which represent the end of striving and which, ideally,
Americans would have liked to associate with their
cities. Restful horizontal lines predominate.

But, in fact, even at this time, as other documents will
testify, American cities were centers of congestion and
turmoil, and farmers as well as city-dwellers often pictured their cities as places of vice where materialism
was rampant and European fashions and follies paraded
shamelessly. Emma Willard, for instance (see doc. 58),
founded a new girls' school in large part to counteract
such evil influences upon American character. Much of
the nostalgia for a simpler age and for republican
virtues (see docs. 104–107) can be explained by
agrarian prejudices against the expansion of urban,
industrial civilization.

DOCUMENT 5

(PLATE 5)

The Triumph of America

We have said that the allegorical mode was congenial to Americans because it explained complex
experience in simple moral abstractions with which they
had been long familiar. Here, however, the progress
of American civilization in its triumph over adversity—
in this case, the triumph over the British at the Peace
of Ghent in 1814—is depicted not in terms of Christian
allegory, but of Greek and Roman mythology. The
appropriateness of such allegory, pagan or Christian,
is argued in documents 31 and 32. The point to be
made here is (1) that the Graeco-Roman example as
a vehicle for allegory was more indigenous to Southern
culture than to the North and (2) that the particular
allegorical representation in this document harmonizes
with the widespread vogue during this period of the
Greek and Roman Revival in architecture. The significance of the Greek and Roman Revival in early American culture is dealt with elsewhere in this volume.

DOCUMENT 6

The Education of William C. Preston

A concern with education was central to the development of a young nation aspiring to greatness. In the vernacular tradition, however, experience has commonly been regarded a greater educator than formal instruction.

William C. Preston (1794–1860) was a well-connected South Carolinian, later a prominent U. S. Senator, whose formal education was supplemented by travel. In the past, the tidewater elite had thought of Europe as the finishing school most proper for a gentleman. The pattern of young Preston's education, including travels in the American West in 1816 as well as in Europe the following year, is an index to the greater sentiment of nationality which was beginning to prevail.

Preston's record of travel contains the only graphic description in this volume of the new life across the Alleghenies. Other notable contemporary accounts of the new West, frequently reprinted, include those of Henry Marie Brackenridge, Timothy Flint, James Hall, and Henry R. Schoolcraft. The most popular record of exploration in the period was Major Stephen Long's *Account of an Expedition from Pittsburgh to the Rocky Mountains* . . . (Philadelphia, 1823).

Preston's description of the West is an untroubled, uncomplicated narrative of romantic adventure. In Europe, however, he shows signs of snarling—for the first time self-conscious of his Americanism, which came into contact with the cosmopolitanism of Washington Irving and with European sophistication. But he also reveals a romantic fascination with Sir Walter Scott and feudal vestiges which anticipates the rise of an exclusive Southern nationality. Preston later developed separatist sentiments.

SOURCE: Minnie C. Yarborough, ed., *Reminiscences of William C. Preston*, 1794–1860, pp. 11–21, 31–36, 43–49, 109–12. Chapel Hill: University of North Carolina Press, 1933.

My father's purpose to have my education finished in Europe was never relinquished. He thought it fit, however, that previous to a visit to Europe I should become acquainted with my own country, to which end with a pair of horses and a servant, he sent me on a journey thro Tennessee, Kentucky, Indiana, Illinois, and Missouri. It was a ride on horseback of four thousand miles with but occasional and accidental companionship. The ride was solitary, thro forests and prairies. It gave occasion for much musing and reveries, not as I think unimportant circumstances in the education of a youth, while my body was hardened by the exercise and exposure and my mind habituated to self-dependence. In Kentucky I made acquaintance with all the principal families, most of whom were variously connected with my own. Portions of Kentucky as it came from the hands of nature are perfectly beautiful, the land apparently a rich alluvian, so that riding thro its magnificent forests of noble trees one has the feeling of being on a rich bottom near a large stream. The principal inhabitants being well born Virginians, retained much of their native and early characteristics, modified, however, by some touch of influence from their new and raw condition. I will not say that the modification was a defect, for that might be a matter of taste and opinion, but it was different from a staid and settled society. The Browns and the Breckenridges and the Howards had lost a portion of Virginia caste and assumed something of Kentucky esteem, an absence of reticence and a presence of presumptuousness. Amongst persons of my own age, who were native to the state, there was a self-dependence not to say self-assertion, and ostentatious suppression of the smaller courtesies of life and minute observances of convention, which was not pleasant. When emigration to a new country takes place even in masses, civilization is not transported or preserved. New physical circumstances induce new developments, and a fermentation of society must take place. An old state of society cannot be propagated in a new country. A certain loss of civilization is inevitable. Stranger and hardier qualities may be superinduced, but they supplant the gentler and more refined. In Indiana and Illinois, society had not begun to be organized. The widely separated colonies surrounded by a small enclosure half field and half patch indicated an incipient comfort, and the worn woman of the house in compliance with the demand of a hungry traveller would in a trice produce a savoury cake and fried chicken or a venison steak, and freely enter upon conversation, until the arrival of another guest would recall her to her usual routine. Let me not omit to add to the real luxuries of chicken and venison, the uniform presence of a capital cup of coffee, not infrequently however sweetened with maple sugar or with wild honey, adulterations not pleasant but tolerable. In the meantime the good man of the house was off some 20 miles for a turn of meal from a mill or more frequently in the prairie with his gun, to get his family supply in the shape of deer, prairie hen or wild turkeys, and no fear that he would return full handed. As to sleeping, the man and wife occupied a sort of truckle bed in a corner, and the hospitable floor presented in its whole extent but scanty room for the numerous guests. I travelled a little more luxuriously than others with a pack horse laden with a little bread, my clothes, several buffalo robes, which last spread on the floor gave me comfortable bedding on which a day's ride of 40, 50 or 60 miles supplied the place of other luxuries. One day I remember I rode 72 miles across the big prairie, completed the journey between a little before day light and sundown, arranged my camp (for that night I camped out) before dark and strolled into the edge of the prairie out of a skirt of woods on a stream which had been designated as my lodging place, and as I stepped into the prairie across a fallen tree

there sprung off a deer that at that distance of 15 or 20
steps stopped, turned, and gazed at me with an enquiring
rather than scared look. I think he had never seen a man
before. I clapped my hands to arouse his instinctive dread
and felt oppressed by the solitude and remoteness of my
situation. My riding horses were exceedingly fine, and the
pack pony, a tough Indian bred animal, of inexhaustible
endurance. I did not nor did my horses seem to suffer
much from this ride of 72 miles. Those under the saddle
were fully protected against the prairie flies by netting,
and the Indian pony's hard hide seemed protected, though
occasionally as we passed a tall clump of grass he would
dash into it and brush off the swarms that beset him.
Late in the night as I slumbered on my buffalo robe I
was aroused by the tread of horses approaching on the
path I had followed. Three mounted men rode up to my
camp fire and called, "Hallo, there traveller." I said, "The
same to you, gentlemen." I saw by the fire light, as they
rode closely up three well mounted men of a grave and
decent aspect. They turned out to be three Methodist
preachers going out to Sangamon, to see if they could not
get up a camp meeting, and establish a church. They
told me that they travelled by night instead of by day to
avoid the cruel annoyance of the prairie flies. They got
down. I shared my supply of jerked venison with them.
They rubbed down and watered their horses, and after an
hour of pleasant talk we had prayers and the gospel way-
farers proceeded on their pious pilgrimage.

Two days afterwards I rode into the old town of Kaskaskia on a pleasant evening just as the people were going
from Vespers. Amongst the men, women and children
my attention was attracted by the tall and stately figure
of an Indian, entirely naked, wending along with the
crowd. Upon inquiry I was told that he was the last of
the Kaskaskia tribe, it having passed away under the usual
influences of contact with the white population. The ride
hence to St. Louis is along the American Bottom, a bottom from six to ten miles wide and more than 100 long,
entirely level, purely alluvial, bounded on the east by

low hills or rather bluffs of Illinois and on the west by the majestic Mississippi close upon whose banks the road generally runs. Opposite St. Louis I crossed the river, standing on a platform erected across two huge canoes of black walnut, which were impelled by paddles like those of a steam-boat, and were worked by hand. Steam was not then (1816) on the Mississippi.

St. Louis was literally overflowing with emigrants, portion of that flood that rolled to the west in 1816. One small tavern was stuffed so full that the nominal guests slept in the piazzas and in hay lofts. Many went out of an evening to camp in the neighbouring prairie. Meeting a gentleman in the door of the tavern he was kind enough to say to me, "I can give you a corner in the room of my printing press until you can look about for better accommodations."

From this hospitable tho not comfortable retreat I was next day extricated by Gov. Clark, (Lewis and Clark) an old friend of my family. The kind gentleman who had given me a roof to sleep under, was Mr. Charles the publisher of a newspaper.

In the elegant quarters of Gov. Clark I was domesticated during my sojourn and found myself most delightfully situated. Besides all appliances of comfort and elegance, I enjoyed the society of that most benevolent and intelligent gentleman, a man of primitive and heroic character, made up of firmness and tenderness, perfectly familiar with everything belonging to the Western Country, having been for years an Indian fighter, then associated in the expedition to the mouth of Columbia, and now for some time governor of the territory of Missouri. His military and civil functions were well and wisely administered. His wide jurisdiction over the Indians extending to the Rocky mountains over a vast and numerous population was efficiently and graciously exercised.

While I was of his household I associated daily with Indian Chiefs and others who came on business and besides had the opportunity of being present at a grand Indian Council held to establish a pacification and make a

treaty with a vast congregation of Indian tribes—Man-
does, Miamis, Osages, Sacs and Foxes, with fragmentary
delegations from all quarters. They were encamped
round about the town in every direction, occasionally tho
rarely drunk in the streets, for they held Gov. Clark whom
they called the Old White Chief in great awe. The Gov.
was of remarkably fair complexion with gray locks and
light blue eyes, hence the epithet *White* Chief. On the
day of the solemn diplomatic session the Governor's large
council chamber was adorned with a profuse and almost
gorgeous display of ornamented and painted buffalo robes,
numerous strings of wampum, every variety of work of
porcupine quills, skins, horns, claws, and bird skins, numerous and large Calumets, arms of all sorts, saddles,
bridles, spears, powder horns, plumes, red blankets and
flags. In the center of the hall was a large long table, at
one end of which sat the governor with a sword lying
before him, and a large pipe in his hand. He wore the
military hat and the regimentals of the army. Occasionally a chief came in, had a little conversation thro the
interpreter with the Governor, and then retired with a
slow and solemn step. By and by came in a somewhat
miscellaneous troop, a sort of rabble, who formed round
the table. The Gov. lit a large pipe; taking a puff or two,
he handed [it] to some of the older men, pipes were
lighted for the rest and they were invited to smoke. This
was a short ceremony, and they were dismissed with a
few kind words and altho mixed with warnings seemed to
be satisfactory. At length there was a long loud roll of
the drum, and an agent marshalled in the delegation of
the Sacs and Foxes. This consisted of eight Chiefs, at the
head of which was a chief leading in the son of the late
King, a youth of 16 years old. His uncle was regent and
guardian to the boy. He and the boy took their places at
the end of the table opposite the Governor, the other
chiefs seated themselves quietly on either side of the table according to rule of precedence that I could perceive.
As they came in the Governor uttered no word nor made
any salutation. Regarding them with a fixed and stern

countenance he half unsheathed his sword and said: "Well, what have you to say?" There was a sort of gruff groan from each, and the regent rising from his seat, with his left hand on the shoulder of the prince, said: "I am not the King—he is dead. I have brought this boy here to our great father, to show you our confidence. The boy is too young to speak in council—these braves and I will speak for him." There was a general grunt of approbation and he sat down. There was a long pause; the interpreter whispered that they expected a pipe to be lit, but the Governor was imperturbable. At length a chief past middle life, rolled up in a long buffalo robe, having a red feather in his hair and his face very much painted, rose and said, "White Chief, we have come down to have a friendly talk with you. There is no more war in our hearts—(a general grunt) We are poor and needy, cold and hungry. We want something to eat, and ammunition to hunt game or we shall starve next winter. We will behave like dutiful children and never again molest our white brethren." "Who are you, you rascal?" exclaimed the Governor interrupting him—"I think I know you, (a general groan)." "I am," said the speaker, "the first man who broke into the settlement on the breaking out of the last war. I killed and scalped two women and a child. Here are the scalps," (taking them out of his pouch), and then I came on down to Pond Fort, where I burnt the stone. Here is my war path," said he, unfolding his robe upon the interior of which was rudely painted in red a long road, with bloody hands splotched along it, and at the end a picture of a conflagration. "I began the war," said he, "I fought thro it, and was the last to consent to peace, but I have consented, and shall be the last to violate it. Small as I seem to you to be I am a great warrior, a very great man, most as great as you. I have taken a great many scalps, stolen a great many horses with bridles and saddles—but now we are beaten and I give up. I have come down to beg peace, and flints and powder that I may hunt deer and buffalo. I have come down as softly as the dew falls at night, but if you refuse these presents the next time I will come like the Missouri in flood. Our horses have trod so gently that not a spark has been struck. If you refuse these presents I will come down like a prairie on fire. I have rode along bare backed on a little skewbald pony with a hickory with bridle, but the next time we will come like a herd of buffalo, when they rush." All this was delivered in an even tone of voice, pausing at each sentence for the interpreter, and using throughout much gesticulation. The Chieftains from time to time had uttered their grunt of approbation. Several of the braves spoke in succession with much less animation, with ample profusions of penitence for the past and deprecation of further resentment, but all urgently begging for presents of ammunition, food, and clothing. When they had finished they asked that a pipe might pass around. The Governor said, "No, you shall not have a whiff—you are rogues, liars, and murderers. (There was a general groan) Go home as you came. I have made a straight path for you, swept it clean,—representing it on the table with the end of his sword— Don't turn on either side to the right or left; if you do my children shall whip you back. So go." They retired with a sorrowful aspect. The Governor sent the Interpreter to recall the Vice-King and the boy prince. They came in and the Governor handing them pipes, said to them, "You have done very wrong to bring that rascal with you on a peace visit. Take this rope to him and tell him that if I ever catch him in my country again I will hang him with such an one. Take these flints and this powder—take your people home and when they get there I will have some things given to them. Instruct this youth to be well behaved and to keep friends with the white men, and I will see that he is cared for."

The Chief who was closely enveloped up to the chin in his buffalo robe and wore no paint (being in mourning) or other ornament except a peacock's feather in his hat, rose to deliver a farewell address to the Governor. I have rarely beheld a more graceful or elegant speaker.

He acknowledged the misconduct of his tribe but extenuated their conduct by setting forth the grievances and oppressions to which the White man had subjected it, and especially he complained that the Whites had associated themselves with the rascally and cowardly Osages, "each one of which big Indians is such a coward that tho he is as big as two men one of my braves can whip three of them." Growing excited in the progress of his speech, he threw the robe from his shoulders and it hung upon the leathern belt round his waist, leaving his whole bust naked except broad silver bands on each wrist and above each elbow making a fine contrast with his rich bronze skin. His gesture was free and graceful, dignified and deliberate, and when he spoke of the recent death of his brother and of the orphanage of the boy upon whose head he tenderly laid his hand, there was a pathos in the tone of his voice and his manner which one would have understood even without the very appropriate and pregnant words which the Interpreter rendered at the end of each sentence. I remembered these speeches for many years and often repeated them to my friends. In general the gestures and personal carriage especially the walk or running of the Indian is very ungraceful, but the whole bearing of this Vice-King was beautiful and majestic. There were several thousand Indians in and about St. Louis with great feasting and frolicking, and such was the influence had by Gov. Clark that there was no instance of violence, tho a good deal of drunkenness.

After a most pleasant sojourn of several weeks, I resumed my journey through Indiana and Missouri, passing Vincennes to Cincinnati—thence to Chillicothe, thence down to the Ohio at Point Pleasant, thence I traversed the wildest and most rugged region of Virginia to my home, having my horses tho wearied in good plight, upon which my father complimented me. I had rode about four thousand miles, had been on horseback nearly five months and had seen something of the New States and of the far West. "Spend the winter," said my father to me, "as diligently reading as you have the summer riding and in the spring you will be fit to go to Europe."

* * *

When I got to the wharf to take the packet for Holyhead, a piteous spectacle was presented. It was a jam of poor and sturdy peasants, trying to get on board for going over to England, to get work in the harvest. The owner of the packet had put the passage at half price and at the instant that the bar was removed enough to cover the whole deck rushed on, many who were not able to pay and when notice being given that such should not be landed at Holyhead, many struggled back. As it was the crowd aboard was prodigious and squalid. The pay passengers bought all the bread in the vessel for their use, and I was drained of my money so as to leave barely enough for me to get to Liverpool on the outside of the coach. When I got there I had but two and sixpence in my pocket. It rained heavily and incessantly the whole way and before we got to the City I was seized with a chill which shook me with great violence. The Coachie seeing it, proposed at one of his drinking places that I should have a glass of hot negus, which may have been a wrong prescription but it gave me presence of mind to tell him that when we got to the City I desired to be driven to the King's Arms and that I was an American. This was a lucky communication for me, for a fever coming on I was somewhat delirious when we got to the King's Arms and lost all consciousness when I was carried into the house, nor had I the slightest recollection for some days. When my delirium passed off at length it was suddenly, and rising on my elbow in bed, I saw standing near me a rosy cheeked, tidy looking girl. Looking at her a moment, and endeavoring to recall my consciousness, I said, "Rosebud, who are you?" She dropped a little curtsey and said in a startled voice, "I am not Rosebud, your honour. My name is Betty," and she left the room. While I was trying to find out if I were not dreaming, the girl returned with a small gentleman dressed in black, [who] said to me in a kind tone: "The doctor said if the anodyne had its expected effect you would probably awake relieved. I hope it is so." "I do not know," said I. "I know nothing about it. Where am I?" He said, "I am your countryman, Washington Irving," and gave me to understand that being ill and delirious at the King's Arms, they had sent for the United States Consul, who, opening my trunk, found my letters one of which was an introduction to him from Mr. Jefferson,—he took possession of me and my effects, employed a Doctor and had me transferred to private lodgings, where he with Mr. Irving and Mr. Brown the banker had been in attendance on me.

* * *

The tenderness and attention which I received from Mr. Irving were consistent with his kind and generous nature. I found him a man of grave, indeed a melancholy aspect, of very staid manners, his kindness rather the offspring of principle and cultivated taste than of emotion. There was an unfailing air of moderation about him, his dress was punctilious, his tone of talking, soft and firm, and in general over subdued, until a natural turn would occasionally run into humour, and laughable delineation of character or events. During my convalescence, which was somewhat tedious, our acquaintance ripened into some degree of intimacy and I freely disclosed to him my condition, my plans, and my purposes. He was eight years my senior, had seen a good deal of society and had made for himself an honourable name. He was then eminently fit to exercise a large influence over me,—especially in restraining the exuberance of my national and natural temper. Of that characteristic of our country he had great dread and distaste. It was foreign to his peculiar idiosyncrasy—he called it whether in conduct or in conversation or in writing *Americanizing* and in himself pushed his opposition to this tendency to the extent almost of affectation. He had a great deal of the English reticence. With them it is, as it was not with him, a surly and ill mannered and unsympathyzing manner.

It is a national character resulting from the false and foolish notion that true dignity is to be always on the watch
for aggression and that *nihil admirari* is elegant and
aristocratic. All emotion is vulgar and ardor horrible.
Towards this Anglicism there was some little tendency in
Irving—propriety, fitness, retention were what he admired.
His great kindness to me made him sensible of my defects in these particulars, and he was free in his ani-
madversions after we had become familiar. I vindicated
myself upon the ground that they were nationalities, but
he replied that they were wrong nationalities and ought
to be suppressed in a gentleman,—that to suppress such
things was one object of travel. Although in the warmth of
such discussions Mr. Irving occasionally grew warm, and
I did not seem to yield, yet he soon became cool and
upon subsequent reflection I saw much truth in what he
said. He was a good deal preoccupied in the first instance,
by the disastrous condition of his pecuniary circumstances. In regard to which I learned from him that he
had set out from America with ample means to meet
the expenses of his European travel, which was projected
for three years and as far as Italy and Greece. Upon getting to Liverpool his brother and brother-in-law thought
that the provision he made was hardly ample enough and
to make it so recommended that he should place his
capital [with them] and become a partner in the then
very prosperous firm, so that he would be entitled to draw
for whatever he might desire. His name was therefore
entered in the books as partner, and at the end of a few
months the flourishing business was suddenly struck by a
disastrous commercial revulsion, which amidst a general
desolation, swept Irving's into utter bankruptcy. "I
found myself," said Irving, "worth much less than nothing, and it was a relief to me to hear that my mother
had died just before the crash. It involved the destruction of some other arrangements that my heart had been
set upon."

Another subject somewhat connected with this was how
he should turn his literary efforts into some profitable

direction. Hitherto literature had been an amusement. He had written Salmagundi, Knickerbocker, and the sketch of the life of Thomas Campbell (Pleasures of Hope) prefixed to an American collection of his works. The sketch of Campbell had brought him in communication with the poet, and led to a pleasant correspondence, in the course of which Campbell had intimated an opinion of Irving's success before the British public if he would attempt some suitable work. Irving decided that literature was to be his profession and the means of support. He had taken lessons in drawing, and had a decided turn for the art. He sketched very well, even in the estimation of Washington Allston, Leslie, and Stewart Newton, and it was perhaps some feeling of this kind that suggested to him the notion of his Sketch Book. He turned it in his mind—spoke a good deal to me about it—occasionally asked me when he gave an account of anything that touched him, how would that do in print. We went to the Athenaeum together and on our return he jotted down what he saw or what had struck him.

* * *

Washington Irving and I took the road for Stirling and the highlands. Our first walk was to Linlithgow, an ancient Royal residence. We walked on steadily, and I flattered myself that I should be able to make the tour successfully. But at Linlithgow I found my feet again broken to pieces, and became assured of what experience has since confirmed, that my feet are disproportionately small and feeble for my size. The next morning they were swollen and inflamed, so of necessity I was compelled to adopt another mode of travelling to this and I hired a sort of large gig drawn by one horse in shafts, capable of holding two persons besides a small driver on a sort of stool in the front. Our driver was a small, red haired, freckled faced fellow 12 or 13 years old, smart, active and good tempered, capable of running by our side on rough or steep road, and always willing to urge the horse faster than we desired. The horse was a stout well set beast, of a grave temper, and not at all inclined to make speedy progress, nor were we inclined to exact it from him,—tho Kelty, as we called him, frequently called out as he trotted by our side, "Give him the whip, Gentlemen."

Bannockburn lay in our way. We of course paused to look at it. I think our minds were more full of the noble poem "Scots wha' hae" than with the battle itself. We saw the rock with a hole in it, in which it is said that Bruce fixed his standard. The fields were quiet under the calm sunlight, and the little brook murmured along, as it did on the day of battle, and will continue its liquid course unchanged, while land and rocks decay and change. I afterwards saw that same unchanging lapse in [–?] by [–?]

We were now in the region of Burns and Scott, and every stream and every rock was vocal with the voice of poetry. Soon

> Gray Stirling with her towers and town
> Upon our wending way looked down.

It was a bright sunset as up the flinty path we strained. The ascent was slow and toilsome so that it was not until the next morning that we could enjoy the glorious prospect from the Castle. We were in the midst of history and poetry—the feudal castle, the moat, the barbican, the palace of a rude and glittering royalty, on the edge of the lowlands and the highlands. From a feverish night we rose at the dawn, to behold the surrounding prospect. North we looked out beyond Callander, to the rugged highlands, on the other side upon the soft and unequalled beauties of the meadows amongst the links of Forth, the river, broad and deep, winding its way through involved mazes slowly as if loath to leave such fair lands. Amongst the links was plain to be seen, Cambus Kenneth gray— and onward little villages and mansions beautiful in the distance. I was pained to have obtruded upon my mind, the ill natured line—'Far as the eye could reach no tree was seen,'—and I rejected it to think of the blue mountains, the green fields, the broad bright water and the touching poetry of bards and patriots that bathed the whole scene. Stirling detained us on its summit for two days rapturously spent. The two days' rest and the good fare had refreshed us as well as our steed Slug, and the boy Kelty. We went nearly thro Dunblane and Callander to Perth.

We decided to take the first canto of "The Lady of the Lake" (the Chase) as the programme of our route, and therefore went to Monan's hill and lone Glenartney's hazel shade, and we could not have made a better choice of a guide, for besides the poetical beauties of the exquisite poem, it is as exact in the description of the scenery and localities as the most minute and painstaking itinerary. In the most glowing and picturesque descriptions of Scott there is beyond any writer since Homer, a minute and accurate representation of real nature. His pictures are all portraits and hence the vividness with which they impress the imagination. We had in our hands "The Lady of the Lake" but the book was hardly necessary, for we knew the poem by heart. We set out at sunrise from Glenartney's hazel shade and having arranged with Kelty and his horse and gig to meet us wherever there was a road, we took the course of the Stag, only deviating from it when the ascents were too precipitous for us to climb. We passed round Benvoirlich, saw the Giant's den on Uam-Var, cooled ourselves amid the

> copsewood gray
> That waved and wept on Loch Achray.
> Where shall *we* find in foreign land
> So lone a Lake so sweet a strand.

The day had far advanced before the Bridge of Turk was seen, and Kelty and his horse as well as ourselves stood in need of refreshment. This we took on the margin of the stream spanned by the old bridge of Turk. Our refreshment was not confined to the cakes and ale we had brought along for that purpose, but stretching ourselves on the margent green we slumbered until it was too late

to prosecute our inspection of the Trossachs, and at a short
distance found very comfortable lodging in the hospitable
mansion of Mr. James Stuart, a stalwart farmer somewhat above the rank of peasants. He said that Walter
Scott's writings had brought so many of "you Southerners"
to visit this region, that he had been compelled in self
defence, and in charity to keep a sort of Inn. "But," said
we, "we are not Englishmen but Americans." "Then,"
said he, "it shall not be an Inn for this night, but a highland cottage in which honoured guests are received by
James Stuart," and surely no entertainment could have
been more hospitable or comfortable. Our host, a most
substantial Scotchman, was shrewd and intelligent. He
told us that he was contemplating emigration to America,
for which his enforced occupation for the last three years
had provided him with the means. He told us many
piquant anecdotes of English humorists, both men and
women, said that Scott had once staid in his house
two days and that notwithstanding his lame foot, he
clambered thro the ravines and over the rocks as actively
as "I or any highland Gilley."

At early morning we went under Stuart's guidance to
explore the dangerous glen. It was as yet gloomy in the
early day, the copsewood where the hunted stag had
eluded his weary pursuers was pointed out, the loose
shingly rocks over which the Gallant Gray had fallen.
Here in this "darksome dell" in the deep "Trossachs'
wilder nook," amidst cold dew and wild flowers, we
hardly knew to which the greatest admiration was due,
the exquisite beauties of the wild nature or the description of them in the Poem. Kelty said, "I think Slug is
hardly as fine as that Gallant Gray you are reading about
but I think he will go safe through." There stood before
us the thunder-splintered pinnacle, near us were the ash
and aspen, and I plucked a fox-glove the dust of which is
yet between the leaves of my portfolio—put there in its
bloom forty years ago.

> "Onward amid the copse gan peep
> A narrow inlet still and deep—

and on it, strange to say, were a pair of small wild ducks. The illusion was so strong that when a short space onward I saw the water of the Lake, I looked to see the Lady of the Lake in her light shallop. With a sort of enthusiasm I stepped forward to the pebbled margin and took a hearty draught of the water. The space of water to the Island seemed an hundred yards or thereabouts. In a moment I was stripped, with the purpose of swimming over where the borderman and Malcolm Graeme had swam, and there was in full view the identical oak behind which Duncraggan's withered dame had stood, when amidst the storm she had dealt the fatal dagger blow to the adventurous spearman. I found the water of the Lake very cold, but I soon accomplished the enterprize. As I stood beside the oak Irving called across to me, "Preston, you may out-swim me, but remember I can out-walk you." I waved adieux to Mr. James Stuart, and Irving quickly crossing in a skiff, we spent the day in rummaging the Island. There was a fantastical little boat house, most inappropriately erected on it, where skiffs were kept for hire. Since that time still more inappropriately has been put upon the Lake a small steam boat, called the Ellen Douglas!! but in our explorations, I think we discovered the identical old tree described by Scott against which Allan Bayne reclined, as blasted, worn and gray as he. I can't but think that this old tree suggested that beautiful picture. Every touch of his pencil draws a real object, and every inspiration springs from nature.

* * *

[Preston's party, without Irving, next proceeded to the Continent.]

A week was spent busily and pleasantly in Rome—and we took the road for the Alps and Gaul. We struck straight for Florence—of all places that I have ever seen, the most beautiful and attractive. Whatever nature could do in her most lavish moods she has done for it, and then it is decorated with all that prodigality of art which wealth and taste for centuries could bestow upon it. Nature has bestowed upon its landscape, the Arno, Fiesole and the Val d'Arno, art has given it the churches and palaces of Michael Angelo and Raphael, Tasso and Dante have conferred upon it the glorious associations of poetry, and the magnificent *Medici* family concentrated in it whatever is beautiful or noble in the productions of the pencil or the chisel—the *Madonna della Seggiola* and the Venus di Medici and all this is enwrapt and enblazoned in a climate the most enchanting and glorious. The surrounding blue covered mountain sides of Albano, Fiesole, uttering the names of Gallileo and Milton, rears its top into the clouds, and the pellucid Arno flows gently thro the city. Surely there is not upon the face of the earth a spot comparable to it, one that so fills at once the soul and the senses with scenes of and sentiments of beauty. Naples with its bay and its volcano is grander—Rome with its solemn memories more awful but neither has that aggregation of beauty which gratifies so intimately all the aesthetic faculties of human nature. To breathe the air was a luxury, to open one's eyes was to see a glory, and if you closed them what memories flowed in upon the soul. Science and Literature and Philosophy—and courage and fortitude. I said to myself a thousand times, "If exile from my native land should be my destiny may it be in *Florence!*"

*   *   *

It was "au courant" with the agreeabilities of Florence [that in] the suite of rooms we had at the Scheidor hotel were a music room, baths and a fine conservatory with a garden attached, all for ten francs a day, our meals being furnished from a neighboring *restaurateur* as we might order.

The Venus did not strike me so agreeably as I had expected—beautiful doubtless—"beautiful exceedingly." My raptures were restrained and modified by those circumstances which seemed to be evolved from a subsequent analysis of my emotions. The statue is too small—below nature. I think she does not seem to be fully grown. The

average height of woman is now and I suppose in all ages
has been above five feet. Venus is below. The attitude is
inexpressive. The countenance has a bad expression—it is
not that of purity and trust. It is not that of a virtuous
woman. The nudity of the figure is not pleasant. With
female beauty we always associate the idea of drapery,
and of colour too. In the male figure we can readily dispense with these accessories of drapery and colours. The
majesty of the male figures may exclude or reject these
things. *Majesty* may supply the place. We can well conceive a grand naked man when wild in woods the native
savage ran—but a naked woman is positively unpleasant.
I doubt whether her configuration is so conformable to
the lines of beauty as that of the male. The majestic is
hid when the man is enveloped in a blanket or a buffalo
robe and revealed when the covering is thrown off, as I
have seen amongst the Indians, and marble or bronze may
fitly represent it, but beauty can't stand the garish and
vulgar light. Modesty is an essential element of female
beauty, at least it is to the civilized and Christian mind.
Woman is picturesque but not statuesque. Upon the
whole the Venus is too *petite*. I take it that Eve was
five feet, an inch, perhaps two, high that before the fall
at least she had a modest look, which Venus has not, and
thus that as the ideal of female loveliness it is defective.
The ancients had not that ideal. It is of Christian origin.
In the gallery of the portraits of eminent painters each
painted by himself, I was proud to see that of our countrymen was Gilbert Stuart, one occupying with all the
characteristics of a fine painting a very conspicuous place
amongst its illustrious compeers, vindicating by its own
merit its right to be here in Florence amongst the illustrious artists deposited by the Italian taste here in this
pantheon.

The lower classes of Florence and the peasantry of
Tuscany were better looking, seemed more contented
and happy than I had seen elsewhere. The eye was offended by fewer priests, prostitutes, and paupers than in
any Italian town. The three classes bear a natural relation

to each other, they flourish under the same form of religion—and civil polity. The reigning Duke is said to be a
good man and a wise ruler, his manners are free and
genial. He is seen frequently at places of public resort,
attended with so little ceremony, that one passes him
without recognizing him. He values himself upon his
horsemanship, keeps a stud of fine English horses, and is
proud to show his skill in riding by dashing amongst
English or American horsemen—his own countrymen
offering no competition with him in the art of riding.
Indeed an Italian on horseback is a ludicrous object and
the ladies astraddle upon their high trotting horses are
horrible.

*   *   *

An American Eve

It may be said that all nude women in art and poetry who embody the feminine ideal are representations of Eve. Henry Adams once asked himself whether any American artist of the nineteenth century had ever "insisted on the power of sex, as every classic had always done, but he could think only of Walt Whitman. . . . All the rest had used sex for sentiment, never for force; to them, Eve was a tender flower, and Herodias an unfeminine horror." He felt that this evasion was part of a fatal dualism in American life which he symbolized by the Dynamo and the Virgin and which such later thinkers as George Santayana have interpreted as a split between the material and the ideal stemming in large part from our Puritan inheritance.

John Vanderlyn's painting of Ariadne in this document, perhaps the finest example of the classic idealized nude in America, seems to us today quite inoffensive—and lifeless; yet it created a public furor when he brought it back with him from Paris in 1815, the Greek and Roman Revival notwithstanding, and in a country where Negroes often went stark naked. In sharp contrast to William Preston, of course, Vanderlyn highly approved of sophisticated European attitudes toward the naked figure and disapproved of American prudishness, which he considered an indelicacy of the mind rather than of art.

DOCUMENT 8

(PLATE 7)

The Other Face of Eve

If John Vanderlyn spent much of his energies railing against the ingratitude, prudishness, and cultural barbarism of his countrymen, another artist of the period, Raphaelle Peale, made much the same point more effectively in a moment of light-heartedness. His painting, "After the Bath," may be interpreted as a clever satire at the expense of a prudish clientele. Actually, however, it was painted as a practical joke to fool the artist's wife, who snatched at what she thought was one of her best napkins covering the painting of a nude. But not even the *trompe l'oeil* was lacking in a broader cultural significance, for it exposed the folly of a countermovement to moralism and abstraction in American art—that is, the slavish rendition of literal fact. "Would you know what is going on here in the way of art?" the painter Thomas Cole was to ask a friend. "It is difficult to say, except that Tom has painted a portrait which shames the old masters; Dick has just finished a red herring to the very life; and Harry has completed his grand historical picture of the Pig-Killing." Cole's poetic landscapes (see, for example, doc. 62) attempted to unite the ideal and the real. The most successful treatments of the female figure during the period, virtually unnoticed by contemporaries, were William Rush's "Comedy" and "Tragedy" (doc. 108).

DOCUMENT 9

The Education of James Guild

The reader may find the following one of the raciest documents of the period. If it seems as formless and sprawling as the nation itself, its sense of immediacy heightens its charm. It was written for the most part immediately after events by a Yankee peddler without William Preston's advantages of social position, education, and hindsight. We know very little about James Guild, except that he was born in Hatfield, Massachusetts, in 1797, gravitated to Europe, where he won several medals for portrait painting and miniatures, spent several years in the West Indies in search of health, and died in New York about 1841.

But Guild reveals himself shamelessly: his poor orthography, his vanity, his petty pride in sharp dealings, his pathetic yearning for respectability. These, together with such other qualities as rare courage, intelligence, humor, and enterprise, suggest that the popular image of the Yankee (see, for example doc. 65) was not entirely myth. On the other hand, like the primitive artist and his wife in documents 10 and 11, he seems almost totally lacking in the idealism of the period.

His picaresque record is more patterned than superficially appears. In the first place, it typifies the great mobility of the period—outwardly, geographical movement; inwardly, an upward movement toward social respectability. It is, then, a success story. Secondly, his social progress parallels roughly the same geographical pattern as William Preston's travels for education, beginning in the West, moving southward to Charleston, South Carolina, and ending in Europe. In other words, it finds its orientation between vernacular and cultivated moorings, ending at the same point of interest as Preston's record, with the innocent, young American's discovery of the naked female body in this wicked Old World—but with such a difference of intention! One wishes that young Guild had continued his story. Subtitles have been added, as also a modified punctuation and paragraphing, in order to help the reader, but the spelling remains unchanged. The only sustained episode which has been omitted is a period of school-teaching.

SOURCE: "The Travel Diary of James Guild," *Vermont Historical Society Proceedings*, new series, Vol. V (1937), pp. 250–313, *passim*.

TUNBRIDGE OCT. 5TH 1818

He Buys a Trunk of Goods

At this time I became of age, July ninth, and freed from a long confined situation, as I used to call it, as I was bound out from 9 years old till I was one and twenty. Then I sough for some happier situation. My disposition would not allow me to work on a farm, and some other employment I must pursue. At this time I was worth a note of $70 Dollars, and I could not command the cash for it. So I had a disposition to sell it for goods which I moved to my great disadvantage. No one knows the feelings of my heart when parting with my little all for a trunk of goods and losing my caricter if I had any by being a pedler. I not only had the disagreable sensations of leaving my friends, but I wondered why why I should stoop so low as to follow so mean a caling. Two things caused many a tear to flow from my eyes, the parting from my beloved Aunt Jenush together with to young Ladies who had happyfied many an hour and the obstinacy which Mr. Hutchinson had or appeared to feel for my wilfare. Although I loved this family dearly and the most of them appeared to have a parting affection for me, I was determined not to shed a tear, and in fact it was a hard matter for me to keep from crying when I see my dear miss shed tears for my departure.

He Stears for the West

After biding all friends adieu I took my little trunk and stears for the west. Now my sorrows began to rise. I went to Rochester in first place. Here I found an old friend where I put up, for a day or two. Previous to this I had engagueed to go in pardenship with one Geo. Youven who was to meet me here in just a week from this time. How to spend one week before I meet him I went to the north. I began my peddleing. You must know it was awkward for a farmer boy who had been confined to the hoe or ax to put on a pedlers face, but I believe I was as apt as any one, I got my things in rotation pedler form, so when I went into a house, do you wish to by some harecombs, needles, buttons, buttonmolds, sewing silk, beeds? If they wished to purchase, they would want to banter untill they could get it for nothing.

Soon I found I had to go through a piece of woods 7 miles through. When I was going through these woods, I began to reflect on my situation, O, says I to myself, what comfort could I take wandering over a lonesome moun tain befriend by no one.

Yet it was as plesant in the solatary wood, as it was to be caling a stranger in different houses in the fair of a pedler. While I consulting my mind, I spied a patrige. I took the trunk of my back and with a stone brought the patridge to the ground and carid it untill I come to a house and gave it for a dish of bread and milk but found my goods ware not salible which increased my sorrows. Then I went on anxious to sell some goods but poor encouragement. I had got within nine miles of where I started, and I was so fild with grief that I was tempted to go back in to some back farmers house where I used to be acquainted and not let the folks know where I lived that I was in town. Sometimes my mind upon one thing and some times an other. The best you could say of me

I was a poor sorry boy. To indulge myself in thinking of home I found was a burden to my sorrows.

I turned my course to northfield and from that on to dog river. Here I found a poor set of inhabitants. I think I traveled 3 days and selling but 30 cent worth of goods, and I believe I gave away more than that, for when I came to a poor house where they wanted a needle atoo or a few pins, I could freely bestow them on the poor although it was but little I posest. After followling down dog river, I found I had to go through a piece of woods 7 miles through. Before I entered these woods I had to cross the river, and there was a freshet a short time before and carried off the bridge, and I had to cross on a log which did not reach across. While crosing this bridge or log I was thinking how I should feel to fall in. Come to the end I had to jump to get a cross and just as I gave a jump, my foot slipt and in went Guile and I. Now this was jumping work to save myself and trunk. When I got out with the water dripping of my nose and chin, sais I to myself this is Guild's luck. I Remember Aunt Jerusha usd to say jim was the most unlucky boy that ever lived, and I caled it my misfortune and went on.

Soon it began to rain and I in the wilderness accompanyed by no friend, and all the consolation I had was in hoping for the better. While I was traveling over the dreary forrest, my mind was not without its thoughts. Some times I was thinking of pleasure I usd to take with my young companions. Some times I would think of my Mother Brothers or sister. Sometimes I would think of my God but not as I ought. Sometimes would sing, but if I sang any thing that was mournful I would burst out in tears. O there was not a sigh from my heart but fetched a tear from the eye. While contemplateing on these things my foot slipt and down went guile, I, trunk and all, and hurt myself and bruised my trunk. I got up and cried out, O heaven what shall I do, was I born for misfortune? O' I am poorer than a beger, and I can never prosper, nor my friends will never more embrace my sosiety with that loveing affection. O misery, I wish my goods were never seen by me, but since I was born for misfortune, I will sit down and sing a song.

* * *

He Journeys to Troy and Eats Parsnips

From this I went to Troy and Laid out all the money I had for more Goods. Here I felt like a green boy, for I never was in so large a place before, and I thought folks new every thing and more to. I was some bashful with all. I reccollect one day as I went to dine with some of the nobilities, I was very much daunted with their look, for I considered myself inferior to them, for I though on my former station as nothing but a plow boy, and now seated with the gay and polished part of that great Citty (as I cauled it). However I thought I was capable of niping and twisting and deceiveing them by affectaton. Soon I was waited upon in great stile. They offered me a plate of boiled vituals consisting of parsnips potatoes & I axcepted of it very freely with the masks of politeness, by thank ye, Sir, although I had as lives take a puke as to taste of a parsnip, but I thought I must eat what they gave me or I should not be a gentleman, although I knew I should not take any comfor of my dinner if I eat that parsnip; so I thought I would eat the parsnip right down and take some good of the rest of my dinner. I made way with it as soon as possible. They perceiving I et it faster than the rest of my vituals concluded I loved it better and they claped another piece on my plate. This is the effect of politeness, and I have thought many times since that I looked more like a hog when I was eating the carrot than I did like a Gentleman in axcepting it, when I did not love it.

I went to Salom, and round about till I came to Bennington again. Then I crossed the green mountains and went to Halifax. Here I found old acquaintance and relation both on Father and Mother side, and I went around amongst them where they seemed to have an affectionate feeling for me. Although I knew I was making nothing, yet I expressed to them I was doing well. I could see in their countenances they noticed I was in trouble, for I think I gave them reason although I was troubled in my mind, and so that when I was out of their sight, my eyes ware filed with tears and my heart with grief thinking on my situation, and when I returned I would chear up the drooping mind with singing or telling stories. I would govil and jolly to drive hence meloncolly, but the heavy load still hung at the heart. Sometimes I think I acked like a crazy person. I know that with this little pen I cannot describe my grief. At last I concluded I would bid them good by and start for boston.

*   *   *

He Crosses the green mountains

While I were crosing the mountain it was very rainy, and I traveled rain or sonshine, but O the heavist grief lay uppon my heart. While I would sing with the tears running down my cheaks, O Mother did you know the sufferings of your son, how woule youre heart ache for me, but I was caful not to let them know of it. Soon I came to a house where I staid over night and found I had meet with some pritty clever folk. Here I told them all my misfortunes. They seemed to feel a tender ness towards me, but I told them that I had concluded to be a poor man the rest of my days and I was going to pursu some employment that would set me below the common class of people. I told them I was agoing to get an old lether apron and some spoon moles and go round a tinkering as I had got to be mean I would be mean. The gentleman replied if this is all you want, I can help you to a lether apron, and I guess my neighbour Thomson has got a pair of spoon moles, and you can by them. I presume I told him I could if I could make a bargain for them, for I told him if I could not be in a situation to live in good society. I wanted appear so mean that no one would take notice of me. He laughed at my nonsense, but I told him to fetch on his lether apron, so he got a lether apron, and I put it on and went and made a bargain for the spoon moles. Now there was laughing enough, my close were become poor, my hat rather mean, and I comed my hare down over my eyes and got me a little sodering iron and and prepared for a tinker. Now I cared not for my looks nor reputation and I had deformed myself so that if I were to meet my mother in the road, I believe she would not know me.

He Goes Atinkering

Now I went on and came to a house and went in and enquired whether they wanted any spoons run or any tinkering done. The reply was, can you run old plates into spoons? O yes, marm, I can mend your arthan ware if you want it mended, for I had got some sement for that purpose, so the old woma fetched on some puter plates, and I went to melting them up. O how my friends would laughed at me could they have seen me in this situation. There was one thing on my side, that was they could not laugh me to scorn, for I was below that. Then however I went to running my spoons, and I run 12 spoons and had 30 cents for doing it.

In the meantime I had a chance to buy four or five dozen sissors at 3 cents each and thought if I could sell them for 12 cents, I was making good profit, so I offerd them for sale, but the reply was they are good for nothing; if they were, you would ask more for them. I tried about a fortnight but sold none, then I took and made two paks of them and marked one 12 and the other 25 cents, new sissors for sale; and when I went into a house it was, do you want any tin cups tin pans tin or puter dishes of any kind mended and do you want to buy some sissors? Yies, if you have got some good ones. Well, marm, I have got some good ones and some poor ones; my best come at 25 cents and the other at 12 cents. So I would show them, to them, and they would look of them. Now mother you must get me a pair of sissors for me, for you never got me a pair. O well dear child I suppose you must have a pair or I shall be teased to death. Now the girl would say mother which is it best to get 12 or 25 cents one? O it is best to get a good pair if any; so they would try them by cutting out paper, and if they cut wet paper, they were good; and in this stile I was spending my time which I thought was a meaner caling than I deserved, but I felt at this time as mean as my employ.

Soon I hurt my foot and caught cold in it, and it was five weeks before I could ware my boot. Now I maintaind myself by running spoons and tinker ing. After this I was entirely discouraged, and I could not stand it no longer. I was so homesick I thought I would give up my carere and return to my friends, and so I started on and wen about fifty miles towards home which brought me within about 70 miles of home. While I were returning, my mind was very much troubled thinking what I should tell for a story, for I felt meaner than you can think.

Now if I tell them I have ben a pedler and a tinker, I shall be no more for my society I usd to enjoy, for they will dispise me. O what shall I do? my life is no more sweet to me and where is a friend? Once I could (when with my master) enjoy the sweetes of society, although I had to work hard and with a discontented mind, but now I must give up my race and work for a living and their society is no more swet to me becaus my company will no more be agreable to them.

While I were thus amusing, the tears ware a faling. O misery what shall I do? O Mother, would you own me any more for your son, and Sister could you any more embrace me in your arms with that affection yousd to? Can I enjoy any society if I return? O my money my reputation, my society, and comfort is all gone and what am I, poor tinker.

It being a rany day I thought I would call in to a house and rest me. Just as I steped into the dore I burst out a crying and went to the table and set down, and if I ever cried I think I did then. I boohood like a little child although I was one and twenty, but all at once it sprang into my head—I wont go back and I said good by, and out dores I flew and right back I went with a determination to get into some business before they should see my face again. Now heads up.

* * *

He Enters a Tavern

. . . I went into a tavern unsuspected of insult and sat down in the corner of the room with a heavy heart thinking on my troubles, while the gang of about 20 ware drinking and carousing with them. I took no part, but as an imposition they they went to pinning papers and rags on my coat which they got from the table of a tailor. I being very busy in in thinking of past times I never noticed them, but soon I found their was a snickering round the room, and I concluded they was doing something to me, for when I looked up there was nothing to laugh at. I ris up from my chair and behold they had pined papers and rags on me so that they hung almost to the ground or flore.

Then I rose up and a terible laugh alover the room. I found I would not answer to resent it but rather fall in with them, so I says to them, my friend, dont you think this is a fine situation for a yanke boy to be in? and I laughed at my looks and says Landlord give me a half pint of your best brandy. Gentlemen here is your health. The very great reason why Im treated in this manner at this time undoubtedly is the long absense from my friends and which caused me to sit in deep study and perhaps my dress and manners are not equal to your honours. Perhaps you look on me with scorn judgeing me by my awkward appearance, but Sir I consider that a sense of our ignorance is the first step to knowledge. Sir your most hearty respect, hopeing if you ever come to vermont (and told them my name to) you will have the goodness to call on me. I will introduce you into the first class of people and you shall receive every thing that is consistant with one friend to another. Gentlemen I have one request, that granted, I will drink with you in the greatest fredom, which is for your to pull off what you have put on me that I may look a little more respectful. By this time one says to another who done this? I dono I dono and finally they all denied it, but they came and pulled them of and we drank round. Thus ended this scrape.

The next day I saw a gentleman from Vermont who was in as bad situation as I was the day before. They imposed him as they'd uppon me and he resented it which gave much sport to them. They black-guarded him and run upon him so it made my heart ache to see him in such a situation. As soon as I got a chance to speak to him, I invited him out to the side of the house and told him that I was usd, as bad as he, but all they wanted was to get him mad. I asked him to treat them and get off as well as he could. He said if I would get a half pint brandy, he would pay one half of it and drink to gether as vermont friends. This I consented to, for to get the man out of difficulty. While were talking the winder happened to be up. Out came a pan of water and wet the man almost all over. Then we went in and I caled for a pint brandy and beged the mans better usage, but the passions of the man ware so great he must dispute with them. Now see what the heart feeling stranger gets for his good intentions to help a stranger out of difficulty when the dificulty was ended. Instead of his paying one half of the treat I caled for it and I might pay for it. He had caled for none, and now all the comfort I got by helping him out of difficulty was pay my own bill and no thank from him.

This learns me human nature. I find you no not who is your friend untill you try them. No, you will find friends enough, only let them live on your purse but when it is drained then you may go.

> Now when a friend appears to view,
> Search him and see if he is true,
> And if he is true then treat him kind,
> For a faithful friend is heard to find.

He Meets the Dutch

Now I started for Casanova. The people and the people on my way ware principely dutch of their costoms and manners I was not usd to, but as night came on I was under the necessity of tarrying here with some of them till morning. Here my curiosity was excited to see a dutch Girl, for I had often heard of them. This was rensing close and it was in the winter and in a cold day, but she would take a basket of close and go down to a brook about forty rods and stand in the brook and rench her close and come up barefoot. This I thought was more than Yanke Girls could do. I told her that I thought she was smarter than Yanke Girls. She would spat her feet and say, Oh Dutch Girls ant afraid of cold weather. With her I had some sport.

Soon supper was ready and the way we had our supper was they made a good large possom or hastipooding an took a pan of milk and mixt it all up together, and so we all sat around and partook of the good thing. After supper was over and we had got through with our conversation, the old Lady lighted me up to bed. She came and turned down the fether bed and told me to get in next to the straw and put the fether bed on top and then you will lay warm. In the morning I started on and came to Casanova.

He Meets a Fortenteller

Here I found a fortenteller who told fortunes for a half of a dollar. The first thing I must have my fortune told, and I went in to her house and she got a pack of cards and told me a thousand fine stories. She said that my fortune has ben just like a Cow giving a good mess of milk and up with her foot and kick it all over, and would be so untill I was fore and twenty. Then I should prosper. She said that in a short time I should learn to paint likenesses, that I should go into a painters shop an my profiles would look so mean to their painting that I should give them a small

sum to learn me to paint. Then I should travel untill I
was 25 years old, then I should marry and sittle down for
life, and live an independant life. She told me some things
that I new was true and some that was not.

She told me a good deal about a certain Girl which who
usd to keep company with me, and after a long time by
the flattering of her friends she turned her back to me, and
says nothing to me. That girl sais she has ben sorry for that
since, and her life will no more be sweet here, but I paid
but little notice of what she said, so I went on to pompy
hill.

He Begins to Cut Profiles

Here I went to cutting profile likenesses. After I had
bin in town about two days, I was traveling on a back road
and passing by a large white House where there ware two
young Lades who had got on their old bonnets for washing.
When they saw me, they thought to have a little fun with
a stranger, for they thought they would never see me again,
and they began to beacon and curtesy and bow and make
all the mocking figures you could mention. All this time I
stood with my mouth wide open and about half bent
and made the appearence of a fool as much as I could.
They seeing my poster concluded I was a fool as perhaps
it is to true.

After they had mocked me enough, I thought I would
let them know I was not so big a fool as they thought, for
in order to get to the back room where they ware, I had to
go through a garden, and over the fence I jumped, and as
hard as I could after them, and followed them into a par-
lor where sat Mrs Semore. Then I was waited uppon in
the greatest politeness. By this time I had attend my deportment and was as polite as you please. No matter,
Marm, about a seat, I only caled because those young
Ladies beaconed to me. I never have young Ladies beacon
to me without I know their desires. One of the girls say I
thought it was some one else. The other says I thought it

was such an one, and their faces coullerd up, and I think they got punished enough for their impodance.

While I ware here I bought me a diamond to cut glases with and of the same man I cut profiles enough to pay for it. Then I went to Elbridge in Camelus. Here I staid 5 week in cutting profiles. While I was here, I sold my diamond for 300 frames to put liknesses in. While here I saw a young Lady who wanted I should give her my profile. O yies you may have my profile and welcome. The object was she thought if I gave her my likness, I would give her my frame, also she being a little imprudent told one of my friends, and he told me. So when I offered it to her, she says O I wont take it unless you give me the frame with it. Well, Marm, I thought you wanted my frame more than my likeness, and I did not give it to her.

* * *

He Goes to Skunk's Misery

Now I went to a place caled skunks misery and I think the place was equal to its name. Here I put up at a tavern, for I was sick and had no appetite for my vituals. While here I had 3 eggs 2/6 a pint of bread and milk 1/7 a little bread and coffee after the rest ware done, 2/6 four lodgins 7/. This I thought unaccountable and told that I was sick and could not eat, but all the reply I got was I had ben there long enough I might calect, but rather than dispute I paid the bill.

At this time a young man of much confidence as well as impodence say, landlord, why dont you lick that fellow if he jaws a word? I would. This starts my dander a little and replied, I'd rather see you do it than tell of. I can, says he. I came out on the floor and told the young man I was ready to exchange a few dry nocks, and I stump you to touch me with your with your little finger, Sir. It was not my object to fite but to scare him. The young man says he would not fight but he would wrastle. Very well, Sir, I will do that. Then he say, I want wrastle unless you will bet a dollar. Very well I will bet a dollar, and I made preparations as fast as possible so as to scare him. Soon he says I wont unless I bet five dollars. Well, I'll bet five, and puled five dollars out of my pocket, and I being in such haste I scart him out of it and he would not any then. I told him as he has imposed on me he might wrestle with me for a little something to treat the company. To this the company was much pleased and caled him a coward and he took hold and I throwed him 4 times and he paid the company a treat and I cleared out.

Now I came to Geneva. From this I went to Gorum. Here I found two Cousins where they was building carding mashines. They was very glad to see me but more for my money than any thing else I presume, for it was but a short time before they wanted to hire some cash. I rejected. But they urged me so hard and I found if I could alow my concience to run such a risk, I could save them from having their property sold at public auction, for their was an attachment on it. Now truly stared me in the face and one Mr Woodward, to assist me in relenting to them, says he would become responsible for the debt 19 day; if they would not pay it, he would. Their flattering looks and words drove away all fear and I let them have 30 dollars.

He Wrastles a Dutchman

Now I went out to bethel to a town meeting, and after meeting was over ther was a wring of wrastling. This I was pleased to see. I stood by untill a number had wrestled, and there was a dutchman had got hold who threw every thing and the observations ware, there was not a man there that could throw him. Just in the ring I saw a brick that I though I would take it a way for fear they would fall on it, and just as I had stooped down the Dutchman threw his opponen against me and kiled to birds with one stone. I jumped up an told him he could not do that again, so I was brought in the next time to throw him. I accepted it very freely, and I could hear the audence saying, he'll throw him you see if he dont, for a stranger would not wrestle unless he was smart. In about one minute I landed him flat on his which made much laughter, but the Dutchman was not satisfied. He thought he could do it next time, so we took hold and in a short time I piled him again, and when I throwed him, I took the to lock of him and his feet was about 3 feet from the ground when his head and shoulders touched. This mad much laugh and no one would take hold of me.

He Visits a Painter of Likenesses

Now I went to canadagua. Here I went into a painters shop, one who painted likenesses, and I my profiles looked so mean when I saw them I asked him what he would show me one day for, how to distinguish the coulers & he said $5, and I consented to it and began to paint. He showed me one day and then I went to Bloomfield and took a picture of Mr goodwins painting for a sample on my way. I put up at a tavern and told a Young Lady if she would wash my shirt, I would draw her likeness. Now then I was to exert my skill in painting. I opperated once on her but it looked so like a rech I throwed it away and tried again. The poor Girl sat niped up so prim and look so smileing it makes me smile when I think of while I was daubing on paint on a piece of paper, it could not be caled painting, for it looked more like a strangle cat than it did like her. However I told her it looked like her and she believed it, but I cut her profile and she had a profile if not a likeness.

Then I traveled on and stoped at every house and inquired if they wanted any profile likeness taken, and if I could not get but a trifle, I would paint for the sake of learning. In about 3 day I was quite a painter for I had one dollar for painting, and when I came to bloomfield I thought I was quite capable of the task. Here I painted this that and the other. After I had got through and ready for a start, one Miss Narvin sent in to have me come in

and see her, for she wanted their little childrens likeness
taken, and I went in and shewd her some painting while
she caled to her husband to come and see them. He came
out and sat down in a chair. Com, Says Miss Marvin,
wont you have our childrens likenesses taken? The reply
was no, get out of my house in a minute, or I will horse
whip you, you dam profiters and pedlers, you ought to have
a good whipping by every one that sees you. Get out of my
house you rasckal. I replied in a soft tone, why now, uncle,
you wont hurt me, will you? I shant go untill I have my
pictures that your wife has got. They gave them to me and
I says now, sir, I will go with pleasur, but I want to take a
little spell with you. I know you are a man who would
have acquaintanc very well and you wont hurt me. I am
one of the best natured fellows you ever see. Now, uncle,
you have one of the finest situations, (her I was inter-
upted). Get out of enclosure, you rascal, or I will horse
whip you and you shall leave the town in one hour or I will
horse whip you all the way out. Stop, says he, give me your
name, Ill warn you out of town. Show me your authority
to demand my name and you shall have it, and not without my authority. I'll let you know my authority. With
that he caught me by the color and with great threats declares a horse whipping while I was very calm and many
pleasant observations which made him the more angry.
He puled me along by the collar and riseing on the second step to enter the house while I was on the first.

Now was a good opportunity for me. I flew my hand
round and caught him I no not where and droped on my
back and with my foot pitched him over my head and
the first that struck was his face on a sharp board purposed
for a goos pen and I gess he carrys the mark untill this
day. Now sir if you will come here I will serve you the
same sauce again, only touch me with your little finger
and I will make you my footstool. After a few minuets of
bustle he recovered and to enter a complaint for hurting
him. So a woman that belonged in the first tavern told me
if I wanted to get a way, she would tell me where to go,

so she pointed the way through a barnyard and into a footpath which in the end prove the same.

* * *

He Goes Southard

Then I made up my mind to go to the southard. I said to myself I will go and either make something or nothing, either gain my health or lose it.

Now I had a Sister whoom I loved ah, yes I loved to dearly. She was the only Sister I had, and when young our father left us, and if I could assist her it was my great pleasure. After getting her a crape gown and a new bonnet & I then must leave and my dear Mother to wander again in the Land of Strangers, and with a heart full of grief not only for my connections, but I had lef a friend who seemed nearer than connections. For particular reasons I have strove to drive her from my mind, but time will decide all all those difficulties. As it is not my object to put down love affairs, I will pass on. Now I came to Charleston where I was sick for a weak, and had a little money stolen from me, and after going to Walpole found it necessary to go back and make him appear guilty. Then I came on to Brattelborough and in a weak made $23. Now I had a good horse and fifty Dollars. Then I came to Albany and sold my horse which was worth $80 for 40. Then I had $90.

I found my health was asusal very poor, and wishing to gain some knowledge in painting I would play truant for awhile, for all the practice that I had had in miniature was when I was at Charlestown. I been in the habit of painting on paper and a Gentleman says, cant you paint on Ivory? Oh yies but I am out of Ivory. Very well I have a piece and you may paint my mineature, so for the first time I attempted Ivory painting and went so much byond my expectations that I thought I soon would be a dabster. I then came to Albany. I then dashed about in this Citty and to gain information in painting, I visited all the dif-

ferent painters and learnt all I could and then started
for New York.

He Goes to New York and Philadelphia

The steemboat left me behind and I took a Sloop where
there was about one Dosen Ladies and Gentlemen. We
left the wharf with the prospects of a fair wind but we
had 6 days Passage. When we had got within 70 miles of
New York there came up a September gale. The gale
struck us just after we had got out of the high Sands, and
we anchored. We found our selves in danger expecting
every moment to be dashed to pieces, the women crying
the Lightening flashing, and the Storm tremendous. After
the storm was over and we came on board we saw the
danger we had been in. Two vessells drove up high and
dry, two in distress and two sunk all in sight. We then
had a fair wind and came down to New York and found
much damage done. Here I dashed around visiting the
different painters and getting all the information I could.
Then I started for Philadelphia. Here was sick for awhile,
then I went to little York where I kept school and painted
miniatures three months, mad $200.

He Meets a Pull Back

I then thought I had improved enough to go to Baltimore. I then came to this City and got one of my best
miniatures and being stranger, I did not know to start
better. I drew up a subscribtion paper and wen round the
Citty stating if I could get 12 engagued I would take
them for half price in order to get start ed. I soon got
the number and meet with very good success. I got just
started in painting and my health failed. I grew very poor
and thought I was going into a consumption. I lost my
ambition my pride and perseverance was lost. No society
was pleasing. I could take no pleasure in the finest society
and sought solitude, but soon found I should die in this
situation. I could not bare to have my ambition lost. I

had made a little money and thought I would make or brake what I had (the latter I soon affected).

I had an opportunity to go in pardenship with a Scotchman whoom I though was worth money who told me many fine tales, pursuaded me to put what I had and goin partenship. This I done, But Oh how soon did I find my self in a pickle. I found that instead of his being worth money, he was $1000, worse than nothing. His father in law arived from London and siezed the thing and just before he lay an attachmen on them, I got wind of it and mad him draw writings that we are disolved and that all debts contracted before our partenship he was responsible &&&. After aranging business as well as I could and getting clear of this fellow, I found I was in debt $25. This was another pull back for awhile.

I was down in the mouth, out of money and in debt was a grevious thing to me, but I soon found I must not loose my ambition but tak to the fence again. I then went to painting and after a little time I made money enough to pay my debts and have $60, in my pocket. I enjoyed myself very well as it was always my rule to keep good company or none, and fortunately I had the good luck to always have that, let my situation be what it might. The people in Baltimore are generally familiar and hospitable, take much notice of strangers, particular if they have a genteel appearance. The Ladies are fond of parties, and spend much of their time in walking with the Gentlemen in the park, & this Gentleman (or scoundrall perhaps is more proper) whose name was Robert Crofford deceived me in every thing that I trusted to his honor. He was the greatest liar I think that I ever knew. He had neith principle or judgement to carry into efect what he undertook. In less than six month after I entered into pardonship with him I found that we ware loosing money very fast and that our debts ware more than we could pay, for he had previous to my partnership borrowed about $600, from one place and and another, and about $800, in debt to his father in Law.

For about three weeks I was in low spirits and sought

solitude. I found my health impairing very fast and to grieve about spilt milk would only shorten my days and deprive me of that independant spirit and ambition which I had to shine in the world. I was and alwas was unhappy because I could not obtain a furtune. I thought that I Should be one of the happiest fellows in the world If I could only be rich, and I thought as others had began with nothin and became men of fortune that I might I threw asside all my dull notions and went to painting and paid off all my debts and a little to clear out. I then left Baltimore and came to Norfolk.

He Makes $300 in Norfolk

Here I said to myself that I will make money. I hired me a room and adver tised to teach writing, and painting miniatures. I had in a short time 40 schollars and as much as I could do in painting. I painted for $5.00, each. I spent six months in this place and made $300. Just beginning to get a better start again, I just got started in business and four or five painters arived, but as I had got the start and they found but little to do except one portrait Painter which did not hurt me much. The inhabitants ware formerly welthy, but owing to the change of times they ware many broken merchants people who had been in the habit of high living, and it is hard for people to give up their pride and stile even rather live poor, than not stilish. Society was very much broken up and family visiting was their greatest amusements. The habits of young men ware very much corrupted. A house in the place was kept where they usd to spend their time in gambling etc. From excessive habit they seem to be more fond of this blackard company than that which was more refined.

While I was here there was a gentleman from curatuck visiting Norfolk. He was introduced to my room and being so well pleased with me he had his miniature taken and said that he would get me work if I would come to curatuck. Not knowing him to well, I thought the sure side was the best. I said to him if he would draw up a sub-scription paper and obtain 20 subscribers I would come. In a few weeks I received a letter from stating that he had got the number. I then considered myself under a pleasing obligation to go from this I went to Curatuck and from thence to Camdin and to Elizabeth City. This was about thirty miles from Norfork. I enjoyed myself very well and mad about $300 in three months, returned to Norfork to spend the fourth of July, and from thence to N. Y. I left Baltimore in Sept, and now it was July. I had made six hundred dollars. After I failed in Baltimore I would not write to my friends to proud to own that I had been taken in and lost all my money. I said to myself money I must and will have. I found I lacked very much for instruction, and I made up my mind to go to N. Y. and receive instruction from the first artists and then take a trip to the south, and when I can go home in Stile then will I go but in any other way I will not show my face.

It now being fourth of July I was invited out to dine where there was a jolly sit. After diner the Ladies retired and then went round the flouring glass. I formed the same resolution as I always had not to get to much. I drank as much as I knew I could carry and did not like to refuse, so when the glass came round I would fill it up and drink the last. I could hold a glass in my mouth an in opeing it I would let it all run into my pocket hankerchief. I drank 7 glasses and spit three out of the windo and three into my hankerchief. The rest of course must have drank some thing like 14. They ware all as drunk as coots but myself, and they all wonderd how I came out so sober, but they attributed it to being more usd to it. I did not undeceive them ———

How often do I think of the famous writer when he was asked what was the greatest thing for a man to learn when he replied one's self; he was asked the second time what was the next, he still replied ones self, and the third, ones self. How true it it man must study himself and practice self denial and if he wishes to be respected, he mus respect himself. How have I learnt human nature by carefully avoiding all those vices which naturally had a man to ruin.

He Starts for New York

Now I started for N.Y. and wishing to appear well in the City, I did not wish to soil my close knowing not who was on board. I fixt myself up in some old duds and looked more a clown than a Gentlemen, but I did not care. I wanted to tumble about the deck. After having got on board I observed four young Ladies, will dressed and of importent manners. They being a little better dresed than the rest of the company ware disposed to treat them with contempt. When dinner was ready I considered myselfas good as them and took my seat at the table, but these Ladies would not sit down although the company was all well behaved. There was about eight or ten other Ladies of the middle Class of people judging from their appearance.

When I found they ware disposed to treat us with so much contempt as to have another table sit for them, I took it as an insult and went to the captain and told him I did not like the appearance of those Ladies. They are more trouble than all the rest of the passengers, said he. Well, said I, let us have some fun with them; I will act the part of a Country fool, not a Soul on board will know to the countrary. He said he had no objections if I would get in no quarrel. I asured him I would not, and I commenced with all my awkwardness, and they soon began to laugh at me, and the more they plaid their pranks, the more I plaid the fool, and in a short time they began to ask me questions such as, was you ever in N.Y? I informed them that I was raised in the back country, never saw such droll things before. In this way I amused them for two days. I then went and dressed up in my best close, fixt up in the best stile, and gave the captain the wink as we had all things pland.

The captain then informed them before I made my appearance that instead of my being the fool, I was a

Gentleman and they ware foold, that I considered it an Insult they refusing to eat at the table. He knew that you took him for some country fellow from his dress, and he has given you a specimen of that caricter, and now he will give you a specimen of a City Gentleman, for such he is. They are all astonished and asked why he should not dress like one. Because he thought it not necessary board a vessel, I think, said he. The best way is for you to fech forward some wine and after this treat him with respect.

At this moment I made my appearance as polite as you can immagin. My apearance was so different they caled for the wine and exclaimed, they never would known it for the same person. I told them that I had been usd to sitting at the table with Genteel people so long that it mortified me when they refused to sit with me. They acknowledged their error and we made friends, and before we arrived at N. Y. those who insulted me was my warmest friends. How easy it is to Quarrel and how easy it is to let it alone. Strive to live in peace with God and man.

* * *

His Sole Object was to Make Money

Now my sole object was to make money. I cared not for this society, nor friendship any more than to have them treat me with politeness, and I do the same to them. I commenced my profession and soon found incourage- ment. I spent 4 months here and in that time I had cleared my expenses and made $400. All went on peacibly with me I had as much Society as I wanted, the best the place afforded. I became acquainted and intimate in the Clergys family, who of couse ware respected. Then when I would to leave Town, it so hapened that they went to Washington the same day I wanted to go myself. They introduced me to the first families in that place and immediately my friends were newmerious and my business very good. Society was rather broken up and although every prospect of success looked dubious to me, but they

entered into the spirit of the thing, and I made money
here. As soon as I found my business dull I was off.

In Washing I boarded at one Dr. Telfares, where I had
one of the sweetest homes I ever had in my life. His
family was modest virtuious and esteemed; they ware prudent discreet and reserved with dignity and respected;
they ware good sensible and indulgent, and ware beloved
and adored by their friends. Such families as this is rare.
They can make a home for a stranger. While I was in this
place a Gentleman of great welth who lived about fifty
miles in the Country on my way to Tarborough was so
pleased with my miniatures offered to carry me to his
house, and from thence when I pleased, if I would go to
his house, and paint his family. I accepted his offer and
went. Here I spent a fortnight in the most agreable manner. Every day we ware sporting with the hounes, hunting
rabits, etc. He was a young Man about my age, (his
name Ashly Atkinson,) then I went to Tarborough.

Here I staid about 3 weeks and made a little cash and
then I was off from this to Fautville where I spend three
weeks. My whole aim was was to make money. I did not
form any acquaintance but made my business my study.
After this, I went to Wilmington. Here I spent about 4
weeks and wound up my business for N. Y. This of all
places is one of the worst for a Young man of a weak
mind, but a strong mind might learn the weakness and
folly of Man. The Young Gentleman appear to be destitute of that society which so much polishes the young
mind (I mean the Ladies). Their time is mostly spent
at a nine pin ally and a place of disipation. I took no part
in their mode of spending their time. My object was
money, and when I had settled up my concerns, I found
I had made one Thousand dollars from, Oct, untill June.
Now I have surmounted the great difficulty I so long
sought. I loved my friends my dear Mother and Sister &
but three years had pased, and I had not seen her.

*   *   *

He is Home Again

I had been absent from them three years, and for two years I had never heard from them nor they from me. I would not wrigt them, because I had failed in business, and unless I could go home in Stile. I Surprised them all very much, for I could go home with my pockets well lined, and of what a happy time I spent with them. I could embrace my dear Mother and Sister with an affectionate kiss, and embrace in my arms, that Mother who watched over my youthful days, and can I Her guardian care forget, nor he my father through bliss or while remembrance shall retain it quiet.

I soon paid my old Master a visit. The family welcomed me with joy. They all seemed pleased to see me, that dear family of, how I love them, four Daughter whoom I usd to carry in my arms. The oldest, is now about sixteen. Ever since I first left them, she never saw me return to pay them a visit but she would with joy, and when I leave them, She would cry with grief. She has alway held the nearest and dearest affections of my heart. With her I had many a sweet and pleasant wride. It usd to seem rather odd to see my old Master, go out and tackle my hors and Cariage for me to wride but it was right. I had to tackle his long enough to pay for it. And wriding about from one house to another and from town to Town I spent two months. in the most agreable maner. How changed the sun seven years before that I was Subject to my masters will, and tied to the hoe and harrow. Now I could wride in my cariage, and ask no man, any favors. I had never done any work since I left him, and had become so accustomed to dressing in stile and keeping Stilish company, it seemed very odd to return to my friends who live as I usd to with a tow Shirt and frock on with a beard a week old. The young Ladies that I usd to think so very nice now look to more like servants Girls. In the stile I had been living and society that I associated with had accostomed me to treat such as was not able to

dress in stile at all times and have the title of Ladies and
Gentlemen, with indifferance, and never thought them
companions for me; but when I saw so much harmony existing in their little family circles, the strong attachments
they held for each other, how happy they ware in, spending their time in industry, contented to please, no ambition to shine, I was ready to exclaim, give me domestic
happiness. I could not help but admire them, and stronger
tachments I have never seen, neither felt in those circles
where they could dress in stile every day After having mad
my visits to all my friends finding them all well, I began
to feel a desire to get back again to N. Y. whire I could enjoy my usual ocupation and visiting those families who
have daughter that play so beautiful on the pianifort, and
where there is constantly some new thing to attrac the eye
and attention.

The country will do for a while but, soon becomes
gloomy for an idle man. Now I must part with the dearest
friends on earth, a here I went to bid them adieu, the
oldest daughter of my Master said she was not agoing to be
so foolish, as to cry this time, but after I got my horse
harnissed and ready for a start, I found her mising. I
found her in the other room, crying, and the little Sisters,
accompanied her. Dear objects of my affections, 'tis had to
part with friends you love so dear But the best friends
must Part.

I bid them an affectionate farwell; then I went to my
Mothers and after a short time, I bid them Farwell. While
here I had some of the most delightful rides I ever had,
with a lovely young Lady, half sister to my Brothers wife.
She possessed all the qualities necessary to make a man
happy in Her society, But as lovely as she was I mus leave
her and all the rest of my friends or I should not be able
to satisfy my ambition to first visit the south and from
thence to Euroup. What seemed surprising to me more
than any thing else was the little affection they seemed to
show each other. My Brothers and Sister never seemed
to embrace my Mother with an affectionate kiss, and yet
in their deportment they Showd the sincerest friendship.

He Goes to Charleston

Now I enter the ship, for Charleston. We had an astonishing quick passage of 70 hours, distance, 700, miles 60 passengers on board, I was sick all the way and made myself a stranger to them. It was not known to the passengers whether I was a painter or a tinker, but after I got established in Charleston, they came one after another and to their astonishment they found me to be a fellow passenger. After a short time I found a little more Stile was necessary in order to get in with the more stilish part of the community. I rented three rooms in an Elegan house, well furnished one for painting and another to receive company and Exibited Some of my finest production at the window. For a short time I found I began to have visitors, and by business increased very fast.

In order to get business from the most wealthy people it becomes necessary to be noticed among them. Being a Stranger I had to do this, by my own merit and genius. To affect this, it becomes necessary to pay great attention to my dress and address. I let no man ride a better horse than myself, dress a little better the most of of them. I soon became acquainted and enjoyed myself very well for about 7 months, made $13,000 and owned my business. The Slaves in this Citty are treated as well as they can be consistently in a Slave holding state. What is most astonishing to me is that the Servants, many of them, are as white as their Masters and no dout many of them are manufactured by them. The country about Charleston is low and marshy and very unhealthy. The best water they have is rain water which is mostly drank. The streets are very narrow and but few of them paved. The inhabitants, many of them, are poor and proud which is a double curse. They are maintained by the income of a few Slaves, and live from hand to mouth.

This is thought by many to be a good place to find a good wife, But my maxim is that a portion in a wife is better than a portion with her. I do not want a Hellin, a St. Cecilia or a Madam Dacur, yit she must be elegant or I should not love her; Sensible or I should not respect her; prudent or I could not confide in Her; well informed or she could not Educate my Children; Well bred or She could not Entertain my friends; Pious or I should not be happy with her, for the delightful hope that she will be a companion for Eternity. Of how much is requisite to make a happy companion; the ornaments which decorate do not support the edifice. Do not indulge romantic idear of super human existence; remember that the fairest creature is a paten creature.

He Sails to Liverpool

Now then I go on board the ship Edward bound to Liverpool, now all the former pleasures I have spent in the sweet society of my relatives and friends, all hover around my heart while I look and gaze to see the last tints of my native shore, but I am in pursuit of not only fame but fortune. Soon I began to suffer with seasickness, and while rowling and tumbling in my burth I would often grown within myself and wish I had never left my native Shore. Soon the sea began to rowl and tumble her waves together while the tempest lowers. Fearfully the vivid lightnings and the rowing thunder and harrow my sorrow. Oh what would I give to set my foot once more on my native land, but soon, the sun is reversed and a calm ensued. Here in the dead sea without a friend to console me, I would sit and meditate upon my former friends. Soon we caught a porpors which waid about 200 lb. This was a little amusement for a while but soon passed away and my days was anxiously spent. Look with anxiety for freedom from this, lonly birth for unfortunately, when I left Charleston I was under the necessity of taking my passage on board a common, merchant vessel, and unfortunately the Captain was a man of a penurious mind and in about 17 days, we ware out of butter sugar and potatoes. Our living was mostly salt codfish, and I got so tired of it I thought I should almost Starve, in a little compact cabin half fited with cotton which created a staunch smell. oh how much I under went.

But after a long time of twenty two days we came in sight of the shores of Ireland, and a fish boat came along side with fish, and I had not had any thing that was good for so long a time. I begen the Captain to buy some fish. He bough enough for one meal, and I told him that we had not had any thing to eat for so long a time that we must get more, and but long pursuading he ofered, a bottle of rum for another another fish. The boat man consented and instead of one brought on board three fine cod, and supposing the Captain would be generous with them, but he being so small refused to give them any more and retired to the cabin. I felt so greatful for the favour that, I wint down and told the Captain I would give them a bottle of my Liquor. The Captain very abruptly said you shant but I will if I like, said I, and after a few words of this sort had pased, I being rather angry, replied, you convince me that I have no wright and I will not, and while I insisted I had a wright to do what I pleased with my own, he insisted that he was the Captain and I had no wrigh to give them without his permission, and although I bought it for my private use that he had a write to do what he pleased with it. This raised my ambition and I caught hold one my bottles and told him I would let him know that I had a wright to do what I pleased with my own, said that I would give them two to pay for his insult. I then took two bottles and gave them while he looked on and saw I was very angry and being a little vext, (or a good deal) I told him I would bolt it out of the Cabin windo before he should have it; And out of the windo went a bottle. The Capt found I would not put up with his meanness and very quietly sat down to dinner and I gave the Boat men two bottles and we had fish for some time.

A tremendous gale sit in and we ware forteen days before we could get up to Liverpool. I wint ashore and viewd the coal mines, saw the poor people at work, got one of the men one side and learnt from him how hard they had to work for a few Shilling a week; and after much fatiage we arived in town. Here I amused myself for a short time, found the place very agreable, had a letter of introduction to a jew, but instead of his being of service to me, he jewd me out of a few pound. Cut him at once; Visited all the places of curiosity; and started for London.

He Goes to London

Got an outside seet so as to see the country. Breakfast ready, stage stop, very dilatory in bringing it in. At last in came a cold chicken. Just as the horn blew to be off paid my reckning. Caught a half chickin in my fist; Not agoing to loose my breakfast fir the company quite amused, and away we went. Stoped to dinner, eat very harty, only just change enough to pay my reckning, no sixpence left for the servant; Servant very impotent; No sixpence for me, sir. Do I ow you any thing, Sir; it is devilish hard that I must pay 18 shilling a week for my situation and no body give me any thing. That your business and if you say anything more to me, I will snub your nose, sir, and away we went. The gard man and waiters cost me more than any passage in the stage; drove into London, put up at the Swans two Weeks, found the, faire very high to stay. I soon got my rooms and boarded myself.

He Commences his Profession as an Artist

I commenced my profession as an artist; I then delivered my letters of introduction; and met with great hospitality, was invited to dine; and became very intimate with Mr Bird. I found him a most hospitable fellow and had a most amible wife in his family. I spent many an hour very pleasantly. I likewise became acquainted with Mr Cethcart; and immediately became acquainted with the most eminent Artist in the Citty; I was introduced into a club of artist where they met once a week for the purpose of painting naked figures; for the purpos of learning the human figure; the first subject we had was a young lady, stript to the beef and placed on a pedistal, and we twenty Artists sitting round her drawing her beautiful figure, perfectly naked; Se Sie————————

DOCUMENTS 10–13

(PLATES 8, 9, 10 AND 11)

Likenesses and National Character

Portraiture—or the "taking of likenesses," as it was sometimes called—was the most popular art form in early America. Itinerant painters like James Guild and Chester Harding ventured as far west as Missouri, bringing their craft to the remotest hamlet, frequently exchanging a "likeness" for their room and board and receiving the highest fees when they became most expert in a camera-like fidelity to life. They concentrated on *faces;* the rest—character, gesture, composition, poetry—was left for high art, which was patronized largely by the gentry of the Eastern seaboard who followed European elite fashions and were willing and able to pay higher prices.

In this period, however, the self-taught takers of likenesses were beginning to compete with the professionals, even in Eastern cities. Documents 10 and 11 express the aspirations of the newly prosperous. The artist and (we assume) his wife have obviously enjoyed considerable material success, which they wish to flaunt. The bodies and background are decorative rather than realistic. The artist has changed the position of his wife's arm in order better to show the decorative flourishes on the arm of the fancy Sheraton chair. He has also eliminated the pleats of her skirt in order to provide a strong contrast between the frenchified gown and porcelain body on the one hand and on the other the chic imported wallpaper borders. The same is true of the artist, who is groomed in the height of fashion and blackly outlined against a decorative, even elegant wainscotting.

Chief interest centers in the faces, which are sensual and arrogant. Obviously, the externals of life matter greatly to these people. The Puritan tradition of

austerity and high-mindedness has undergone a transformation. The older cultivated tradition in American portraiture is represented in documents 12 and 13.
Here, composition and character are quite as important
as facial likenesses. These, too, represent success and
prosperity, but quite as much attention has been paid
to the inwardness of their lives. Robert Fulton is in-
tense in chiaroscuro, full-bodied, his inventive qualities
suggested not only by the expression on his face and
the containment with which he holds himself, but also
by the explosion in the background of one of his tor-
pedoes on target. The woman in document 13, by
contrast, is quizzical, relaxed, fashionable without arro-
gance. She feels undoubtedly secure in her social position. Nevertheless, one senses here that the artist, a
pupil of Benjamin West, is concerned with the social
fripperies.

Document 14

The Education of Chester Harding

With a background very similar to that of James Guild, Chester Harding (1792–1866) became a fashionable portrait painter of English dukes and American notables. The following document is also a success story. Yet it reveals a mind more conventional than Guild's, and Harding's portrait style was not more distinguished than that of half a dozen portrait artists less popular than he during the period. Why, then, should the one succeed so exceptionally, while the others fell behind, Guild disappearing altogether?

Harding conscientiously tries to explain the secret of his success, which he attributes to his ability to embody the myth of the West. He apparently had the kind of personality, physical presence, and rough integrity that went along with this fiction. Yet there is something ironically revealing about this frontier democrat's pride in being lionized by nobility. He *was* conventional —and became more so as he came more under the influence of the cultivated tradition. His early picture of Daniel Boone (doc. 102) is more interesting than portraits painted after benefit of study in England.

Notice his emphasis, below, on "likenesses," one of the very revealing words of the period.

SOURCE: William Dunlap, *History of the Rise and Progress of the Arts of Design in the United States*, Vol. II, pp. 289–95. New York: 1834.

I was born in the town of Conway, Mass. Sept. 1st, 1792. My childhood and youth were spent in the way common to children of poor parentage, in this portion of the country; the winter months devoted to the acquisition of the rudiments of education, and the remainder of the time to agricultural pursuits.

At the age of twenty-one I began the trade of chair-making with my brother. This mode of life I followed for about two years; but as I did not entirely fancy the calling, I embraced the first fair prospect that presented itself of my bettering my means of living. I tried various ways of accumulating property, amongst which was keeping a tavern in a country village in the western part of New-York. This and all others failing, I embarked at the head of the Aleghany river in a 'flat,' with my wife and one child, and floated down this beautiful stream in search of adventures.

Pittsburgh was now to become the theatre for the new part I was to take in the great drama of life. I had no distinct notion of what I was to do for a living, and I felt for the first time in my life that I was a penniless stranger. After overcoming a great many difficulties, I opened a sign painter's shop, and continued in that branch of the useful arts until July 1817. During this period (a year and a half) I conceived the idea of painting portraits. I had become acquainted with a Mr. Nelson, 'an ornamental sign and portrait painter,' as his advertisement ran, and was much enamoured of his pictures. I sat to him for my own portrait, and also caused my wife to sit for hers, although I was by no means in a condition to afford the money they cost, which was ten dollars each. Mr. Nelson was one of that class of painters who have secret modes of painting faces, and would sell a 'receipt,' but saw no advantage that could possibly grow out of his *giving* his experience to another; so that I never saw my own portrait in an unfinished state, nor would he let me be present at the painting of my wife's portrait. Here I must date the commencement of my present line of life. These pictures, although as bad as could well be produced in any new country, were, nevertheless, models for my study and objects of my admiration. Soon after I took these pictures home, I began to analyze them; and it was not long before I set a palette, and then seating myself before my wife, made my first attempt. In this I was eminently successful; and I question if I have ever felt more unalloyed pleasure in contemplating what I might consider at the time my pet-picture, than I did when I first discovered a likeness to my wife in my own work. This success led me to think much of portrait painting, and I began to grow disgusted with my vocation, neglected my customers, and thought seriously of following my newly discovered goddess, regardless of consequences. I now conceived the plan of going to Kentucky, which was almost as soon executed as formed. During my residence in Pittsburgh I painted a few portraits, perhaps ten or twelve, and in each I could always trace some remote resemblance to the originals. This gave me some confidence in myself, so much so that I ventured, though with some misgivings, to announce myself as a *portrait painter* in the town of Paris, Kentucky.

Here my mode of life underwent a great change. I was now pursuing a profession which had always been deemed honourable, though of that circumstance I had not the most remote idea. I regarded it in a more favourable light than I did the calling I had just abandoned, because it gave me more pleasure in the prosecution of it, not that it was more honourable. I took rooms and commenced business at once. My price was $25, which to the highminded Kentuckians was a trifle, though to me it seemed exorbitant; but that price I was advised to charge, and at that price I opened my new shop.

In this small town I painted near a hundred heads, and found that I was sufficiently in funds to enable me visit Philadelphia. I forthwith set off, and passed five or six weeks in looking at the portraits of Mr. Sully and others, and then returned to Kentucky to renew my labours with increased strength. I had now begun to think more favourably of my profession, and I determined to distinguish myself in it. I felt at the same time that there were more difficulties in the way than I had dreamed of before I went to Philadelphia. A knowledge of these difficulties I believe for a while impeded my progress. I

thought that my pictures, after my return, were not
as good as those I painted before I had thought so much of
the art and its intricacies; and I am now persuaded that
the knowledge of the many obstacles that I must overcome before I could arrive at distinction in the art, had
the effect of intimidating me, and it was a good while before I could get into my former free style of painting.
About this time too, the currency of the state became
sadly deranged, and all classes were obliged to curtail
their expenses, so that my affairs did not prosper so well
after I returned from Philadelphia as they did before I
went.

I shifted my place of residence several times, but failing
to produce any very considerable interest in my favour,
I made a grand move to St. Louis, Missouri.

I had the good fortune to meet with constant occupation, and at the advanced price of forty dollars. I remained
in this place until July, 1821. During my stay here, I
greatly improved my pecuniary circumstances, and for the
first time began to think of visiting Europe. In the autumn
after I left St. Louis, I made my debut in the city of
Washington. I painted a few heads for exhibition; so that
by the time congress met, I made something of a display. I was successful beyond my most sanguine expectations. I painted something like forty heads, during this
winter and spring. The autumn following I went to Boston,
chiefly on a pilgrimage to Stuart. I saw him and many of
his works, and felt, as every artist must feel, that he was
without a rival in this country. I spent a week or so in
Boston, and then went back to my native country, Massachusetts, with my mind filled with feelings very foreign
to those I started into the world with, many years before.
I had while at Washington become acquainted with Mr.
E. H. Mills, our senator at that time in congress, who
induced me to open rooms in Northampton. Here I
painted a number of heads; and while in that town I was
employed by some gentlemen living in Boston, who
thought so favourably of my pictures, that they urged me
to go to that city and establish myself. I said no—not

while Stuart was there. But they urged me so much, and at the same time offered to procure several sitters for me, that my reluctance was overcome, and I accordingly found myself in the same city with Stuart, seeking employment from amongst his admirers.

The gentlemen who urged me to come to Boston, more than fulfilled their promises. They brought me many sitters, and in all respects were deserving of my highest gratitude. My room became a place of fashionable resort, and I painted the enormous number of eighty heads in six months; and I verily believe, I had more than twice that number of applicants for portraits in that time. Mr. Stuart is too well known to allow of the supposition, that my portraits could bear any sort of comparison with his; yet, such was the fact, that while I had a vast deal more offered than I could execute, Mr. *Stuart* was allowed to waste half his time in idleness, from want of sitters. Is not this a hard case? I can account for this public freak only in the circumstances of my being a back-woodsman, newly caught; then the circumstance of my being self-taught was trumpeted about much to my advantage.

Perhaps, to the superficial observer, there is no circumstance in the history of an artist, that carries such a charm with it, as that of being self-taught—while to those competent of judging, it conveys no other virtue with it, than that of perseverance. By self-taught, is here meant not having any particular instructor. It matters little how an artist arrives at a sort of midway elevation, at which all with common industry may arrive. But it is the man of genius, who soars above the common level, and leaves his less favoured brethern to follow in his track with mingled feelings of envy and admiration.

I now found myself in funds sufficient for a trip across the Atlantic, and notwithstanding the thousand times I had been told that I could learn nothing by going to London, and the pressing business I must give up, I set sail for Liverpool the first of August, 1823.

On arriving in London, I found myself in a wilderness of art, and an equally dense wilderness of people. For a month or two my mind was in the greatest confusion. I was perfectly solitary; and from seeing so much of art, instead of being stimulated to exertion by it, became in a degree indifferent to all the sublime works that were within my reach. I felt that the old masters had been much over-rated, and that the greatest merit their works possessed was, that they bore the undoubted marks of antiquity. I don't know whether any other artist, on his first visiting the treasures of art in the old world, has been for a time satiated with them as I was. But my experience proves satisfactorily to me the truth of the hackneyed quotation of, "Drink deep, or taste not," &c. By degrees, however, as I became familiar with the works of Sir Thomas Lawrence, Sir Joshua and others, I began to perceive a change of feeling towards the old masters. I began to see new beauties every day in Raphael's cartoons, which at first struck me as little better than scene-painting at the theatre.

If I was peculiar in my feelings of indifference, I cannot account for it to myself. I am willing to confess, however, that on my first arrival in London, my solitary life was made more so by the contrast that I was forced to draw between my lonely situation in London, and that I so lately left in Boston. I was now left to myself, and my thoughts naturally turned upon myself; and perhaps I felt more mortification than I was willing to admit, at discovering that I was not so rich in acquirements as my friends had very innocently led me to think. While in this state of mind, I did not derive all the advantage from my opportunities that I might have done, had my mind been bent on improvement alone.

In a short time I began to get rid of this apathy, and it soon became my greatest pleasure to visit those very works, which had at first so disappointed my expectations. I soon found that my funds were insufficient to support me *one* year in London, though I thought them ample for two; and it became necessary that I should paint portraits, or shorten my contemplated visit. Amongst my first, was a head of Mr. Rush, our minister in London at that time.

I was more than usually successful in the likeness. It had the effect of inducing others to sit, and it was the indirect means of introducing me to the Duke of Sussex, whose patronage I subsequently enjoyed to a considerable extent. I was indebted to his royal highness for an introduction to the Duke of Hamilton, who was particularly kind to me during the whole of my stay in Great Britain. He sat to me for several portraits of himself, and invited me to stay with him at Hamilton Palace, which invitation I gladly accepted. I spent near three weeks at this splendid place. There are few richer galleries in Great Britain than that of Hamilton Palace; and amongst its rare gems is the original "Daniel in the Lions' Den," by Rubens, many splendid Vandyks, &c.

During my stay in England I had the good fortune to spend a few weeks at Holkham, the seat of Mr. Coke. Here I saw a great deal of high life; and it requires but little imagination to see, that the transition from the back woods of Missouri to this seat of luxury and elegance, was most imposing, and, in some respects, embarrassing. My mornings were spent chiefly in looking at the "old masters," and the afternoons in shooting. In early life I had been in the frequent habit of shooting bears and other large game; but on this occasion I felt almost as ignorant of the fashions of the field as I was of those of the dinner-table and drawing-room. However, the sport of killing pheasants and partridges, that at first seemed to me so trifling, became, in a short time, very interesting. I met a good many noblemen of high rank during my visit here; and one of the most distinguished by the distinguished, was Mr. Chantry. I had the pleasure of shooting by his side by day, and sitting by his side at dinner.

I was an exhibitor at Somerset House, every year while I was in England. I always profited by the comparison of my pictures with those about them, although it was always at the expense of my vanity. I invariably found that my pictures looked better to me, while in my own

room, than they did by the side of the distinguished
artists of the day. I used sometimes to indulge the feeling, that I had not justice done me in the hanging of my
pictures at the Royal Academy: but I was compelled to
admit, after due reflection, that the committee had done
me more justice in placing me where they did, than if
they had placed me more conspicuously in comparison
with better painters. And I am led to believe, that the
body of artists who have the management of this great
institution are actuated by feelings entirely liberal, free
from jealousy or envy. There is a charm in the bare walls
even of Somerset House, that excites a student to emula-
tion: but when those walls are filled with the works of
contemporary artists, one cannot but feel proud of his
profession, and disposed to give himself up to its study,
caring for nothing else. Unfortunately for that state of
mind, which is such perfect bliss, the worldly cares about
house-rent, food, and clothing, for his wife and children,
will break the spell. I am thoroughly convinced, that had
I been a bachelor, when I was in London, I should have
been there at this time. But I then had a wife and four
children, which rendered it necessary that I should realize
a certain amount of money every year. When an artist is
harassed in his financial concerns, his mind is in no state
to pursue the arts with pleasure or profit. In the course
of the three years I was abroad I painted to the amount
of 12,000 dollars; which sum was just sufficient for my
expenses.

I visited Paris; but my stay was so short, and my total
ignorance of the language of the country so great, that I
will make no comment upon the artists or the schools in
that city. I returned to Boston in the autumn of 1826;
since which I have made it my head quarters.

DOCUMENT 15

(PLATE 12)

The Apocalyptic Mood

The artist Chester Harding referred to the "great drama of life." For most Americans life was indeed a drama—if not a wrestling with fiends for admission to the heavenly city, at least a struggle against adversity for access to an earthly paradise. Some Americans, indeed, believed the Second Coming of Christ to launch the Millennium to be imminent. This character of thinking, directly or indirectly, colored American thought in all areas of endeavor. Ralph Waldo Emerson and Henry David Thoreau early imbibed their idealism in such a climate of faith; Hawthorne and Melville in its partial rejection.

Document 15 depicts a Methodist revival meeting on the frontier. In the foreground of the picture, communicants are shown experiencing the "jerks" and "shakes" prior to conversion. It was an emotional religion. The tenor of American life as a whole was more emotional than intellectual, and Americans lived from the crisis of the War of 1812 to the Panic of 1819 in constant expectation of a climax to their individual dramas.

Hints on the Fulfillment of Prophecy

The mission of America was to build a New Jerusalem and second Paradise from which to launch the
redemption of mankind from the sins of the hellish Old
World. This reading of the gospel, still reverberating
from the seventeenth and eighteenth centuries, was
paralleled by more secular interpretations of the same
mission. For some, the reforming mission was to be
achieved through individualistic enterprise, for others
through utopian communities. For Lorenzo Dow
(1774–1834), an independent preacher who introduced
the American-style camp revival meeting to England and
Ireland, it was to be achieved, according to prophecy,
by a cataclysmic upheaval, followed by the Second
Advent of Christ and the Millennium. His reading of
prophecy appears below.

The first thing to note is that it makes all history
converge on America, the land of nature and godliness.
The second point of significance is that it is polarized
by the same contrast of forest and city, America and
Europe, that appears in other documents of the period.
It was, in fact, the over-arching myth of America as a
second Garden of Eden which has made these poles so
meaningful throughout American history.

Lorenzo Dow was, of course, a predecessor of the
Millerites and Mormons, but many contemporaries
with even greater social prestige had similar ideas.
Jedidiah Morse, father of the inventor, in his tract
Signs of the Times (Charleston, Massachusetts, 1810)
expected the Millennium to begin about 1866. It
would begin in the West, according to Elias Boudinot,
former President of the Continental Congress, whose
much quoted *Star in the West* (Trenton, 1816) located

the famed lost tribes of Israel there. His *The Second Advent, or Coming of the Messiah in Glory* (Trenton, 1815) was the most comprehensive treatment of the subject in the first half of the century. Many writers considered the War of 1812 a sign of the great coming event, as typified by Alexander McLeod's *Scriptural View of the Character of the War* (New York, 1815).

Lorenzo Dow was more doctrinal and opinionated in this matter than the great circuit rider, Peter Cartwright, whose *Autobiography* has been reprinted, but both greeted the earthquake at New Madrid (see docs. 19 and 22) similarly as an omen for the nation. The emotional quality of their kind of religion is conveyed well in the picture of a typical Methodist revival meeting (doc. 15), which again associates American destiny with western forests. This picture should be contrasted with the ritualistic solemnity (doc. 62) with which white officials treated with the original inhabitants of the forest. A reaction against both the enthusiasm of frontier religions and the thorny dialectics of orthodox Calvinism is William Ellery Channing's influential "Moral Argument against Calvinism" (1820), reprinted in Robert E. Spiller, ed., *The Roots of National Culture: American Literature to 1830*, pp. 542–48 (New York: The Macmillan Company, 1933).

SOURCE: Lorenzo Dow, *History of Cosmopolite . . . His Experience and Travels, in Europe and America . . .* , pp. 530–32, 533–34. Cincinnati: 1858.

* * *

Babylon—mentioned in Revelation; the term is borrowed and transferred from Babylon of old to Rome, consequently when Babylon sunk in the East she rose in the West. And if a transfer be admitted once, if need be it may be admitted again with propriety without any thing twisted or far-fetched.

Now I ask, where can a city be found, the destruction of which would cause such a general cry and lamentation, &c., to commence and affect the whole world, as it is described in the xviiith chapter of Revelation from the

10th to the 19th verses inclusive; which the reader must pay attention to.

Rome in the political and commercial world has scarcely but a name, and her destruction could not produce such a general lamentation. Therefore we must look for some other city of a like description, the destruction of which would be universally felt. London may be styled the mother of trade, having her concomitants mediately or immediately throughout the world in every place of trade; of course her fall would produce such an effect; therefore a transfer thither may be admitted with propriety.

Again; England having been a province under the civil government of Rome Pagan, and under the influence of Rome Papal; consequently it is *one*; the "ten horns," therefore we must look for reunion under the second beast, that the prophecy may be completely fulfilled throughout the whole.

What does this argue? And what times are we to expect at hand?

It was observed that the woman fled into the wilderness; that is, those countries northwest of the Danube, where the gospel had not been received before, but when she had the wings as eagles, I must believe America to be the place referred to in prophecy.

Reason 1st. The first settlers of New England, &c., evidently came for conscience' sake, and many others have come here for the sake of peace and "liberty" from the intolerant hand of persecution and oppression.

Reason 2d. The earth helped the woman, which by commentators here is allowed to signify civil government. Therefore, whatever toleration has been given in Europe, is equal to that in America; for they have some kind of national established religion, which tends to bind the consciences of men and restrict their privileges, in consequence of which virtue is oppressed and vice triumphs.

But not so in America; all are protected, though none established; that if a religion be false, she shall not have the civil sword to uphold her; and if genuine and true, shall not be persecuted nor depressed.

Reason 3d. The eagle and stars are in our banners of liberty.—America may well be styled a wilderness, naturally, when compared to the old world, and considering our infancy.

Reason 4th. Whoever believes in a Providence must acknowledge a particular Providence of God in the separation, preparation and independence of the United States; when compared with the affairs of Europe. A whole is composed of parts, and the parts form the whole; therefore, the particular providences compose the general providence as much as the individuals compose a general family; of course the term general providences, without the particular providences considered and implied, is a great swelling phrase without meaning; it is like half a dozen cyphers, which make an appearance, but count nothing. Therefore we must admit a Providence, or be atheists, and suppose *nothing* could put forth the act of power and beget something; and *that* something jumped together and formed men and things, and so argue that effects may be produced without causes.

I would advise such as wish to be profited by reading history, to become well acquainted with the history of their own times and country, and view the Providential hand of God in our deliverance and preservation. One instance only out of many I will now hint. The first time the British invaded Charleston, S. C., it was expected they would attack them in the rear; but the preventative was afterwards discovered to be the water rising some feet higher than it was wont to do—thus the place was saved. Also, when every man's hands seemed to hang down, except the great Washington, when the American cause appeared so gloomy and desperate, the night the council of war was held at Trenton, relative to the attack on Princeton. Also, Cornwallis to deliver his sword to the son whose father was in that tower, of which he was the constable. And even when on the verge of falling into the general commotions of Europe, God has kept us by his providential hand, more than once or twice beyond human probability.

There is such a thing as national privileges, of course national blessings, which when abused, generally become national sins—which merit national judgments, that must be poured out for punishment in this world, unless there be a national repentance—for we shall not be judged at the bar of God as nations (for nations will then cease to exist) but as individuals, and punished accordingly; but national sins must be punished here, seeing it cannot be done hereafter.

General Burgoyne in the course of his defence, when on his trial, made the following remark—"I once thought the Americans were in the wrong, but now I am convinced that nothing short of the over-ruling hand of Providence could unite the hearts of three millions of people so perseveringly to stand or fall together as what the Americans are." [The present war is only an appendix of the former—a continuation of those opposite principles in theory, brought to the test. But where does "natural justice" lay?]

* * *

It must be observed by all who study this book, that what John describes relative to the two beasts, &c., he viewed first in heaven, and afterwards fulfiled upon the earth, and a clear distinction must be kept, otherwise our ideas will be confused, or else the subject will appear as tautology. [Compare Rev. xv, 1, with chapter xvi, 1, and then reading from chapter xiii, 11, to the end of the 15th chapter, (for heaven) and the following ones to the 20th, as fulfilled (on earth.) This may serve in a measure as a key to an inquiring mind.]

I have no doubt but we have arrived towards the closing of the sound of the trumpet of the sixth angel, and the commencement of the seventh, and also the pouring out of the seven last plagues. And however much the earth, or political, civil or religious and Christian world, may now be convulsed or confused, I apprehend worse times are at the door; and what has passed for the last twenty years, only as a few drops before a shower, in comparison to what is to come. I therefore intreat all into whose hands these hints may fall to take timely warning; and particularly the true Christian, that he may have suffering grace in the day of evil, and be preserved as the seed of the Gospel, and found in a state of readiness against the coming of our Lord and Saviour Jesus Christ, . . .

These things, when taken in conjunction with the state of Europe, a few years ago, and what it is now, with the probable consequence of what is at the door, denotes something impressive indeed, and ought to stimulate every thinking mind on the continent of America to prize their privileges, and improve them accordingly; for where can a country be found, with peace, plenty, and religious liberty, but these United States; and how soon we may be called to trial, is in the womb of futurity. As I do not believe that a country was ever given up to the sword and destruction, where *pure religion* was on the progression; therefore we need to pray for peace, that we may be kept from the *deluge* of the *old* world, which is fast progressing. And should the Euphrates, or Turkish Empire receive an overthrow, as other nations of late have fared, we should know *exactly* the *time* of the church; and it is not improbable but Bonaparte will avail himself of the prejudices of the Jews to answer his own designs, who amount to 9,000,000 in his jurisdiction; and in doing this, in the establishment of them at Palestine, it will cut up the Turkish Empire, afford him money, men, and a half way house to the Indies. Thus the "Euphrates would be dried up, that the way of the Kings of the East might be prepared," Rev. xvi, 12. I add no more, only give a recapitulation of the subject.

DOCUMENT 17

Books, Books, Books

The author of the story of Washington and the
cherry tree, Mason Locke Weems (1759–1825), though
he once studied theology in London, was an ignorant
man. Nevertheless, his letters have considerable personal
and cultural interest. Parson Weems' mission was to
serve God (and himself) by selling his countrymen
books to improve their morals, an enterprise in which
he was extraordinarily successful. Letters like the following to his employer Mathew Carey, Philadelphia
publisher and bookseller, furnish excellent guides to
the popular reading taste of the period.

For more than twenty years he castigated Carey for
"sending wrong books to the wrong places," complaining that "heavy books" like Samuel Miller's *Retrospect of the Eighteenth Century* or John Adams' *Defense of the Constitutions*—"books the like of which
any even the commonest Carpenter might 'saw &
plane' out of a maple slab of pine"—were dead weights
in his wagon. On the other hand, one of Carey's own
publishing ventures of 1820, Shaw and Hill's *Picturesque Views of American Scenery* (see doc. 63), was
light enough, but "too tame" for people who were beginning to link national destiny with wild, sublime nature (see doc. 62). The popularity in all parts of the
country of Weems' own reforming tracts and idealizing
biographies further testifies to the close connection between religion and patriotism. The great reform movements and utopian experiments of the next period grew
out of this background.

SOURCE: Mason Locke Weems, *His Works and Ways*, Vol. III:
Letters, 1784–1825, edited by Emily Ellsworth Ford Skeel, pp.
23, 320–22. New York: 1939.

[To Mathew Carey]

Augusta, July 30. 1810

. . . This is no time to be wrangling. The Country is in darkness. Men's minds are uninform'd, their hearts bitter, and their manners savage. Humanity and Patriotism both cry aloud, Books Books, Books. If you want me to do much good, this *fall*, for the Country or yourself—send me immediately $100 Bucks Theological Diety. 300 Russells 7 sermons, no more Blairs.—20 Whitfields sermons. 12 village sermons, 50 Bunyan's Visions, 50 Rippons hymns. 12 Pilg. progress, 100 Doz Webster's spell^g. . . . 4 Reams writing paper—it sells well, 20 Doz testaments—10 Doz Bibles—and 1 to 150 4°. Bibles @ $4.25. 50 destruction of Jerusalem, *no more plays*, great many of Josephus . . . 1 to 200 Websters small d° (grammar) . . . 20 Bards Compend.* . . .

. . . Thank God there is at last some appearance of a calm. And far be it from me to think of pulling out the plugs of Eolus. But I can't bear the touch of blame where no blame is deserv^d. You will tell me of deception towards you in not instantly saying yea or nay to your proposition to break the magna charta of my rights to have the books carried at your cost to the Court houses &c &c. I have told you that it is to be accounted for very plainly by my long absences from this place. . . . *All haste.*

[To Mathew Carey]

Dumf. Oct. 12, 1821

Dear Sir— . . . You ask— . . .
3^d. *Cant you obtain* 500 subs "for Atlas in S. Carol^a?"
Answer. No doubt there are *rich men* enough in that state to subscribe for that number—if they were properly *work^d upon—all depends on that*—and, thank God, my chances are good.
4th. "*We wish to know what are y^r views*"

* Bard's Compendium of the Theory and practice of Midwifery, 12 mo.——1 25' *Carey's Catalogue*, 1816, p. 98, LC.—Samuel Bard, 1742–1821, was President of the New York College of Physicians and Surgeons. Ed.

Answer. I have told you once or twice since I return^d, that I am *willing to* cooperate with you. Owing to most unfortunate errors in times past we have done but little, with great means. Those errors are now detected. And from good will to you & good wishes for my Country & own Family, I am ready to commence de novo & con Spirito proportion^d to the Greatness of the aim & the Shortness of the time to do it in. My idea is as it ever has been, that, *two birds may be kill^d at a throw.* To set up throughout the Nation large parcels of miscellaneous books, heavy priced & badly assorted, is, I very well know an unfailing receipt to make a Rich man poor: But still it is not less true that there are books that will sell. The brave & virtuous fathers of our Republic, as, Washington, Franklin, & Marion, will sell, and indeed by proper management might be made School Books—these you possess. Besides this, every Parent knows that, after all his labours for his son, that son may quickly be thrown to the Dogs & the dung hill by drinking, Gambling, Wenching & Duelling: hence, with all considerate Parents, there is good hope that *short, cheap, ad captand. pamphlets* on those most interesting subjects will ever be popular. [Such a pamphlet was his *Looking Glass Against Duelling,* represented by doc. 29–Ed.] The trial has been made, & with a success abundantly sufficient to encourage perseverance. Now to say nothing of motives arising from Philanthropy & Patriotism of which you possess a stock equal to the most, I think on principles purely pecuniary you ought with Lavoisne & the Grand Bible to run y^r Wash. Frank. Marion & the Look^g Glasses especially as my uncommonly extensive travels & acquaintance furnish me such good opportunities to make establishments, & my past experiments must bind me to do it in the safe & right way. You have b'ot the Biograph^s. I will sell you the Looking Glasses, at the most reasonable rates; and as I am very strongly affected with a sense of the exceeding charity of setting before young minds the examples of such Virtues as are delineated in the Biograph^s and such Vices as the Look^g

Glasses hold up I will take *any commission* that you shall think perfectly warranted by your own prudence. It is our lot to live in a time uncommonly important to Posterity—a time when the sacred fire of Liberty is confin^d to one torch, and that burning in our own country. Vice is the Azote, and Virtue the Grand vital element of that fire, and my belief is that the day will surely come when to minds enlighted^d like ours, nothing but what we have done to maintain that holy fire will afford us any pleasure. I have great advantages—such as habitual Exercise, Temperance, cheerfulness, extensive acquaintance, general acceptableness to the World & much Experience, and if you will, as you are wont, show yourselves good friends to me by settling with me liberally & lending me a little money for a needful purpose, I shall be willing to be as one with you, for the next 2 or 3 years, which may, thro' a concurring Providence, be the Best we have yet had. You have sent me several boxes, but unless the Show bills, as directed, were sent, *nothing will be done!!!* I have had 10000 trials & yet you LACK FAITH!

In the morning I set off. Hope to see you by the 18th.

The Steamboat Comes to God's Country

One often wonders to what extent people are aware of contemporary events to which posterity later attaches special significance. The steamboat, like the locomotive, was to become a favorite literary symbol of the coming of the Industrial Revolution to America, greeted as both a national blessing and a national tragedy. Something of both reactions is contained in the following document, a faithful rendering of first-hand reports. The author, John Latrobe (1803–1891), was eight years old when his sister, Mrs. Nicholas Roosevelt, accompanied her husband on this first steam-boat voyage down the Mississippi.

All nature, including its forest inhabitants, stands aghast at the sudden intrusion of this fire-belching infernal machine into the tranquil scene. The coinci-dence of its appearance at the same time as a fiery comet in the sky and a spectacular earthquake which attracted much attention throughout the United States helped to invest it with almost apocalyptic significance (see again docs. 19 and 22). But the author, who in his later life became a devoted champion of progress, is careful to attribute to Indians the view that the steam-boat is an "omen of evil." Documents 20 and 83, how-ever, may suggest that it was also a view endorsed by many Americans then living whose sensibilities were shocked by numerous steamboat explosions and fatali-ties. An interesting emphasis in the following document on tension and nervous strain anticipates poetic reactions to the Industrial Revolution, treated for the most part not as a gradual historical process of betterment, but as a sudden traumatic change, usually for the worse.

SOURCE: John H. B. Latrobe, *The First Steamboat Voyage on the Western Waters*, pp. 20–28. Baltimore: Maryland Historical Society, 1871.

*   *   *

The anchor was weighed. To get into the Indiana channel, which was the best, a wide circuit had to be made bringing her head down stream, completing which, the New Orleans began the descent. Steerage way depended upon her speed exceeding that of the current. The faster she could be made to go, the easier would it be to guide her. All the steam the boiler would bear was put upon her. The safety valve shrieked: The wheels revolved faster than they had ever done before; and the vessel, speaking figuratively, fairly flew away from the crowds collected to witness her departure from Louisville. Instinctively, each one on board now grasped the nearest object, and with bated breath awaited the result. Black ledges of rock appeared only to disappear as the New Orleans flashed by them. The waters whirled and eddied, and threw their spray upon the deck, as a more rapid descent caused the vessel to pitch forward to what at times seemed inevitable destruction. Not a word was spoken. The pilots directed the men at the helm by motions of their hands. Even the great Newfoundland dog seemed affected by the apprehension of danger, and came and crouched at Mrs. Roosevelt's feet. The tension on the nervous system was too great to be long sustained. Fortunately, the passage was soon made; and, with feelings of profound gratitude to the Almighty, at the successful issue of the adventure, on the part of both Mr. Roosevelt and his wife, the New Orleans rounded to in safety below the Falls. There was still the same leaden sky—the same dim sun during the day—the same starless night;—but the great difficulty had been overcome, and it was believed that there would now, be nothing but plain sailing to the port of destination. It was yet to be seen how far the expectations of those on board, in this respect, would be realized.

Hitherto, the voyage had been one of pleasure. Nothing had marred the enjoyment of the travellers. The receptions at Louisville and Cincinnati had been great events. But, now, were to come . . . "those days of horror." The comet of 1811, had disappeared, and was followed by the earthquake of that year, of which the atmospheric phenomena just mentioned were the prognostics; and the earthquake accompanied the New Orleans far on her way down the Mississippi.*

The first shock that was observed was felt on board the New Orleans while she lay at anchor after passing the Falls. The effect was as though the vessel had been in motion and had suddenly grounded. The cable shook and trembled, and many on board experienced for the moment a nausea resembling sea sickness. It was a little while before they could realize the presence of the dread visitor. It was wholly unexpected. The shocks succeeded each other during the night. When morning came, the voyage was resumed; and, while under way, the jar of the

---

* In the language of a very intelligent traveller of those days: "Many things conspired to make the year 1811, *the annus mirabilis* of the West. During the earlier months, the waters of many of the great rivers overflowed their banks to a vast extent, and the whole country was in many parts covered from bluff to bluff. Unprecedented sickness followed. A spirit of change and recklessness seemed to pervade the very inhabitants of the forest. A countless multitude of squirrels, obeying some great and universal impulse, which none can know but the Spirit that gave them being, left their reckless and gambolling life, and their ancient places of retreat in the North, and were seen pressing forward by tens of thousands in a deep and solid phalanx to the South. No obstacles seemed to check their extraordinary and concerted movement. The word had been given them to go forth and they obeyed it, though multitudes perished in the broad Ohio which lay in their path. The splendid comet of that year long continued to shed its twilight over the forests, and as the autumn drew to a close, the whole valley of the Mississippi, from the Missouri to the Gulf, was shaken to its centre by continued earthquakes."—C. J. *Latrobe's Rambler in North America.*

machinery, the monotonous beating of the wheels and the steady progress of the vessel, prevented the disturbance from being noticed.

. . . In his voyage of exploration, Mr. Roosevelt had found coal on the Ohio, and he had caused mines to be opened in anticipation. Their value was now realized; and, when he reached them on his way down the river, he took on board as much coal as he could find room for.

Some miles above the mouth of the Ohio, the diminished speed of the current indicated a rise in the Mississippi. This was found to be the case. The bottom lands on either shore were under water, and there was every sign of an unwonted flood. Canoes came and went among the boles of the trees. Sometimes, the Indians attempted to approach the steamboat; and, again, fled on its approach. The Chickasaws still occupied that part of the State of Tennessee lying below the mouth of the Ohio. On one occasion, a large canoe, fully manned, came out of the woods abreast of the steamboat. The Indians, outnumbering the crew of the vessel, paddled after it. There was at once a race, and for a time the contest was equal. The result, however, was what might have been anticipated. Steam had the advantage of endurance; and the Indians with wild shouts, which might have been shouts of defiance, gave up the pursuit, and turned into the forest from whence they had emerged.

While the crew of the New Orleans were more amused than alarmed at this incident of the voyage, Mr. Roosevelt, who had not forgotten the visit to the flatboat on the preliminary exploration, was not sorry, now, when he lost sight of the canoe. That he bestowed a second thought upon the matter, illustrates the nervous excitement that prevailed on board. Mrs. Roosevelt and himself were still discussing the adventure when they retired to rest. They had scarcely fallen asleep, when they were aroused by shouts on deck, and the trampling of many feet. With the idea of Indians still predominant, Mr. Roosevelt sprang from his bed, and seizing a sword

—the only weapon at hand—hurried from the cabin to join battle, as he thought, with the Chickasaws. It was a more alarming enemy that he encountered. The New Orleans was on fire; and flame and smoke issued from the forward cabin. The servant who attended there, had placed some green wood too close to the stove in anticipation of the next day's wants; and, lying down beside it, had fallen sound asleep. The stove becoming over heated, this wood had taken fire; the joiners work close by had caught, and the entire cabin would soon have been in flames, had not the servant, half suffocated, rushed on deck and given the alarm. By dint of great exertion, the fire, which, by this time, was making rapid headway, was extinguished; but not until the interior wood work had been either destroyed, or grievously defaced. Few eyes were closed for the remainder of the night; nor did the accident tend to tranquilize the nerves of the travellers.

A supply of provisions had been taken on board the New Orleans, at Louisville, amply sufficient for the voyage to Natchez, and this was occasionally supplemented by purchases at settlements along the river. These, however, were few and far between, and not at all to be relied on. The crew, accustomed to the simple fare of boatmen on the Mississippi, were easily provided for. The commissariat of the voyage, therefore,—longer than a voyage to Europe now,—gave no trouble.

Early in the afternoon of each day, the steamer was rounded to, and fastened to the bank, the crew going ashore to cut the wood required, after the coal was exhausted, for the next day's consumption. On some of these occasions, squatters came on board with tales of their experience upon the land, which they insisted shook and trembled under their feet. At New Madrid [see doc. 19— Ed.] a great portion of which had been engulphed, as the earth opened in vast chasms and swallowed up houses and their inhabitants, terror stricken people had begged to be taken on board, while others dreading the steamboat, even more than the earthquake, hid themselves as she approached. To receive the former was impossible.

The would be refugees had no homes to go to; and ample
as was the supply of provisions for Mr. Roosevelt and his
wife, it would have been altogether insufficient for any
large increase of passengers: and as to obtaining provisions
on the way, the New Orleans might as well have been
upon the open sea. Painful as it was, there was no choice
but to turn a deaf ear to the cries of the terrified inhabitants of the doomed town.

One of the peculiar characteristics of the voyage was
the silence that prevailed on board. No one seemed disposed to talk; and when there was any conversation, it
was carried on in whispers, almost. Tiger, who appeared,
alone, to be aware of the earthquake while the vessel was
in motion, prowled about, moaning and growling; and
when he came and placed his head on Mrs. Roosevelt's
lap, it was a sure sign of a commotion of more than usual
violence. Orders were given in low tones; and the usual
cheerful "aye, aye, sir," of the sailors, was almost inau-
dible. Sleeplessness was another characteristic. Sound,
continuous sleep, was apparently unknown. Going ashore
for wood was the event of each twenty-four hours, and was
looked forward to by the crew with satisfaction, notwithstanding the labor that it involved. And yet the men,
if not sullenly, toiled silently; and if the earth shook,
as it often did, while they were at work, the uplifted axe
was suspended, or placed quietly on the log, and the
men stared at each other until it ceased. Nor was this
depression confined to the steamer. Flat boats and
barges were passed, whose crews instead of bandying
river wit, as they had done when met on the voyage
from Pittsburg to Louisville,—uttered no word as the
New Orleans went by. Before the travellers had been
many days on the Mississippi, they fancied, as they looked
at each other, that they had become haggard. Mrs. Roosevelt records "that she lived in a constant fright, unable
to sleep or sew, or read."

Sometimes, Indians would join the wood choppers; and
occasionally one would be able to converse in English
with the men. From these it was learned that the steam-

boat was called the "Penelore," or "fire Canoe," and was supposed to have some affinity with the Comet that had preceded the earthquake,—the sparks from the chimney of the boat being likened to the train of the celestial visitant. Again, they would attribute the smoky atmosphere to the steamer, and the rumbling of the earth to the beating of the waters by the fast revolving paddles. To the native inhabitants of the boundless forest that lined the river banks, the coming of the first steamboat was an omen of evil.

*   *   *

Document 19

(Plate 13)

The Great Earthquake at New Madrid

The great earthquake which shook the entire Mississippi Valley in the autumn of 1811 may not have made history, but it sent a shock of delightful horror through the hearts of thousands of people across the nation who read about it in letters and newspapers and saw it depicted in lurid pictures like the following. They were pictures out of nightmare—or the Revelation of St. John—and had special appeal for preachers of doom, watchers for the Second Coming, practitioners of phrenology, believers in spiritualism and animal magnetism, and all the lovers of sensation with which the country thronged, even then, before the days of the yellow press. Even then, to be an American was in no small part to thrill to great expectations, to read portents in the sky, and breathe an air that was tonic.

Document 20

(Plate 14)

The Explosion of the Washington

Another event, too, sent thrills of horror through
readers of eyewitness reports. It was one of the numerous steamboat explosions of the period which led to a
public investigation into the causes and correctives for
such explosions (see doc. 83). Unlike earthquakes,
these were man-made and not acts of God. Nevertheless,
there were those who regarded the steamboat and steam
engines as infernal machines. To such people, a steamboat explosion was as much a rent in nature as an
earthquake, a portent of things to come, a sign, even,
of God's displeasure with His chosen people. The
banner "Washington" in this picture links the event
with patriotic destiny.

Captain Shreve survived this disaster of 1816 to profit
by it. For his contribution to the development of the
high-pressure steam engine, see doc. 84. The majority
of Americans were too committed to material comfort
and convenience to turn their backs on technological
progress, however great the risks to body and soul.

The Richmond Theatre Fire

This memorable fire broke out Christmas Night, 1811, the year of the great earthquake. More than ten years after the event, Henry Cogswell Knight recorded in his *Letters from the South and West* a visit to Richmond, Virginia. He went "to see where the awful fire appalled the Theatre, and crowded above three score of shrieking victims from the scenes of time, into the scenes of eternity; and among them the governor, and a brave officer and his beloved. The new Monumental Church, over the ruins and ashes of the dead, is nearly completed, but is not to be compared with many churches at the north." A picture of the Monumental Church, which replaced the theatre, is found in doc. 99.

DOCUMENT 22

Signs of the Times

Many of the elements in the preceding documents are brought together below by Washington Irving (1783–1859) in the form of notes for a story which was never, finally, written. As an imaginative projection of the public temper which prevailed on the eve of the War of 1812, it helps us to understand the force of unreason which swept us into that war. It is also a charming demonstration of the artistic imagination at work trying to invest the disparate materials of culture with meaning.

SOURCE: Washington Irving, "Personalia," in *Tour in Scotland and Other Manuscript Notes*, edited by Stanley T. Williams, pp. 108–10. New Haven: Yale University Press, 1927.

Various circumstances had occasioned to give a melancholy tone to the public mind & to excite the public imagination—The Dreadful conflagration of the Theatre of Richmond which had wrapped beauty & talents in flames. Tornado which had swept the southern coast & desolated the country &c The continual succession of earthquakes—all had produced a feverish excitement & filled the imagination with dreams of horror & apprehensions of sinister & dreadful events

About this time a man published a prophesy—predicting the end of the world on 4 June. effect of it on the country people Work suspended many did not grow corn for they knew not that they should reap it—In the town where our college was situated a Butcher had been made the depository of many of the pamphlets—He was resorted to by all those of diseased & alarmed minds—from con-

tinually reading them & conversing with every variety of
melancholy & forlorn being his intellects became confused
& he went mad.

The diseased state of the public mind was caught in
the college. some went home others lodged about in small
wooden houses.—Some took up a desperate mode of dis-
sipating thought & played cards incessantly—One man was
stationed at a pendulum to give warning of the approach
of a shock—that we might fly to the fields. He got a
bugle & used to sound three blasts. Never did any thing
sound to me more disastrous—He was nicknamed *Gabriel*
by one of the profligates. I used to take my bible & read.

Alarm of earthquake at night. We all fled to the college
court. Chimney falls with dreadful crash—exclamation
that the earth had opened before us—lurid look of the
heaven—stillness & oppressiveness of air Wall of one of the
bigger apartments falls—Exclamation that the earth had
opened. behind—dreadful state of alarm. Meteor streams
over the College. Glare a baleful light over the court yard
& bursts with tremendous report—gave myself up for lost—
thought I was annihilated—

Howling of dogs Screams of domestic fowls—Shrieks of
women & wailing of children

Butcher runs frantically about the street foaming at the
mouth—& crying Woe Woe Woe the destruction of Columbia is at hand &c—prepare for the presence of the
Lord. . . .

DOCUMENT 23

Hard Times in Ohio

The next document records something of the disillusionment which swept the country in the wake of the Panic of 1819. The caption on the cartoon reads, "I have been . . . I am going to Ohio." Its author, Doctor Jeremiah Smipleton, published his *Journal* to counteract what he felt to be the gross exaggerations in the promotional tracts and emigrant guides which had lured so many unsuspecting settlers to that region. Two years later, Zerah Hawley also published an account of his experience in Ohio, which he called sardonically "the *fabled region* of the West." "I say *fabled region*," he wrote, "because more, much more has been said about the State, than has any foundation in truth. It has been compared to Canaan, and even extolled above it. It has been called the *Garden* of America, and many other high sounding titles. . . ." This sense of the disjunction between myth and reality is an early example of the impulse underlying the later critical Midwestern realism of Joseph Kirkland, Hamlin Garland, and Zona Gale.

SOURCE: *Journal of Doctor Jeremiah Smipleton's Tour to Ohio.* Boston: 1819.

WESTERN EMIGRATION.

:❖:

JOURNAL

OF

DOCTOR JEREMIAH SMIPLETON's

TOUR TO OHIO.

CONTAINING

An account of the numerous difficulties, Hair-breadth
Escapes, Mortifications and Privations, which the
DOCTOR and his family experienced on their
Journey from Maine, to the 'Land of Pro-
mise,' and during a residence of three years
in that highly extolled country.

BY H. TRUMBULL.

Nulli Fides Frontis.

BOSTON--PRINTED BY S. SEWALL.

Hard Times in Ohio, 1819. Courtesy of the American Anti-
quarian Society.

DOCUMENT 24

A Firebell in the Night

Not even Thomas Jefferson, in deep retirement at Monticello, could refrain from reacting in an apocalyptic mood to public events. He regarded the Missouri question not only as "a firebell in the night," but a potential source of treason "against the hopes of the world." His two letters below to a friend in Congress, Hugh Nelson, link the Missouri problem in his fears to the widespread distress occasioned by the Panic of 1819. These letters should be read in conjunction with a contemporary satire on Western migration (doc. 23), because the greater fears as well as highest hopes for the future development of the nation seemed to hinge on events in the West. For the important relationship of disillusionment to high expectations in this period, one should also read Zerah Hawley's "Journal of a Tour" to Ohio in 1821, reprinted in Warren S. Tryon, *A Mirror for Americans,* Vol. III, pp. 496–508. Chicago: University of Chicago Press, 1952.

SOURCE: *The Works of Thomas Jefferson,* edited by Paul Leicester Ford, Vol. XII, pp. 157–58. New York: the Knickerbocker Press, 1904–5.

[To HUGH NELSON]

Monticello, Feb. 7, 1820

Dear Sir,–. . . . I thank you for your information on the progress & prospects of the Missouri question. It is the most portentous one which ever yet threatened our Union. In the gloomiest moment of the revolutionary war I never had any apprehensions equal to what I feel from this source.

I observe you are loaded with petitions from the Man-

ufacturing commercial & agricultural interests, each praying you to sacrifice the others to them. This proves the
egotism of the whole and happily balances their cannibal
appetites to eat one another. The most perfect confidence
in the wisdom of Congress leaves me without a fear of the
result. I do not know whether it is any part of the petitions of the farmers that our citizens shall be restrained
to eat nothing but bread, because that can be made here.
But this is the common spirit of all their petitions. My
ill-health has obliged me to retire from all public concerns. I scarcely read a newspaper. I cannot therefore tell
you what is a doing in the state, but this you will get fully
from others. I will therefore add only the assurances of
my great & friendly esteem and respect.

Monticello, March 12, 1820

I thank you, dear Sir, for the information in your favor
of the 4th instant, of the settlement, *for the present*, of
the Missouri question. I am so completely withdrawn from
all attention to public matters, that nothing less could
arouse me than the definition of a geographical line,
which on an abstract principle is to become the line of
separation of these States, and to render desperate the
hope that man can ever enjoy the two blessings of peace
and self-government. The question sleeps for the present,
but is not dead. This State is in a condition of unparalleled
distress. The sudden reduction of the circulating medium
from a plethory to all but annihilation is producing an
entire revolution of fortune. In other places I have known
lands sold by the sheriff for one year's rent; beyond the
mountains we hear of good slaves selling for one hundred
dollars, good horses for five dollars, and the sheriffs generally the purchasers. Our produce is now selling at market for one-third its price, before this commercial catastrophe, say flour at three and a quarter and three and a half
dollars the barrel. We should have less right to expect
relief from our legislators if they had been the establishers
of the unwise system of banks. A remedy to a certain degree was practicable, that of reducing the quantum of

circulation gradually to a level with that of the countries with which we have commerce, and an eternal abjuration of paper. But they have adjourned without doing anything. I fear local insurrections against these horrible sacrifices of property. In every condition of trouble or tranquillity be assured of my constant esteem and respect.

Like half a Rainbow rising on yon shore
While its twin partner spans the semi o'er
And makes a perfect whole that need not part
Till time has furnish'd us a nobler art.

PART II

Reflections of Nationalism

DOCUMENT 25

(PLATE 16)

The Burning of Washington: A British View

The burning of Washington in 1814 by British troops, hardly before a proud nation was able to celebrate the city's completion, was another of the calamitous events which contributed to the feverish public imagination during this period.

Here the event is pictured from a British point of view. It is a stirring moment, filled, like the scene of the Richmond theatre fire in document 21, with vivid action, throngs of people, moving masses of light and dark. Yet there is no panic or hysteria, since the government and most of the citizens have been evacuated from the capital and also the British artist wishes to emphasize the serried orderliness of the foot soldiers, the methodical calm of their officers, the civilized restraint of his countrymen in doing what they thought they had to do to end the war victoriously. From an American point of view, of course, it seemed an act of vicious barbarity. Contemporary American Federalist cartoons of the event satirized the weakness of Madison's government.

DOCUMENT 26

(PLATE 17)

The Ruins of the Capitol: An American View

An American viewpoint of the destruction of the national capitol attributes a cosmic significance to that event by showing America's patron goddesses of justice and liberty aghast at the spectacle of manacled slaves being led to help rebuild the capitol. The author of the anti-slavery tract in which this picture appeared observed of it, "Would it be superstitious to presume, that the Sovereign Father of all nations, permitted the *perpetuation* of this apparently execrable transaction, as a *fiery,* though salutary signal of his displeasure at the conduct of his Columbian children, in erecting and idolizing this splendid fabric as the temple of freedom, and at the same time oppressing with the yoke of captivity and toilsome bondage, twelve or fifteen hundred thousand of their African *brethren* . . . , making merchandize of their *blood,* and dragging their bodies with *iron chains,* even under its towering walls? Yet is it a fact, that *slaves* are employed in rebuilding this sanctuary of *liberty*."*

* Jesse Torrey, Jr., A *Portraiture of Domestic Slavery in the United States,* pp. 33–34. Philadelphia: 1817.

The Star in the West: Astoria

The fur-trading enterprise of John Jacob Astor (1763–1848), a penniless German immigrant in 1784, helped the United States to acquire Oregon. The following letter shows how closely Astor identified his private interests with those of the nation. It may also suggest that however broad of vision he may have been, he was essentially lacking in the graceful accomplishments and culture typified by Jefferson's leadership. The future of America lay increasingly with men like Astor—practical, energetic, acquisitive men of action whose vocabulary was sprinkled with such words as "profit," "property," "interest," "calculation," and "enterprise."

Their effort to color their economic views with an idealizing national interest received considerable assistance in this period from Chief Justice John Marshall, particularly in his decisions against the impairment of private contracts in the case of Fletcher *vs.* Peck (1810) and the Dartmouth College case (1819). The War of 1812 itself reflected a new community of interest between the federal government and landed capitalism, in that strongest support for the war came from parts of the country characterized by agrarian discontent and speculative "land hunger."

When Astor's activity in the Far West brought him into conflict with British interests, however, the American government was, for the moment, too weak to bail him out, and he finally sold Astoria to the British North West Company, though without abandoning the fur trade. It is significant that both Astor and Andrew Jackson were products of westward expansion, yet had rather little to do with the kind of primitive pioneering which James Fenimore Cooper was to romanticize.

SOURCE: Kenneth Wiggins Porter, *John Jacob Astor, Business Man*, 2 vols. Vol. I, pp. 541–43. Cambridge, Mass.: Harvard University Press, 1931.

New york 18 ac^r 1813

Thomas Jefferson Esqr
Sir

From the corect view which you had of the Importanes of my undertaking Relative to the trade in the Indian country and Particularly our establishment near the mouth of Columbia River I am Lead to belive that it would have aforted you pleasure to have heard of our Sucess which I had hopes to have Comunicated to you & which I Should have had in my Power to have Done had we not fallen a Sacrifies to Political events tho the Restrictive Measurs adopted by Congress prevented our oprating from this quater in the Interio yet we ware going on well from the other Side of the Land all our Pepol those who went out by Land aCross the Country & those who went by Watter Round Cape Horn had meet at Columbia River where In 1811 thy Establishd tham Selfs thy had build a forte & & & and had Cleard Some Land from which thy ware Raissing Considerable Suplys— thy found the Indians in the vecenity Peaceble & friendly and thy had in 1811 Send Several parties in the Interior and a Long the coast to explor the country which thy found to abound with fish & game and the quantity of valuable furrs fare exceeding our most Sangguine exspectations thy had Establishd Several trading houses or post in the Interior & all Seemd to Promise well—the north west Compay of Canada became Sencible that in consequece of our arrangements thy would have to abandon a great part of thire Indian trade made Representation to the British government which ever being Ready to graps at & to monopolize the commerce of the world readly Listond to thire Representations & thy have Send out a frigate to Destroy

aur establishment & no Doubt to blunder us of aur property from the Information which I have Recid I am Lead
to belive that the British government means to take pos-
sistion of Columbian River & to protect the north west
Company in fixing a post for trade—

I have Long Sence ben fearefull of [interlineated: that]
Such Steeps would be taking & I did Inform our government of it 12 months ago. Soliciting Some protection and
Recomending that a Smal Garison might be plaisd there
which with what we had and could have Done would have
Securd the plaise for at Least Some few years to com I
hope yet that government will Do Something and if So
we may yet hold our possion which if Peace would in
4 or 5 years Prove of very great Importanis

you may have Seen by the publick papers the arrivl of
Mr Stuart & others from Columbia the former gentleman
had resited there 15 months & had During that time ex-
plord a considerable part of the country he keep a journal
& of his voyage across the country which he Left with the
President should you feel a Desire to read it I am Sure the
President will Send it to you you will See that thire are
Large & extensive Rivers in that part of the country of
which we we [sic] had no Knowladge before— I belive in
the cours of 4 or 5 years if we had remaind at Peac we
Should have Drawn furrs from that country to amount of
Some Millions of Dollars p annum—and we should most
Certainly have confind the British traders to British Dominions—but as it is unless we have a Speedy Peace & that
than we are permitted to carry on a trade to there we must
exspect to abandon our plan & Loss aur Property & the
Labour & time which has ben Spent in the undertaking
which is very Considerable—in the mean time I am fear-
full that our pepol will be Driven off & perhaps Dispers
and it may not be easey to get tham to gether again thire
number is obaut 120 and about 30 to 40 Sandwich Island-
ers who apear to be an excellent pepol Since the war I have
Send two ships to Columbia River to give noties of the
war and to furnish tham with Suplys—which if thy have

arrivd in Safty may be the means to Safe the place tho I have greate fears—I am with very great Respt Sir your most obt Servent

John · Jacob · Astor

Plate 1. *View in Nootka Sound*, by John Webber, ca. 1792. Courtesy
of the William Robertson Coe Collection of Western Americana, Yale
University Library.

Plate 2. *Pioneer's Progress*, first view, from Orasmus Turner, PIONEER HISTORY OF THE HOLLAND PURCHASE, p. 563 (Buffalo: 1849). Photo by Rensselaer Polytechnic Institute.

Plate 3. *Pioneer's Progress*, second view, from Orasmus Turner, PIONEER HISTORY OF THE HOLLAND PURCHASE, p. 567. Photo by Rensselaer Polytechnic Institute.

Plate 4. *View of Boston*, a lithograph after Jacques Milbert, 1826. Courtesy of the Library of Congress.

Plate 5. *The Peace of Ghent 1814 and Triumph of America*, an engraving of Madame Plantou's painting, 1818. Courtesy of the Library of Congress.

Plate 6. *Ariadne of Naxos,* by John Vanderlyn, 1814. Courtesy of the Pennsylvania Academy of the Fine Arts.

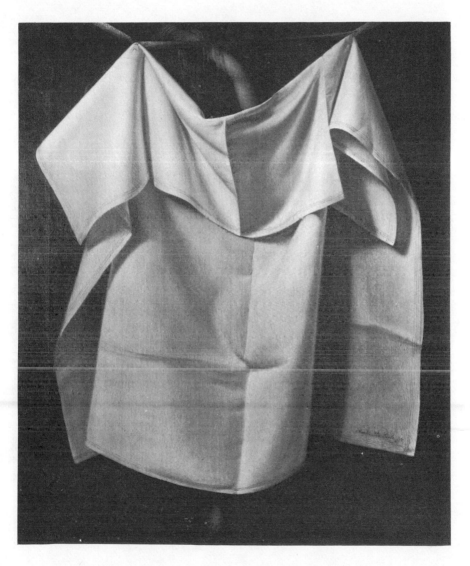

Plate 7. *After the Bath*, by Raphaelle Peale, 1823. Nelson Gallery—
Atkins Museum (Nelson Fund), Kansas City, Missouri.

Plate 8. *The Artist*, anonymous, ca. 1810. Courtesy of the New York State Historical Association, Cooperstown, New York.

Plate 9. *The Artist's Wife*, anonymous, ca. 1810. Courtesy of the New York State Historical Association, Cooperstown, New York.

Plate. 10. *Robert Fulton*, by Benjamin West, 1806. Photograph by courtesy of the New York State Historical Association, Cooperstown, New York.

Plate 11. *Mrs. David C. DeForest*, by Samuel F. B. Morse, 1823.
Courtesy of Yale University Art Gallery.

Plate 12. *Camp Meeting of the Methodists in North America*, after Jacques Milbert, 1819. Courtesy of the Library of Congress.

Plate 13. *The Great Earthquake at New Madrid*, from Henry Howe, HISTORICAL COLLECTIONS OF THE GREAT WEST, p. 237 (Cincinnati: 1853). Photo by the New York State Library.

Plate 14. *The Explosion of the Washington*, 1816, from LLOYD's STEAMBOAT DIRECTORY, p. 56 (Cincinnati: 1856). Photo by Rensselaer Polytechnic Institute.

Plate 15. *The Burning of the Richmond Theatre*, by B. Tanner, 1812. Courtesy of the Library of Congress.

Plate 16. *The Burning of Washington*, a British view, from Henry Robertson's continuation of RAPIN's HISTORY OF ENGLAND, Vol. II, opp. p. 773 (London: 1816). Photo by the Burns Studio.

Plate 17. *The Ruins of the National Capitol*, an American view, frontispiece to Jesse Torrey, Jr., A PORTRAITURE OF DOMESTIC SLAVERY IN THE UNITED STATES (Philadelphia: 1817). Photo by the Burns Studio.

Plate 18. *Challenge to a Duel*, from Mason Locke Weems, God's Revenge Against Duelling, p. 16 (Philadelphia: 1821). Photo by the New York State Library.

Plate 19. *Like Master, Like Man*, frontispiece to Mason Locke Weems, God's Revenge Against Duelling. Photo by the New York State Library.

Plate 20. *Fourth of July in Centre Square*, by John L. Krimmel, 1819. Courtesy of the Pennsylvania Academy of the Fine Arts.

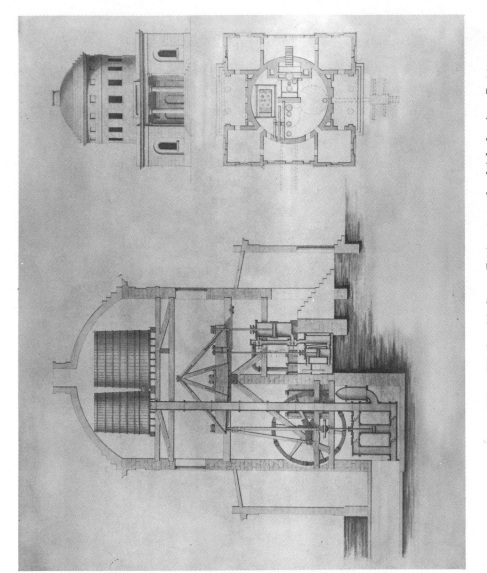

Plate 21. *Centre Square Water Works with Steam Engine*, an undated ink drawing. Courtesy of the Historical Society of Pennsylvania.

Plate 22. *Declaration of Independence*, by John Trumbull, 1786–1797. Courtesy of Yale University Art Gallery.

Plate 23. *Declaration of Independence*, by John Trumbull, 1818. Courtesy of the Library of Congress.

Plate 24. *Peale in His Museum*, by Charles Willson Peale, 1822.
Courtesy of the Pennsylvania Academy of the Fine Arts.

Plate 25. *Exhuming the First American Mastodon*, by Charles Willson Peale, 1806. Courtesy of the Peale Museum, Baltimore, Maryland. Gift of Mrs. Henry J. White.

DOCUMENT 28

A Naval Hero: Stephen Decatur

The real meaning of events is inward. The character of a people or nation is revealed through its arts, its architecture, literature, and not least through its heroes. When victories on land were so few, it is not strange that the naval heroes, who did so much to salvage national honor in a war believed to be fought for honor, should be singled out for acclaim. Among the many naval heroes, Stephen Decatur was easily the most popular.

By contrast with Andrew Jackson, who became the outstanding hero of the war with his spectacular victory at New Orleans, Decatur was a hero in the classical tradition: young, handsome, aristocratic, accomplished. Is it not likely that he owed his elevation in part to the impulse which raised Greek and Roman temples? After the war, he lived in a house designed by Benjamin Latrobe, architect of the Classical Revival.

Decatur's fervent concern for honor, reflected in his famous toast ending, "may she always be in the right; but our country, right or wrong," later involved him in a fatal duel, an account of which appears below. Its author, John Quincy Adams, was Minister to Russia in 1813, when the account begins. The reader may also wish to consult the published *Correspondence between the Late Commodore Stephen Decatur and Commodore James Barron* . . . (Washington, 1820). Document 29 presents a further commentary upon Decatur's death. Adams did not consider such anti-dueling tracts very effective, because they did not go to the roots of the problem.

SOURCE: *The Diary of John Quincy Adams, 1794–1845,* edited by Allan Nevins, pp. 106, 234–35. New York: Charles Scribner's Sons, 1951.

May 11, 1813.— At dinner I was seated between Count Kotschubey and General Bétancourt, with both of whom I had some conversation. That with the Count was chiefly political, on our war with England. My feelings on this subject, and some remarks and questions of the Count, urged me to a degree of warmth bordering at least on indiscretion. Count Romanzoff, who was unusually marked in his attentions to me, said, in a tone of pleasantry, "How happens it that you are constantly beating at sea the English, who beat all the rest of the world, and that on land, where you ought to be the strongest, the English *do what they please?*" I answered him in the same manner, that I knew not how to account for it, unless by supposing that these times were reserved to keep the world in a continued state of wonder, and to prove that there is something new under the sun. He replied that there had once been a confusion of tongues, and now, he believed, was the time for a confusion of minds.

March 22, 1820.— Before I left my house this morning to go to my office, W. S. Smith came in and told me that Commodore Decatur had just been brought in from Bladensburg, mortally wounded in a duel with Commodore James Barron, who was also wounded, but not dangerously. I went immediately to Decatur's house: on the way met Captains McDonough and Ballard, who were coming from it, and whose information was discouraging but not decisive. At the house I saw Generals Brown and Harper, Colonel Bomford, and E. Wyer. Brown and Harper were flattered by some uncertainties of Dr. Lovell the Surgeon-General, who, I suppose, thinks it humane to keep Mrs. Decatur and her father, who is with her, in suspense as long as possible. Wyer, who had seen Decatur, told me that he could not survive the day. He died between nine and ten o'clock this evening. The nation has lost in him one of its heroes—one who has illustrated its history and given grace and dignity to its character in the eyes of the world . . .

The sensation in the city and neighborhood produced by this catastrophe was unusually great. But the lamentations at the practice of duelling were, and will be, fruitless, as they always are. Forbes called at my house this evening: he had been sitting an hour with Barron, who is at Beale's Congress Hotel on Capitol Hill. He has a ball in his body, which spared his life by hitting and glancing from the hip-bone. The cause of the duel is said to have been Decatur's resistance, as one of the Commissioners of the Navy, to the restoration of Barron to the naval service. Barron had been suspended for five years, from 1807, by the sentence of a court-martial, of which Decatur was a member, for the unfortunate affair of the *Chesapeake* frigate with Berkeley's squadron. The five years expired during our late war with Great Britain. Barron was then in Europe, and did not return to the United States during our war with Great Britain: though he made application for a passage in the *John Adams*, from Gottenburg, in June, 1814. After the peace he came back, and claimed to be restored to active employment, which it is said Decatur prevented him from obtaining. He has also spoken of him in slighting and contemptuous terms. A correspondence of mutual crimination and defiance has been passing between them since last June, and is now to be published.

March 24, 1820.— I went to my office; and attended the funeral of Decatur. There were said to be ten thousand persons assembled. An order of procession had been announced in the newspapers, and was inverted at the house. The procession walked to Kalorama, where the body was deposited in the family vault of the Barlows. A very short prayer was made at the vault by Dr. Hunter, and a volley of musketry from a detachment of the Marine Corps closed the ceremony over the earthly remains of a spirit as kindly, as generous, and as dauntless as breathed in this nation, or on this earth. I walked with Mr. Crawford. John Randolph was there; first walking, then backing his horse, then calling for his phaeton, and lastly crowding up to the vault as the coffin was removed into it from the hearse—tricksy humors to make himself conspicuous.

DOCUMENT 29

(PLATES 18 AND 19)

The Vice of Dueling

Crusading against vice had become a traditional expression of the national mission, which began with the early settlers, to bring about a reformation of man and society. The author of the tract in which these cartoons appeared, Parson Weems (see doc. 17), was much influenced by the apocalyptic vision of a new heaven and a new earth, which he was industriously and profitably engaged in bringing about. But his vision was inevitably clogged by worldly considerations, of which anti-foreign prejudices and the acceptance of slavery were a part, as the cartoons show. Weems also wrote crusading tracts against gambling, wenching, drunkenness, and murder. His "Looking Glasses," as he called them, purported to be mirrors of truth, presenting case histories in palatable fictional form. "The Case of Peter and John Hay" in his *Drunkard's Looking Glass*, for instance, stressed the awful retribution which overtook two richly endowed brothers of Charleston, South Carolina, who took to drink. They were burned to death when a barn where they went to sleep off their hangover caught fire. Parson Weems' *Looking Glasses* captured the popular imagination and became best sellers.

DOCUMENT 30

Commodore Perry

Washington Irving seemed to understand better than
most Americans the main source of the naval heroes'
appeal and wrote about it in the following analysis of
Commodore Perry, who was second only to Decatur in
popularity. If Irving is right, his countrymen liked a
simple, comprehensible unity of event dominated by a
single dynamic individual who professed a simple
faith in God's helping providence. They wanted to
believe, above all, in a triumph of virtue which left
nothing to chance, for were they not a chosen people?
In the image-making process, Perry enjoyed one advantage over Decatur which was shared by General
Jackson—namely, an association with the virgin landscape of the interior.

Irving's treatment stresses the great American theme
of the invasion of the wilderness by civilization. A
Rhode Islander, Perry was not really cut out for an
Adamic role, and he had fewer opportunities than
Decatur to distinguish himself in naval action. When
Samuel Waldo, who wrote an early *Memoir* of General
Jackson as well as painting Jackson's portrait, decided
to write a popular naval biography, he chose Stephen
Decatur as his subject rather than Oliver Perry.

SOURCE: Washington Irving, "Commodore Perry," *Works*, 27
vols. Vol. XIX, pp. 105–11. New York: 1865–69.

* * *

There is . . . a distinctness of character about a naval
victory that meets the capacity of every mind. There is
such a simple unity in it; it is so well defined, so complete
within itself, so rounded by space, so free from those in-

tricacies and numerous parts that perplex us in an action on land, that the meanest intellect can fully grasp and comprehend it. And then, too, the results are so apparent. A victory on land is liable to a thousand misrepresentations; retreat is often called falling back, and abandoning the field called taking a new position; so that the conqueror is often defrauded of half the credit of his victory; but the capture or destruction of a ship is not to be mistaken, and a squadron towed triumphantly into port, is a notorious fact that admits of no contradiction.

In this battle, we trust, incontrovertible proof is given, if such proof were really wanted, that the success of our Navy does not arise from chance, or superiority of force; but from the cool, deliberate courage, the intelligent minds and naval skill of our officers, the spirit of our seamen, and the excellent discipline of our ships; from principles, in short, which must insure a frequency of prosperous results, and give permanency to the reputation we have acquired. We have been rapidly adding trophy to trophy, and successively driving the enemy from every excuse in which he sought to shelter himself from the humiliation of defeat; and after having perfectly established our capability of fighting and conquering in single ships, we have now gone further, and shown that it is possible for us to face the foe in squadron, and vanquish him even though superior in force.

In casting our eye over the details of this engagement, we are struck with the prominent part which the commander takes in the contest. We realize in his dauntless exposure and individual prowess, what we have read in heroic story, of the warrior, streaming like a meteor through the fight, and working wonders with his single arm. The fate of the combat seemed to rest upon his sword; he was the master-spirit that directed the storm of battle, moving amid flames, and smoke, and death, and mingling wherever the struggle was most desperate and deadly. After sustaining in the *Lawrence* the whole blaze of the enemy's cannonry; after fighting until all around him was wreck and carnage; we behold him, looking forth from his shattered deck, with unruffled countenance, on the direful perils that environed him, calculating with wary eye the chances of the battle, and suddenly launching forth on the bosom of the deep, to shift his flag on board another ship, then in the hottest of the action. This was one of those master-strokes by which great events are achieved, and great characters stamped, as it were, at a single blow,—which bespeak the rare combination of the genius to conceive, the promptness to decide, and the boldness to execute. Most commanders have such glorious chances for renown, some time or another, within their reach; but it requires the nerve of a hero to grasp the perilous opportunity. We behold Perry following up his daring movement with sustained energy,—dashing into the squadron of the enemy,—breaking their line,—raking starboard and larboard,—and in this brilliant style achieving a consummate victory.

But if we admire his presence of mind and dauntless valor in the hour of danger, we are no less delighted with his modesty and self-command amidst the flush of triumph. A courageous heart may carry a man stoutly through the battle, but it argues some strong qualities of head to drain unmoved the intoxicating cup of victory. The first care of Perry was to attend to the comfort of the suffering crews of both squadrons. The sick and wounded were landed as soon as possible, and every means taken to alleviate the miseries of their situation. The officers who had fallen, on both sides, were buried on Sunday morning, on an island in the Lake, with the honors of war. To the surviving officers he advanced a loan of one thousand dollars, out of his own limited purse; but, in short, his behavior in this respect is best expressed in the words of Commodore Barclay, who, with generous warmth and frankness, has declared that "the conduct of Perry towards the captive officers and men was sufficient, of itself, to immortalize him!"

The letters which he wrote announcing the intelligence were remarkably simple and laconic. To the Secretary of the Navy he observes, "It has pleased the Almighty to give to the arms of the United States a signal victory over their enemies on this Lake. The British squadron, consisting of two ships, two brigs, one schooner, and one sloop, have this moment surrendered to the force under my command, after a sharp conflict." This has been called an imitation of Nelson's letter after the battle of the Nile; but it was choosing a noble precedent, and the important national results of the victory justified the language. Independent of the vast accession of glory to our flag, this conquest insured the capture of Detroit, the rout of the British armies, the subjugation of the whole peninsula of Upper Canada, and, if properly followed up, the triumphant success of our northern war. Well might he say "It has pleased the Almighty," when, by this achievement, he beheld immediate tranquillity restored to an immense extent of country. Mothers no longer shrunk aghast, and clasped their infants to their breasts, when they heard the shaking of the forest or the howling of the blast; the aged sire no longer dreaded the shades of night, lest ruin should burst upon him in the hour of repose, and his cottage be laid desolate by the firebrand and the scalping-knife; Michigan was rescued from the dominion of the sword, and quiet and security once more settled on the harassed frontiers, from Huron to Niagara.

But we are particularly pleased with his subsequent letter giving the particulars of the battle. It is so chaste, so moderate and perspicuous; equally free from vaunting exultation and affected modesty; neither obtruding himself upon notice, nor pretending to keep out of sight. His own individual services may be gathered from the letter, though not expressly mentioned; indeed, where the fortune of the day depended so materially upon himself, it was impossible to give a faithful narrative without rendering himself conspicuous.

We are led to notice these letters thus particularly, because that we find the art of letter-writing is an accomplishment as rare as it is important among our military gentlemen. We are tired of the valor of the pen, and the victories of the ink-horn. There is a common French proverb, "Grand parleur, mauvais combattant," which we could wish to see introduced into our country, and engraven on the swords of our officers. We wish to see them confine themselves in their letters to simple facts, neither swaggering before battle nor vaunting afterwards. It is unwise to boast before, for the event may prove disastrous; and it is superfluous to boast afterwards, for the event speaks for itself. He who promises nothing, may with safety perform nothing, and will receive praise if he perform but little; but he who promises much will receive small credit unless he perform miracles. If a commander have done well, he may be sure the public will find it out, and their gratitude will be in proportion to his modesty. Admiration is a coin which, if left to ourselves, we lavish profusely, but we always close the hand when dunned for it.

Commodore Perry, like most of our naval officers, is yet in the prime of youth. He is of a manly and prepossessing appearance; mild and unassuming in his address, amiable in his disposition, and of great firmness and decision. Though early launched among the familiar scenes of naval life (and nowhere is familiarity more apt to be licentious and encroaching), yet the native gentility and sober dignity of his deportment always chastened, without restraining, the freedom of intimacy. It is pleasing thus to find public services accompanied by private virtues; to discover no drawbacks on our esteem, no base alloy in the man we are disposed to admire; but a character full of moral excellence, of high-minded courtesy, and pure, unsullied honor.

Were anything wanting to perpetuate the fame of this victory, it would be sufficiently memorable from the scene where it was fought. This war has been distinguished by new and peculiar characteristics. Naval warfare has been carried into the interior of a continent, and navies, as if by magic, launched from among the depths of the forest. The bosoms of peaceful lakes which, but a short time since, were scarcely navigated by man, except to be skimmed by the light canoe of the savage, have all at once been ploughed by hostile ships. The vast silence that had reigned for ages on those mighty waters, was broken by the thunder of artillery, and the affrighted savage stared with amazement from his covert, at the sudden apparition of a sea-fight amid the solitudes of the wilderness.

The peal of war has once sounded on that lake, but probably will never sound again. The last roar of cannonry that died along her shores was the expiring note of British domination. Those vast internal seas will, perhaps, never again be the separating space between contending nations; but will be embosomed within a mighty empire; and this victory, which decided their fate, will stand unrivalled and alone, deriving lustre and perpetuity from its singleness.

In future times, when the shores of Erie shall hum with busy population; when towns and cities shall brighten where now extend the dark and tangled forest; when ports shall spread their arms, and lofty barks shall ride where now the canoe is fastened to the stake; when the present age shall have grown into venerable antiquity, and the mists of fable begin to gather round its history; then will the inhabitants of Canada look back to this battle we record as one of the romantic achievements of the days of yore. It will stand first on the page of their local legends, and in the marvellous tales of the borders. The fisherman, as he loiters along the beach, will point to some half-buried cannon, corroded with the rust of time, and will speak of ocean warriors that came from the shores of the Atlantic; while the boatman, as he trims his sail to the breeze, will chant in rude ditties the name of Perry—the early hero of Lake Erie.

DOCUMENT 31

An Allegorical Peace of Ghent

The cult of war heroes produced by the War of 1812 had much in common with the "monumental" style in the arts as an expression of national feeling. The monumental style, typified by Trumbull's grandiose historical paintings (doc. 37), by classical public buildings and monuments, Greek and Roman place names and pen names, Greek-letter fraternal societies, stilted epics, and fanciful allegories, represented attempts to link American destiny with a glorious past and eternal truths.

Benjamin Latrobe (1764–1820), in the piece below, finds something ludicrous about Mrs. Plantou's attempt to picture the Peace of Ghent allegorically (see doc. 5). But the problem of adapting American experience to universal themes was a more general one. One wonders, for example, whether Latrobe's own design for the Center Square pump house (docs. 34 and 35) was not equally ludicrous—indeed, whether the whole Classical Revival was not a mistake.

A comparison of the Plantou picture with Trumbull's more realistic treatment of a similar historical occasion, the signing of the Declaration (doc. 37), suggests, perhaps, a widening split in the American psyche between the real and the ideal with the advance of industrial civilization. Recent commentators have generally regarded the realistic vein of artistic creation more authentically American, because closer to the vernacular, but it remains nonetheless true that

the greatest artists have always sought to embody the
ideal in the familiar.

SOURCE: Benjamin H. B. Latrobe, *Impressions Respecting New
Orleans*, edited with an introduction by Samuel Wilson, Jr.,
pp. 102–5. New York: Columbia University Press, 1951.

March 18th, 1819. I went this morning with Mr. Plantou
to see his wife's picture of the treaty of Ghent. It is an excellent painting in many points of view. . . . But its inherent sin, especially in America, is its being an allegorical
picture. When the mythology of antiquity was the substance of its religion, & the character & history of every
deity was known to every individual of the nation, allegorical representations were a kind of *written description* of
the subject represented, & might be generally understood.
But since Hercules & Minerva & the rest of the deities are
in fashion only as decorations of juvenile poetry, & are
known by character only to those few who have had classical educations, an allegorical picture stands as much in
need of an interpreter as an Indian talk.

Mrs. Plantou has painted exceedingly well, but has
judged very ill. In another respect also her American feeling has betrayed her into error. She has painted a picture
of the largest size in oil, of course a picture calculated for
duration, & forming an historical record, to represent
evanescent feelings, the feelings of unexpected & of course
riotous & unreasonable triumph. Brittania is represented
as laying at the feet of America, who approaches in a tri-
umphal car, her flag, her rudder (emblems of naval superiority), her laurels, & other symbols of victory &
dominion. She kneels in the posture of an humble sup-
pliant, while Hercules & Minerva threaten her with the
club & the spear—all this is caricature. But the whole of
this group excepting Hercules is admirably painted. The
figure of Brittania is very graceful & well drawn, & the
drapery has superior merit. The group on the right is also
uncommonly well conceived & executed. The whole picture does, indeed, infinite credit to the artist & to her
country, for she is a Philadelphian. The great fault is the

choice of the subject, for the signing or negotiation of a treaty, *as a matter of fact*, can at best be but a collection of expressive likenesses of persons writing or conversing, & has nothing picturesque about it. Strength, fortitude, courage, & some good luck, on our side, were not wanting "to conquer the treaty," in the French fashionable phrase, and admirable talent was displayed in the negotiation. But these are not very well *paintable*.

As to *allegory* generally it is a most difficult branch of the art of the painter & sculptor, & belongs rather to the poetical department. Yet sometimes the sculptor & painter have succeeded in rendering sentiment intelligible by the chisel & pencil. For instance, in the personification of peace, by Canova, where a pair of doves make their nest in a helmet.

Some years ago Dr. Thornton of Washington described, in a large company, the allegorical group which it was his intention as Commissioner of the city of Washington, to place in the center of the Capitol, around the statue of the general.

"I would," said he, "place an immense rock of granite in the center of the dome. On the top of the rock should stand a beautiful female figure, to represent Eternity or Immortality. Around her neck, as a necklace, a serpent— the rattlesnake of our country—should be hung, with its tail in its mouth, the ancient & beautiful symbol of endless duration. At the foot of the rock another female figure stretching her hands upwards in the attitude of distressful entreaty should appear ready to climb the steep. Around her a group of children representing agriculture, the arts & sciences, should appear to join in the supplication of the female. This female is to personify time, or our present state of existence. Just ascending the rock, the noble figure of General Washington should appear to move upwards, invited by immortality; but also expressing some reluctance in leaving the children of his care. "There," said he, "Mr. Latrobe, is your requisite in such works of art; it would represent *a matter of fact*, a *truth*, for it would be the very picture of the General's sentiments, feelings, &

expectations in departing this life: regret at leaving his people, but hoping & longing for an immortality of happiness & of fame. You yourself have not ingenuity sufficient to pervert its meaning, & all posterity would understand it."

The Doctor was so full of his subject that I was unwilling to disturb his good humor. But I said that I thought his group might tell a very different story from what he intended. He pressed me so hard that at last I told him: that supposing the name & character of General Washington to be forgotten, or at least that the group being found in the ruins of the Capitol, the learned antiquarians of 2000 years hence were assembled to decide its meaning. I thought then that they would thus explain it.

There is a beautiful woman on the top of a dangerous precipice, to which she invites a man, apparently well enough inclined to follow her. Who is this woman? Certainly not a very good sort of one, for she has a snake about her neck. The snake indicates assuredly her character, cold, cunning, & poisonous. She can represent none but some celebrated courtisan of the day. But there is another woman at the foot of the rock, modest & sorrowful, & surrounded by a family of small children. She is in a posture of entreaty, and the man appears half-inclined to return to her. She can be no other than his wife. What an expressive group! How admirable the art which has thus exposed the dangerous precipice to which the beauty & the cunning of the abandoned would entice the virtuous, even to the desertion of a beautiful wife & the mother of a delightful group of children! I was going on, but the laughter of the company & the impatience of the Doctor stopped my mouth. I had said enough, & was not easily forgiven.

DOCUMENT 32

Another View of Allegory

Like Benjamin Latrobe, John Quincy Adams (1767–1848), a future President of the United States, was struck by the inappropriateness of the reigning allegorical mode, but for a different reason. Charles Bulfinch (1763–1844), to whom he refers below, was Latrobe's successor as chief architect for the federal buildings. One cannot attribute to Adams a wholly sectional point of view, for Bulfinch also came from Massachusetts.

SOURCE: *The Diary of John Quincy Adams, 1794–1845,* edited by Allan Nevins, p. 347. New York: Charles Scribner's Sons, 1951.

May 31, 1825.— Bulfinch and Persico came at one o'clock, and we discussed the new design [for the tympanum of the Capitol], which was a personification of the United States standing on a throne, leaning upon the Roman fasces, surmounted with the cap of liberty, with Justice at her right hand, blindfolded, holding the suspended balance, and in the other hand an open scroll, and Hercules at her left, seated on a corner of the throne, embracing the fasces, and emblematical of strength; to which were added, separately drawn, and to fill up the space, Plenty seated with her cornucopia, in one corner, and Peace, a flying angel, extending a garland of victory towards America with one hand, and bearing a palm in the other.

These two last figures I advised should be discarded, as well as the Roman fasces and the cap of liberty. The Hercules had also too much of the heathen mythology for my taste, and I proposed to substitute in his place a figure of Hope, with an anchor—a Scriptural image, indicating that this Hope relies upon a Supreme Disposer of events; "which hope we have as an anchor to the soul, sure and steadfast." Instead of the fasces I proposed a pedestal, with 4th July, 1776, inscribed on its base, and 4th March, 1789, upon its upper cornice. The whole design then would represent the American Union founded on the Declaration of Independence and consummated by the organization of the general government under the Federal Constitution, supported by Justice in the past, and relying upon Hope in Providence for the future.

DOCUMENT 33

A National Style for Architecture

An oft-heard complaint during the early years of the
nineteenth century was that the chief practitioners of
the fine arts in the United States were foreign-born.
Many of Latrobe's troubles in Washington, resulting
finally in his dismissal, he owed to his foreign birth.
The native architect, Robert Mills (1781–1855),
who was a pupil of Latrobe, wrote in the following
document one of the most succinct statements of the
philosophy and origin of the Classical Revival.

In it, he draws a sharp distinction between the Greek
and Roman styles, a distinction which turned chiefly
on the use of a rotunda, or dome, in Roman-type buildings (see again doc. 34) and one which has since
been largely obscured. Here he seems unconscious of
the kind of difficulty which his design for the Monumental Church in Richmond represented (see doc. 99)
in adapting Greek forms to American needs. He is also
unconscious of irony in recommending an architecture
which was both suited to the character of the nation
and "universally approved throughout civilized Europe."

On the other hand, there is a suggestion that he was
struggling toward the more vernacular view that
"form follows function," and he certainly had a clear
conception of the organic nature of architecture. His
plea for including architecture in liberal education unfortunately never reached the public.

Another authoritative statement of the philosophy of
the Classical Revival, longer and less well-organized,
is Benjamin Latrobe, *Anniversary Oration Pronounced
before the Society of Artists of the United States . . .*
(New York, 1811). The opposite view, that the Classi-

cal Revival was alien to the American spirit, received significant expression in an article in *The Analectic Magazine*, Vol. VI, pp. 363–76 (1815), and in an address of 1824 by Gulian C. Verplanck, reprinted in his *Discourses and Addresses*, pp. 123–54 (New York, 1832).

SOURCE: H. M. Pierce Gallagher, *Robert Mills, Architect of the Washington Monument, 1781–1855*, pp. 168–71. New York: Columbia University Press, 1935.

The author, having the honor of being the first native American who directed his studies to architecture as a profession, may have some claim to the favourable mention of his fellow citizens, and having acted as a pioneer in the cause, his more enlightened brethren of the profession will be less severe in their criticisms than they would otherwise be on these, his original efforts.

The author is altogether American in his views—his studies having never been out of the United States and consequently had very little advantage of and from a personal examination of the celebrated works of antiquity, or of more modern date, except that which is to be found in books, and even these were few and difficult to procure at the time he was a student, as architecture was then in its infancy in this country and no invitation was held out for the importation of works of art.

Fortunately for the author, Mr. Jefferson, then President of the United States (befriended him), to whose library he had the honor of having access, where he found some few works of eminent Roman architects but no Grecian writers.

Mr. Jefferson was an amateur and a great admirer of architecture. He was therefore much gratified to find an American turning his attention to its study, and he gave him every encouragement in the pursuit of his profession. Through his recommendation and advice, the author entered into the office of that celebrated Architect and Engineer, Benjamin H. Latrobe, whom Mr. Jefferson had lately appointed Surveyor of the Public Buildings. With this gentleman, the author pursued and completed his studies and practiced in both branches of his profession, as Mr. Latrobe was, at this time, acting engineer of the Chesapeake and Delaware Canal.

The talents of this gentleman were of the first order; his style was purely Greek, and for the first time in this country was it introduced by him in the Bank of Pennsylvania—a building much admired for its chasteness of design and execution.

It was fortunate that this style was so early introduced into our country, both on the ground of economy and of correct taste, as it exactly suited the character of our political institutions and pecuniary means. Mr. Jefferson was a Roman in his views of architecture, as evidenced in Monticello House, his late residence, which was designed by him, and for the execution of which he furnished with his own hands all the detail drawings.

The example and influence of Mr. Jefferson at first operated in favour of the introduction of the Roman style into the country, and it required all the talents and good taste of such a man as Mr. Latrobe to correct it by introducing a better. The natural good taste and the unprejudiced eye of our citizens required only a few examples of the Greek style to convince them of its superiority over the Roman for public structures, and its simplicity recommended its introduction into their private dwellings.

During this period also, Europe, which for centuries had adapted the Roman and mixed style, began to emerge out of its prejudices and the light which had been thrown upon the Greek architecture by such men as Stewart caused it to be early substituted in their place. Since then it has been universally approved throughout civilized Europe, and in our own country we now find the simple and chaste style of the Grecian buildings generally adopted.

The author has contributed his mite in this important work, and has acted as a pioneer in the undertaking. He had many and great difficulties to contend against which those who may succeed him in the profession will never be subject to. In a new country like ours, where everything had to be done and little means to accomplish it with, it will readily be seen that the architect would receive little encouragement and the value of his labours be little appreciated. The increasing prosperity of the Union, the wealth and good taste of our citizens, are every day aiding the cause of the fine arts, and we may anticipate the time when the United States will rival the most enlightened country of the old world, if not in the splendor, yet in the magnitude, utility, and good taste of its public works.

The nature of our public institutions, the independent character of our people, their liberal education and the wide field for successful enterprise opened in the various pursuits of life, all tend to enlarge the mind and give the most exalted views on every subject of art and science. Taken in the aggregate, there is not a more liberal and enlightened people on the face of the globe than the people of the United States.

The professional labours of the author are distributed in various parts of the Union. The principal part of the designs found in his work were executed in Philadelphia, Baltimore, Washington, Richmond, Charleston, Columbia, Camden and other towns of South Carolina, Augusta, Ga., New Orleans, Mobile, etc., etc.

Utility and economy will be found to have entered into most of the studies of the author, and little sacrificed to display; at the same time his endeavors were to produce as much harmony and beauty of arrangement as practicable. The principle assumed and acted upon was that beauty is founded upon order, and that convenience and utility were constituent parts. In the cases of private buildings it is of special importance that convenience, utility and economy should be associated, and the author was generally successful in developing these. European works of architecture were, some years ago, very deficient in plans for private houses, and those laid down were both unsuitable and wanting in economy and convenience. The author experienced no aid in this important . . . , and was obliged to refer to his own resources for assistance. The subject of domestic economy in the arrangement of private houses has since undergone considerable improvement, particularly in France, and many useful hints now are to be gathered from French works on Architecture; but the author has made it a rule never to consult books when he had to design a building. His considerations were,—first, the object of the building; second, the means appropriated for its construction; third, the situation it was to occupy; these served as guides in forming the outline of his plan. Books are useful to the student, but when he enters upon the practice of his profession, he should lay them aside and only consult them upon doubtful points, or in matters of detail or as mere studies, not to copy buildings from.

The science of Architecture is perhaps the most difficult, important, and interesting of all branches of study, where it is intended to form the ground work of practice. There is no other profession that embraces so wide a field of research and practical operation. Some idea may be formed of the nature of these researches when the requisites to constitute an accomplished architect are taken into consideration. The student, after going through the usual collegiate course, will find himself on the threshold of the temple. Besides having an intimate acquaintance with the different styles of building, ancient and modern, and a thorough knowledge of the five orders (as they are termed), which necessarily demand an acquaintance with drawing, he must study the infinite detail which make up the endless variety of parts constituting the higher class of structure. There is not a mechanic art, from the laborer who excavates the foundation to the highest artisan who decorates the interior of the building, but should acquire such knowledge as would enable him to give direction and judge whether the work executed is done in proper manner. There is scarcely a science but is embraced in greater or less degree in this profession; mathematics, natural philosophy, chemistry, geology, botany, natural history, jurisprudence and theology. In short to be an accomplished architect is to be not only an accomplished scholar but an accomplished artist and mechanic. There is not a more fascinating study in the whole range of the liberal professions than that of architecture, even considered in the light of study only; but when its utility is examined, and that it offers one of the most honourable pursuits, it cannot be too highly commended to our youth. If it constituted a part of liberal education, we should see a better taste and a more attractive character of buildings adopted in our country. Until our citizens can distinguish between the crude drawings of the illiterate artist and the designs of the regular bred architect, it is not to be expected that a judicious selection of plans would always be made. It is all important, therefore, that architecture should constitute one of the sciences taught in our colleges and academies.

DOCUMENT 34

(PLATE 20)

Fourth of July in Centre Square

Here we find one of the most interesting paintings
of the period, interesting in its revelation of the national
style in a variety of modes functioning together in a
naturalistic communal setting. First, we have the style
of the Fourth of July celebration itself—its festive gre-
gariousness, its leveling of the classes and age groups
for the public occasion, its display of Sunday dress
and holiday informality, its semi-official setting in an
important public square whose Roman temple, sculptured waternymph, and stately trees stamp the scene
with the seal of the Republic. The temple and fountain, designed respectively by Benjamin Latrobe and
William Rush, are, of course, examples of the republican vogue in architecture. Then there can be seen the
reigning fashions in dress and comportment. The men
and women have for the most part segregated themselves from one another, with the small children and
dogs serving as links between them. The dandies in
the picture have their eyes on the girls, who pretend
to ignore them. Finally, the painting itself is an interesting early example of genre painting: the discovery
of the common man in his local habitat by the vernacular artist. The locale is Philadelphia.

Document 35

(Plate 21)

Centre Square Waterworks With Steam Engine

This drawing of the Roman temple at Centre Square helps to direct our attention to certain incongruities in the foregoing scene which may have escaped our notice. There is smoke rising out of the great nipple of a dome. The chaste, antique structure breathes something more palpable than classic poetry because it houses a modern water pump and steam engine designed especially for it by Oliver Evans. Republican simplicity has not yet caught up with technological innovation in structural design—indeed, seems hardly aware of the problem of assimilating the new technology to traditional forms or of creating new forms to express the changing spirit of the times. The people thronging the square in the foregoing scene obviously feel quite at home with this cultural monstrosity. Nor are they aware of the ludicrousness of having a classical nymph holding a goose with water squirting from its mouth to represent the Schuylkill River. They seem to be living in an arcadian past, their only concession to the present being a certain affectation in dress which the new material prosperity encourages.

This basic incongruity can be highlighted further by comparing the busy Fourth of July scene with document 89, which shows an uncongested Centre Square, in the foreground of which lumbers Oliver Evans' combination scow-steamdredge-locomotive, puffing up a cloud of steam as it overtakes a horse-drawn covered wagon.

DOCUMENT 36

John Trumbull's "Declaration of Independence"

The great dialogue about the nation's self-identity was carried on in painting as in architecture and other aspects of culture. The controversy aroused by Trumbull's four national paintings which were commissioned to hang in the Capitol Rotunda begins below with an acidulous comment by John Quincy Adams. Since document 37 shows both versions of the picture in question, the reader is able to test Adams' judgment for himself. Wherein does the believed superiority of the earlier, more impressionistic picture lie? John Randolph, the brilliant, eccentric Virginian who had been an early sponsor of Trumbull's project, came to consider them a *"Shin-piece,* for surely, never was there, before, such a collection of legs submitted to the eyes of man."

SOURCE: *The Diary of John Quincy Adams, 1794–1845,* edited by Allan Nevins, p. 201. New York: Charles Scribner's Sons, 1951.

New York, Sept. 1, 1818.— Called about eleven o'clock at Mr. Trumbull's house, and saw his picture of the Declaration of Independence which is now nearly finished. I cannot say I was disappointed in the execution of it, because my expectations were very low: but the picture is immeasurably below the dignity of the subject. It may be said of Trumbull's talent as the Spaniards say of heroes who were brave on a certain day: he has painted good pictures. I think the old small picture far superior to this large new one. He himself thinks otherwise. He has some books on the President's table which the Abbé Correa advised him to letter on the backs, Locke and Sidney. I told him I thought that was not the place for them. They were books for the members to read at home, but not to take with them there. I advised him to letter them simply "Journals."

DOCUMENT 37

(PLATES 22 AND 23)

Two Versions of "The Declaration of Independence"

The earlier first picture of the Signing of the Declaration which John Trumbull painted measured only twenty-one by thirty-one inches. The second version, one of the series of four historical paintings for which he received thirty-two thousand dollars, measured more than eighteen feet by twelve feet, with figures as large as life. Both versions are shown here. It would seem that, considering the painstaking detail and realism for which Trumbull was striving, the larger picture would have been easier to execute. This was not altogether true, however, for Trumbull suffered from monocular vision, a physical defect which made it difficult to perceive spatial relationships in a large-scale work.

Document 38

A *Favorable Review of "The Declaration of Independence"*

Benjamin Silliman (1779–1864), author of the following critique and a well-known chemist at Yale University, had recently founded the scientific journal in which this review first appeared. He was a close friend of the painter. That he was also an ardent patriot is certain; his qualifications as an art critic are submitted to the reader. The sense of responsibility which led him to report on developments in the arts as well as in science reflected the encyclopedic character of early nationalism (see also doc. 42).

SOURCE: *The American Journal of Science and Arts,* Vol. I, pp. 200–3 (1818).

"It is proper that some mention of this great national work should be made, in publications less transient than newspapers; and as the fine arts are included within the design of this Journal, it may with propriety be noticed here. This is the greatest work which the art of painting has ever produced in the United States. The picture is magnificent both in size and in execution. The dimensions of the canvass are eighteen feet by twelve.

"This picture forms one of a series long since meditated by Mr. Trumbull, in which it was intended to represent the most important events, civil and military, of the American revolution, with portraits of the most distinguished actors in the various scenes. The materials for this purpose were collected many years ago, and two plates have been engraved from paintings of the deaths of Gen.

Warren and Gen. Montgomery;* but the work was suspended, in consequence of the political convulsions, which, during twenty-five years, were so fatal to the arts of peace.

"The government of the United States have ordered four of the subjects originally proposed by Mr. Trumbull, to be painted by him, and to be deposited in the capitol.

"No event in human history ever shed a more salutary influence over the destinies of so great a mass of mankind: the wisdom of no political act was ever so soon and so powerfully demonstrated, by such magnificent consequences. And justly may the nation be proud of the act itself; and of those eminent men, its authors, whose patriotism (rising above enthusiasm, and the passions which have so often bewildered mankind) was calm, dignified, persevering, and always under the guidance of reason and virtue.

"The painting represents the congress at the moment when the committee advance to the table of the president to make their report.

"It contains faithful portraits of all those members who were living when the picture was begun, and of all others of whom any authentic representation could be obtained. Of a small number, no trace could be discovered; and nothing was admitted which was not authentic."

This picture is now, by permission of government, exhibited in the Academy of Arts in New-York, and will probably be shown in some of our other principal cities, before it receives its final location at Washington.

It exhibits the interior of the then Congress Hall at Philadelphia. Most of the members are represented as sitting in their respective chairs, or, in various instances, as standing in different parts of the room. Almost all the portraits were taken by Colonel Trumbull *from the living men*, and their accuracy may therefore be relied on.

The president, John Hancock, sitting at a table, and elevated somewhat by a low platform, is receiving the

---

* These pictures, as is well known, represent the assault on Quebec, and the battle of Bunker's Hill.

report of the committee declaring the independence of
the colonies; that committee, individually illustrious,
and in this august transaction collectively memorable, was
composed of Franklin, Adams, Sherman, Jefferson, and
Livingston. Mr. Jefferson, in the prime of life, is in the
act of laying upon the table the great charter of a nation's
liberties; while his companions support him by their
silent but dignified presence, and the venerable Franklin,
in particular, imposes new obligations on his country's
gratitude.

The figures are as large as the life; and it may safely be
said, that the world never beheld, on a similar occasion, a
more noble assemblage. It was the native and unchartered
nobility of great talent, cultivated intelligence, superior
manners, high moral aim, and devoted patriotism. The
crisis demanded the utmost firmness of which the human
mind is capable—a firmness not produced, for the moment, by passion and enthusiasm, but resting on the most
able comprehension of both duties and dangers, and on a
principled determination to combat the one and to fulfil
the other.

This moral effect has been produced in the fullest and
finest manner by this great painter; and no true American can contemplate this picture without gratitude to the
men who, under God, asserted his liberties, and to the
artist who has commemorated the event, and transmitted
the very features and persons of the actors to posterity.
Such efforts of the pencil tend powerfully also to invigor-
ate patriotism, and to prompt the rising generation to
emulate such glorious examples.

The composition and execution in this picture are in a
masterly style. The grouping of so many full length portraits, in a scene in which there could scarcely be any
action, and in such a manner as to dispose of them without monotony, was an attainment of no small difficulty.
The painter could not even avail himself of the adventi-
tious relief of splendid costume and furniture, and of
magnificence or rich decorations in architecture; for on
this occasion both were characterized by an elegant sim-

plicity only, such however as became the actors and the crisis.

The composition has all the variety of which it is susceptible; and there is also enough of it in the style of dress and of features to relieve the eye from any danger of satiety.

It is believed, that in this picture, the United States possess a treasure to which there is no parallel in the world. In no instance, within our knowledge, is there an exhibition to an equal extent, of the actual portraits of an illustrious assembly, concerned in so momentous a transaction.

It was a great thing to assert, *in principle*, the liberties of this country; but it was also a great thing to vindicate them by arms; and we rejoice that Colonel Trumbull is still to proceed, under the sanction of government, to delineate other scenes, in which Washington and his illustrious American coadjutors, and the flower of French chivalry, were the actors. In the maturity of his experience, skill, and fame—possessed, as he is, of the portraits of most of the great men of that period, taken principally from the life, and having been himself largely and personally conversant with them in their great deeds, we trust that the government will promptly second what we doubt not the united voice of the nation will demand—that the illustrious artist should dedicate the evening of his life to his country's honour and glory.

DOCUMENT 39

"The Declaration of Independence":
An Exchange of Views

The following exchange illustrates a major problem in so-called realistic art, the temptation to be diverted by the important consideration of subject matter from the even more important considerations of artistry and the creative imagination. Could Colonel Trumbull have defended himself on the higher ground of creative imagination? He was quite as sensible as Mrs. Plantou of trying to evoke sentiments of the ideal, yet he belongs to the tradition of American artists who have chiefly exploited subject matter and in a rather literal way. The major patriotic subject of Trumbull's period was the great moments of American history, soon to be followed by the grandeur of American landscape (see doc. 62). Portraiture, a more humble art, led gradually, toward the end of the period, to the ennobling discovery of the Common Man in genre painting. This discovery of the social classes by such artists as John Krimmel and Henry Sargent (docs. 59 and 80–81) belongs perhaps within the same frame as the steamboat and the locomotive and the Lowell factories, all expressive of new middle-class aspirations.

SOURCE: *The Port Folio*, Vol. VII, pp. 84–86 (1819).

Great National Picture.—I have lately seen the painting by colonel Trumbell, "representing the Declaration of Independence," which is said to contain "portraits of forty seven of the members present in Congress on that memorable occasion."

This picture has been drawn by direction of Congress,

and is now submitted to public inspection by permission of the government.

It is not my intention to examine the merits of this production as a specimen of the arts. It may, perhaps, be *a very pretty picture*, but is certainly no representation of the Declaration of Independence. The errors in point of fact, with which it abounds, ought to exclude it from the walls of the capitol, where its exhibition will hereafter give to the mistake of the artist the semblance and authority of historical truth.

The manifest intention of Congress, in directing the preparation of this picture was to perpetuate accurate recollections of one of the greatest events in history, and to hand to posterity correct resemblances of the men who pronounced our separation from Great Britain. In tracing such a sketch, the fancy of the painter has a very limited indulgence. Some latitude is allowed him, as respects design and embellishment; but the very object of his effort enjoins a scrupulous adherence to fact, in all that regards the actors and main incidents of his subject. If he overleaps this boundary, he violates the plain rules of propriety and common sense; and his piece sinks from the grade of a great historical painting into a sorry, motley, mongrel picture, where truth and fiction mingle, but cannot be discriminated. To make the "national painting" in question subservient to a display of the likeness of any American, however distinguished, who was not both a member of Congress and present in that body when Independence was declared, is no less ridiculous than it would be to introduce into it the head of lord Chatham, or that of Col. Barre.

Among "the portraits of forty-seven of the members present in Congress on that memorable occasion," colonel Trumbull has given those of George Clinton of New-York, and Benjamin Rush and George Clymer of Pennsylvania.—Now, the truth happens to be, that neither of these gentlemen was present when Independence was declared, and never gave a vote for or against the Declaration. Mr. Clinton, if I am not mistaken, was appointed a general in June, 1776, and was serving, when Congress pronounced our severance from Great Britain, in a military capacity, in the province of New-York,—Messrs. Rush and Clymer were not elected to Congress until the 20th of July, 1776, that is to say, sixteen days after the final passage of the Declaration, and nineteen days subsequent to its approval in committee of the whole. The names of the two gentlemen last mentioned, together with those of James Smith, George Taylor and James Ross, appear among the signatures to the Declaration of Independence in consequence of the following circumstances:—On the 19th day of July, 1776, (the day before the election of Mr. Rush, and his associates above mentioned) Congress passed a resolution that each of its members should sign that instrument. It was not, however, engrossed on parchment and prepared for signatures until the 3d of August. The new members from Pennsylvania having taken their seats in the interim, signed the Declaration in obedience to the resolution of the house.

The persons who are believed to have been present when the independence was declared, and whose portraits do not appear in the paintings of colonel Trumbull, are—

Henry Wisner, of New-York; John Hart, of New-Jersey; John Morton and Charles Humphreys, of Pennsylvania; Cæsar Rodney, of Delaware; Thomas Stone, of Maryland; Thomas Nelson, Jun. Richard Lightfoot Lee, and Carter Braxton, of Virginia, John Penn, of North Carolina; Button Gwinnet and Lyman Hall, of Georgia.

That portraits of these distinguished men are not contained in the piece is not a fault of the artist, who has been unable to obtain accurate likenesses of them. But it is particularly to be regretted, that an authentic representation of Cæsar Rodney, of Delaware, could not have been found to substitute for one of the faces which have no pretensions to a place. To the vote of this gentleman, on the 4th of July, and to the accidental or intentional absence from their seats of Robert Morris, of Pennsylvania, and John Dickenson, also of Pennsylvania, (not of

Delaware, as the artist has it in his prospectus,) it is owing that *the vote of the states* was unanimous in favour of the national charter on its final adoption. The delegates of Delaware present in Congress on the 1st of July, when the Declaration of Independence passed in committee of the whole, were divided in opinion—Mr. Reed, one of the attending delegates from that state, being *against* the measure, and Mr. M'Kean, the other attending delegate, being *for* it. The vote of Pennsylvania, in committee of the whole was unfavourable to independence, Mess. Morris, Dickenson, Willing, and Humphreys, declaring against it, in opposition to Messrs. Franklin, Morton and Wilson.

I have thought proper to offer these few remarks, both because the permission given by the government to exhibit the painting in N. York, seems to be an invitation to dispassionate criticism, and because the artist still has time before the removal of his picture, to make it, if practicable, accord with historical truth. To exhibit it in its present form on the walls of the capitol at Washington, would be a severe satire on our ignorance of our own history, and would justly expose our legislative councils to the scoffs and sneers of every intelligent foreigner who may visit us.

DETECTOR.

MR. TRUMBULL returns his thanks to "Detector," for having given him an opportunity of laying before the public some account of the origin and progress of the Painting of the Declaration of Independence, which he could not otherwise have done, without being liable to censure for egotism.

After the termination of the war of the revolution, Mr. T. determined to study the art of painting, for the purpose of recording the great events and great men of that period. In the year 1786, the paintings of the battle of Bunker's Hill, and the attack on Quebec, were finished, were seen by and received the most flattering approbation of, the first artists and connoisseurs in England, France,

Germany, and Prussia. Considering the success of his general plan thus secured, he proceeded to determine the other subjects which should form his series; and among these the Declaration of Independence was considered as the most important.

At this time, Mr. Trumbull enjoyed the friendship and hospitality of Mr. Jefferson, then minister of the United States at Paris; and it was under his roof, and with the aid of his advice, that the arrangement and composition of this picture was settled. In the following summer of 1787, the head of Mr. John Adams, then minister of the United States in London, was painted, a few days previous to his return from his mission; and shortly after the head of Mr. Jefferson was painted in Paris.

The question immediately occurred, which "*Detector*" has so shrewdly discovered, who were the men actually present on the 4th of July? The journals of Congress are silent; it would be dangerous to trust the memory of any one—and the only prudent resource was to take as a general guide, the signatures to the original instrument, although it was as well known to Mr. Jefferson and Mr. T. then as it is now to the sagacious "*Detector*," that there were on that instrument the names of several gentlemen who were not actually present on the 4th of July; and also, that several gentlemen were then present who never subscribed their names.

The record was therefore taken as a general guide; and with regard to all the most important characters represented in the painting, there was, and (begging my sagacious friend's pardon) there is no doubt.

In 1789 Mr T. arrived in this town from Europe, and passed the winter here, Congress being then in session. Here the portraits of Richard Henry Lee, Roger Sherman, Lewis Morris, Francis Lewis, &c. &c. were painted, and at this time he was informed that George Clinton, then governor, had been a member present in Congress on the 4th of July, although his name was not among those subscribed to the instrument. He therefore waited on governor Clinton to ascertain the fact, *and was by*

him assured that he was present on that memorable oc-
casion. The governor consented with pleasure to sit for
his portrait—and on this testimony the portrait was
painted.

This session of Congress was peculiarly important, and
had collected in this city many eminent men; military as
well as civil; and Mr. T. thus had a fair opportunity not
only of advancing the picture in question, but of collect-
ing the materials for other subjects. He was of course
well known to president Washington, and to all the distinguished characters of the day. He made it his duty,
and his business, to ask the advice and criticism of all
those who did him the honour to sit for their portraits;
and not only the Declaration of Independence, but the
battles of Trenton and Princeton, and the surrender of
Yorktown, were very much advanced under the eye, with
the criticism, and with the approbation, of the men who
had been the great actors in the several scenes.

In May, 1790, Mr. T. went to Philadelphia, where,
during three months, he added considerably to his stock
of materials.—Here he was informed that Mr. Thomas
Willing was a member present in Congress on the 4th of
July, although his name was not on the list of signatures.
On application to Mr. Willing, he assured Mr. T. that
he was present but opposed to the measure, and therefore had not signed.—Mr. T. did not feel it to be his duty
to record only those who had been supporters of the
measure, and therefore requested Mr. W. to sit, which
he did.

In November of the same year, Mr. T. went to Boston
and New-Hampshire, and obtained portraits from the life
of John Hancock, Samuel Adams, R. T. Paine, Josiah
Bartlett, and many others.

In February 1791, he went to Charleston, S. C. and
obtained from the life, portraits of Edward Rutledge and
Thomas Heyward—and copies of pictures of Thomas
Lynch, and Arthur Middleton, who were dead—as well
as many heads of men eminent in other scenes, military
as well as civil, which entered into his plan. On his re-

turn, he went to Yorktown, in Virginia, and made a correct drawing of the scene of lord Cornwallis's surrender—at Williamsburg, obtained a portrait from the life of George Wythe, &c. &c.

Mr. T. afterwards made two visits to the east, went to Saratoga, and passed the winters of 1792 and 3 in Philadelphia, where congress then sat—always endeavouring to obtain correct information; and when men whose memory it was desirable to preserve, were dead, using all the means in his power, to obtain from their surviving friends whatever memorial existed.

During this period Mr. T. had, and solicited, no other patronage or assistance in his arduous undertaking than subscriptions for those prints which have been long since published from his pictures of the death of Warren and Montgomery.

He was known, during these four years to be employed in this pursuit. He enjoyed the friendship and advice of the most eminent men in the country, and he was not idle. The men of those days are now almost all gone to their reward; and but for the indefatigable perseverance of Mr. T. in a pursuit which his friends often smiled at as visionary, it would at this moment be impossible to obtain even such imperfect pictures as "Detector" considers this to be.

One word more to this most estimable, kind and impartial critic. Two years ago Mr. T. was advised to submit the small picture of this subject (to which all that has been said refers) to the view of the government, in the expectation that it might attract their attention. In consequence, the Declaration of Independence, the surrender of lord Cornwallis, the battle of Trenton, and that of Princeton, were taken to Washington, and, by permission of the Speaker, hung up in the Hall of the Representatives, where they remained subject to criticism for several days—and there is no doubt that the honourable testimony borne to their authenticity and correctness by many contemporaries in both houses of Congress, as well as by Mr. Madison, then president, and Mr. Monroe, then secretary of state, was the cause of that employment which is the source of undissembled satisfaction to Mr. T. and which, he proudly trusts, gives him a title to be remembered hereafter with the events which it has been the occupation, and is now the delight, of his life to have so commemorated.

Mr. T. still solicits candid and liberal criticism, and will thank any person who will point out an error in his work, and kindly supply him with the means of information by which he may correct it. But he holds malignity and envy in profound contempt.

New-York, 19th Oct. 1818.

Col. Trumbull's painting of the Declaration of American Independence, was exhibited in New-York one day for the benefit of the Deaf and Dumb Institution lately established there—The receipts were 350 dollars, from 1328 persons.

Document 40

"The Declaration of Independence" and Others

Here the cultural dialogue finds expression in the pages of a novel. The fictional technique for presenting serious art criticism was a novelty in this period, repeated much later by William Dean Howells. On the other hand, both Hugh Henry Brackenridge and James Fenimore Cooper had already used the novel as a vehicle for social criticism when John Neal's *Randolph, A Novel,* from which the following selection is taken, first appeared.

John Neal (1793–1876), though an inferior novelist, was an able Baltimore editor and a singularly perceptive critic. At the same time, one wonders whether he too was not seduced by subject matter, finding his aesthetic criterion chiefly in fidelity to life. Unlike most of his contemporaries, however, he did not judge art on narrow moral and ideological grounds, for he instinctively understood, like Poe after him, that the American utilitarian atmosphere supplied little enough nourishment for artistic growth.

Neal's nearest rival in critical sanity was George T. Tucker of Virginia, whose collected *Essays on Various Subjects of Taste, Morals, and National Policy* appeared in 1822. The dominant critical assumption of the period was that the artist should adapt his work to the morality of the society.

SOURCE: John Neal, *Randolph, A Novel,* 2 vols. Vol. II, pp. 125–28, 132–33, 136–37, 202–3. Philadelphia: 1823.

* * *

Let us now look in upon Mr. Trumbull. You have seen his SORTIE OF GIBRALTAR; and nothing that I could say

of it now, would be of any avail, to elevate it in your
opinion. It is his best picture. Indeed, his Death of Montgomery; Battle of Lexington; Bunker Hill, and all of his
late pictures, are, altogether, not worth so much as that
—so vigorous, and so full of action, as it is.

His DECLARATION OF INDEPENDENCE, is a plain, substantial affair, with an aspect of inveterate reality about
it; but exhibiting not one feature of sublimity, or grandeur. The countenances are strong and varied;—but the
awful gravity and wisdom of legislation; the moment of
tremendous passiveness, when the travail is all over; and
the thought of liberty has become a Declaration of Independence—*that* is not to be found in the picture. There
is no passion—no majesty—no emotion; and no especial
seriousness, except in the sculptured face of Samuel
Adams; not so much, as you will see at any long dinner
table, when the dishes are all uncovered, at once. You
stand before it without any feeling of awe or delight. You
see the interiour of an old-fashioned apartment, with
the light coming through the windows behind—and a
number of figures, seated and standing, like men that
think it about time to break up, and go home to a comfortable bed. I wish, heartily, that I could say something
in favour of the picture; but I cannot—it does not deserve
it. It is only a collection of strongly painted portraits; assembled together, without any common feeling or expression; but, as if by accident, and just as well behaved-
men may come together, any where, without design.

The next is the SURRENDER OF CORNWALLIS. On the
right of the picture, running off to a point, is a litter of
American troops; and, on the left, diminishing in the
same way, as if to make the perspective correspond, is
another litter of Frenchmen. They are all of a family.
All of his strong men, are strong with the same expression. You are struck with a strange family likeness in the
whole. The first four or five faces, seem to be brothers, at
least, if not different views of the same head.

In the centre, is general Lincoln, mounted on a beautiful white horse, sitting to receive the sword, that a Brit-

ish officer, general O'Hara, surrenders. The common notion is, that Washington, himself, received the sword
from the hands of Cornwallis. But neither Washington
nor Cornwallis, was on the ground. General Lincoln was
appointed to receive it, in the name of Washington, from
the representative of Lincoln's haughty conquerour, Cornwallis; for, not long before, the latter had meted to the
brave Lincoln, a full measure of unsparing and bitter
humiliation, at the south; and this was the hour of retribution.

The first thing that strikes the eye, forcibly, is this
—the unpleasant continuity of the lines; and the amazing
variety of attitudes, into which Mr. Trumbull has thrown
his horses' heads. One has a nose in the air—the next, his
a little lower—and the third, a little lower yet—while a
fourth, is biting his own knee, with his leg advanced, and
held, as if he had the cramp. This was done, undoubtedly,
to break the line; and to give more action to the picture;
but the design is too evident. We see the art—it does not
deceive us for a moment. Here and there, too, are sundry
ricketty and ill-formed horses, that, as I live, Stafford,
reminded me of nothing, except the wooden cuts, in
Geoffry Gambado's lessons for grown horsemen. There
is not one good horse in the picture, except that in the
centre; and his left fore hoof, is so turned in, upon a spot
in the canvass, of the same colour, that it looks deformed
and almost pointed; but the heads of the horses are admirable. A singular defect—one that will make you smile,
is apparent in all—they are *all* too low in the shoulder;
their fore-legs are too short, in almost every case.

His SURRENDER OF BURGOYNE, I lately saw. As I live,
Stafford, I begin to be ashamed of my countryman. When
I look at these three national pictures, for which Congress have paid twenty-four thousand dollars; and think
of their being shown in the capitol, at Washington, I
could almost weep with shame and vexation. They are,
altogether, a reproach to the country; and—I say it de-
liberately, Stafford—were I in congress, I would move for
their being set fire to, before the great front of the build-

ing, which they help to make ridiculous. I cannot trust myself to speak of this last picture, as I feel. It is execrable. The heads are too big for the bodies. There is neither dignity nor character in it. It looks like bad tapestry, where a patch-work landscape is made up of fragments, picked out of different pieces; where the heads, cut out of old pictures, are pasted to bodies—and the bodies grouped by different people, each with a design of his own. Col. Morgan, the rifleman, looks like a target; and a captain from Connecticut, mounted, for the purpose of showing his profile, has been made to break his own neck; and general Burgoyne is tilting over upon his nose.

*　*　*

I have now done with Mr. Trumbull, lamenting that a man of such strength, when young, should be, in his dotage, or, if not in his dotage, that he should be contented with such labour. There are now some other pictures, particularly of Mr. Alston, Leslie, and Morse, of which, were I a little better acquainted with them, I would speak at large. They were all pupils of Mr. West; or, at least, students in the Royal Academy; and all, I believe, have carried off some prizes. Mr. Morse, I know, had one; and would have obtained another, had he remained in the country, *with* his picture; for the rules of the society required that. But he could not. The subject had been given out to sixteen pupils—and he could not feel very certain of the gold medal, whatever were the merit of his picture; and, beside that, his father had been pressing him, with great earnestness, and for a long time, to return home;—he did return, leaving his picture, which Mr. West, himself, afterward wrote to him, would have obtained the prize, had *he* remained. Mr. West has always shown himself warmly disposed toward his young countrymen; and all of them speak of him, with affection and reverence. He it was, that influenced Mr. Sully to abandon *copying;* and to begin manufacturing for himself, while he was literally working, and starving himself to death, in London for some of his American *patrons.*

Was he not right? A man might as well hope to learn how to make a poem, by *copying* poems, as a picture, by copying pictures.

Mr. Morse's prize was obtained for the DYING HERCULES. I have never seen it; but I have heard it spoken of, as a bold and excellent piece of naked anatomy—but with too much convulsion in the sinews and flesh, even for Hercules. It was first modelled in clay, by Mr. Morse;— nay, I believe that it was for that model, and not for the painting, that he received the medal. But his style is beautiful and warm; strong, rich, and fanciful. His portraits, such as I have seen, were small, and hastily done up; but they were excellent:—and one, making a large picture, with some broken architecture, I have dwelt upon, with great pleasure, again and again. It was the portrait of a young girl of South Carolina, where Mr. Morse has now gone to reside.

*   *   *

Stafford, why is this?—Is it the nature of man to overlook whatever is near and familiar to him—to court whatever is rare, and of difficult attainment? Why are strangers met, as they are, with incense and wine, while our own children are languishing?—Yet, so it is—a new face, like a new planet, is apt to make us forget the old ones. Thus, Mr. Alston [Allston Ed.], who is from the south, goes to the north, for sustenance; and Mr. Morse, who was born at the north, goes to the south. Thus, too, if girls want to be married, they must go, no matter how amiable and excellent they are, where they are *not* known;—where people are not familiar with their loveliness. How many a young man, unknown and unhonoured at home, is found, steadily and proudly, among the great, when he is abroad, and dependent only upon his own merit. Excuse the digression, dear Stafford—there was an indignant feeling at my heart, and I thought it safest to give it vent, when I reflected on the miserably reluctant spirit, with which we award to them that we have known, the encouragement of genius. Why is it?—Are we unwilling to be beaten in

the race, by them that learnt their alphabets out of the
same book with ourselves; trundled hoops; and flew kites,
just exactly as we did?—Yes—it is.—If we be beaten by
strangers; eclipsed by the unknown, we conceal our mortification, under the pretence that, *they* were born with
some peculiar faculty, which we wanted. But, we cannot
lull our shame with this unction, when we have *known*
our conquerors, from the cradle; and know that they have
beaten us, not by any inherent power, peculiar to themselves, but by their industry, and perseverance. This, I
believe, is the secret. But, to return.—

* * *

We have now come to Mr. Vanderlyn—and I must tell
you something about him, too. It will assist you in remembering him, and his worth. When Aaron Burr was
in his zenith, he happened to be travelling, somewhere in
the western parts of New York; and stopping, one day, at
a tavern, he saw what he took to be, a line engraving, of
uncommon vigour. He spoke of it to the landlord; and was
not a little amazed, when the latter told him that it was
a drawing, made with a pen, by a stupid boy of his; an
apprentice to the blacksmith's trade, of whom he feared
that he should never be able to make anything. Burr sent
for the boy, and was so pleased with him, that he tried to
obtain him—but the master, suspected some secret value,
in his stupid apprentice, and would not part with him, at
last, on any terms. "Put a shirt into your pocket," said
Col. Burr, in passing the boy; "come to New York, when
you can get a chance, and ask for Aaron Burr—he will
take care of you."

Some time had passed, and Col. Burr had forgotten
the incident; when, one morning, in came a strange-look-
ing boy, while he was sitting at breakfast; and, as he approached, plucked out a bundle from his pocket, and gave
it to him. The colonel was not a little amused to find it
a shirt. Here began the acquaintance; and here, the eminence of Vanderlyn; and heaven so ordered it, that, when
colonel Burr, the Julius Caesar of our country—the greatest evil spirit of his age—was in the wane, Vanderlyn,

who had just left Paris, warm with favour, and rich with all that makes life comfortable, encountered him, in his desolation; and, in his turn, ministered to the necessities of his benefactor.

Such is the anecdote, as I have heard it; and such, I believe, is the truth, in all the material facts.

The only two pictures of Vanderlyn, that I have seen, are his MARIUS, sitting amid the Ruins of Carthage; and his ARIADNE, deserted by Theseus [see doc. 7—Ed.]. The former obtained a medal from the national academy, in France. It is a stern, strange, natural picture; with a finish of unexampled perfection. The figure is larger than life, sitting like a giant, intruded upon by some vision of conquest and rebellion. There is nothing visionary, nothing intellectual, about MARIUS. All is the barren and bleak expression of the tyrant man, when his heart is iron, and his nature hardened in blood. It is a great picture—but too elaborately finished.

His Ariadne is very beautiful; but you feel no emotion, no trembling, when you approach her. You do not feel that slight, tremulous quivering of the heart, which you ought to feel, when trespassing upon the sleep of even a *pictured* woman—in her innocence, timidity, and loveliness.

* * *

No—we have no "dramatists"—no "architects"—no "sculptors"—no "musicians"—no "tragedians." And why? It is not for want of natural genius. There is enough of that among my countrymen. It is for the want of encouragement, riches, a crowded population, luxury, and corruption. These arts are of the last, to which a people turn their attention. And when we turn ours to them, we shall succeed, as we have, in everything else, to which we have applied our hand, seriously. I know of more than one man, at this moment, who is capable of writing great drama. We have many builders, who have studied architecture, and would excel, if they could feed themselves and their families upon the chameleon diet, meanwhile.

* * *

DOCUMENT 41

A National *Journal of Art and Science*

Unlike literature and the fine arts, the sciences have been little understood in their cultural matrix. The following documents will suggest that the pursuit of the sciences in early nineteenth-century America was greatly influenced by the cultural and natural environment. The strong nationalistic drive to establish a preeminence in science as in art, for example, had to overcome a traditional lack of public interest and support. And the more important achievements of the period were connected with the scientific explorations of the wilderness, initiated earlier by Thomas Jefferson.

The polarity of America and Europe, moreover, was quite as important an organizing principle in scientific thought as in art and other aspects of culture. Thus, we find William Maclure (1763–1840), whose *Observations on the Geology of the United States* in 1809 won him an international reputation, challenging the Wernerian system of classification in Europe which supported a volcanic theory of earth upheaval from under water. The New World utopianism of such scientists is suggested also by the fact that Maclure later tried to establish an agricultural school in the socialistic community of New Harmony. *The American Journal of Science and Arts* in which his letter appears, founded in 1818, remained for many years the leading organ in the United States for the dissemination of scientific knowledge.

SOURCE: *The American Journal of Science and Arts*, Vol. II "Preface," (1820); Vol. V, pp. 197–98 (1824).

Preface

As two volumes of this work are now completed, the public are in a situation to judge how far the execution has corresponded with the original plan. Not a *local*, but a *national* undertaking, its leading object is to advance the interests of this rising empire, by exciting and concentrating original American effort, both in the sciences, and in the arts, and it may with truth be said, that no Journal was ever more fully sustained by *original* communications. They have been forwarded from our cities, towns and villages, from our academies and colleges, from the East and the West, the North and the South, and even occasionally from other countries, so that the Editor feels himself justified in believing, that this work is regarded as a *national Journal*. If therefore this view be one which patriotic and honourable men can approve, and if the execution has in any good degree corresponded with the design, it is to be hoped that the American public will not permit the work to languish, for want of pecuniary patronage. This is the only material difficulty which it has encountered, and this is far from being removed. A more extended patronage is indispensable to its permanent establishment, and, should it fail on this ground, who can wonder if our national character should be even more severely (perhaps even more *deservedly*) reproached than ever.

The Editor, although called upon to sustain the *pecuniary*, as well as the more *appropriate* responsibilities of the work, is determined not lightly to abandon the undertaking. He will persevere, until it is ascertained, whether the vast American Republic, with ten millions of inhabitants, with wealth scarcely surpassed by that of the most favoured nations, and with immensely diversified interests, growing out of those physical resources, which the bounty of God has given us, will permit this effort, devoted to the advancement of its wealth and its power, its honor and its dignity, to become abortive, with the gloomy presage that it *may* be *very long* before any similar enterprize can be successfully prosecuted.

Yale College, November 1, 1820.

Extracts of a letter from Wm. M'Clure, Esq. to the editor, dated, Madrid, Dec. 4, 1821.

Progress of American Science.

"I am glad to hear of the rapid progress science in general, (and mineralogy and geology, in particular) makes in the United States. The men of science in Europe, are astonished at the rapidity with which one discovery succeeds another, and cannot conceive, how, in so short a time, so many hands, and heads are occupied with the exact sciences, and mechanics.

"The vast advantages attached to freedom, are unknown on this side of the Atlantic, and the spirit of energy with which a free people pursue whatever they perceive to be for their interest, are only beginning to be understood by the few.

(From the same, to the same.)
Comparative features of American and European Geology.

"The most striking, and strongly marked difference between the geology of North America, and Europe, is the regularity, continuity, and uninterrupted state of the stratification, for almost the whole length of the continent; and the absence of all rocks of disputed origin.

The trappose hornblendish rock which partially, and in patches, and ridges, covers the old red sandstone from the Connecticut river to the Rappahannock; and where the sandstone has been washed away in the states of New-York, Maryland, and Virginia, loose masses of the trappose rock cover the surface, as evidence of the continuity of the sandstone formation—this hornblendish rock is the nearest to a volcanic formation, of any I have ever seen in the United States, both from structure and relative position; it is found covering puddingstone, and sandstone aggregates, of rounded particles, made so, most probably, by water; while we have not caught nature forming any rocks by water, at all similar to the Hornblendish rock; but we find many volcanic rocks almost similar in structure, and exactly corresponding in relative situation. This gives probability to the supposition, that it is of volcanic origin, and throws many difficulties, and doubts on the supposition of Neptunian origin, for after the waves on the sea-coast, or the action of running waters had formed the sand, and rolled pebbles; to make the waters return in sufficient quantities to form a rock partly crystalline (which by the Wernerian system would require a great depth) is a forced supposition, that does not appear natural: but such is the forced theory of that system respecting Basalt, and all the newest floets-trap formation, which Werner supposes to be of aqueous origin, while their resemblance, both in structure and relative position, renders the supposition of their volcanic origin, much more simple and natural.

The geology of the United States, where every primitive transition, and secondary rock is found (except the basalt, and the newest floets-trap formation) that is found in Europe; at the same time, that no volcanoes are in action, is a strong argument against the Wernerian system —all these theories have had their day, and are fast going out of fashion."

DOCUMENT 42
(PLATE 24)

A National *Museum of Art and Science*

Peale's Museum in Philadelphia and its founder, Charles Willson Peale, helped to make Philadelphia a leading center of the country's intellectual and artistic life. The artist here proudly lifts the curtain on one of his major achievements, with gesture and benign countenance inviting the spectator inward to view his various exhibits, which are surmounted by portraits of the heroes of the American Revolution painted by himself and his sons. In the foreground lies a stuffed specimen of the wild turkey, the native fowl which Benjamin Franklin had preferred to the eagle as a symbol of American nationality. Franklin, Washington, Lafayette, and other great men associated with the destinies of the early Republic—all had given their patronage to this museum. Jefferson and Hamilton had served on its board of directors. Peale failed in his ambition to mount specimens of "the human animal" for display in order to complete his "world in miniature," but he became rich and famous with his exhibition of the first mastodon skeleton ever assembled (see the next document). Peale's Museum was perhaps the most spectacular success of the encyclopedic movement in America.

DOCUMENT 43

(PLATE 25)

Exhuming the First American Mastodon

Organizer in 1801 of the first scientific expedition
in American history, Charles Willson Peale preserved
a dramatic record of its work in this picture. Peale's
discovery made the word "mammoth" a synonym for
almost everything of extraordinary size, and, of course,
Americans liked to boast about the size and quantity
of the many wonders in their country. Visitors who
came to see the gigantic skeleton, both at its unearthing
and later in the Museum, were told that it was a relic
from Noah's Flood. This opinion not only befitted the
apocalyptic temper of the times, but was also comfort-
ing to those who hoped that the scientific study of
American geological formations would produce evidence to support the Biblical account of the Flood.

Though Peale felt himself in the presence of awesome, even miraculous History, he depended upon
realism rather than the stilted histrionics of the grand
manner for his dramatic effect. Still, the baleful, murky
light, the frantic stir of activity before an impending
storm, the great tripods which support the ingeniously
improvised pumping system—all contribute to the sense
of a climactic incident in the progress of American
civilization.

DOCUMENT 44

Nationalism in Ornithology

Another significant American contribution to science was Alexander Wilson's *American Ornithology*, reviewed here by Governor De Witt Clinton of New York. Wilson's contribution was followed a few years later by Thomas Nuttall's *The Genera of North American Plants . . . to the Year 1817.* Dr. James E. De Kay called attention to the effect of the War of 1812 in awakening the spirit of inquiry, while a physician in Cincinnati, Daniel Drake, acknowledged in his 1820 *Discourse on the Prospects of the Western Museum Society* the inspiration of nature: "Let the architects of our national greatness conform to the dictates of science; and the monuments they construct will rise beautiful as our hills, imperishable as our mountains, and lofty as their summits, which tower sublimely above the clouds."

Not the least remarkable achievement of the period was De Witt Clinton's mastery in the natural sciences, of which the following document is but a small sample. He was a powerful patron of both the arts and sciences, a leader of educational reform, a founder and president of the New-York Historical Society, a promoter of manufacturing, and a great political leader who narrowly missed election to the presidency of the United States in 1812.

SOURCE: De Witt Clinton, *An Introductory Discourse before the Literary and Philosophical Society of New York . . .* , pp. 81–84. New York: 1815. An appendix reprinted from *The American Medical and Philosophical Register.*

AMERICAN ORNITHOLOGY; *or the Natural History of the Birds of the United States: illustrated with plates, engraved and colored from original drawings taken from nature.* By ALEXANDER WILSON. Philadelphia. Inskeep & Bradford. Imperial 4to. vols. 5th, 6th, 7th, 8th, and 9th. About 120 pages each: 1812–14.

THE author of the American Ornithology having closed his earthly career before he finished that important work, the task of completing the ninth and last volume, devolved upon his friend and executor, mr. George Ord, who has prefixed to it an interesting biography of mr. Wilson. Having, on former occasions, noticed several of the volumes, it now remains for us to pay the last tribute of respect to a man whom we esteem, and to an author whose works will always occupy an important rank among the writings on Natural History.

The life of mr. Wilson exhibits the complete triumph of genius over the want of education, and of persevering industry over the evils of poverty. Without any other reliance than on his own faculties, and with a force of exertion which nothing could check or retard, he has obtained a celebrity in science to which few men, in this country, can aspire; although many may be more highly favored with the endowments of genius, and more extensively gifted with the advantages of early education, and the bounties of fortune. The life of Wilson shows, conclusively, that the temple of fame is open to the most humble individual in the community, if he only attempts it with zeal and industry and with a judicious selection of the part which he intends to act on the theatre of the world: and it may not be amiss to add, in opposition to the complaints of his biographer, that notwithstanding he experienced, in some few instances, the slights of ignorance, and the sneers of impertinence, yet that a liberal and enlightened community bore witness to his merits by a munificent subscription which, after satisfying all expenses, would have placed him, if living, on the enviable ground of independence.

The science of ornithology is involved in considerable difficulty and confusion. The arrangement of animals according to the principles of the Linnæan system, is an admirable contrivance to extricate the science of zoology from the darkness which surrounded it. The classes and orders of the great naturalist are arbitrary: the genera and species are natural; but when we consider that the generic characters of birds are taken from the bill, tongue, nostrils, cere, caruncles, and other naked parts—and that the characters of the species are derived principally from the plumage and habitudes, we must be sensible that here is a wide field for a difference of opinion. Besides, the nomenclature adopted, in endeavouring to compress the descriptions of animals within the shortest compass, is frequently a mystery to most readers. Take, for instance, an account of a bird by Linnæus, Latham, or Pennant, and it will require considerable industry to penetrate the exact meaning of the author. The generic characters frequently run so closely into each other, that it is no easy task to make the appropriate arrangement. The plumage of birds varies according to seasons, to age, and to climate; and their manners assume a different appearance at different times, and in different countries. The sexes exhibit, almost invariably, a diversity. The male is frequently smaller than the female, and is generally arrayed in a more beautiful dress. Genera are confounded together; varieties are represented as distinct species; the male is placed in a different species from his mate; and the same bird, at different ages and seasons, is considered a different species. The names of birds vary in different places.

In the same district of country the same bird frequently goes by different appellations, and the scientific name is also not uniform; Linnæus, Brisson, and Buffon oftentimes disagree. We may add to this, the absurd custom adopted in this country of naming our birds after those in Europe, to which they are supposed to have some likeness, although, in most respects, they are dissimilar.

There are three modes in which we may obtain a knowledge of birds. From personal observation of these animals in their natural state; from preserved subjects in cabinets of natural history; and from books. The first is undoubtedly preferable, so far as it goes; but it is necessarily limited by our range of travelling. The second supplies this defect, but it is liable to this great objection; the subjects are often not only imperfectly prepared in the first instance, but generally decay and dissolve. In Cayenne, which has furnished more subjects for the cabinets of european naturalists, than any other country; the birds are steeped in spirits for a long time, and dried by the heat of an oven. This must undoubtedly, in many instances, sully the glossy beauty of their plumage, and give them an appearance different from their natural one. Books must be resorted to in order to complete and extend our knowledge; but to place our sole reliance on them, would be as absurd as to attempt to attain a knowledge of mankind by the meditations of contemplative retirement.

Our author has, with unparalleled industry, and singular sagacity of observation, surmounted all the disadvantages which we have enumerated, and availed himself of all the sources of information: every state in the union has witnessed his labours: on our alpine hills; in our most distant forests; on the borders of our rivers and lakes; on the shores of the Atlantic, the footsteps of his enterprising industry may be seen. He first examined the feathered creation with his own eyes; he traced them in their most secluded haunts; he watched their migrations; he observed their seasons of song, and of love, and of incubation; he noticed their food, their instinct, and their habits.

After having explored this source of information, he next had recourse to cabinets of natural history, to the aviaries of amateurs, and to the observations of inquisitive and ingenious men. The museum of Peale furnished him with various and extensive knowledge; the methodical and comprehensive writings of Linnæus; the extensive information of Pennant, Brisson, Edwards, and Latham, and the splendid elucidations of Buffon, were also familiar to him.

Thus furnished with information, he has produced a

work which excels all that precedes it, whether we have
reference to the style and matter, or the drawings. It is
in vain to attempt to form ideas from written descriptions
of animals, sufficiently distinct, so as to distinguish them
in all cases from each other: we must have recourse to
the delineations of the pencil, and to the preservations
of the museum. The number of species of birds has undoubtedly been greatly multiplied from the generality
and confusion of descriptions; let the same bird be described after the Linnæan manner by two different persons, and it is an equal chance if they do not vary in some
essential respects; but a faithful representation of the
pencil will at once remove all ambiguity. The delineations
of Wilson are done in such a masterly style, that the bird
is at once recognised. He also excels in his account of the
manners of birds: although he cannot boast of the splendid eloquence of Buffon, yet there is such a fascination
in his style, such a simplicity in his manner, and so much
truth and nature in all his remarks, that we are compelled to give him the preference.

To form a just estimate of the extensiveness of this
work, we have only to compare it with the celebrated
natural history of Mark Catesby, published in 1754. Although the drawings of this writer are eminently beautiful, and generally correct, yet they are greatly inferior to
those of Wilson. His descriptions also will not bear a
comparison, either in interest or extent: the whole number of birds which he describes amounts to 113, which
contained all the land birds he saw in North America,
between the 30th and 45th degrees of latitude. Wilson
has figured and described 278 species, 56 of which were
not known before: his untimely death has prevented the
full execution of his plan. The swan, the turkey, and the
crane, the most interesting of the feathered race, did not
come under his review; a loss that cannot be supplied.
With what interest would we read his remarks on the
turkey? [See document 42—Ed.] What light would he not
have cast upon those controverted questions, whether the
turkey is of exclusive american origin? and whether the

domestic is a distinct species from the wild turkey? and whether, contrary to the general operation of cultivation and domestication upon animals and plants, this bird has dwindled in size, and sustained a deterioration by its domestic state?

Although Wilson has done much, yet much more remains to be done, in order to complete our ornithology. The whole number of species, according to Latham, is three thousand. Considering that the american republic, including our Louisiana acquisition, extends from the Atlantic to the Pacific, embraces the greatest and most spacious inland seas in the world, comprehends every variety of climate and soil, innumerable and boundless forests; prairies, or natural meadows, of several days journey; deserts like those of Africa; mountains dividing the country into an eastern and western section; and rivers equalled in size by none in the old world: considering also its vicinity to numerous islands of a warm temperature, and the approximation of America to Europe and Asia, by which the land birds of the old world can have easy access to our continent: it is not unreasonable to suppose, that we may claim at least one thousand species of birds, who either reside among us, or occasionally visit us. If this calculation be correct, what an extensive field yet remains for the ornithologist? and if another Wilson shall arise, endowed with genius and invincible industry, the rich treasures of natural science, which are now hidden from our view, will be drawn from the darkness which covers them, and exposed to the full view of an admiring world.

DOCUMENT 45

Nationalism in Medicine: A Frontier Doctor

The best-known doctors of the period were Benjamin
Waterhouse in Boston and Benjamin Rush and Philip
Physick in Philadelphia. But contrary to impressions
created by James Fenimore Cooper's satire of frontier
medicine in *The Pioneers,* some of the best medicine
was practiced on the frontier. The reader may be
amused to contrast the ineptitude of Dr. Todd in Cooper's novel with the professional virtuosity of Dr. William Beaumont revealed below in his case record,
which ends on the threshold of one of the great experiments in the annals of medicine. Dr. Beaumont
(1785–1853) was a U. S. Army doctor stationed at
the post of Mackinac, Michigan Territory, in June
1822, when the fateful accident occurred.

Another significant frontier contribution to medicine
in this period was Daniel Drake's study of contagious
disease. Cultural historians have overrated Benjamin
Rush's *Medical Inquiries and Observations upon the
Diseases of the Mind* (Philadelphia, 1812) as a pioneering psychiatric study. At least, De Witt Clinton
once insisted that "the connexion between the mind,
and the body, is universally admitted." The proportion
of careful scientific observation to general statement is
so much higher in Beaumont's work than in Rush's
that, indeed, the reader may well wonder where to
find in it sentiments of nationality. These break through
toward the end in his expression of concern for "the
principles of justice to poor human nature" when his
patient was refused poor relief by the county. The
rhetorical fear that the Territory was being delivered
over to the Kingdom of Satan derives, of course, from

religious conceptions of America's mission into the wilderness.

SOURCE: J. S. Meyer, *Life and Letters of Dr. William Beaumont,* pp. 107–17, *passim.* St. Louis: C. V. Mosby Company, 1912.

Alex Samata, St. Martin, San Maten, a Canadian lad about 19 years old, hardy, robust and healthy, was accidentally shot by the unlucky discharge of a gun on the 6th of June, 1822. The whole charge, consisting of powder and duck shot, was received in the left side at not more than 2 or 3 feet distance from the muzzle of the piece, in a posterior direction, obliquely forward and outwards, carrying away by its force the integuments more than the size of the palm of a man's hand; blowing off and fracturing the 6th rib from about the middle anteriorily, fracturing the 5th, Rupturing the lower portion of the left lobe of the Lungs, and lacerating the Stomach by a spicula of the rib that was blown through it[s] coat, Lodging the charge, wadding, fire in among the fractured ribs and lacerated muscles and integuments, and burning the clothing and flesh to a crisp. I was called to him immediately after the accident. Found a portion of the Lungs as large as a turkey's egg protruding through the external wound, lacerated and burnt, and below this another protrusion resembling a portion of the Stomach, what at first view I could not believe possible to be that organ in that situation with the subject surviving, but on closer examination I found it to be actually the Stomach, with a puncture in the protruding portion large enough to receive my forefinger, and through which a portion of his food that he had taken for breakfast had come out and lodged among his apparel. In this dilemma I considered any attempt to save his life entirely useless. But as I had ever considered it a duty to use every means in my power to preserve life when called to administer relief, I proceeded to cleanse the wound and give it a superficial dressing, not believing it possible for him to survive twenty minutes. On attempting to reduce the protruding portions, I found the Lung was prevented from returning by the sharp point of the fractured rib, over which its membrane had caught fast, but by raising up the Lung with the front of the forefinger of my left hand I clipped off with my penknife, in my right hand, the sharp point of the rib, which enabled me to return the Lung into the cavity of the Thorax, but could not retain it there on the least efforts of the patient to cough, which were frequent.

After giving the wound a superficial dressing, the patient was moved to a more convenient place, and in about an hour I attended to dressing the wound more thoroughly, not supposing it probable for him to survive the operation of extracting the fractured spicula of bones and other extraneous substances, but to the utter astonishment of every one he bore it without a struggle or without sinking.

After taking away the fragments of the ribs, old flannel, wad and the principal charge of shot, all driven together under the skin and into the muscles, and replacing the lungs and stomach as much as practicable, I applied to the wound the carbonated fermenting poultice, composed of flour, hot water, charcoal, and yeast, changing once every 8, 10, or 12 hours, according to the quicker or slower process of fermentation, keeping the parts around constantly bathed with a solution of muriate of ammonia in Spirits and vinegar. This was done with an intention to excite local reaction as soon as possible upon the surface and occasional sloughing of contused, lacerated and burnt muscles and integuments, which had the desired effect in less than 84 hours, with assistance of the Camphorated Aq. Amon. Acet. given internally in liberal quantities. Under the above treatment a lively reaction commenced in about 24 hours, accompanied with strong arterial action and high inflammatory symptoms of the system generally, more specially of violent pneumonia and inflammation of the Lungs, with great dyspnoea and distressing cough. At the commencement of those symptoms I opened a vein and took 12 or 14 oz. of blood from the arm. Gave a mild cathartic. The bleeding abated the action and gave relief. The cathc. had no effect, having escaped from the stomach through the wound. I continued the Caphd. Aq. Acetat. every hour for the first 72 internally and the carbonated poultice and wash externally, omitting the muriate. The fever continued for 8 or ten days, running into the Typhoid type and the wound becoming very fetid. Nothing passed his bowels after the 2d day, and they became impervious and inactive, scarcely to be excited by stimulating injections. From the 2d day till the 10th nothing passed, no reaction from his bowels at all, everything he took into his stomach was either absorbed or made its exit at the wound externally.

About the 5th day a partial sloughing took place in the wound and the febrile symptoms abated. The protruded portion of the lungs and the small lacerated piece of the stomach also sloughed off, and left the puncture of the Stomach plain to be seen, and large enough to admit my forefinger its whole length directly into the cavity of the stomach, and a passage into the cavity of the Thorax half as large as my fist, exposing to plain view the action of the left lobe of the Lungs, and admitting at every respiration full escape of air, bloody mucus, froth, etc.

About the 10th day a more extensive sloughing took place. The febrile symptoms all subsided, and the whole surface of the wound put on a healthy, granulating appearance. The fractures of the ribs commenced exfoliating, and nature kindly performing what human foresight viewed as hopeless and professional skill might calculate upon with dubious odds. All that entered his stomach came out again at the wound for 12 or 15 days, and the only means of sustaining him was by nutritious injection given per anus until all was sloughed, and compresses and adhesive strap could be applied to stop the orifice in the stomach and retain the food and drinks.

A lucky and perhaps the only circumstance to which his miraculous survival can be attributed was the protruded portion of the Stomach, instead of falling back into the cavity of the abdomen to its natural position, adhered by the first intention to the intercostal muscles, and by that means retained the orifice in the wounded stomach in contact with the external wound, and afforded a free passage out and a fair opportunity to apply the dressings. The carbon poultice was continued constantly until the sloughing was complete and the granulating process established. They were afterwards occasionally applied as a corrective when the wound was becoming ill conditioned or languid. The Aq. Am. Acetat. was continued for several weeks, in proportion to the febrile symptoms or fetid condition of the wound.

No sickness or peculiar irritability of the Stomach was ever experienced, not even nausea, during the whole time; and after 3 weeks the appetite regular and healthy, alvine evacuation became regular, and all the functions of the system seemed as regular and healthy as in perfect health, excepting the wounded parts.

Cicatrization and contraction of the external wound commenced about the 5th week, and continued gradually and almost uninterruptedly. The Stomach at the wounded part became more and more firmly attached to the intercostals by its external coats, but showed not the least disposition to close its puncture by granulations forming from its own lacerated coats any more than is in the anus or mouth. By applying the nitrate of silver to the edges of the wounded muscles of the stomach, I could extend the attachments by its external and cellular coats more firmly to the intercostals or external integuments, which seemed rather to enlarge than contract the orifice in the Stomach, bringing it more and more external as its adhesions to the external wound increased, resembling in its appearance (all but the Sphincter) a natural anus, with a slight prolapse every time I removed the dressings, and the contents of the Stomach would run out fairly in proportion to the quantity received. If the Stomach happened to be empty when I dressed it, a prolapse and partial invertion of the Stomach would follow the removal of the compresses of lints from the wound, unless prevented by the application of my thumb, finger, or something else to its orifice while the dressing was reapplying. Frequently upon removing the dressings, when they had become looser than usual by some derangement of the bandages, the stomach would be inverted and the inner coats protruded through the orifice large as a hen's egg. No difficulty occurred in reducing it; a gentle pressure with the thumb or finger upon the protruded portion would quickly return it to its place without giving the least pain and almost without sensation. Nitrate of silver, applied to the lips of the wound and upon the inner coats of the Stomach so as to produce sloughing, occasioned less sensation than when applied to the most common fungus or ulcer upon the surface of the body or limbs, a conclusive evidence in my opinion that the Stomach is not so exquisitely sensible an organ as is represented by anatomists and Physiologists in general.

About the 6th or 7th week exfoliation from the fractured ribs and the separation of the ribs from the cartilagenous ends began to take place; spiculae of bones and fragments of old cloth and shot also were working out from among the muscles and integuments. The 6th rib, that was worst injured and blown off entirely in the first place, was also abraded of its periostium for about three inches back of the fracture towards the Spine and became carious at its fractured extremity. So that I was obliged to amputate it about midway between sternum and spine, which I did by dissecting around, separating and retracting the intercostals to the sound portion of the rib, and then sawing it off by introducing between the ribs a very narrow, short saw, which I had made for the occasion. In this operation I succeeded admirably, beyond my most sanguine expectations, taking the rib off smoothly without injuring any parts whatever. The granulations shot immediately out and formed soundly over the amputated end. About half of the interior edge of the other rib exfoliated longitudinally from about the center to the Sternum, and then the healthy granulation formed soundly over the other part and continued so.

After removing all the exfoliations and extraneous substances that were to be found about the wound, my next object was to contract the external wound and close up the puncture in the stomach if practicable, which I attempted by drawing the edges of the wound as near together as I could by adhesive straps laid on in radiative form, the circumference of the external wound being at least 12 or 14 inches, the orifice in the Stomach about in the center. To retain the food and drink as much as possible, I kept to the orifice a firm compress of lint, fitted to the shape and size of the puncture, and confined by the straps. Under these dressings and management cicatrization went on rapidly, his health improving, and all functions of the system regular. Digestion was as completely performed as in the most healthy person in the vicinity (and I could even see it go on every time I dressed the wound). I kept the granulating surface duly stimulated by applying sometimes Cincona pulv., sometimes Mirc. precip. Rub., and sometimes Nit. Silver, as the state of the granulation indicated.

After trying every means within my power to close the puncture of the Stomach by exciting adhesions between the lips of the wound of its own proper coats, without the least appearance of success, I gave over trying, convinced that the Stomach of itself will not close a puncture in its coats by granulations, and the only alternative left seemed to be to draw the external wound together as fast as cicatrization would form and contracting as much as possible the orifice in the Stomach, and make the granulations from the intercostal muscles and integuments shoot across and form over and close it that way. But to this method there seemed an insuperable difficulty, for, unless there be kept constantly upon the orifice a firm plug of lint compound, all the contents of the Stomach flow out and the patient must die for want of aliment, and this lint, intersepting, prevents the granulation from forming across.

The lacerated portion of the lungs sloughed off and digested away, leaving a surface suppurating in the lobe of the lungs large as the concave surface of a teacup, from which continued to issue much purulent matter for two or three months until it became completely filled up with healthy granulations and cicatrized over externally, with the lower portion of the left lobe firmly adhering to the Pleura costalis. Four months after the injury an abscess formed about two inches below the wound, anteriorly, over the cartilaginous ends of the 1st and 2d false ribs, very painful and extremely sore, producing a violent symptomatic fever, checking the process of cicatrization, rendering the granulation languid and pale, and the wound ill-conditioned and unfavorable to the prospects of recovery. After applying emolient poultices for several days, the swelling pointed externally, and I punctured and laid it open with the bistoury and director for about 2 or 3 inches. It discharged copiously very fetid, purulent matter for the first 2 days. On the 3d I could feel with the probe a small extraneous substance, which in the course of 3 or 4 days, by the use of the soap plaster and compresses, proved to be a shot and a small portion of the wad. After the exit of these I could introduce a common pocket-case silver probe nearly its whole length in the longitudinal direction of the ribs, and a great soreness and pain extended from the opening in the abscess upon the track of the cartilaginous ends of the false ribs to the spine, with a copious discharge from a long fistulous sinus. In the course of about 5 or 6 days [appeared] the cartilaginous end of a rib about an inch long; soon after this followed some small spicula of bone. The discharge, soreness and inflammation continued in the same direction. In about 6 or 7 days longer came away another similar cartilage about an inch and a half long, and in about the same length of time another 2 inches, and so continued to come away every 5 or 6 days, increasing in length in about the same proportion until five had made their exit through the same passage. The last was about three inches long, and seemed to be separated from the last false rib, as the soreness terminated at that point, and after which the sinus commenced closing, the discharge diminished, and the soreness subsided from that point forward with regular progression. The discharge, pain and irritation during the 4 or 5 weeks all those cartilages

were working out reduced the strength of the patient very
much, induced a general febrile habit, and stopped the
healthy healing process of the original wound. Directly
after exit of the last mentioned cartilage an inflammation
appeared at the lower end of the sternum, about over
the ensiform cartilage, from the anterior end of the original wound, extremely irritable and very painful. By the
use of emolient poultice a few days it terminated in a
large abscess, which I punctured and laid open an inch or
two with the bistoury. About half a pint of very offensive
matter discharged from this, and in a few days followed a
cartilaginous substance about 3 inches long, after which
the inflammation subsided. In a day or two after this came
away another small cartilage and the discharge abated. To
support the patient's strength under all these debilitating
incidents, I gave him the diluted muriatic acid and wine,
which very much improved his health and increased his
strength.

It is now going on the 7th month since the injury was
received, and the orifice in the stomach is still visible and
but little contracted. The integuments are all cicatrized,
smooth to within the circumference of a half eagle, immediately around the wound in the Stomach. His health
daily improving, his spirits good, his appetite regular, his
sleep refreshing, and all the functions of the system natural and healthy.

*   *   *

The County refusing any further assistance to the patient (who has become a pauper from his misfortune),
I took him into my own family from mere motives of
charity and a disposition to save his life, or at least to
make him comfortable, where he has continued improving
in health and condition, and is now able to perform any
kind of labour from the whitling of a stick to the chopping
of Logs, and is as healthy, active and strong as he ever was
in his life, or any man in Mackinac, with the apperture of

the Stomach in much the same condition as it was at the
last mentioned date. June 1, 1824.

* * *

Charity.

Happy are they that die in the poor-house of this place,
and three times doubly happy are the people of the
Borough who reluctantly contribute to their wretched
support while living upon the public charity! Were I reduced to the necessity of existing upon the charity of this
Borough, I would commit suicide without scruple or hesitation, from principles of justice to poor human nature,
from no other motive than to rescue her from the op-
probrious ignominy of suffering a fellow being to perish
in distress for want of comfortable and timely assistance!
It is truth, abhorrent to human nature and too melancholy
to be recorded, that, in my opinion, the public officers of
the Borough, whose duty it is to provide relief for the
distressed, would sooner pay a round sum for the extinc-
tion of life of a pauper than to make an exertion or take
any trouble to procure the necessary assistance.

"May the Lord deliver us from evil," than which a
greater could never befall a human being than to become
dependent upon the charity and benevolence of the people for relief in time of distress, for this is the Kingdom of
Satan, the power of Tyrants, the Benevolence of Turkey
and the Glory of Heathens! Amen! & Amen!

* * *

When he lies on the opposite side I can look directly
into the cavity of the Stomach, and almost see the process
of digestion. I can pour in water with a funnel, or put in
food with a spoon, and draw them out again with a
syphon. I have frequently suspended flesh, raw and wasted,
and other substances into the perforation to ascertain the
length of time required to digest each; and at one time
used a tent of raw beef, instead of lint, to stop the orifice,
and found that in less than five hours it was completely

digested off, as smooth and even as if it had been cut with a knife.

*   *   *

This case affords an excellent opportunity for experimenting upon the gastric fluids and process of digestion. It would give no pain, nor cause the least uneasiness, to extract a gill of fluid every two or three days, for it frequently flows out spontaneously in considerable quantities. Various kinds of digestible substances might be introduced into the stomach, and then easily examined during the whole process of digestion. I may, therefore, be able hereafter to give some interesting experiments on these subjects.

Document 46

A National System of Weights and Measures?

The next document demonstrates a popular belief of the period that the pursuit of science contributed to the physical, moral, and intellectual improvement of mankind. The U. S. Senate Resolution which launched John Quincy Adams in 1820 upon an inquiry into the possibility of a uniform standard of measurements was related to the reforming sense of mission in other areas of American culture. The desire to improve upon, or even abandon, the inherited British system of weights and measures, for example, paralleled the effort of Edward Livingston in the succeeding document to reform American penal codes so as to free them from an antiquated English common law.

Adams' major reason, finally, for retaining British practices was that they conformed to long habit as well as to "the nature of things," insofar as diversity was a law of nature. So he worked out his solution between the poles represented by the standard of nature and the customs of civilized Europe. The result of his inquiry is an outstanding example, incidentally, of the possibility of investing the driest subject with interest.

SOURCE: John Quincy Adams, *Report Upon Weights and Measures*, pp. 6–13, 46–48, 74–75, 90–94. Philadelphia: 1821.

* * *

In the order of human existence upon earth, the objects which successively present themselves, are man—natural, domestic, civil society, government, and law. The want, at least, of measures of length, is founded in the physical organization of individual man, and precedes the

institution of society. Were there but one man upon
earth, a solitary savage, ranging the forests, and supporting his existence by a continual conflict with the
wants of his nature, and the rigor of the elements, the
necessities for which he would be called to provide would
be *food, raiment, shelter*. To provide for the wants of food
and raiment, the first occupation of his life would be the
chase of those animals, the flesh of which serves him for
food, and the skins of which are adaptable to his person
for raiment. In adapting the raiment to his body, he
would find at once, in his own person, the want and the
supply of a standard measure of length, and of the proportions and subdivisions of that standard.

But, to the continued existence of the human species,
two persons of different sexes are required. Their union
constitutes natural society, and their permanent cohabitation, by mutual consent, forms the origin of domestic society. Permanent cohabitation requires a common place of
abode, and leads to the construction of edifices where the
associated parties, and their progeny, may abide. To the
construction of a dwelling place, superficial measure becomes essential, and the dimensions of the building still
bear a natural proportion to those of its destined inhabitants. Vessels of capacity are soon found indispensable for
the supply of water; and the range of excursion around the
dwelling could scarcely fail to suggest the use of a measure
of itinerary distance.

Measures of *length*, therefore, are the wants of individual man, independent of, and preceding, the existence
of society. Measures of surface, of distance, and of capacity, arise immediately from domestic society. They
are wants proceeding rather from social, than from individual, existence. With regard to the first, *linear* measure,
nature in creating the want, and in furnishing to man,
within himself, the means of its supply, has established a
system of numbers, and of proportions, between the
man, the measure, and the objects measured. Linear
measure requires only a change of direction to become a
measure of circumference; but is not thereby, without

calculation, a measure of surface. Itinerary measure, as it needs nothing more than the prolongation or repetition of linear measure, would seem at the first view to be the same. Yet this is evidently not the progress of nature. As the want of it originates in a different stage of human existence, it will not naturally occur to man, to use the same measure, or the same scale of proportions and numbers, to clothe his body, and to mark the distance of his walks. On the contrary, for the measurement of all objects which he can lift and handle, the fathom, the arm, the cubit, the hand's-breadth, the span, and the fingers, are the instruments proposed to him by nature; while the pace and the foot are those which she gives him for the measurement of itinerary distance. These natural standards are never, in any stage of society, lost to individual man. There are probably few persons living who do not occasionally use their own arms, hands, and fingers, to measure objects which they handle, and their own pace to measure a distance upon the ground.

Here then is a source of *diversity*, to the standards even of linear measure, flowing from the difference of the relations between man and physical nature. It would be as inconvenient and unnatural to the organization of the human body to measure a bow and arrow for instance, the first furniture of solitary man, by his foot or pace, as to measure the distance of a day's journey, or a morning's walk to the hunting ground, by his arm or hand.

Measures of capacity are rendered necessary by the nature of fluids, which can be held together in definite quantities only by vessels of substance more compact than their own. They are also necessary for the admeasurement of those substances which nature produces in multitudes too great for numeration, and too minute for linear measure. Of this character are all the grains and seeds, which, from the time when man becomes a tiller of the ground, furnish the principal materials of his subsistence. But nature has not furnished him with the means of supplying this want in his own person. For this measure he is obliged to look abroad into the nature of things; and his first measure of capacity will most probably be found in the egg of a large bird, the shell of a cetaceous fish, or the horn of a beast. The want of a *common* standard not being yet felt, these measures will be of various dimensions; nor is it to be expected that the thought will ever occur to the man of nature, of establishing a proportion between his cubit and his cup, of graduating his pitcher by the size of his foot, or equalizing its parts by the number of his fingers.

Measures of length, once acquired, may be, and naturally are, applied to the admeasurement of objects of surface and solidity; and hence arise new diversities from the nature of things. The connection of linear measure with *numbers*, necessarily, and in the first instance, imports only the first arithmetical rule of numeration, or addition. The mensuration of surfaces, and of solids, requires the further aid of multiplication and division. Mere numbers, and mere linear measure, may be reckoned by addition alone; but their application to the surface can be computed only by multiplication. The elementary principle of decimal arithmetic is then supplied by nature to man within himself in the number of his fingers. Whatever standard of linear measure he may assume, in order to measure the surface or the solid, it will be natural to him to stop in the process of addition when he has counted the tale equal to that of his fingers. Then turning his line in the other direction, and stopping at the same term, he finds the square of his number a hundred: and, applying it again to the solid, he finds its cube a thousand.

But while decimal arithmetic thus, for the purposes of *computation*, shoots spontaneously from the nature of man and of things, it is not equally adapted to the numeration, the multiplication, or the division, of material substances, either in his own person, or in external nature. The proportions of the human body, and of its members, are in other than decimal numbers. The first unit of measures, for the use of the hand, is the *cubit*, or extent from the tip of the elbow to the end of the middle finger; the motives for choosing which, are that it presents more definite terminations at both ends than any of the other superior limbs, and gives a measure easily handled and carried about the person. By doubling this measure is given the ell, or arm, including the hand, and half the width of the body, to the middle of the breast; and, by doubling that, the fathom, or extent from the extremity of one middle finger to that of the other, with expanded arms, an exact equivalent to the stature of man, or extension from the crown of the head to the sole of the foot. For subdivisions and smaller measures, the span is found equal to half the cubit, the palm to one third of the span, and the finger to one fourth of the palm. The cubit is thus, for the mensuration of matter, naturally divided into 24 equal parts, with subdivisions of which 2, 3, and 4, are the factors; while, for the mensuration of distance, the foot will be found at once equal to one fifth of the pace, and one sixth of the fathom.

Nor are the diversities of nature, in the organization of external matter, better suited to the exclusive use of decimal arithmetic. In the three modes of its extension, to which the same linear measure may be applied, length, breadth, and thickness, the proportions of surface and solidity are not the same with those of length· that which is decimal to the line, is centesimal to the surface, and millesimal to the cube. Geometrical progression forms the rule of numbers for the surface and the solid, and their adaptation to decimal numbers is among the profoundest mysteries of mathematical science, a mystery which had been impenetrable to Pythagoras, Archimedes, and Ptolemy; which remained unrevealed even to Copernicus, Galileo, and Kepler, and the discovery and exposition of which was reserved to immortalize the name of Napier. To the mensuration of the surface and the solid, the number ten is of little more use than any other. The numbers of each of the two or three modes of extension must be multiplied together to yield the surface or the solid contents: and, unless the object to be measured is a perfect square or cube of equal dimensions at all its sides, decimal arithmetic is utterly incompetent to the purpose of their admeasurement.

Linear measure, to whatever modification of matter applied, extends in a straight line; but the modifications of matter, as produced by nature, are in forms innumerable, of which the defining outward line is almost invariably a curve. If decimal arithmetic is incompetent even to give the dimensions of those artificial forms, the square and the cube, still more incompetent is it to give the circumference, the area, and the contents, of the circle and the sphere.

There are three several modes by which the quantities of material substances may be estimated and compared; by number, by the space which they occupy, and by their apparent specific gravity. We have seen the origin and character of mensuration by space and number, and that, in the order of human existence, one is the result of a necessity incidental to individual man preceding the social union, and the other immediately springing from that union. The union of the sexes constitutes natural society: their permanent cohabitation is the foundation of domestic society, and leads to that of government, arising from the relations between the parents and the offspring which their union produces. The relations between husband and wife import domestic society, consent, and the sacred obligation of promises. Those between parent and child, import subordination and government; on the one side authority, on the other obedience. In the first years of infancy, the authority of the parent is absolute; and has, therefore, in the laws of nature, been tempered by parental affection. As the child advances to mature age, the relations of power and subjection gradually subside, and, finally, are dissolved in that honor and reverence of the child for the parent, which can terminate only with life. When the child goes forth into the world to make a settlement for himself, and found a new family, civil society commences; government is instituted—the tillage of the ground, the discovery and use of metals, exchanges, traffic by barter, a *common* standard of measures, and mensuration by *weight*, or apparent specific gravity, all arise from the multiplying relations between man and man, now superadded to those between man and things.

The difference between the specific gravities of different substances is so great, that it could not, for any length of time, escape observation; but nature has not furnished man, within himself, with any standard for this mode of estimating equivalents. Specific gravity, as an object of mensuration, is in its nature *proportional*. It is not like measures of length and capacity, a comparison between different definite portions of space, but a comparison between different properties of matter. It is not the simple relation between the extension of one substance, and the extension of another; but the complicated relation of extension and gravitation in one substance to the extension and gravitation of another. This distinction is of great and insuperable influence upon the principle of *uniformity*, as applicable to a system of weights and measures. *Extension* and *gravitation* neither have, nor admit of, one common standard. *Diversity* is the law of their nature, and the only *uniformity* which human ingenuity can establish between them is, an uniformity of proportion, and not an uniformity of identity.

The necessity for the use of *weights* is not in the organization of individual man. It is not essential even to the condition or the comforts of domestic society. It presupposes the discovery of the properties of the balance; and originates in the exchanges of traffic, after the institution of civil society. It results from the experience that the comparison of the articles of exchange, which serve for the subsistence or the enjoyment of life, by their relative extension, is not sufficient as a criterion of their value. The first use of the balance, and of weights, implies two substances, each of which is the test and the standard of the other. It is natural that these substances should be the articles the most essential to subsistence. They will be borrowed from the harvest and the vintage: they will be corn and wine. The discovery of the metals, and their extraction from the bowels of the earth, must, in the annals of human nature, be subsequent, but proximate, to the first use of weights; and, when discovered, the only mode of ascertaining their definite quantities will be soon perceived to be their weight. That they should, themselves, immediately become the common standards of exchanges, or otherwise of value and of weights, is perfectly in the order of nature; but their proportions to one another, or to the other objects by which they are to be estimated, will not be the same as standards of weight, and as standards of value. Gold, silver, copper, and iron, when balanced each by the other in weight, will present masses very different from each other in value. They give rise to another complication, and another diversity, of weights and measures, equally inaccessible to the uniformity of identity, and to the computations of decimal arithmetic.

Of the metals, that which, by the adaptation of its properties to the various uses of society, and to the purposes of traffic, by the quantities in which nature has disclosed it to the possession of man, intermediate between her profuse bounties of the coarser, and her parsimonious dispensation of the finer, metals, holds a middle station between them, wins its way as the common, and at last as the only, standard of value. It becomes the universal medium of exchanges. Its quantities, ascertained by weight, become themselves the standards of weights. Civil government is called in as the guardian and voucher of its purity. The civil authority stamps its image, to authenticate its weight and alloy: and silver becomes at once a weight, money, and coin.

With civil society too originates the necessity for common and uniform standards of measures. Of the different measures of extension necessary for individual man, and for domestic society, although the want will be common to all, and frequently recurring, yet, the standards will not be uniform, either with reference to time or to persons. The standard of linear measure for each individual being in himself, those of no two individuals will be the same. At different times, the same individual will use different measures, according to the several purposes for which they will be wanted. In domestic society, the measures adaptable to the persons of the husband, of the wife, and of the children, are not the same; nor will the idea of reducing them all to one common standard press itself upon their wants, until the multiplication of families gives rise to the intercourse, exchanges, and government, of civil society. Common standards will then be assumed from the person of some distinguished individual; but accidental circumstances, rather than any law of nature, will determine whether identity or proportion will be the character of their uniformity. If, pursuing the first and original dictate of nature, the cubit should be assumed as the standard of linear measure for the use of the hand, and the pace for the measure of motion, or linear measure upon earth, there will be two units of long measure; one for the measure of matter, and another for the measure of motion. Nor will they be reducible to one; because neither the cubit nor the pace is an aliquot part or a multiple of the other. But, should the discovery have been made, that the *foot* is at once an aliquot part of the pace, for the mensuration of motion, and of the ell and fathom, for the mensuration of matter, the foot will be made the common standard measure for both: and, thenceforth, there will be only one standard unit of long measure, and its uniformity will be that of identity.

Thus, in tracing the theoretic history of weights and measures to their original elements in the nature and the necessities of man, we have found linear measure with individual existence, superficial, capacious, itinerary measure, and decimal arithmetic, with domestic society; weights and common standards, with civil society; money, coins, and all the elements of uniform metrology, with civil government and law; arising in successive and parallel progression together.

When weights and measures present themselves to the contemplation of the legislator, and call for the interposition of law, the first and most prominent idea which occurs to him is that of *uniformity*: his first object is to embody them into a system, and his first wish, to reduce

them to one universal common standard. His purposes are
uniformity, permanency, universality; one standard to be
the same for all persons and all purposes, and to continue
the same forever. These purposes, however, require powers
which no legislator has hitherto been found to possess.
The power of the legislator is limited by the extent of his
territories, and the numbers of his people. His principle
of universality, therefore, cannot be made, by the mere
agency of his power, to extend beyond the inhabitants of
his own possessions. The power of the legislator is limited
over time. He is liable to change his own purposes. He is
not infallible: he is liable to mistake the means of effecting his own objects. He is not immortal: his successor ac-
cedes to his power, with different views, different opinions, and perhaps different principles. The legislator has
no power over the properties of matter. He cannot give a
new constitution to nature. He cannot repeal her law of
universal mutability. He cannot square the circle. He
cannot reduce extension and gravity to one common measure. He cannot divide or multiply the parts of the surface,
the cube, or the sphere, by the uniform and exclusive number ten. The power of the legislator is limited over the
will and actions of his subjects. His conflict with them is
desperate, when he counteracts their settled habits, their
established usages; their domestic and individual economy,
their ignorance, their prejudices, and their wants: all
which is unavoidable in the attempt radically to change,
or to originate, a totally new system of weights and measures.

In the origin of the different measures and weights, at
different stages of man's individual and social existence;
in the different modes by which nature has bounded the
extension of matter; in the incommensurable properties of
the straight and the curve line; in the different properties
of matter, number, extension, and gravity, of which measures and weights are the tests, nature has planted sources
of diversity, which the legislator would in vain overlook,
which he would in vain attempt to control. To these
sources of diversity in the nature of things, must be added

all those arising from the nature and history of man. In the first use of weights and measures, neither universality nor permanency are essential to the uniformity of the standards. Every individual may have standards of his own, and may change them as convenience or humor may dictate. Even in civil society, it is not *necessary*, to the purposes of traffic, that the standards of the buyer and seller should be the same. It suffices, if the proportions between the standards of both parties are mutually understood. In the progress of society, the use of weights and measures having preceded legislation, if the families, descended from one, should, as they naturally may, have the same standards, other families will have others. Until regulated by law, their diversities will be numberless, their changes continual.

These diversities are still further multiplied by the abuses incident to the poverty, imperfections, and deceptions, of human language. So arbitrary and so irrational is the dominion of usage over the speech of man, that, instead of appropriating a specific name to every distinct thing, he is impelled, by an irresistible propensity, sometimes to give different names to the same thing, but far more frequently to give the same name to different things. Weights and measures are, in their nature, relative. When man first borrows from his own person a standard measure of length, his first error is to give to the measure the name of the limb from which it is assumed. He calls the *measure* a cubit, a span, a hand, a finger, or a foot, improperly applying to it the name of those respective parts of his body. When he has discovered the properties of the balance, he either confounds with it the name of the weight, which he puts in it to balance the article which he would measure, or he gives to the definite mass, which he assumes for his standard, the indefinite and general name of *the weight*. Such was the original meaning of the weight which we call a *pound*. But, as different families assume different masses of gravity for their unit of weight, the pound of one bears the same name, and is a very different thing from the pound of another. When nations fall into the use of different weights or measures for the estimation of different objects, they commit the still grosser mistake of calling several different weights or measures by the same name. And, when governments degrade themselves by debasing their coins, as unfortunately all governments have done, they add the crime of fraud to that of injustice, by retaining the name of things which they have destroyed or changed. Even things which nature has discriminated so clearly, that they cannot be mistaken, the antipathy of mankind to new words will misrepresent and confound. It suffers not even numbers to retain their essentially definite character. It calls sixteen a dozen. It makes a hundred and twelve a hundred, and twenty-eight, twenty-five. Of all the tangles of confusion to be unravelled by the regulation of weights and measures, these abuses of language in their nomenclature are perhaps the most inextricable. So that when law comes to establish its principles of permanency, uniformity, and universality, it has to contend not only with the diversities arising from the nature of things and of man; but with those infinitely more numerous which proceed from existing usages, and delusive language; with the partial standards, and misapplied names, which have crept in with the lapse of time, beginning with individuals or families, and spreading more or less extensively to villages and communities.

In this conflict between the dominion of usage and of law, the last and greatest dangers to the principle of uniformity proceed from the laws themselves. The legislator having no distinct idea of the uniformity of which the subject is susceptible, not considering how far it should be extended, or where it finds its boundary in the nature of things and of man, enacts laws inadequate to their purpose, inconsistent with one another; sometimes stubbornly resisting, at others weakly yielding to inveterate usages or abuses; and finishes by increasing the diversities which it was his intention to abolish, and by loading his statute book only with the impotence of authority, and the uniformity of confusion.

This inquiry into the theory of weights and measures,

as resulting from the natural history of man, was deemed
necessary as preliminary to that statement of the proceedings of foreign countries for establishing uniformity in
weights and measures, called for by the resolution of the
Senate.

It presents to view certain principles believed to be
essential to the subject, upon which the historical statement required will shed continual illustration, and which
it will be advisable to bear in mind, when the propositions supposed to be proper for the adoption of the United
States are to be considered.

* * *

From the year 1757 to 1764, in the years 1789 and
1790, and from the year 1814 to the present time, the
British parliament have, at three successive periods, instituted inquiries into the condition of their own weights
and measures, with a view to the reformation of the system, and to the introduction and establishment of greater
uniformity. These inquiries have been pursued with ardor and perseverance, assisted by the skill of their most
eminent artists, by the learning of their most distinguished
philosophers, and by the contemporaneous admirable exertions, in the same cause of uniformity, of their neighbouring and rival nation.

Nor have the people, or the Congress of the United
States, been regardless of the subject, since our separation from the British empire. In their first confederation,
these associated states, and in their present national constitution, the people, that is, on the only two occasions
upon which the collective voice of this whole Union, in its
constituent character, has spoken, the power of *fixing* the
standard of weights and measures throughout the United
States has been committed to Congress. A report, worthy
of the illustrious citizen by whom it was prepared, and,
embracing the principles most essential to uniformity, was
presented in obedience to a call from the House of Representatives of the first Congress of the United States. The
eminent person who last presided over the Union, in the

parting message by which he announced his intention of retiring from public life, recalled the subject to the attention of Congress with a renewed recommendation to the principle of decimal divisions. Elaborate reports, one from a committee of the Senate in 1793, and another from a committee of the House of Representatives, at a recent period, have since contributed to shed further light upon the subject: and the call of both Houses, to which this report is the tardy, and yet too early answer, has manifested a solicitude for the improvement of the existing system, equally earnest and persevering with that of the British parliament, though not marked with the bold and magnificent characters of the concurrent labors of France.

After a succession of more than sixty years of inquiries and experiments, the British parliament have not yet acted in the form of law. After nearly forty of the same years of separate pursuit of the same object, *uniformity*, the Congress of the United States have shown the same cautious deliberation: they have yet authorized no change of the existing law. That neither country has yet changed its law, is, perhaps, a fortunate circumstance, in reference to the principle of uniformity, for both. If this report were authorized to speak to both nations, as it is required to speak to the legislature of one of them, on a subject in which the object of pursuit is the same for both, and the interest in it common to both, it would say—Is your object *uniformity*? Then, before you change any part of your system, such as it is, compare the uniformity that you must lose, with the uniformity that you may gain, by the alteration. At this hour, fifteen millions of Britons, who, in the next generation, may be twenty, and ten millions of Americans, who, in less time, will be as many, have the same legal system of weights and measures. Their mile, acre, yard, foot, and inch—their bushel of wheat, their gallon of beer, and their gallon of wine, their pound avoirdupois, and their pound troy, their cord of wood, and their ton of shipping, are the same. They are of the nations of the earth, the two, who have with each other the most of that intercourse which requires the constant use of weights and measures. Any change whatever in the system of the one, which would not be adopted by the other, would destroy all this existing uniformity. Precious, indeed, must be that uniformity, the mere promise of which, obtained by an alteration of the law, would more than compensate for the abandonment of this.

If these ideas should be deemed too cold and cheerless for the spirit of theoretical improvement; if Congress should deem their powers competent, and their duties imperative, to establish uniformity as respects weights and measures in its most universal and comprehensive sense; another system is already made to their hands. If that universal uniformity, so desirable to human contemplation, be an obtainable perfection, it is now attainable *only* by the adoption of the new French system of metrology, in all its important parts. Were it even possible to construct another system, on different principles, but embracing in equal degree all the great elements of uniformity, it would still be a system of diversity with regard to France, and all the followers of her system. And as she could not be expected to abandon that, which she has established at so much expense, and with so much difficulty, for another, possessing, if equal, not greater advantages, there would still be two rival systems, with more desperate chances for the triumph of uniformity by the recurrence to the same standard of all mankind.

The system of modern France originated with her Revolution. It is one of those attempts to improve the condition of human kind, which, should it even be destined ultimately to fail, would, in its failure, deserve little less admiration than in its success. It is founded upon the following principles:

1. That all weights and measures should be reduced to one *uniform* standard of linear measure.
2. That this standard should be an aliquot part of the circumference of the globe.
3. That the unit of linear measure, applied to matter, in its three modes of extension, length, breadth,

and thickness, should be the standard of all measures of length, surface, and solidity.

4. That the cubic contents of the linear measure, in
distilled water, at the temperature of its greatest
contraction, should furnish at once the standard
weight and measure of capacity.

5. That for every thing susceptible of being measured
or weighed, there should be only one measure of
length, one weight, one measure of contents, with
their multiples and subdivisions exclusively in
decimal proportions.

6. That the principle of decimal division, and a proportion to the linear standard, should be annexed
to the coins of gold, silver, and copper, to the
moneys of account, to the division of *time*, to the
barometer and thermometer, to the plummet and
log lines of the sea, to the geography of the earth
and the astronomy of the skies; and, finally, to
every thing in human existence susceptible of comparative estimation by weight or measure.

7. That the whole system should be equally suitable
to the use of all mankind.

8. That every weight and every measure should be designated by an appropriate, significant, characteristic name, applied exclusively to itself.

This system approaches to the ideal perfection of *uniformity* applied to weights and measures; and, whether
destined to succeed, or doomed to fail, will shed unfading
glory upon the age in which it was conceived, and upon
the nation by which its execution was attempted, and
has been in part achieved. In the progress of its establishment there, it has been often brought in conflict with the
laws of physical and of moral nature; with the impenetra-
bility of matter, and with the habits, passions, prejudices,
and necessities, of man. It has undergone various important modifications. It must undoubtedly still submit to
others, before it can look for universal adoption. But, if
man upon earth be an improveable being; if that universal
peace, which was the object of a Saviour's mission, which

is the desire of the philosopher, the longing of the phi-
lanthropist, the trembling hope of the Christian, is a blessing to which the futurity of mortal man has a claim of
more than mortal promise; if the Spirit of Evil is, before
the final consummation of things, to be cast down from
his dominion over men, and bound in the chains of a
thousand years, the foretaste here of man's eternal felicity;
then this system of common instruments, to accomplish
all the changes of social and friendly commerce, will furnish the links of sympathy between the inhabitants of the
most distant regions; the metre will surround the globe
in use as well as in multiplied extension; and one language
of weights and measures will be spoken from the equator
to the poles.

*   *   *

If the project of reforming weights and measures had
extended, as was proposed by the French system, to the
operations of astronomy, geography, and navigation; if the
quadrant of the circle and of the sphere had been divided into one hundred degrees, each of one hundred
thousand metres; the assumption of that measure would
have been an advantage much more important than it is,
or can be, in the present condition of the system. Whether
it would have compensated for disturbing that uniformity
which exists, and which has invariably existed, of the division into ninety degrees, with sexagesimal subdivisions
of minutes and seconds, is merely matter of speculation.
At least, it has been found impracticable, even in France,
to carry it into effect: and, without it, the metre, as the
natural standard of the system, has no sensible advantage
over the foot. To a perfect system of uniformity for all
weights and measures, an aliquot part of the circumference
of the earth is not only a better natural standard unit
than the pendulum, or the foot, but it is the only one that
could be assumed. Every voyage round the earth is an
actual mensuration of its circumference. All navigation is
admeasurement: and no perfect theory of weights and
measures could be devised, combining in it the principle

of decimal computation, of which any other natural standard whatever could accomplish the purpose. Its advantages
over the pendulum are palpable. The pendulum bears no
proportion to the circumference of the earth, and cannot
serve as a standard unit for measuring it. Yet a system of
weights and measures, which excludes all geography, astronomy, and navigation, from its consideration, must be
essentially defective in the principle of uniformity.

But, if the metre and its decimal divisions are not to be
applied to those operations of man, for which it is most
especially adapted; if those who circumnavigate the globe
in fact are to make no use of it, and to have no concern
in its proportions; if their measures are still to be the
nonagesimal degree, the marine league, the toise, and the
foot; it is surely of little consequence to the farmer who
needs a measure for his corn, to the mechanic who builds
a house, or to the townsman who buys a pound of meat,
or a bottle of wine, to know that the weight, or the measure which he employs, was standarded by the circumference of the globe. For all the uses of weights and measures,
in their ordinary application to agriculture, traffic, and the
mechanic arts, it is perfectly immaterial what the natural
standard, to which they are referable, was. The foot of
Hercules, the arm of Henry the First, or the barley-corn,
are as sufficient for the purpose as the pendulum, or the
quadrant of the meridian. The important question to
them is, the correspondence of their weight or measure
with the positive standard. With the standard of nature,
from which it is taken, they have no concern, unless they
can recur to it as a test of verification. However imperfect
for this end the human foot, or the kernel of wheat or
barley, may be, they are at least easily accessible. It is a
great and important defect of the systems which assume
the meridian or the pendulum for their natural standard,
that they never can be recurred to without scientific operations.

This is one great advantage which a natural standard,
taken from the dimensions and proportions of the human
body, has over all others. We are perhaps not aware how

often every individual, whose concerns in life require the
constant use of long measures, makes his own person his
natural standard, nor how habitually he recurs to it. But
the habits of every individual inure him to the comparison
of the definite portion of his person, with the existing
standard measures to which he is accustomed. There are
few English men or women but could give a yard, foot, or
inch measure, from their own arms, hands, or fingers, with
great accuracy. But they could not give the metre or decimetre, although they should know their dimensions as well
as those of the yard and foot. When the Russian General
Suwarrow, in his Discourses under the Trigger, said to his
troops, "a soldier's step is an arsheen;" he gave every
man in the Russian army the natural standard of the long
measure of his country. No Russian soldier could ever
afterwards be at a loss for an arsheen. But, although it is
precisely twenty-eight English inches, being otherwise divided, a Russian soldier would not, without calculation,
be able to tell the length of an English yard or inch.

Should the metre be substituted as the standard of our
weights and measures, instead of the foot and inch, the
natural standard which every man carries with him in his
own person would be taken away; and the inconvenience
of the want of it would be so sensibly felt, that it would
be as soon as possible adapted to the new measures: every
man would find the proportions in his own body corresponding to the metre, decimetre, and centimetre, and
habituate himself to them as well as he could. If this
conjecture be correct, is it not a reason for adhering to that
system which was founded upon those proportions, rather
than resort to another, which, after all, will bring us back
to the standard of nature in ourselves.

* * *

To despair of human improvement is not more congenial to the judgment of sound philosophy than to the
temper of brotherly kindness. Uniformity of weights and
measures is, and has been for ages, the common, earnest,
and anxious pursuit of France, of Great Britain, and, since

their independent existence, of the United States. To the attainment of one object, common to them all, they have been proceeding by different means, and with different ultimate ends. France alone has proposed a plan suitable to the ends of all; and has invited co-operation for its construction and establishment. The associated pursuit of great objects of common interest is among the most powerful modern expedients for the improvement of man. The principle is at this time in full operation, for the abolition of the African slave-trade. What reason can be assigned, why other objects, of common interest to the whole species, should not be in like manner made the subject of common deliberation and concerted effort? To promote the intercourse of nations with each other, the uniformity of their weights and measures is among the most efficacious agencies: and this uniformity can be effected only by mutual understanding and united energy. A single and universal system can be finally established only by a general convention, to which the principal nations of the world shall be parties, and to which they shall all give their assent. To effect this, would seem to be no difficult achievement. It has one advantage over every plan of moral or political improvement, not excepting the abolition of the slave-trade itself: there neither is, nor can be, any great counteracting *interest* to overcome. The conquest to be obtained is merely over prejudices, usages, and perhaps national jealousies. The whole evil to be subdued is diversity of opinion with regard to the means of attaining the same end. To the formation of the French system, the learning and the genius of other nations did co-operate with those of her native sons. The co-operation of Great Britain was invited; and there is no doubt that of the United States would have been accepted, had it been offered. The French system embraces all the great and important principles of uniformity, which can be applied to weights and measures: but that system is not yet complete. It is susceptible of many modifications and improvements. Considered merely as a labor-saving machine, it is a new power, offered to man, incomparably greater than that which he has acquired by the new agency which he has given to steam. It is in design the greatest *invention* of human ingenuity since that of printing. But, like that, and every other useful and complicated invention, it could not be struck out perfect at a heat. Time and experience have already dictated many improvements of its mechanism; and others may, and undoubtedly will, be found necessary for it hereafter. But all the radical principles of uniformity are in the machine: and the more universally it shall be adopted, the more certain will it be of attaining all the perfection which is within the reach of human power.

Another motive, which would seem to facilitate this concert of nations, is, that it conceals no lurking danger to the independence of any of them. It needs no convocation of sovereigns, armed with military power. It opens no avenue to partial combinations and intrigues. It can mask, under the vizor of virtue, no project of avarice or ambition. It can disguise no private or perverted ends, under the varnish of generous and benevolent aims. It has no final appeal to physical force; no *ultima ratio* of cannon balls. Its objects are not only pacific in their nature, but can be pursued by no other than peaceable means. Would it not be strange, if, while mankind find it so easy to attain uniformity in the use of every engine adapted to their mutual destruction, they should find it impracticable to agree upon the few and simple but indispensable instruments of all their intercourse of peace and friendship and beneficence—that they should use the same artillery and musketry, and bayonets and swords and lances, for the wholesale trade of human slaughter, and that they should refuse to weigh by the same pound, to measure by the same rule, to drink from the same cup, to use in fine the same materials for ministering to the wants and contributing to the enjoyments of one another?

These views are presented as leading to the conclusion, that, as final and universal uniformity of weights and measures is the common desideratum for all civilized nations; as France has formed, and for her own use has es-

tablished, a system, adapted, by the highest efforts of
human science, ingenuity, and skill, to the common purposes of all; as this system is yet new, imperfect, susceptible
of great improvements, and struggling for existence even
in the country which gave it birth; as its universal establishment would be a universal blessing; and as, if ever
effected, it can only be by consent, and not by force, in
which the energies of opinion must precede those of legislation; it would be worthy of the dignity of the Congress of
the United States to consult the opinions of all the civilized nations with whom they have a friendly intercourse;
to ascertain, with the utmost attainable accuracy, the existing state of their respective weights and measures; to
take up and pursue, with steady, persevering, but always
temperate and discreet exertions, the idea conceived, and
thus far executed, by France, and to co-operate with her to
the final and universal establishment of her system.

But, although it is respectfully proposed that Congress
should immediately sanction this consultation, and that
it should commence, in the first instance, with Great
Britain and France, it is not expected that it will be attended with immediate success. Ardent as the pursuit of
uniformity has been for ages in England, the idea of extending it beyond the British dominions has hitherto received but little countenance there. The operation of
changes of opinion there is slow; the aversion to all innovations, deep. More than two hundred years had elapsed
from the Gregorian reformation of the calendar, before it
was adopted in England. It is to this day still rejected
throughout the Russian empire. It is not even intended to
propose the adoption by ourselves of the French metrology
for the present. The reasons have been given for believing,
that the time is not yet matured for this reformation.
Much less is it supposed adviseable to propose its adoption
to any other nation. But, in consulting them, it will be
proper to let them understand, that the design and motive
of opening the communication is, to promote the final
establishment of a system of weights and measures, to be
common to all civilized nations.

In contemplating so great, but so beneficial a change, as the ultimate object of the proposal now submitted to the consideration of Congress, it is supposed to be most congenial to the end, to attempt no present change whatever in our existing weights and measures; to let the standards remain precisely as they are; and to confine the proceedings of Congress at this time to authorizing the Executive to open these communications with the European nations where we have accredited ministers and agents, and to such declaratory enactments and regulations as may secure a more perfect uniformity in the weights and measures now in use throughout the Union.

The motives for entertaining the opinion, that any change in our system at the present time would be inexpedient, are four:

First, That no change whatever of the system could be adopted, without losing the greatest of all the elements of uniformity, that referring to the persons using the same system. This uniformity we now possess, in common with the whole British nation; the nation with which, of all the nations of the earth, we have the most of that intercourse which requires the constant use of weights and measures. No change is believed possible, other than that of the whole system, the benefit of which would compensate for the loss of this uniformity.

Secondly, That the system, as it exists, has an uniformity of proportion very convenient and useful, which any alteration of it would disturb, and perhaps destroy; the proportion between the avoirdupois and troy weights, and that between the avoirdupois weight and the foot measure; one cubic foot containing of spring water exactly one thousand ounces avoirdupois, and one pound avoirdupois consisting of exactly seven thousand grains troy.

Thirdly, That the experience of France has proved, that binary, ternary, duodecimal, and sexagesimal divisions, are as necessary to the practical use of weights and measures, as the decimal divisions are convenient for calculations resulting from them; and that no plan for introducing the latter can dispense with the continued use of the former.

Fourthly, That the only *material* improvement, of which the present system is believed to be susceptible, would be the restoration of identity between weights and silver coins; a change, the advantages of which would be very great, but which could not be effected without a corresponding and almost total change in our coinage and moneys of account; a change the more exceptionable, as our monetary system is itself a new, and has hitherto been a successful institution.

Of all the nations of European origin, ours is that which least requires any change in the system of their weights and measures. With the exception of Louisiana, the established system is, and always has been, throughout the Union, the same. Under the feudal system of Europe, combined with the hierarchy of the church of Rome, the people were in servitude, and every chieftain of a village, or owner of a castle, possessed or asserted the attributes of sovereign power. Among the rest, the feudal lords were in the practice of coining money, and fixing their own weights and measures. This is the great source of numberless diversities existing in every part of Europe, proceeding not from the varieties which in a course of ages befell the same system, but from those of diversity of origin. The nations of Europe are, in their origin, all compositions of victorious and vanquished people. Their institutions are compositions of military power and religious opinions. Their doctrines are, that freedom is the grant of the sovereign to the people, and that the sovereign is amenable only to God. These doctrines are not congenial to nations originating in colonial establishments. Colonies carry with them the general laws, opinions, and usages, of the nation from which they emanate, and the prejudices and passions of the age of their emigration. The North American colonies had nothing military in their origin. The first English colonies on this continent were speculations of commerce: they commenced precisely at the period of that struggle in England between liberty and power, which, after long and bloody civil wars, terminated in a compromise between the two conflicting principles.

The colonies were founded by that portion of the people, who were arrayed on the side of liberty. They brought with them all the rights, but none of the servitudes, of the parent country. Their constitutions were, indeed, conformably to the spirit of the feudal policy, charters granted by the crown; but they were all adherents to the doctrine, that charters were not donations, but compacts. They brought with them the weights and measures of the law, and not those of any particular district or franchise. The only change which has taken place in England with regard to the legal standards of weights and measures, since the first settlement of the North American colonies, has been the specification of the contents of measures of capacity, by prescribing their dimensions in cubical inches. All the standards at the exchequer are the same that they were at the first settlement of Jamestown; with the exception of the wine gallon, which is of the time of queen Anne: and the standards of the exchequer are the prototypes from which all the weights and measures of the Union are derived.

*   *   *

DOCUMENT 47

A New Penal Code

Americans considered English common law, like the laws of entail and primogeniture, a barbarous inheritance from the days of feudalism. Nevertheless, except for the Zenger case of 1733, when truth was admitted as evidence in libel cases, little was done to overhaul English common law until the early nineteenth century. Trade union associations, for instance, could be indicted as conspiracies under common law as late as 1840. Slowest progress in modifying the English common law came in areas vital to the invested interests of property. The laws of entail and primogeniture, on the other hand, in spite of Thomas Jefferson's celebrated law abolishing them in Virginia, had never been widely established in the American colonies.

Gradually during the nineteenth century the practice was adopted, particularly in the new western states, of prohibiting English common law except when expressly reaffirmed by state legislatures. A leader in this movement was Edward Livingston (1764–1836) in New Orleans, where the problem was aggravated by the presence of conflicting French and Spanish procedures. By 1828, the leadership had been taken over by Livingston's native state of New York. An interesting contemporary discussion of the conflict-between property rights and the doctrine of equality growing out of common law cases of the period can be found in John R. Commons, et al., eds., *Documentary History of American Industrial Society*, 10 vols. Vol. III, p. 343; Vol. IV, pp. 71–73 (Cleveland: Arthur H. Clarke Company, 1910–11). The following document is an anonymous review of Livingston's *Report of the Plan of the Penal Code* to the Louisiana legislature in 1822.

SOURCE: *North American Review*, Vol. XVII, pp. 242–68, *passim* (1823).

Report made to the General Assembly of the State of Louisiana, of the Plan of the Penal Code for the said State. By Edward Livingston, Member of the House of Representatives from the Parish of Plaquemines. 8vo. New Orleans, 1822.

THE preceeding numbers of our journal have contained ample evidence, we trust, of our hearty cooperation in the furtherance of an object, which, while it is the cause of enlarged and enlightened humanity all over the civilized world, is emphatically so in this country, where every thing conducive to the improvement of man as a social being, is a kind of indigenous production of the soil. We allude to the generous endeavors of philanthropic individuals in the present age, to investigate, establish, and spread abroad a liberal and rational theory of penal jurisprudence, and to the zeal with which those endeavors have been seconded by the legislative bodies of America at least, if not of Europe. In examining the work now before us, and transferring to our pages such extracts from it as may suffice to exhibit a specimen of its character and execution, of the high-minded views of public policy, the strain of manly and animated eloquence, the powerful reasoning, the comprehensiveness and accuracy in details, by which it is every where pervaded and marked, we shall only be continuing our humble exertions to contribute to the diffusion of genuine principles of benevolence and justice.

* * *

The code is divided into six books. The first is composed of definitions of technical words, and directions with regard to the promulgation of the code; the second contains a preamble, and certain dispositions of a general and

introductory nature; the third defines offences and desig-
nates their punishment; the fourth establishes a system
of criminal procedure; the fifth contains rules of evidence
applicable to trials for the several offences made punish-
able by the code; and the last relates to the establishment
and government of a penitentiary.

* * *

Mr Livingston proposes, among other smaller changes,
four principal deviations from the crimes designated by
the common law, all which deviations are defended with
great eloquence, and with a cogency of reasoning which
it is certainly difficult to withstand. The first of them is a
modification of the law respecting complicity. Our
juridical readers will recollect that, by the common law,
any 'person, who, knowing a felony to have been committed, receives, relieves, comforts, or assists the felon,' is
styled an accessory after the fact, and in most cases subjected to the same punishment as the principal offender.
By the provisions of the new code of Louisiana, such
an act is to cease to be criminal in relations of the principal in the ascending or descending line, or in the collat-
eral, as far as the first degree, or in persons united to him
by marriage, or owing him obedience as a servant.

'Our law now calls for the punishment of acts, which,
if not strictly virtues, are certainly too nearly allied to
them to be designated as crimes. The ferocious legislation,
which first enacted this law, demands, and sometimes
under the penalty of the most cruel death, the sacrifice of
all the feelings of nature, of all the sentiments of humanity; breaks the ties of gratitude and honor; makes
obedience to the law to consist in a dereliction of every
principle that gives dignity to man; and leaves the unfortunate wretch, who has himself been guilty of no offence,
to decide between a life of infamy and self-reproach, or a
death of dishonor. Dreadful as this picture is, the original
is found in the law of accessories after the fact. If the
father commit treason, the son must abandon or deliver
him up to the executioner. If the son be guilty of a crime,

the stern dictates of our law require that his parent, that the very mother who bore him, that his sisters and brothers, the companions of his infancy,—should expel nature from their hearts and humanity from their feelings; that they should barbarously discover his retreat; or with inhuman apathy abandon him to his fate. The husband is even required to betray his wife, the mother of his children; every tie of nature or affection is to be broken, and men are required to be faithless, treacherous, unnatural, and cruel, in order to prove that they are good citizens and worthy members of society.' *Report*, pp. 30, 31.

Perhaps the common law goes too far in making it criminal to afford the least aid or shelter to a felon, although it would evidently be difficult to draw the line between those acts which tend, in a greater or less degree, to obstruct the course of justice; but we doubt whether Mr Livingston's amendment would be found safe in operation. If the persons particularized in the code have a right to exercise all their ingenuity, nay, to have recourse to violence itself, to enable their kinsman to elude the pursuit of justice, felons might easily set the laws at defiance. We do not say that the laws ought to go the length of asking a parent to abandon his child, or a husband his wife, much less to assist in their apprehension; it may be wrong to look, in every father, for the stern justice of a Junius Brutus. But we should hesitate in granting men protection and indemnity, while they were rescuing the guilty from that punishment, which the good of society required they should suffer. Besides, Mr Livingston confines the privilege to certain specified relations, leaving cases of other 'ties of gratitude or friendship,' to 'the consideration of the pardoning power.' Now it is clear that the principle, on which Mr Livingston would excuse persons in the cases referred to,—that it is unjust to demand of men to do what is incompatible with the natural feelings of humanity,—applies with equal force to many relations, for which he does not and cannot provide. How often are 'the ties of gratitude or friendship' stronger than those of birth;—and yet he, who should yield to the dic-

tates of nature for the protection of his friend or benefactor, must still be subjected to suffer as an accessory.

Whatever doubt there may be, however, with respect
to the expediency of this change, there can be none as
to the two next proposed by Mr Livingston. The reasons,
which induced him to expunge from his code the act of
suicide, and another*, whose name ought never to pol-
lute the laws of a civilized people, we think are un-
answerable. For his remarks on the latter, we refer to the
Report itself; on the former, he observes:

'Melancholy, misfortune, and despair sometimes urge
the unhappy to an act, which, by most criminal codes, is
considered as an offence of the deepest die; and which,
being directed principally against the offender himself,
would have required a separate division, if it had been
admitted in this code. It has not; because its insertion
would be contrary to some of the fundamental principles,
which have been laid down for framing it.

'Suicide can never be punished but by making the
penalty, whether it be forfeiture or disgrace, fall exclusively upon the innocent. The English mangle the remains of the dead. The inanimate body feels neither the
ignominy nor pain. The mind of the innocent survivor
alone is lacerated by this useless and savage butchery,
and the disgrace of the execution is felt exclusively by him,
although it ought to fall on the laws which inflict it. The
father, by a rash act of self-destruction, deprives his
family of the support he ought to afford them; and the
law completes the work of ruin, by harrowing up their
feelings, covering them with disgrace, and depriving them,
by forfeiture, of their means of subsistence.

'Vengeance, we have said, is unknown to our law; it
cannot, therefore, pursue the living offender, much less,
with impotent rage, should it pounce like a vulture on

---

* Livingston himself called it a species figuring in "every code,
from the Mosaic downward, to those of our own days, and generally with capital punishments denounced against its commission." For the cultural meaning of this evasiveness, see docs. 7
and 8. [Ed.]

the body of the dead, to avenge a crime which the
offender can never repeat, and which certainly holds out
no lure for imitation. The innocent, we have assumed,
should never be involved in the punishment inflicted on
the guilty; but here not only the innocent, but those most
injured by the crime, are exclusively the sufferers by the
punishment. We have established, as a maxim, that the
sole end of punishment is to prevent the commission of
crime; the only means of effecting this, in the present
case, must be by the force of example. But what punishment can be devised to deter him, whose very crime consists in the infliction upon himself of the greatest penalty
your law can denounce? Unless, therefore, you use the
hold which natural affection gives you on his feelings, and
restrain him by the fear of the disgrace and ruin with
which you threaten his family, your law has no effective
sanction. But humanity forbids this; the legislator that
threatens it, is guilty of the most refined tyranny; if he
carries it into execution, he is a savage. It is either a vain
threat, and therefore cannot operate; or if executed,
with an ill-directed rage, strikes the innocent because the
guilty is beyond its reach.' pp. 35, 36.

The three changes on which we have commented, are
omissions of crimes recognized by the common law, as it
exists in England and is adopted in most of the United
States. The last change in the enumeration of public offences recommended by Mr Livingston, is the creation of
a new class, against the freedom of the press. He remarks:

'It has generally been thought a sufficient protection
[of the liberty of the press] to declare that no punishment should be inflicted on those who legally exercise the
right of publishing; but hitherto no penalties have been
denounced against those who illegally abridge this liberty.
Constitutional provisions are, in our republics, universally introduced to assert the right, but no sanction is given
to the law. Yet do not the soundest principles require it?
If the liberty of publishing be a right, is it sufficient to
say that no one shall be punished for exercising it? I have
a right to possess my property, yet the law does not con-

finc itsclf to a dcclaration that I shall not be punished for
using it; something more is done; and it is fenced round
with penalties, imposed on those who deprive me of its
enjoyment.

* * *

'All violence, or menace of violence, or any other of the
means which are enumerated in the code; all exercise of
official influence or authority, which may abridge this
valuable privilege is declared to be an offence. Nay, the
project which will be presented to you, goes further, and
considering the constitutional provision as paramount to
any act of ordinary legislation, and consequently that all
laws in derogation of it are void;—it declares all those
guilty of an offence, who shall execute any law abridging
or restraining the liberty of the press, contrary to the
privilege secured by the constitution.' pp. 39–41.

We confess that this improvement strikes us as being
rather fanciful, and, what is worse, as unnecessary and
incapable of answering any useful purpose. Mr Livingston
cannot be more ardently attached to a free press than
ourselves, nor more resolute to maintain it to the best of
our ability, in its full integrity, at every hazard. Most
fervently do we respond to the declaration of our own
constitution, that 'the Liberty of the Press is essential to
the security of freedom in a state.' But we think this
liberty is sufficiently guarded by the removal of all re-
strictions on its legitimate use. From whom are we to
apprehend any infringement of it, which a penal sanction
in the laws could prevent? Not surely from persons in
their private, individual capacity; because the liberty is of
such a nature, that no direct invasion of it can be made
by private persons. It is not in the power of man to
impede us in the mere publication of our sentiments, by
any immediate act, for which the laws do not sufficiently
provide. In revenge of what we have published, or in
anticipation of what we intend to publish, he may attack,
seize, imprison our persons; he may denounce our principles and defame our characters; he may deface or de-

stroy our manuscripts, or sheets, or scatter their fragments abroad to the winds of heaven; he may break up
our apparatus for printing, and disperse our types or shake
them together into inextricable confusion: but who would
pretend that either of these acts was, properly speaking,
an invasion of the freedom of the press? They are all in-
fringements of the rights of personal security, liberty, or
property, for which the comprehensive remedies of the
common law already afford adequate redress. No direct
attack can be made on the freedom of the press *as such*,
but by some branch of the government. Now if the
executive or judicial authorities attempt to debar a citizen
from the free use of a privilege accorded him by the laws,
the injured party may proceed against the wrong-doer as
a private individual, amenable, like other individuals, to
the municipal laws of his country; or he may pursue the
constitutional remedy of an impeachment of such wrong-
doer for the illegal act as perpetrated in his official capacity; or he may do both; and in this alternative, he certainly
has most ample opportunity to obtain legal indemnifica-
tion for his injury. In short, there is but one source in our
republics, from which any serious attack on the liberty of
the press can be rationally apprehended, and that is the
legislature. Should our legislative halls ever become a field
for the ambitious efforts of unprincipled men, it would
evidently be for their interest, and would probably be
their endeavor, to abridge and circumscribe the operations of the press, which, if free, could not fail to oppose
the most formidable resistance to the execution of any
project for subverting the constitution. Now if such a crisis
in the affairs of Louisiana should hereafter occur, how is it
that the penal denunciations in the new code can chain
the hands of the General Assembly? They do not become
incorporated in the constitution. The same power which
enacts the code, may repeal it. Nor do we think it sufficient
to reply to this objection, as Mr Livingston does, that 'the
repeal of this part of the code would be an acknowledgment, on the part of those who procured it, that they

were hostile to the right secured by the constitution;' and
that this no representative would dare to avow.

* * *

We have enlarged on this topic considerably, both because of its importance in itself, and because we entertain such high respect for the judgment and opinions of
Mr Livingston, that we were unwilling to differ from him
materially without assigning our reasons at some length.
Mr Livingston next proceeds to consider a portion of
criminal law, which is undoubtedly the most important,
namely, the means of securing obedience to its pro-
hibitory and mandatory provisions, or the punishment of
crimes. In this branch of his duty, he investigates his
principles with great care and faithfulness, and then
fearlessly follows them out through all their consequences.

'It would be disgusting and unnecessary to pass in review all the modes of punishment, which have, even in
modern times, been used, rather it would seem to gratify
vengeance, than to lessen the number of offences. A spirit
of enlightened legislation, taught by Montesquieu, Bec-
caria, Eden, and others,—names dear to humanity,—has
banished some of the most atrocious from the codes of
Europe. But it has happened in this branch of jurisprudence, as it has in most other departments of science, that
long after the great principles are generally acknowledged,
a diversity of opinion exists on their application to particular subjects. Thus, although the dislocation of the
joints is no longer considered as the best mode of ascertaining innocence or discovering guilt; although offences against the Deity are no longer expiated by the
burning faggot; or those against the majesty of kings
avenged by the hot pincers, and the rack, and the wheel;
still many other modes of punishment have their advocates, which, if not equally cruel, are quite as inconsistent with the true maxims of penal law. It may, therefore,
be proper to pass some of them in review.' pp. 43, 44.

We need not follow our author through his exposition
of the defects of the ordinary modes of punishment,

which the example of Europe has sanctioned too long, but which now meet with few advocates in America. Banishment, deportation, simple imprisonment or imprisonment in chains, confiscation of property, exposure to public derision, labor on public works, mutilation or other indelible marks of disgrace, stripes or the infliction of other bodily pain,—are all of them punishments, which the good sense of the people of our country in general, no less than the sober conviction of men who make this a subject of philosophical inquiry, has almost universally condemned, as alike inconsistent with the principles of justice and humanity, unsuited to the temper of the times, and hostile to the liberal spirit of all our laws, customs, habits, and institutions. Mr Livingston has done, we apprehend, what the great mass of his countrymen will cordially approve, in throwing these altogether out of the question in the compilation of his code; and in abolishing, at the same time, the punishment of death, he has ventured upon the trial of a system, whose efficacy all humane men will rejoice to see thoroughly tried, whatever doubt may exist with regard to the issue.

* * *

He contends that the fear of the privation of life does not exert so powerful an influence on the mind as many other motives, which are within the control of a legislator; and that, if you make the spectacle of the infliction of death common, it debases and brutalizes the public sentiment,—if you make it rare, it converts the criminal into a martyr,—and in either alternative does more evil than good. A few extracts will fully explain his ideas on the subject.

'Let us have constantly before us, when we reason on this subject, the great principle, that the end of punishment is the prevention of crime. Death, indeed, operates this end most effectually as respects the delinquent; but the great object of inflicting it is the force of the example on others. If this spectacle of horror is insufficient to deter men from the commission of slight offences, what good reason can be given to persuade us that it will have this operation where the crime is more atrocious? Can we believe that the fear of a remote and uncertain death will stop the traitor in the intoxicating moment of fancied victory over the constitution and liberties of his country? While, in the proud confidence of success, he defies heaven and earth, and commits his existence to the chance of arms, that the dread of this punishment will check his pride,—force him, like some magic spell, to yield obedience to the laws, and abandon a course which he persuades himself makes a virtue of his ambition? Will it arrest the hand of the infuriate wretch, who, at a single blow, is about to gratify the strongest passion of his soul in the destruction of his deadly enemy? Will it turn aside the purpose of the secret assassin, who meditates the removal of the only obstacle to his enjoyment of wealth and honors? Will it master the strongest passion and counteract the most powerful motives, while it is too weak to prevent the indulgence of the slightest criminal inclination? If this be true, it must be confessed that it presents a paradox, which will be found more difficult to solve when we reflect that great crimes are, for the most part, committed by men, whose long habits of guilt have familiarized them to the idea of death, or to whom strong passions or natural courage have rendered it in some measure indifferent; and that the cowardly poisoner or assassin always thinks that he has taken such precautions as will prevent any risk of discovery. The fear of death, therefore, will rarely deter from the commission of great crimes. It is, on the contrary, a remedy peculiarly inapplicable to those offences. Ambition, which usually inspires the crime of treason, soars above the fear of death; avarice, which whispers the secret murder, creeps below it; * * * * threats of death will never deter men, who are actuated by these passions; many of them affront it in the very commission of the offence, and therefore readily incur the lesser risk of suffering it in what they think the impossible event of detection. But present other consequences more directly opposed to the enjoyments which were anticipated in the commission of the crime, make those consequences permanent and certain, and then, although milder, they will be less readily risked than the momentary pang attending the loss of life. Study the passions, which first suggested the offence, and apply your punishment to mortify and counteract them. The ambitious man cannot bear the ordinary restraints of government,—subject him to those of a prison; he could not endure the superiority of the most dignified magistrate,—force him to submit to the lowest officer of executive justice; he sought by his crimes a superiority above all that was most respectable in society,—reduce him in his punishment to a level with the most vile and abject of mankind. If avarice suggested the murder, separate the wretch forever from his hoard; realize the fable of antiquity; sentence him, from his place of penitence and punishment, to see his heirs rioting on his spoils; and the corroding reflection that others are innocently enjoying the fruits of his crime will be as appropriate a punishment in practical, as it was feigned to be in poetical justice. The rapacious spendthrift robs to support his extravagance, and murders to avoid detection; he exposes his life, that he may either pass it in idleness, debauchery, and sensual enjoyments, or lose it by a momentary pang; —disappoint his profligate calculation; force him to live, but to live under those privations, which he fears more than death; let him be reduced to the coarse diet, the hard lodging, and the incessant labor of a penitentiary.' pp. 51–55.

After remarking on the importance of adopting some system of punishment capable of reforming the delinquent and of affording room for correcting a false judgment, both of which are precluded by taking away the convict's life, our author proceeds to consider the influence of the example of capital executions on society at large, in these words:

'Another consequence of the infliction of death is, that if frequent it loses its effect; the people become too much

familiarized with it to consider it as an example; it is
changed into a spectacle, which must frequently be repeated to satisfy the ferocious taste it has formed. * * * *
Human sufferings are never beheld for the first time but
with aversion, terror, and disgust. Nature has strongly im-
planted this repugnance on our minds, for the wisest purposes; but this once conquered, it happens in the intellectual taste as it does in that of the senses; in relation to
which last it is observed, that we become most fond of
those enjoyments, which required, in the beginning, some
effort to overcome the disgust produced by their first use;
and that our attachment to them is in proportion to the
difficulty which was conquered in becoming familiarized
to them. Whatever may be the cause of this striking fact in
the history of the human mind, its effects ought to be
studied by the legislator, who desires to form a wise and
permanent system. If the sight of one capital execution
creates an inhuman taste to behold another; if a curiosity,
satisfied at first with terror, increases with its gratification,
and becomes a passion by indulgence, we ought to be
extremely careful how, by sanctioning the frequency of
capital punishments, we lay the foundation for a depravity
the more to be dreaded, because, in our government, popular opinion must have the greatest influence on all its
departments, and this vitiated taste would soon be discovered in the decisions of our courts and the verdicts
of our juries.

But if this punishment be kept for great occasions, and
the people are seldom treated with the gratification of
seeing one of their fellow-creatures expire by the sentence
of the law, a most singular effect is produced; the sufferer,
whatever be his crime, becomes a hero or a saint; he is
the object of public attention, curiosity, admiration, and
pity. Charity supplies all his wants, and religion proves her
power by exhibiting the outcast and murderer, though
unworthy to enjoy existence upon earth, yet purified from
the stain of his vices and crimes, converted by her agency
into an accepted candidate for the happiness of heaven.
He is lifted above the fear of death by the exhortations

and prayers of the pious; the converted sinner receives the tender attentions of respectability, beauty, and worth; his prison becomes a place of pilgrimage,—its tenant, a saint awaiting the crown of martyrdom; his last looks are watched with affectionate solicitude; his last words are carefully remembered and recorded; his last agonies are beheld with affliction and despair; and after suffering the ignominious sentence of the law, the body of the culprit, whose death was infamy and whose life was crime, is attended respectfully and mournfully to the grave by a train that would not have disgraced the obsequies of a patriot or a hero. This sketch, though highly colored, is drawn to the life; the inhabitants of one of the most refined and wealthy of our state capitals sat for the picture; and although such exalted feelings are not always excited, or are prudently repressed, yet they are found in nature; and in whatever degree they exist, it cannot be doubted that in the same proportion they counteract every good effect, that punishment is intended to produce. The hero of such a tragedy can never consider himself as the actor of a mean or ignoble part; nor can the people view, in the object of their admiration or pity, a murderer and a robber, whom they would have regarded with horror, if their feelings had not been injudiciously enlisted in his favor. Thus the end of the law is defeated, the force of example is totally lost, and the place of execution is converted into a scene of triumph for the sufferer, whose crime is wholly forgotten, while his courage, resignation, or piety marks him as the martyr, not the guilty victim of the laws.' pp. 59–63.

Our author next goes into a variety of considerations in support of his views, all tending to show that the infliction of death at any time as a punishment is unnecessary, impolitic, unjust and hurtful to the good order of society. He concedes, however, and we think wisely, that governments have an undoubted right to inflict it, provided it can be proved necessary to the preservation of public and private peace.

*   *   *

Mr Livingston concludes his argument by refuting, with much more eloquence than they deserved to have bestowed upon them, the reasons usually urged in favor of capital punishment independent of the question as to the force of its example. The Jewish laws, which the mild spirit of the Gospel has long ago stripped of their authority as positive institutions,—the practice of most nations from the remotest antiquity, which might, with equal justice, be alleged in vindication of all the worst abuses in government and all the weakest and vilest prejudices in the whole category of human error,—and the danger of innovation in an age and a country, which owe whatever is most admirable in science or the arts and in social condition to the irrepressible workings of the genius of improvement, objections such as these to abolishing the punishment of death have but a poor chance of success in America. What then are the substitutes proposed to supply the place of the old system of punishment discarded as so objectionable? They are:

'Pecuniary fines.—Degradation from office.—Simple imprisonment.—Temporary suspension of civil rights.—Permanent deprivation of civil rights.—Imprisonment at hard labor.—Solitary confinement during certain intervals of the time of imprisonment to be determined in the sentence.

The advantage of this scale of punishment is, that it is divisible almost to infinity; that there is no offence, however slight, for which it does not afford an appropriate corrective; and none, however atrocious, for which, by cumulating its different degrees, an adequate punishment cannot be found.' p. 83.

We have followed Mr Livingston so closely thus far, that, for what remains of his code, where there is less of novelty and more of the uncontested principles of law, we content ourselves with referring to the pages of the Report. We have been attracted to the discussion of the subject by the consideration that even at this day, widely and profoundly as the researches of philosophers have been pushed, there is still much to learn of a subject, which

embraces the entire range of man's actions, his physical
and moral constitution, habits, feelings, propensities,
destiny;—which ascends to the palaces of the rich and
powerful, but disdains not to search the cottage of the
meanest villager, in quest of useful illustrations;—which
lays bare alike the heart of the prince and the peasant,
the weak and the mighty, to scrutinize the inmost re-
cesses of the human breast, and view there, undisguised,
the passions, the master-springs, that move the vast
machinery of the world;—which is of the most deep and
vital interest to society, inasmuch as it involves the great
question of the preservation of social tranquillity, security,
and order, and of the moral discipline of the whole human race. Nor is it the intricacy of the subject alone, that
renders it inexhaustible. Where truths in the science of
remedial law are so clearly demonstrated as to be fundamental axioms, still the improvements, which they dictate, remain to be adopted, and men yet obstinately and
pertinaciously cling to their inveterate prejudices. The
names of two hundred capital offences continue recorded
in the statute-book of England. In that country, ministerial influence has not yet ceased to elude, nor ministerial
sophistry ceased to resist, the repeal of laws the most absurd in principle, the most pernicious in operation. But
in America, all the most odious features in the penal
laws of our father-land, with but few exceptions, have
yielded themselves up, and what remains cannot long
maintain itself in opposition to the healthful influences
of the young Spirit of Freedom. Our emancipation from
the tyranny of the feudal institutions is fast approaching
its full accomplishment. And Mr Livingston's code, although confined in the immediate sphere of its operation to Louisiana, will sensibly contribute, we doubt not,
to the diffusion of an unexceptionably liberal system of
criminal law throughout the United States.

DOCUMENT 48

The American System

The next document, though not widely influential, is nevertheless one of the finest, most original expressions of Whig nationalism. It raises the sectional and economic debates of the period high above the level of self-interest, justifying almost all groups except supporters of the U. S. Bank in their plea for government support, on the ground of national interest. Although its philosophy was too advanced—indeed, is as modern as the New Deal—to be suited to the individualistic temper of a basically laisser-faire nation, it was praised for refusing to do "homage to the theories advanced in Europe." In much the same spirit of Livingston's modification of English common law, Daniel Raymond (1786–1849?), a New England lawyer transplanted to Baltimore, here undertook to modify the classical economics of Smith, Ricardo, and Malthus.

Like John Quincy Adams in the treatise on weights and measurements, moreover, Raymond took a middle position in his thinking between a savage state of nature and the advanced civilization of Europe. His view that social principles, far from being absolute and universal, are relative always to time and place puts him squarely in the American vernacular tradition. He is one of the few theorists in that tradition.

SOURCE: Daniel Raymond, *Thoughts on Political Economy*, pp. 112–31, 223, 286–94. Baltimore: 1820.

The comparative advantages of Agricultural and Manufacturing labour.

If, according to the established laws of nature the earth is the only source of wealth, and labour the only cause by which it is produced; and if a capacity for acquiring the necessaries and comforts of life be the true definition of national wealth; the first question that presents itself to the political economist, is whether one species of labour* is better calculated to promote national wealth, than another. Whether it be the duty of government to encourage one species of labour in preference to another, or in other words, whether agricultural or manufacturing labour is most conducive to national wealth, or whether they stand upon equal ground in point of utility.

The most effectual mode of augmenting a nation's capacity for acquiring the necessaries and comforts of life, is the proper subject of inquiry for the political economist; and a more extensive or important subject cannot be presented to the consideration of the philosopher. It embraces not only the political and municipal regulations of a nation, properly so called, but also the character of man—the principles of human nature, and the motives of human action.

The capacity of a nation for acquiring the necessaries and comforts of life, depends on the development of the moral and physical energies of man. The most effectual means of developing these energies, constitutes the very gi[s]t of the inquiry. The laws of nature must be studied— The principles of nature are the fundamental principles of political economy, and he who adheres to these prin-

* Although there is, in fact, but one species of labour, yet there are different subjects upon which it may be bestowed, which produces a difference in the effect; and the established laws of rhetoric authorise a figure of speech, which puts the effect for the cause. By different species of labour, therefore, is not meant any difference in labour itself, but in the effect produced, according to the subject upon which the labour is bestowed.

ciples the most strictly, and traces them out the most successfully, will entitle himself to the highest rank among
the professors of this august and sublime science.

The only rational division, that can be made of labour,
is, into that which produces the necessaries, and that
which produces the comforts of life. No man ever has,
or ever will be able to draw the line of distinction between the comforts and luxuries of life. It is useless,
therefore, to attempt it. The distinction which Adam
Smith makes between the *necessaries* and the *luxuries* of
life, is whimsical enough. He makes *a linen shirt* a *necessary* of life, and *butchers' meat* a *luxury*. He makes no
distinction between the *necessaries* and *comforts* of life.

Whether the one species of labour or the other, be
most productive of national wealth, depends entirely
upon accidental and arbitrary circumstances. In one sense
that species which produces the necessaries of life, is the
most important, and entitled to the rank of pre-emi-
nence. Without it human life could not be sustained—
Consequently it supports the whole fabric of life, and
civilization. Without it all other labour would be useless.

The immediate cause of this labour, is however so remote from the immediate objects of legislation—Those
concerned in it have so little consideration of the important function they are performing; (which is no less than
sustaining the whole superstructure of human society,)
they are themselves influenced by so many other more immediate motives for their labour, that it is hardly worth
while to puzzle one's brain, to establish the relative importance of the two kinds of labour.

There is another distinction vastly more important to
have established. The distinction between the labour that
tends to preserve, and that which tends to corrupt the
morals of society. Let political economists cease their
disputes about productive and unproductive labour, and
employ their talents in ascertaining what kinds of labour
have a moral, and what an immoral tendency, and then
they may render some service to mankind.

Whether one species of labour is more productive to

national wealth than another, depends entirely upon the circumstances of each particular nation. At one period agricultural labour may be the most productive, at another manufacturing labour, nor can there be any rules laid down before hand, for ascertaining whether the one or the other kind will be most productive.

Suppose the comforts of life not taken into the definition of national wealth, and it be defined a capacity for acquiring the necessaries of life alone. Even according to this definition, it would not, by any means follow, that manufacturing labour was unproductive of national wealth. According to this definition, manufacturers for home consumption would be unproductive labourers; but manufacturers for foreign consumption would not. So far as national wealth is concerned, a nation may as well export manufactures as provisions—it may as well purchase provisions, by exporting manufactures, as to raise those provisions by agriculture. If the same quantity of labour, which would be necessary to raise a hundred thousand bushels of wheat, by being bestowed on manufactures, could always procure the same quantity of wheat from foreign countries, what difference can it make, so far as national wealth is concerned, in which way the labour is employed? It may make a material difference, as to the moral character of the people, and the political safety of the nation; and for these reasons, agricultural labour may be preferable, though not on the score of its being more productive or profitable.

As a general rule, manufacturing labour is the most profitable, because it requires the most skill. A man can, ordinarily, earn more corn in a day, by spinning and weaving, than by ploughing, notwithstanding all that economists may say of the unproductiveness of manufacturing labour: and if an individual can do this, so may a nation.

So long as the comforts and luxuries of life constitute a portion of our natural or artificial wants, so long will every species of labour which contributes to their gratification, be productive; and as a general rule, the more refined the luxury, and the more unnecessary the gratification, the better will the labour be paid which produces it.—Hence, stage-players, and mountebanks, are always better paid than the cultivators of the soil,—dancing masters and fiddlers, better paid than teachers of the sciences. In a rude and unsophisticated state of society, one would naturally enough suppose, that dancing and stage playing were a species of labour not very well adapted to the production of corn; but in this refined age, they are found to be more productive of that article than turning up the virgin soil.*

But although it is perfectly immaterial, so far as national wealth is concerned, whether the people raise their own corn by cultivating the earth, or whether they manufacture toys and trinkets to purchase it with, so long as toys and trinkets will purchase it; yet, in regard to national security and independence, there is a vast difference between the two modes.—A nation that raises its own corn, need not fear having its supplies cut off. A nation that depends on purchasing it from foreign nations, by a sale of its manufactures, is liable to two very probable, and very fatal contingencies—that of having its supplies interrupted by foreign hostility, and that of losing the market for its manufactures, which would deprive it of the means of purchasing corn. Their occupation is liable to be usurped or interfered with, by others.

Such is, in some measure, the present predicament of England. For the last twenty-five years, she has not only enjoyed the benefit of her colonial monopoly, but also a monopoly to a great extent, of the trade with the whole

* The labour of the fiddler, and stage-player produces a comfort of life, real or imaginary, to the audience, who are the consumers, and who pay for it, as much as labour bestowed in manufacturing lace, produces a comfort of life to those who wear or consume the lace. In both cases, the labour produces a comfort of life to the consumer, and the price paid for the labour, is a certain portion of the necessaries of life. This kind of labour, therefore, produces the comforts of life to the consumer, and the necessaries to the producer, strange result! but no more strange than true.

world, which she has supplied with her manufactures. A large portion of her population have come to depend on their manufacturing labour, for their support—they procure their bread by spinning, and not by ploughing. The market for their manufactures has become very much circumscribed, and they are thrown out of employment—their occupation is gone; and although there may be, or might be, corn enough raised in England, for the support of all her inhabitants, yet these people who have been thrown out of employment by the change of the times—by the curtailment of their market, have got nothing, and can get nothing to buy with.

The last twenty-five years has been a period of great prosperity in England, in consequence of her extensive commerce—the necessaries and comforts of life were abundant, and easily procured, because the whole product of her labour was annually consumed—because there was no surplus of produce above consumption. The consequence has been, a most rapid increase of population, for an old country; and now, when the political storm has subsided, and things return to their natural state—when she no longer enjoys a monopoly of the commerce of the world, she finds herself encumbered with a surplus population; not a population which the island is incapable of supporting, and supplying with the necessaries and comforts of life, but one which it cannot with comfort support under present circumstances; with their present pursuits, manners, customs, and habits. As soon as these can be changed to suit the times, they can all live as comfortably as the unequal division of property, and form of government, will admit of; but before this can be done, there must be much suffering.

The same causes which have produced the present embarrassment and distress in England, have produced a similar effect, though in a less degree in this country. The stagnation of business has produced an inordinate degree of national wealth, according to the theories of our profound political economists.—It has produced a great accumulation of the surplus of produce above consumption.

The body politic is overwhelmed with a quantity of the product of labour, which it cannot consume.

There is, however, this material difference between the effects which the same causes have produced in this country, and in England. The difference arises from the different kinds of labour most prevalent in the two countries. The exports of England consist, principally, of the comforts of life, or the product of manufacturing labour —the exports of the United States, consist of the necessaries of life, or the product of agricultural labour. Destroying the market for these different kinds of products, causes the same mercantile embarrassment and distress, but it does not cause the same distress to the people. The commercial embarrassments are probably as great in this country, as in England, because commercial prosperity depends on the facility with which one commodity can be exchanged for another, and not on the kind of commodities exchanged. But a surplus of the product of agricultural labour has a very different effect upon the labourers who produce it, from what a surplus of the product of manufacturing labour, has upon those by whose labour it is produced. The latter is useless, unless it can be sold—the former may be eaten and will sustain life. As a general rule manufactures are as useless to those whose labour produces them, as gold and silver would have been to Robinson Crusoe. This is not the case with the surplus of agricultural labour—if it cannot be sold or exchanged, it can be eaten. We may be obliged to forego some of the comforts of life, according to our refined notions, but we are not obliged to forego life itself.

We are very much in the habit of confounding embarrassments in trade and commerce, with national distress. We are perpetually mistaking a few prominent noisy individuals in a nation, for the nation itself. There is a great stagnation in trade and commerce—the facility of exchanging commodities is interrupted, or constrained, and the merchants make a great outcry, which we mistake for the moanings of national distress. This however is not always the case. Mercantile distress may be the distress of the nation, or it may not. When the surplus produce which the merchants cannot dispose of, consists of manufactures or the comforts of life, then the embarrassment and distress of the merchants will be the distress of the nation—But when that surplus consists of the necessaries of life, then the distress of the merchants will not be the distress of the nation. National distress consists in the want of the necessaries of life. Pauperism and starvation are the signs of national distress. But half the merchants in the country may fail, and still pauperism not prevail to any uncommon extent. Commercial embarrassment of itself, is not a species of distress which touches life. Merchants are not a class of people, likely to want the necessaries of life, whatever may be the extent of their embarrassments. National distress must always be sought for among the labouring poor—Distress among them, is a distress which touches life.

Whether agricultural or manufacturing labour will be most productive of national wealth, for the time being, depends entirely on accidental, arbitrary circumstances, which no political economist can foresee. It would have been impossible, in 1814, to have told whether in 1818, agricultural or manufacturing labour would be most productive of national wealth in England.

The demand, however, for agricultural labour, that is for the produce of it, is not liable to such fluctuations, as the demand for manufacturing labour, nor are the fluctuations when they happen, so fatal in their consequences. The former has, therefore, a great advantage over the latter, as regards national security and independence.

It has also a great advantage as to its moral effect upon the people. Agriculturists are a superior class of men to manufacturers. They enjoy more vigorous health, and possess more personal courage. They have more elevated and liberal minds. It is much more congenial to man's nature; to be abroad in the fields, breathing a pure air, and admiring the works of creation, and the beauties of nature, than to be confined in the unwholesome, impure air of a workshop. The former softens the heart and liberalizes the mind—the latter hardens the heart, contracts the mind, and corrupts the passions.

It does not, however, follow that agricultural labour should be encouraged and patronized by the government, and manufacturing labour neglected, or discouraged. Universal experience proves, that the two species of labour, are a mutual advantage to each other, and that those nations are the most flourishing and prosperous, where a proper medium is preserved between them. They produce a re-action upon each other, and in this way, infuse into the body politic, a much greater degree of energy, than would otherwise be produced. To encourage manufactures, is often the most effectual mode of encouraging agriculture. Agriculture is never carried to so great a degree of perfection, in countries, exclusively agricultural, as in countries, where agriculture and manufactures flourish together, and receive the equal protection and encouragement of the government. This is manifest not only from experience, but also from the very nature of things.—Nature, when she planted in the breast of man a desire for the comforts of life, intended this desire, should be gratified upon the same terms and conditions, that his desire for the necessaries of life was to be gratified. It is, therefore, in pursuance of the dictate of nature, that man labours for the comforts of life! This is the provision of nature for raising man from a state of savageism to civilization. If nature had not planted in the breast of man, a desire for the comforts and luxuries of life, the arts and sciences would never have been cultivated. Had such been the case, manufacturing labour would have been unproductive, and there would have been none of it; there would have been no employment for man, but agriculture, hunting, and fishing. With human nature thus modified, mankind would always have remained in a state of barbarism; for there could have been no motive for the exertion of his faculties, for any other purpose, than to obtain the necessaries of life. Every man must have provided his own food by his own labour; for there would have been nothing which he would give in exchange for it.

Among a people whose wants are confined to the necessaries of life, as is almost entirely the case with all savage nations, it is notorious that agriculture is never carried to any degree of perfection. Our industry is always in proportion to our wants, or to our motives to labour; and where his wants are confined to the mere necessaries of life, man is an indolent, slothful animal. But the case is entirely changed when the comforts and luxuries of life, come to constitute a portion of his wants. Skill in the arts, then becomes a means of acquiring food; manufactures come to have a value; manufacturing labour becomes productive; its product stimulates the agriculturist to greater exertion; a re-action is produced; the wilderness is converted into a fruitful field; and savage man into the polished enlightened citizen.

In this way artisans and manufacturers perform their full share, in multiplying the fruits of the earth, and in ameliorating the condition of man; not, however, by accumulating the surplus product of labour, but by consuming it.

That is the best regulated community, where agriculture and manufacturing labour, bear a due proportion to each other; and when one preponderates in too great a degree, as is often the case, it becomes the duty of the government, to interpose and restore the equilibrium, by encouraging and protecting the other.

In England, manufactures have acquired too great a preponderance, either from the particular circumstances of the times, or from an unwise interposition of the government in their behalf. In the United States agriculture has acquired too great a preponderance, from the particular situation of our country, and from the unwonted demand for the product of agriculture, in consequence of the unexampled condition of the world, for the last thirty years. In both cases ought the government to interpose, to restore that just equilibrium, so essential to the health of the body politic, and so conducive to national prosperity and wealth.

The principal, or at least one of the principal objects

of government, should be to preserve the body politic, from the disease of *accumulation*, not by stifling industry, or preventing production, (for that would be like a physician, who should think to preserve the vigour of the human body, by constant depletion,) but by making effectual provision for the complete consumption, within the time which nature dictates, of the whole product of industry.

The time dictated by nature for this consumption, is the year following the production. It matters not by whom this product is consumed, provided it be but consumed. It may be consumed at home or abroad; by one nation or another, but consumed it must be, or the nation will not remain in vigorous health, any more than a man would, who had a quantity of food on his stomach, which he could not digest.

If all the manufactures are worn out, and all the provisions are eaten up clean, annually; we shall have no occasion to trouble ourselves about their value, or the price they would sell for; nor any occasion to inquire whether money is plenty or scarce; whether interest is high or low; whether the circulating medium be paper or gold; whether the national debt be great or small; or, whether one kind of labour be more productive than another; we may be very sure whatever be the case in these other respects, that in the present condition of the civilized world, the nation will be in a prosperous and flourishing condition.

It may, perhaps, be said that among all savage people the annual product of their labour is always consumed as soon as obtained, and that with them there is never any accumulation, and yet they suffer all the horrors of poverty and want. This is admitted, and it is also further admitted, that if this cannot be accounted for, upon principles consistent with the above doctrine, then the doctrine is erroneous.

What then are the points of contact or resemblance, between a horde of savages, and a nation of civilized men? For if there be no resemblance between the two, we cannot reason correctly from one to the other.

If the wants of a nation of civilized men, and the mode

of supplying those wants, are entirely different, from the wants of a tribe of savages, and their mode of supplying them, then the principles which apply to, and govern one, will not apply to, and govern the other.

In the first place, the wants of savages consist entirely of the necessaries of life; they know nothing of the arts and sciences; nor do they desire, or if they desire, they know not how to procure any of those articles which we denominate the comforts of life; manufacturing labour is altogether unknown to them. If they can get wherewith to satisfy hunger, it is all they expect of the product of labour; and their natural indolence and sloth is so great, that they never procure or enjoy an abundance, even of food. Poverty and want is the inevitable lot of all savages.

Very different are the wants of civilized man. They are innumerable, and insatiable. The necessaries of life, constitute a very small portion of them. The wants of the humblest individual, in civil life, are so numerous, that the labour of himself could supply but a very small portion of them. Could any one man build the house he lives in, and prepare the materials of which it is built? Could he make the furniture for it? Could he make even the clothes, which he considers necessary to his comfort? What man is there in civil society, who would not think himself in a deplorable state of poverty, if his articles of food were limited to the production of his own labour? If he could obtain no greater variety than that, which contents the savage?

But great as is the difference between the wants of the savage and the citizen; the difference between the manner in which they are supplied, is still greater. This difference places them in such totally different circumstances, that the principles which govern the one cannot govern the other.

The savage supplies all his wants by his own labour. He depends on the labour of others for no part of them. His *individuality* is in this respect as complete as if he did not belong to any nation or tribe. Unless he hunts or fishes for himself, he goes without food. In such a state of things, it is very manifest, that no evil consequences can arise from accumulation. He can accumulate nothing but the necessaries of life, the benefit of which he is to enjoy himself, and if he fails to accumulate, he suffers the consequence of a dearth, famine, or other casuality.

The case, however, is very different with a man in civil society. Not one in five hundred of his wants is, or can be supplied by his own labour. He depends on the labour of others, perhaps, for all the necessaries of life, and, perhaps, for ninety-nine in a hundred of the comforts of life, and these he probably depends on being able to procure, by his own labour, on an article, which is to him, neither a necessary or a comfort of life. If then, the article accumulates upon his hands, and he cannot sell or exchange it for the necessaries of life, he must starve, or live upon the bounty of others. What is true of one individual, is true of thousands of others, and of a nation.

The most prosperous times for this individual, is when the product of his labour is consumed as fast as it is produced. As soon as the demand for it slakens, it begins to accumulate on his hands, and pinch him with distress; or in order to prevent its accumulation, (the evil consequences of which, he is fully aware of, in spite of all the theories of political economists,) he perhaps dismisses some of his workmen, and thus throws the evil from his own shoulders, upon theirs. This causes, if not an accumulation of the commodity itself, upon the hands of the labourers, at least an "accumulation of superfluous labour,"* (another definition of national wealth) upon their hands, equally as destructive in its consequences, as the accumulation of the commodity itself. Thus, this evil, like all others, in human society, descends according to the laws of gravitation, from the higher to the lower grades of society, and with a force accumulated, in proportion to the height from which it descends.

* This might, with more propriety, be called superfluous idleness; and indeed, I cannot imagine what is meant by an "accumulation of superfluous labour," unless it is an accumulation of idleness.

There is, to be sure, no danger that a nation will either starve, or be compelled to live upon charity.—As there is no such thing as national wealth, in the absolute sense of the word, neither is there absolute national poverty. Wealth, and poverty, are comparative expressions, when applied to a nation, and the degree depends upon the number, which those who suffer want, bear to those who enjoy a competency. The parallel, therefore, between an individual and a nation, is not complete, but it is sufficiently so, to show the effect of accumulation on national wealth and happiness.

Although it is a matter of indifference, by whom the annual product of labour is consumed, provided there is a certainty that it always will be consumed, yet it is all-important to guard against probable, or even possible contingencies, which may affect this certainty of consumption. For this reason, domestic, is preferable to foreign consumption,—the latter, depending in some measure on the will of others—the former, on the nation's own will alone. Home consumption, and a home market, is, therefore, always to be preferred to a foreign one.

This affords a solution of that much vexed and long agitated question of free trade. It is not my intention to discuss that question at present it will be the subject of a future chapter. I will, however, here remark, that the true principles upon which that question ought to be settled, have never yet been developed. The question, whether individuals should be permitted to sell, where they can sell *dearest*, and buy, where they can buy *cheapest*, ought not to be decided upon the narrow, contemptible principles of private interests, but upon the more expanded and noble principles of public interests. Public and private interests, are often directly at variance; but when at variance, I presume, it is not to be made a question, which ought to prevail.

It is the duty of legislators, to foresee the public evil consequences of any particular policy, and guard against them. Private citizens can only be expected to be wise for themselves—it is not their duty to look after the public interests—they are not the conservators of national wealth. This belongs to the department of legislation.

If, from particular circumstances, from a state of war, or a state of peace, one species of industry is more profitable than another, it must be expected that individuals will embark in it, without any regard to the evil consequences it may produce to succeeding generations; but it does not become a legislator, either to be blind to their consequences, or not to guard against them.

Hitherto, individuals have found it extremely profitable to import slaves from Africa, to cultivate their lands in America; and in the earlier periods of this accursed traffic, when there was a scarcity of labourers in America, it was no doubt, greatly conducive both to public and private wealth. This being the case, and admitting that there was no injustice, or moral iniquity in the trade, it could not have been expected of individuals to forego the advantages to themselves, on account of the pernicious effects of slavery, upon future generations. No man can be expected to forego a present advantage to himself, provided there is no immorality in the enjoyment of it, upon the ground that it may be prejudicial to posterity. He may have no posterity, or if he has, their interests at the distance of two or three generations, is too remote to influence his conduct. The influence of self interest on human conduct, like the laws of gravitation, is in the inverse compound ratio of distance and quantity.

Legislators, however, are not permitted to take such limited, short-sighted views of things—they are placed on a more elevated station—they move in a higher sphere— they are traitors to their high trust, if they do not look to the future, as well as the present—they are in one sense, (though, in a very humble one,) the vicegerents of God on earth; and, as he regulates and governs the world, by the laws of eternal justice and wisdom, in regard to the future, as well as the present; by the same laws, ought legislators to regulate and govern the nations of the earth, over whom they preside. Even, according to the laws of self interest, the remoteness of the interests of future generations, should be counterbalanced by the magnitude of those interests.

Had the legislators of former ages been as just and as wise as they ought to have been, they would have foreseen the dreadful consequences of slavery to succeeding generations; and foreseeing them, it would have been their imperious duty (admitting slavery to be innocent in itself,) to have abolished the slave trade, and slavery. Had they done so, how much greater reason should we have had to bless their memory, than we now have?

It does not, however, follow, (as some have absurdly supposed,) that, because the legislators of those days, were not as wise, or as just as they should have been, or because they neglected their duty in not abolishing the slave trade, that those persons concerned in it were guiltless. Our forefathers are not exonerated from the guilt of carrying on the slave trade, upon the ground, that the English government permitted it. They were, on the contrary, guilty of the most atrocious crimes, against both God and man. They violated the law of God, written upon the heart of every human being. The nation, or state, as contradistinguished from the people, may not have been guilty, because it may not have had the power of offending, but the people themselves, were not the less guilty on that account.

What is true, as it respects the duty of government, in regard to the slave trade, so far as national interests alone are concerned, is true of every other measure, relating to national industry, which has a remote tendency to affect national wealth and prosperity. The true policy for every wise legislator is, to consider the nation immortal, and to legislate for it, as though it was to exist for ever; but, unfortunately, most legislators act as though they thought the nation as short lived as themselves; and, instead of adopting a policy, which looks prospectively to future generations and centuries, they adopt one which looks only to themselves, and the present race; and, too frequently, one which looks only to the interests of some particular individuals, or classes, in the community, instead of the interests of the nation.

Legislation should always be national, and not individual; instead of which, it is more frequently individual than national. This is not to be wondered at, when we consider what a mass of stupidity and ignorance is ordinarily selected for the administration of public affairs. It seems almost to have grown into a maxim, that "when a man is fit for nothing else, he is fit for a legislator,"—that neither talents, education, or experience, are at all necessary to qualify a man to take charge of a nation's interests.

Stimulants to National Industry

In the first part I have examined into the nature, source and cause of national wealth. I have dared to give a definition of national wealth different from any hitherto given. I have traced it to one simple *source*—the earth, and have endeavoured to show that it is the *effect* of one single *cause*—labour.

I have also presumed to controvert some of the most popular theories, on the subject of national wealth; and have endeavoured to prove that the prevailing one, which confounds national with individual wealth, and makes national wealth to consist in *accumulation*, of the surplus of production above consumption, is not only erroneous, absurd and impossible, in the nature of things, but that it is also positively pernicious; and that, consequently, every legislative act which proposes the accomplishment of such an object, must necessarily be detrimental to the community, in proportion as it is successful in attaining its object.

* * *

Most writers on political economy suppose, that war has a prejudicial effect on national wealth, by causing the consumption of the product of labour, and thereby preventing *accumulation*. This, however, so far from being prejudicial, is in fact one of the modes in which war promotes national wealth. In this way it affords a motive for industry, and a stimulus to greater exertion, and often causes an increased production, much greater than the war expenditure.

If a war expenditure be equal to ten millions, and, in consequence of the war, national industry is stimulated to such a degree, as to cause an increased production equal to fifteen millions, it will follow, that national wealth would be augmented five millions, in consequence of the war, according to the doctrine which makes national wealth to consist in accumulation of the surplus of production above consumption. Such an augmentation of the product, would increase national wealth, although the accumulation of it would prevent it from being as beneficial as it might be. A stream of water spread over a field, may have a happy effect in fertilizing it, but if suffered to accumulate upon it, it may produce quite a contrary effect. So increasing the product of labour will have the effect to augment national wealth; but in order to be most salutary in its effects, it must be annually consumed, and not suffered to accumulate.

War affords a stimulus to industry, by increasing the demand for labour. The consumption of the product of labour, by an army, prevents accumulation, and often causes a still greater increase of population. This explains the phenomenon of England's always increasing in wealth, during a period of war with the maritime nations of Europe. Having a naval superiority on the ocean, war gives her the commerce of the world, and in addition to the excitement and energy which war is calculated to infuse into the body politic, she enjoys the additional advantage of supplying the world, or the greater part of it, with her manufactures, which gives an impulse to the industry of the nation, and causes an increase of production, much greater than the war expenditure. War may, therefore, enrich England, while it impoverishes other nations.

It is altogether a mistaken notion to suppose, that the evils of war, consist in a useless consumption of the product of labour. If this was the only evil, war would be a very harmless amusement, or perhaps, a useful luxury. The

252 OF AMERICA, 1810-1824

devastation and desolation which it occasions, is of quite a different character. In this respect, it has an immediate and lasting effect to diminish national wealth. It has also an injurious effect on public morals, and therefore, tends to enervate and weaken the arm of industry. The influence of war also, is irregular and fluctuating in its operation. It furnishes, for a time, a strong demand for particular species of labour; but as war cannot be permanent or lasting, that demand may be suddenly withdrawn, and then distress is produced among those classes of people, to whom it had given employment. All fluctuations are unfavourable to national wealth and happiness—the more permanent the demand for any article, the better. This is one cause of the present distress in England, and this country. An unnatural demand had been occasioned, by war, for the product of the labour of the two countries. Peace has interrupted the demand, and thousands of people are thrown out of employment in consequence of it.

PUBLIC WORKS. The expenditure of public money, in public works, frequently has not a less invigorating influence than war, on national industry.

It is a common opinion, that all expenditures in public works, of all descriptions, whether in building fortifications, ships, making roads, canals, or any other permanent improvement, is a real tax upon the community, to the amount of money expended, and that the public can only be remunerated by the advantage it may derive from the use of the building or improvement.

According to this doctrine, it would follow, that if the fortification, ship, road, canal, or other improvement was, when finished, either useless, or should be destroyed, the expense of building would have been an actual drain upon the wealth of the nation, equal to the amount of money expended. Nothing can be more erroneous than such a doctrine.

If the fortification, or ship, should be destroyed, the day they were finished, it would not follow, that national wealth would have been lessened, in consequence of building them. Should a road, or canal, be perfectly useless, when finished, it would not follow, that the nation was the poorer for the money expended upon them. It would, undoubtedly, be better for the nation, that the fortification, or ship, should remain, when built, than be destroyed; nevertheless, it may be better for the nation to have built, than not to have built them, even though they should be immediately destroyed. The capacity of the nation, for acquiring the necessaries and comforts of life, may be none the less, for having built a ship, that sinks to the bottom of the ocean, as soon as she is off the stocks, or for having made a road, or canal, which are perfectly useless. If public money is to be expended, it is no doubt better that it should be expended prudently, than imprudently, profitably, than unprofitably; although it does not follow, that national wealth is lessened by its being expended either imprudently, or unprofitably. To those who have been in the habit of confounding national with individual wealth, and of considering national wealth to consist in the accumulation of superfluous labour, or in other words, of idleness, these may seem to be strange opinions, although they are perfectly reconcileable with those theories, which make national wealth to consist in the *surplus of production above consumption*, or in the accumulation of gold and silver.

If a canal is made with a nation's own means, there will be just as much money in the nation, after, as before it was made, or, as there would have been, had it not been made, even though it should be perfectly useless when made. The money may belong to different individuals, in consequence of making the canal, still it will belong to the nation; and so far as national wealth is concerned, even upon the principles of accumulation, it matters not, whether it be in the possession of A. or B.; and as there will be just as much money in the country after, as before building the useless canal, or road, or a ship that is sunk to the bottom of the ocean; so there may be just as much, or as great a *surplus of production above consumption*.

If the expenditure of the public money, in these public works, has caused an increase of the quantity of labour,

equal to what was required to build them, then the production will be just as great with, as it would have been
without building them. The number of people to be supported out of the product of labour, is not increased; and
therefore, the surplus, if any, will be as great in the one
case, as in the other. In this case, the expenditure affords
such a stimulus to national industry, as to augment the
quantity of labour, equal to what was required in the public works; and of course, there will not be a bushel less
of wheat, or a pound less of tobacco, cotton, or sugar, than
there would have been, but for the public works. It is
very clear, that this may be the case in all countries. There
is not a country on earth, that has not a large quantity of
surplus labour, or in other words, a large number of people, who are either idle the whole, or some part of their
time, and who might be employed in labour. As every nation, therefore, possesses a quantity of unexerted, or un-
expended labour, or power; a measure of government,
which shall have the effect to call this labour into action,
may expend it in the erection of public works, without
diminishing the annual product of labour, or preventing
as great an accumulation of the surplus of it, as would
have taken place, without such expenditure. Suppose the
United States was to employ ten thousand men during
the next ten years, at an annual expense of two millions
of dollars, in making roads, canals, and other permanent
improvements, in the country; is there any reason to suppose, that any portion of that labour would be withdrawn
from other branches of industry? The particular individuals, employed upon the public works, would, no doubt,
be withdrawn from other branches of industry; but others
would either take their places, or those who remained,
would labour more, so that the quantity of labour would
be as great as though none had been withdrawn. In other
words, a stimulus would be applied to the energies of the
nation, which would augment the quantity of labour equal
to what had been applied to the public works. The nation
is capable of exerting a power, annually, to a much greater
extent than this. Fifty thousand men might, no doubt, be

employed on public works, without lessening the annual product of labour a single pound. It is, therefore, possible for the nation to expend a large amount of labour and money, on public works, without, in other respects, diminishing public wealth.

But this is not all; the expenditure of labour and money, in this way, may be the means of augmenting public wealth, in other respects; it may cause a greater annual product of labour, than there would otherwise have been; it may make the necessaries and comforts of life still more abundant among the people. It may produce this effect, by infusing into the nation a degree of industry, which will more than supply the labour expended upon the public works. It may excite the energies of the nation, to a much greater degree than is required for the performance of this additional labour, and thereby augment the annual product of the necessaries and comforts of life.

Was the state of Maryland to expend a million of dollars, in making a canal from the Susquehanna to Baltimore, there is not the slightest reason to suppose, there would be a bushel less of wheat or corn, or a pound less of tobacco, raised in the state, in consequence of the labour bestowed upon the canal; nor would there be a dollar less money in the state. It might, on the contrary, be the means of augmenting the quantity of both. The canal then would cost the state, in reality, nothing. Public wealth would be just as great after the canal was made, exclusive of the canal itself, as it would have been, had the canal not been made, and the national wealth would, therefore, at all events, be augmented to an amount equal to the value* of the canal to the public.

If making the canal should cause an increase of industry equal only to half the labour bestowed on it, then public wealth would be augmented only to half the amount of the value of the canal to the public. In other words, if the labour expended in building the canal was equal to

* The word *value* is here used in its popular or figurative sense, for a canal can have no *value* in the technical sense of the word, any more than national territory.

the value of a million of dollars, and in consequence of building it, labour should be withdrawn from other branches of industry, to the value of half a million of dollars, which would cause a diminished product of wheat, corn, tobacco, &c. equal to half a million of dollars; then the actual expense to the state, of the canal, would be half a million of dollars.

If then, the real value of the canal, to the state, when finished, should be only half a million of dollars, there would be nothing lost or gained, as it regards public wealth, by building it. But if the real value of the canal, to the state, should be seven hundred thousand dollars, then the state would have gained two hundred thousand. But should the canal be worth, to the state, a million and a half dollars, then there would be a gain of a million. Should the canal, however, be worth only three hundred thousand dollars, then there would be a loss of two hundred thousand; unless this loss should be counterbalanced by the greater habits of industry and skill, which the people would have acquired in consequence of the work, which would augment their capacity for acquiring the necessaries and comforts of life.

This is taking it for granted, that making the canal would withdraw a quantity of labour equal to half the quantity expended on the canal from other branches of industry; but upon the supposition that no labour would be withdrawn from other branches of industry, which would probably be the case; should the canal, when finished, be of no value to the state, still public wealth would not be diminished.

There is every reason to believe that the New-York canals will increase the quantum of industry, in the state, equal to the whole amount of labour bestowed upon them, and that the product of labour in agriculture, manufactures, and commerce, will be as great, as it would have been, had the canals not been built, so that in reality they will cause no drain on public wealth, even though they should be worth nothing to the state, when finished; and it is even more than probable, that these enterprises have infused into the body-politic, a degree of energy and industry, which will more than supply all the labour required to build the canals, and that there will be a greater product of labour in other branches of industry, in consequence of making them. The public wealth of the state will, therefore, be augmented, independent of the value of the canals.

The body-politic like the natural body is liable to fall into a state of comparative lethargy and torpor. It then becomes necessary to arouse its dormant energies, by administering stimulants. The expenditure of public money, in public works, will often produce this effect.

The Monroe Doctrine

Cultural nationalism, whetted by the War of 1812 and reflected in the arts and sciences, made its way into domestic policy with Henry Clay's American system of protective tariffs and internal improvements. John Quincy Adams would have paid for these internal improvements with the proceeds from the sale of western public lands. The counterpart of these developments in foreign policy was the Monroe Doctrine, of which Adams, then Monroe's Secretary of State, was the principal author. The most succinct statement of the Monroe Doctrine, however, came from the pen of Thomas Jefferson and is presented below. Of special interest today is his attitude toward Cuba in the context of the Monroe Doctrine.

SOURCE: *The Works of Thomas Jefferson*, edited by Paul Leicester Ford, 12 vols., Vol. XII, pp. 318–21. New York: G. P. Putnam's Sons, 1904–5.

To James Monroe

Monticello, October 24, 1823

Dear Sir,— The question presented by the letters you have sent me, is the most momentous which has ever been offered to my contemplation since that of Independence. That made us a nation, this sets our compass and points the course which we are to steer through the ocean of time opening on us. And never could we embark on it under circumstances more auspicious. Our first and fundamental maxim should be, never to entangle ourselves in the broils of Europe. Our second, never to suffer Europe to intermeddle with cis-Atlantic affairs. America, North, and South, has a set of interests distinct from those of Europe, and peculiarly her own. She should therefore have a system of her own, separate and apart from that of Europe. While the last is laboring to become the domicil of despotism, our endeavor should surely be, to make our hemisphere that of freedom. One nation, most of all, could disturb us in this pursuit; she now offers to lead, aid, and accompany us in it. By acceding to her proposition, we detach her from the bands, bring her mighty weight into the scale of free government, and emancipate a continent at one stroke, which might otherwise linger long in doubt and difficulty. Great Britain is the nation which can do us the most harm of any one, or all on earth; and with her on our side we need not fear the whole world. With her then, we should most sedulously cherish a cordial friendship; and nothing would tend more to knit our affections than to be fighting once more, side by side, in the same cause. Not that I would purchase even her amity at the price of taking part in her wars. But the war in which the present proposition might engage us, should that be its consequence, is not her war, but ours. Its object is to introduce and establish the American system, of keeping out of our land all foreign powers, of never permitting those of Europe to intermeddle with the affairs of our nations. It is to maintain our own principle, not to depart from it. And if, to facilitate this, we can effect a division in the body of the European powers, and draw over to our side its most powerful member, surely we should do it. But I am clearly of Mr. Canning's opinion, that it will prevent instead of provoking war. With Great Britain withdrawn from their scale and shifted into that of our two continents, all Europe combined would not undertake such a war. For how would they propose to get at either enemy without superior fleets? Nor is the occasion to be slighted which this proposition offers, of declaring our protest against the atrocious violations of the rights of nations, by the interference of any one in the internal affairs of another, so flagitiously begun by Bonaparte, and now continued by the equally lawless Alliance, calling itself Holy.

But we have first to ask ourselves a question. Do we wish to acquire to our own confederacy any one or more of the Spanish provinces? I candidly confess, that I have ever looked on Cuba as the most interesting addition which could ever be made to our system of States. The control which, with Florida Point, this island would give us over the Gulf of Mexico, and the countries and isthmus bordering on it, as well as all those whose waters flow into it, would fill up the measure of our political well-being. Yet, as I am sensible that this can never be obtained, even with her own consent, but by war; and its independence, which is our second interest (and especially its independence of England), can be secured without it, I have no hesitation in abandoning my first wish to future chances, and accepting its independence, with peace and the friendship of England, rather than its association, at the expense of war and her enmity.

I could honestly, therefore, join in the declaration proposed, that we aim not at the acquisition of any of those possessions, that we will not stand in the way of any amicable arrangement between them and the mother country; but that we will oppose, with all our means, the forcible interposition of any other power, as auxiliary, stipendiary, or under any other form or pretext, and most especially, their transfer to any power by conquest, cession, or acquisition in any other way. I should think it, therefore, advisable, that the Executive should encourage the British government to a continuance in the dispositions expressed in these letters, by an assurance of his concurrence with them as far as his authority goes; and that as it may lead to war, the declaration of which requires an act of Congress, the case shall be laid before them for consideration at their first meeting, and under the reasonable aspect in which it is seen by himself.

I have been so long weaned from political subjects, and have so long ceased to take any interest in them, that I am sensible I am not qualified to offer opinions on them worthy of any attention. But the question now proposed involves consequences so lasting, and effects so decisive of our future destinies, as to rekindle all the interest I have heretofore felt on such occasions, and to induce me to the hazard of opinions, which will prove only my wish to contribute still my mite towards anything which may be useful to our country. And praying you to accept it at only what it is worth, I add the assurance of my constant and affectionate friendship and respect.

DOCUMENT 50

American School Instruction

In spite of the importance which leaders like Thomas Jefferson attached to learning, the American Adam tended to be contemptuous of formal education, which he associated with European refinement. His limited outlook, reinforced by geographical isolation, a glorification of practical achievement, and the example of unlettered preachers who considered head-religion inferior to heart-religion, was often reflected in school instruction. Thomas Low Nichols (1815–1901), journalist and nutrition pioneer whose quarrels with convention resulted finally in his expatriation to England, describes below the content of education in a typical New Hampshire common school.

SOURCE: Thomas Low Nichols, *Forty Years of American Life*, pp. 62–63. London: 1864.

* * *

The education we got was solid enough in some respects, and very superficial in others. In arithmetic, geometry, surveying, mechanics, and such solid and practical matters, we were earnest students; but our geography was chiefly American, and the United States was larger than all the universe beside. In the same way our history was American history, brief but glorious. We despised monarchical countries and governments too thoroughly to care much about their histories; and if we studied them, it was that we might contrast their despotisms with our own free and happy institutions. We were taught every day and in every way that ours was the freest, the happiest, and soon to be the greatest and most powerful country in the world. This is the religious faith of every American. He learns it in his infancy, and he can never forget it. For all other countries he entertains sentiments varying from pity to hatred; they are the down-trodden despotisms of the old world. There is a certain admiration for France, and that respect for Russia which one great and growing power gives to another. But a genuine American does not think much of Europe anyhow.

How should we? Great Britain was the most powerful country of Europe, and had we not beaten her twice? One of our great lakes would drown the whole United Kingdom. And what could we think of a people who submitted to be governed by a hereditary aristocracy,—who did not own the land they worked on, and were not allowed to vote, who had not even guns, a great many of them?

Our education was adapted to intensify our self-esteem, and to make us believe that we were the most intelligent, the most enlightened, the freest, most Christian, and greatest people the sun ever shone upon. Ours was the model Government of the world; our institutions were the model institutions, our country the model Republic. I do not in the least exaggerate. We read it in our books and newspapers, heard it in sermons, speeches, and orations, thanked God for it in our prayers, and devoutly believed it always.

* * *

DOCUMENT 51

American School History

The following example of textbook writing went through at least three editions. Its Biblical quality is perhaps unusual but nonetheless indicative of the widespread influence of religion on national feeling in this period. Note especially the reference to Jefferson's mastodon (see doc. 43), the stress on the wilderness origin of American liberty and Jackson's triumph at New Orleans, and the poetic, almost Old Testament flavor of such phrases as "the green fields blushed." The main Biblical sources for such associations were prophetic and historical writings about the chosen people's restoration to an earthly paradise.

SOURCE: Gilbert J. Hunt, *The Historical Reader, Containing "The Late War between the United States and Great Britain . . ."* pp. 70–73, 208–9, 211. New York: 1819.

Sketches of the History of America.

1 THE voice of many years shall drop upon the children of men; and our children's children shall hearken unto it in the days to come.

2 The country of Columbia is a wide extended land, which reacheth from the north to the south more than eight thousand miles; and the breadth thereof is about three thousand.

3 Moreover, the name of the country was called after the name of a great man, who was born in a place called Genoa; being in Italy, on the sea-coast.

4 His name was Christopher, sur-named Columbus.

5 As the righteous man struggleth against wickedness, so did he against ignorance and stupidity.

6 Nevertheless it came to pass, in the fourteen hundred and ninety-second year of the Christain [*sic*] Era, that he crossed the waters of the mighty deep, a thing that had never been known among the sons of men.

7 And the place where he landed was an island in the sea, nigh unto the continent of Columbia, called San Salvador; which, being interpreted, signifieth a place of safety.

8 And the place was inhabited by wild savages, and they were naked.

9 Now when the people heard that Columbus had found a new land, they were astonished beyond measure, for it was many thousand miles off; moreover, some of them strove to rob him of the honor, and he was treated wrongfully.

10 But his name was lifted up above his enemies, and it shall not be lost.

11 Now the land of Columbia is a most plentiful land, yielding gold and silver, and brass and iron abundantly.

12 Likewise, all manner of creatures which are used for food, and herbs and fruits of the earth:

13 From the red cherry and the rosy peach of the north, to the lemon and the golden orange of the south.

14 And from the small insect that cheateth the microscopic eye, to the huge mammoth that once moved on the borders of the river Hudson, on the great river Ohio, and even down to the country of Patagonia in the south.

15 Now the height of a mammoth is about seven cubits and a half, and the length thereof fourteen cubits; and the bones thereof, being weighed, are more than thirty thousand shekels, and the length of the tusks is more than six cubits.

16 It is more wonderful than the elephant; and the

history thereof, is it not recorded in the book of Jefferson, the scribe?*

17 The fierce tiger and the spotted leopard dwell in the dark forests, and the swift-footed deer upon the mountains and high places.

18 Now the number of inhabitants that are spread over the whole continent, is more than a hundred million.

19 And the people of Columbia, who are independent of the tyrants of the earth, and who dwell between the great river which is called Mississippi in the south, and the province of Canada in the north, being numbered, are about ten thousand times ten thousand souls.*

20 The men are comely and noble, and cowardice hath forgot to light upon them: neither are they a superstitious people; they are peace-makers, they love the God of Israel, and worship him; and there are no idolaters amongst them.

21 The women are passing beautiful; they are like unto fresh lilies; their cheeks are like wild roses; their lips as a thread of scarlet; nature hath gifted them with Roman virtue and patriotism; and they have spread goodness with a plentiful hand.

22 Now it happened in times past, that the king of Britain had made war upon the people of Columbia, even forty years ago.

23 For the riches and prosperity of Columbia had become great, and the king coveted them.

24 And the war raged with the might of Britain, even in the heart of the land of Columbia, for about the space of seven years, when the army of Columbia became triumphant; neither could the power of Britain conquer the sons of liberty.

25 Accordingly, a part of those who remained of the armies of Britain returned home to the king, their master;

* Jefferson's Notes on Virginia.
* The last census, in 1810, stated the amount at about 8,000,000; the number may now probably be increased to 10,000,000.

but a great number refused to return, prefering a country whose mild laws are equally and righteously dispensed, and where the hard earnings of industry are not taken away by the tax-gatherer:

26 So there was peace throughout the United States, and a covenant made between the nations.

27 But the names of the wise men of the Great Sanhedrim in those days, and the names of those who fought hard in battle, and spilt their blood in the cause of liberty, are they not written in the books of the chronicles of those days?

28 Now the fatness of the land of Columbia bringeth people from all nations to dwell therein.

29 The people of Columbia use no persuasion; the sacred cause of LIBERTY IS THE STAR OF ATTRACTION; and the time shall come, when the eyes of all men shall be opened, and the earth shall rejoice.

30 Their laws are wholesome, for the people are the lawgivers, even as it was in the days of Cæsar; but they know no kings.

* * *

[The Battle of New Orleans]

9 And the army rested upon the plains of Mac Piardies, nigh unto the cypress swamp, being distant from the city about forty and eight furlongs.

10 And it was about the rising of the sun, when the battering-rams of the king began to utter their noises; and the sound thereof was terrible as the roaring of lions, or the voice of many thunders.

11 Moreover, they cast forth bombs, and Congreve rockets, weapons of destruction, which were not known in the days of Jehoshaphat.

12 Nevertheless, the soul of Jackson failed him not, neither was he dismayed, for he was entrenched round about; and when he raised his hand, he held every man's heart therein.

13 And Jackson spake, and said unto his captains of fifties, and his captains of hundreds, Fear not; we defend our lives and our liberty, and in that thing the Lord will not forsake us:

14 Therefore, let every man be upon his watch; and let the destroying engines now utter forth their thunders in abundance:

15 And ye cunning back-woodsmen, who have known only to hunt the squirrel, the wolf, and the deer, now pour forth your strength upon the mighty lion, that we may not be overcome.

16 And as the black dust cast upon a burning coal instantly mounteth into a flame, so was the spirit of the husbandmen of the back-woods of Columbia.

17 Now the brave men from Tennessee and Kentucky set their shining rifles at work, and the destroying engines began to vomit their thunders upon the servants of the king.

18 Twice did the host of Britain, in solid columns, come against the entrenchments of Jackson, and twice he drove them back.

19 Moreover, Daniel the brave, who had raised up defences upon the banks of the river, likewise let his engines loose upon them, and shot into the camp of the king.

20 And the men of Britain strove to scale the ramparts, and get into the strong hold of Jackson; but the husbandmen drove them back with great slaughter.

21 The fire and the smoke, and the deafening noise that sounded along the battlements, were tremendous, for more than the space of two hours, when the dreadful roarings ceased; for the warriors of the king fled in confusion.

22 But when the sulphureous vapor arose, behold! the battle-ground was covered with the slain and the wounded officers and soldiers of the kingdom of Great Britain!

23 Humanity shuddered at the awful scene, whilst the green fields blushed.

24 Seven hundred of the servants of the king were slain; and their whole loss that day was two thousand six hundred valiant men, who had fought under Wellington, the champion of England.

* * *

32 Moreover, Jackson was honored with great honor by the people throughout the land of Columbia; even the Great Sanhedrim were pleased with him, and exalted his name.

33 And the inhabitants of New Orleans were greatly rejoiced, and carried him through the streets of the city above the rest; and the virgins of Columbia strewed his path with roses.

34 For, lo! he had defended them from the violence of savages, who came in search of BEAUTY and BOOTY.

35 And when the wounded of the host of Britain were brought into the city, the fair daughters of Columbia took their fine linen and bound up the wounds of the poor, fainting officers and soldiers of the king, and sat bread and wine before them, to cheer their drooping spirits.

36 Now again were the servants of the king disappointed; for, as they were sent upon an evil, as well as a foolish errand, they expected not mercy.

37 And when they saw the goodness that was showered upon them, they said, Surely, ye are angels sent down from heaven, to heal the wounds inflicted by the folly of the nations!

38 And should we again be led on to battle against your country, with propositions to violate your happiness, our swords, as by magic shall be stayed, and drop harmless at the feet of VIRTUE and BEAUTY!

Cobb's Spelling Book

The preceding account of the Battle of New Orleans ended with a tribute to the virtuous daughters of Columbia who repaid evil with good. Spelling books were often equally moralistic and included moral fables as reading exercises. The great emphasis on morality, whether in school or workshop (see doc. 74) stemmed not only from the Protestant religious heritage of the citizens, but also from their self-righteous assumption of the superiority of their unsullied, natural, uncivilized world over the supposed corruption of civilized Europe. Indeed, this polar contrast was the essence of the Protestant mission in the New World.

The Cobb spelling book made it clear, however, that natural virtue was not to be confused with vulgar vernacular pronunciations. Education was, after all, a civilizing process, a pathway to success and social respectability. Noah Webster (1758–1843), author of the most popular spelling book and also of the great American dictionary which incorporated many native usages, was better able to reconcile the civilizing mission with the standard of nature. A sample page from his spelling book appears in the succeeding document.

SOURCE: Lyman Cobb, *Cobb's Spelling Book, Being a Just Standard for Pronouncing the English Language*, pp. 143, 164–65. Albany, N.Y.: 1828.

The following chapter is composed of words which are generally pronounced in an *improper* and *vulgar* manner, even by many who *profess* to be *correct* speakers.

Note.—As the words in the following chapter are contained in the preceding chapters, and the *proper* pronounciation of them given, I have only given the *vulgar* pronounciation of them in this chapter.

Proper.	Vulgar.	Proper.	Vulgar.
	1		4
Boil	bile	clinch	klensh
broil	brile	creek	krik
brooch	brotshe	cringe	skrinj
char	tshore	curse	kuss
chives	sivez	dint	dent
chine	tshime	far	fur
cloy	kli	film	felm
drain	dreen	fleam	flem
edge	aje	get	git
ewe	yo	girth	gert
groin	grine	gripe	grip
hoist	histe	harsh	hash
jest	jeest	hearth	hurth or hath
join	jine	hiss	siss
joint	jinte	home	hum
joist	jiste	hoof	huff
loin	line	just	jest
loo	lu	lid	led
milc	mild	marsh	mash
oil	ile	nape	nap
peep	peek	pith	peth

*   *   *

An Address to Youthful Females

Listen, fair daughter of innocence, to the instructions of prudence, and let the precepts of truth sink deep into thy heart; so shall the charms of thy mind add lustre to the elegance of thy form; and thy beauty, like the rose it resembles, shall retain its sweetness when its bloom is withered.

It is a melancholy truth, that *man* too often prostitutes his boasted faculties to the destruction of female happiness. How necessary, then, to fortify your minds against the attacks of such vile seducers! Blemishes in female characters seldom are effaced. Not so with man. He tarnishes his name and brightens it again.

But if *woman* chance to swerve from the strictest rules of virtue,

> "Ruin ensues, reproach and endless shame
> "And *one* false step forever blasts her fame.
> "In vain with tears the loss she may deplore,
> "In vain look back to what she was before,
> "She sets, like stars that fall, to rise no more."

Remember thou art made man's reasonable companion, not the slave of his passions. The end of thy being is to assist him in the toils of life, to sooth him with thy tenderness, and to recompense his care with soft endearments. . . .

Happy is the man whose life is blessed with such a partner; happy is the child who calls her mother.

That such may be thy happy state, fair daughter of America, listen to the directions of wisdom, and regulate thy heart and life by the principles of piety and virtue.

DOCUMENT 53

The American Spelling Book

The polar tension between America and Europe had a central place in the thinking of Noah Webster, as the very name of his spelling book implies. In a newspaper advertisement of 1828 giving notice of the completion of his dictionary, he mentions a visit to England, partly "to ascertain the real state of the language." "English dictionaries," he continues, "are all, half a century behind the state of science," and he hopes "that his fellow citizens will be furnished with something better in the one which he is about to publish." He notes, finally, that "not less than 7 *millions* of copies of his Spelling Book have been sold."

The reforming zeal which inspired Webster's dictionary is also apparent in his spelling book. Here it takes the form of a moral fable. The fable itself is expressed through dialogue which is more or less vernacular, as is the crude woodcut which illustrates it, while the tidy moral appended to the end smacks of gentility.

SOURCE: Noah Webster, *The American Spelling Book*, p. 83. Albany: 1808.

FABLE I.

Of the Boy that stole Apples.

AN old Man found a rude Boy upon one of his trees stealing Apples, and desired him to come down; but the young Sauce-box told him plainly he would not. Won't you? said the old Man, then I will fetch you down; so he pulled up some tufts of Grass, and threw at him; but this only made the Youngster laugh, to think the old Man should pretend to beat him down from the tree with grass only.

Well, well, said the old Man, if neither words nor grass will do, I must try what virtue there is in Stones; so the old man pelted him heartily with stones; which soon made the young Chap hasten down from the tree and beg the old Man's pardon.

MORAL.

If good words and gentle means will not reclaim the wicked, they must be dealt with in a more severe manner.

DOCUMENT 54

The National Government in Higher Education

Although George Washington had left money in his will for the founding of a national university, although every administration from Washington to John Quincy Adams supported the idea of a national university, although a number of proposals envisaged public land grants for the endowment of state universities, although the nation was smarting from foreign criticism of its cultural backwardness and such prominent leaders as Jefferson in Virginia and De Witt Clinton in New York were urging that the very survival of democratic government was bound up with education, the federal government did almost nothing.

The following documents will suggest other reasons besides anti-intellectual prejudices for its failure to act in this period, reasons related to the westward expansion of capitalistic enterprise and to the individualistic philosophy enunciated in 1819 in the Dartmouth College case (see doc. 27) as well as in the various vetoes of bills for internal improvements. But individualistic enterprise was itself anti-intellectual in spirit. When the federal government finally acted in 1862 to provide land grants to the states, the emphasis was upon practical, utilitarian education.

SOURCES: *Annals of Congress*, 14th Congress, 1st Session, pp. 1031–32. Washington: 1856. *American State Papers*, 38 vols., Vol. III (*Public Lands*), p. 363. Washington: 1833–61.

A Bill for the Establishment of a National University, 1816

Be it enacted, by the Senate and House of Representatives of the United States of America in Congress as-

sembled, That the President of the United States be, and he is hereby, authorized to cause to be erected, on such site within the District of Columbia as he shall select, the buildings necessary for a National University; and, for defraying the expense thereof, the sum of ––– thousand dollars is hereby appropriated, to be paid out of any money in the Treasury of the United States not otherwise appropriated by law.

Sec. 2. And be it further enacted, That the President of the United States be, and he is hereby, authorized and required to cause to be surveyed and laid into building lots the whole, or such parts as he may think proper, of the ground reserved for the use of the United States, in the City of Washington; and to cause the same to be sold, at such times and places, and in such proportions, and under such regulations as he shall prescribe; and the proceeds thereof, after defraying the charges of survey and sale, to be invested in such stocks or public securities as shall by him be deemed most advisable; and the same, when so invested, and the dividends thereon arising, shall constitute a fund for the support of a National University.

Sec. 3. And be it further enacted, That the President of the United States be, and he is hereby, requested to cause to be prepared and laid before Congress, at its next session, a plan for the regulation and government of the said university.

Congressional Objections to the Proposal to Grant Public Lands for the Endowment of State Universities, 1819

Mr. Poindexter, from the Committee on Public Lands, to whom was referred a resolution instructing said committee to inquire into the expediency of appropriating one hundred thousand acres of land to each State, for the endowment of a university in each State, reported:

That they are fully impressed with the propriety and importance of giving every encouragement and facility to the promotion of learning, and the diffusion of knowledge over the United States, which can be done without a violation of the principle of the constitution, and the system of policy heretofore adopted for the advancement of the general welfare. The proposition under consideration is, whether it be or be not expedient to authorize a grant of one hundred thousand acres of land to each State in the Union, making in the whole two million three hundred thousand acres, to be vested in bodies corporate, created by the several States having the care and management of their respective universities. Your committee have no specific knowledge of the necessity which exists for this appropriation, in reference to any particular State whose resources may not be adequate to the support of literary institutions, as no petitions or memorials have been referred to them on the subject. In the absence of these it is fair to presume that the internal wealth and industry of the population, composing the several States, have been found sufficient to answer all the purposes of public education and instruction, so far as they have deemed it prudent and necessary to apply the means they possess to those objects. But if the aid of the General Government should, at any time, be required to enable a particular State, or every member of the Union, to carry into effect a liberal and enlarged system of education, suited to the views, capacities, and circumstances, of all classes of society; and if it should be thought wise and constitutional to extend to them the national bounty, the donation of extensive tracts of lands in the unappropriated Territories of the United States appears to your committee to be the most exceptionable form in which the requisite assistance could be granted. To invest twenty-three corporations, acting under State authority, with a fee simple estate in two million three hundred thousand acres of land, to be located in the Western States and Territories, would put it in their power to impede the settlement of that section of the Union by withholding these lands from market; to interfere with the general regulations now in force for the disposal of the public lands; to divide settlements which would otherwise be contiguous; and, consequently, to lessen the value of the lands offered for sale by the United States in the neighborhood of these large grants, which may remain unoccupied for any length of time, at the discretion of the Legislature of the State to which the donation is made. Your committee are of opinion that, besides these strong objections to the donations proposed in the resolutions submitted to their consideration, it does not comport with sound policy, or the nature of our republican institutions, to grant monopolies of large and extensive tracts of the public domain, either to individuals or bodies corporate. The lands of the United States ought, as far as practicable, to be distributed in small quantities among the great body of the people for agricultural purposes; and this principle ought in no instance to be violated, where the grantee is exempted from the payment of a valuable consideration to the Government. Your committee are sensible that it may be found necessary and useful, for the promotion of learning in this growing republic, either to endow a national university, or to extend its benevolence in a reasonable and proper proportion to individual States; but, in either case, they are of opinion that the requisite aid should be given in money and not in the mode pointed out in the resolution referred to them. They, therefore, recommend the following resolution to the House: *Resolved*, That it is inexpedient to grant to each State one hundred thousand acres of land for the endowment of a university in each State.

DOCUMENT 55

(PLATE 26)

A *View of the University of Virginia*

The national government, beginning with the state of Ohio in 1802, granted two townships to each new Western state for a university; yet by 1860 there were only 17 state universities out of a total of 246 institutions of higher learning. The only state university founded during the period surveyed by this volume, the University of Virginia, was conceived and brought to fruition by Thomas Jefferson. Among the more important new private institutions were Amherst College (1821), Colby College (1813), George Washington University (1821), Hamilton College (1812), Kenyon College (1824), Norwich Military Academy (1819), Rensselaer Polytechnic Institute (1824), and Trinity College (1823).

This lithograph of the University of Virginia stresses the arcadian classicism of its architecture and rural setting. One would little suspect that its curriculum was one of the most advanced in the nation. The artist, moreover, has exaggerated the size of the Rotunda, suggested by Benjamin Latrobe, who felt that Jefferson's original rectangular plan was too uniform and needed a dominant building. The formalistic purism of Jefferson is also seen in his modeling of the professors' houses after the various classic orders.

DOCUMENT 56

(PLATE 27)

A Comparable View of Lowell Factory Town

In spite of Jefferson's formalism, it did not disturb him, as a recent critic has observed, "to hang a practical balcony from the center of the columns in an otherwise classical facade." This dichotomy between the practical man and idealist is also sensed in those who projected the factory town at Lowell, Massachusetts, at about the same time as the University of Virginia. They tried to recreate in their factory town an idyllic village life. They forbade grog shops, taverns, and other corrupting city resorts. They imported virtuous farm girls for operatives and sheltered them in attractive boarding houses, sent them to school and church, and chaperoned their conduct.

The town, like the mill which dominates it, was built after rational principles; yet it faces two different ways. The dwelling units reflect sharp social and class divisions (see docs. 75–78): the unskilled operatives lived in late colonial cubes, for instance, while the agent-executive occupied a high-Georgian block with a Greek facade. The individualistic New England architecture conflicts with the company group and both with the baroque of the central plaza, the English gothic church tower, and the alternating double wooden houses and quadruple brick houses. Another way of looking at this company town, however, is to see that it represented a new "kingdom of force" in American life, the machine, which was already beginning to influence traditional patterns of education in the direction of the practical and scientific, as evidenced in the founding of Rensselaer Polytechnic Institute.

Document 57

Thomas Jefferson and the University of Virginia

Thomas Jefferson thought of the University of Virginia, founded in 1819, as a substitute for a national university. His idealism was embodied not only in its architecture (see doc. 55), but also in such innovations as an inclosed student-faculty community, scientific instruction, a provision for free electives, and a carefully integrated system of education for the whole state. The states, however, were not much more vigorous in the support of education than the federal government, for Virginia refused to implement the proposal for a statewide system of graduated schools and De Witt Clinton's experiment with state subsidies and Lancasterian reforms was allowed to languish in New York after his retirement.

The following glimpse of Jefferson and the University of Virginia derives from Jefferson's friendship with George Ticknor (1791–1871), author and educator, who introduced the thorough German methods of study into the United States. Ironically, his attempt at Harvard to establish an elective system like Jefferson's failed, except in his own department of French and Spanish. William H. Prescott (1796–1859), to whom he describes below Jefferson's educational reforms, was just beginning his career as a historian of Spanish conquest.

SOURCE: *Life, Letters, and Journals of George Ticknor*, 2 vols. Vol. I, pp. 300–3, 348–49. Boston: 1876.

FROM MR. JEFFERSON.
POPLAR FOREST, near LYNCHBURG, November 25, 1817.

* * *

I am now entirely absorbed in endeavors to effect the establishment of a general system of education in my native State, on the triple basis: 1. of elementary schools which shall give to the children of every citizen, gratis, competent instruction in reading, writing, common arithmetic, and general geography; 2. Collegiate institutions for ancient and modern languages, for higher instruction in arithmetic, geography, and history, placing, for these purposes, a college within a day's ride of every inhabitant of the State, and adding a provision for the full education, at the public expense, of select subjects from among the children of the poor, who shall have exhibited at the elementary schools the most prominent indications of aptness, of judgment, and correct disposition; 3. A university, in which all the branches of science deemed useful at this day, shall be taught in their highest degree. This would probably require ten or twelve professors, for most of whom we shall be obliged to apply to Europe, and most likely to Edinburgh, because of the greater advantage the students will receive from communications made in their native language. This last establishment will probably be within a mile of Charlottesville, and four from Monticello, if the system should be adopted at all by our Legislature, who meet within a week from this time. My hopes, however, are kept in check by the ordinary character of our State legislatures, the members of which do not generally possess information enough to perceive the important truths, that knowledge is power, that knowledge is safety, and that knowledge is happiness. In the mean time, and in case of failure of the broader plan, we are establishing a college of general science at the same situation near Charlottesville, the scale of which, of necessity, will be much more moderate, as resting on private donations only. These amount at present to about 75,000 dollars; the buildings are begun, and by midsummer we hope to have two or three professorships in operation. Would to God we could have two or three duplicates of yourself, the original being above our means or hopes. If then we fail in doing all the good we wish, we will do, at least, all we can. This is the law of duty in every society of free agents, where every one has equal right to judge for himself. God bless you, and give to the means of benefiting mankind which you will bring home with you, all the success your high qualifications ought to insure.

TH. JEFFERSON.

FROM MR. JEFFERSON.
MONTICELLO, October 25, 1818.

DEAR SIR: I received, two days ago, your favor of August 10, from Madrid, and sincerely regret that my letter to Cardinal Dugnani did not reach you at Rome. It would have introduced you to a circle worth studying as a variety in the human character. I am happy, however, to learn that your peregrinations through Europe have been successful as to the object to which they were directed. You will come home fraught with great means of promoting the science, and consequently the happiness of your country; the only obstacle to which will be, that your circumstances will not compel you to sacrifice your own ease to the good of others. Many are the places which would court your choice; and none more fervently than the college I have heretofore mentioned to you, now expected to be adopted by the State and liberally endowed under the name of "the University of Virginia." . . . . I pass over our professorship of Latin, Greek, and Hebrew, and that of modern languages, French, Italian, Spanish, German, and Anglo-Saxon, which, although the most lucrative, would be the most laborious, and notice that which you would splendidly fill, of Ideology, Ethics, Belles-Lettres, and Fine Arts. I have some belief, too, that our genial climate would be more friendly to your constitution than the rigors of that of Massachusetts; but all this may possibly yield to the *hoc cœlum, sub quo natus educatusque essem.* I have indulged in this reverie the more credulously, because you say in your letter that "if there were a department in the central government that was devoted to public instruction, I might have sought a place in it; but

there is none, there is none even in my State government." Such an institution of the general government
cannot be, until an amendment of the Constitution, and
for that, and the necessary laws and measures of execution, long years must pass away. In the mean while we
consider the institution of our University as supplying its
place, and perhaps superseding its necessity.

With stronger wishes than expectations, therefore, I
will wait to hear from you, as our buildings will not be
ready under a year from this time; and to the affectionate
recollections of our family, add assurances of my constant
and sincere attachment.

TH. JEFFERSON.

To WILLIAM H. PRESCOTT
MONTICELLO, December 16, 1824

*   *   *

Yesterday we formed a party, and, with Mr. Jefferson
at our head, went to the University. It is a very fine establishment, consisting of ten houses for professors, four eat-
ing-houses, a rotunda on the model of the Parthenon,
with a magnificent room for a library, and four fine lecture-
rooms, with one hundred and eight apartments for students; the whole situated in the midst of two hundred and
fifty acres of land, high, healthy, and with noble prospects
all around it. It has cost two hundred and fifty thousand
dollars, and the thorough finish of every part of it, and the
beautiful architecture of the whole, show, I think, that it
has not cost too much. Each professor receives his house,
which in Charlottesville—the neighboring village—would
rent for $600, a salary of $1,500, and a fee of $20 from
every student who attends his instructions, which are to be
lectures, three times a week. Of the details of the system
I shall discourse much when I see you. It is more practical
than I feared, but not so practical that I feel satisfied of
its success. It is, however, an experiment worth trying, to
which I earnestly desire the happiest results; and they
have, to begin it, a mass of buildings more beautiful than

anything architectural in New England, and more appropriate to an university than can be found, perhaps, in the world.

Mr. Jefferson is entirely absorbed in it, and its success would make a *beau finale* indeed to his life. He is now eighty-two years old, very little altered from what he was ten years ago, very active, lively, and happy, riding from ten to fifteen miles every day, and talking without the least restraint, very pleasantly, upon all subjects. In politics, his interest seems nearly gone. He takes no newspaper but the Richmond Enquirer, and reads that reluctantly; but on all matters of literature, philosophy, and general interest, he is prompt and even eager. He reads much Greek and Saxon. I saw his Greek Lexicon, printed in 1817; it was much worn with use, and contained many curious notes. . . .

Mr. Jefferson seems to enjoy life highly, and very rationally; but he said well of himself the other evening, "When I can neither read nor ride, I shall desire very much to make my bow." I think he bids fair to enjoy both, yet nine or ten years. . . . Write to us, my dear William, as soon as you can, and very often, and we will do all we can to send you speedy and pleasant answers.

Yours always,

GEO. TICKNOR.

Document 58

A Plan for Female Education

Such public support for secondary education as existed was for men. Women received no public aid. The few private schools for women were run for profit, with results that living and study accommodations were often skimpy and educational standards suffered, stressing showy accomplishments over solid achievement. The attempt of Emma Willard (1787–1870) to repair this situation helped launch the long crusade for women's rights. Her main contention was that nature had intended women to be companions of men rather than mere satellites moving in an orbit of duty "around the Holy Center of perfection." She was also concerned for the great moral influence which women exerted as mothers.

The following document was originally addressed to the legislature of New York, to which Emma Willard had come from Vermont, attracted by the greater liberality to be expected of the state which had undertaken the Erie Canal and had already done so much to promote public education. Although the legislature failed to act upon her petition, she received assistance from citizens of nearby Troy, where she founded her new school. Some of the same citizens contributed to the founding of Rensselaer Polytechnic Institute in 1824.

What Emma Willard has to say about the corrupting influence of wealth and fashion finds echoes in many documents of the period. The reader is referred in particular to documents 10–11, 59, and 104. Emma

Willard coupled her plea for equal rights with the national mission of reform.

SOURCE: Emma Willard, *An Address to . . . the Legislature of New York Proposing a Plan for Improving Female Education*, pp. 25–35. Albany: 1819.

* * *

In inquiring, concerning the benefits of the plan proposed, I shall proceed upon the supposition, that female seminaries will be patronized throughout our country.

Nor is this altogether a visionary supposition. If one seminary should be well organized, its advantages would probably be found so great, that others would soon be instituted; and, that sufficient patronage can be found to put one in operation, may be presumed from its reasonableness; and from the public opinion, with regard to the present mode of female education. It is from an intimate acquaintance, with those parts of our country, whose education is said to flourish most, that the writer has drawn her picture of the present state of female instruction; and she knows, that she is not alone, in perceiving or deploring its faults. Her sentiments are shared by many an enlightened parent of a daughter, who has received a boarding school education. Counting on the promise of her childhood, the father had anticipated her maturity, as combining what is excellent in mind, with what is elegant in manners. He spared no expense that education might realize to him, the image of his imagination. His daughter returned from her boarding school, improved in fashionable airs, and expert in manufacturing fashionable toys; but, in her conversation, he sought in vain, for that refined and fertile mind, which he had fondly expected [see doc. 59—Ed.]. Aware that his disappointment has its source in a defective education, he looks with anxiety on his other daughters, whose minds, like lovely buds, are beginning to open. Where shall he find a genial soil in which he may place them to expand? Shall he provide them male instructors?—Then the graces of their persons and manners, and whatever forms the distinguishing charm of the feminine character, they cannot be expected to acquire.—Shall he give them a private tutoress? She will have been educated at the boarding school, and his daughters will have the faults of its instruction second-handed. Such is now the dilemma of many parents; and it is one, from which they cannot be extricated by their individual exertions. May not then the only plan, which promises to relieve them, expect their vigorous support?

Let us now proceed to inquire, what benefits would result from the establishment of female seminaries.

They would constitute a grade of public education, superior to any yet known in the history of our sex; and through them, the lower grades of female instruction might be controlled. The influence of public seminaries, over these, would operate in two ways; first, by requiring certain qualifications for entrance; and secondly, by furnishing instructresses, initiated in these modes of teaching, and imbued with their maxims. Female seminaries might be expected to have important and happy effects, on common schools in general; and in the manner of operating on these, would probably place the business of teaching children, into hands now nearly useless to society; and take it from those, whose services the state wants in many other ways.

That nature designed for our sex the care of children, she has made manifest, by mental, as well as physical indications. She has given us, in a greater degree than men, the gentle arts of insinuation, to soften their minds, and fit them to receive impressions; a greater quickness of invention to vary modes of teaching to different dispositions; and more patience to make repeated efforts. There are many females of ability, to whom the business of instructing children is highly acceptable; and, who would devote all their faculties to their occupation: for they would have no higher pecuniary object to engage their attention; and their reputation as instructors they would consider as important. Whereas, whenever able and enterprizing men, engage in this business, they consider it, merely as a temporary employment, to further some object, to the attainment of which their best thoughts and calculations are all directed. If then women were properly fitted by instruction, they would be likely to teach children better than the other sex; they could afford to do it cheaper; and those men who would otherwise be engaged in this employment, might be at liberty to add to the wealth of the nation, by any of those thousand occupations, from which women are necessarily debarred.

But the females, who taught children, would have been themselves instructed either immediately or indirectly by the seminaries. Hence through these, the government might exercise an intimate, and most beneficial control over common schools. Any one, who has turned his attention to this subject, must be aware, that there is great room for improvement in these, both as to the modes of teaching, and the things taught; and what method could be devised so likely to effect this improvement, as to prepare by instruction, a class of individuals, whose interest, leisure, and natural talents, would combine to make them pursue it with ardor. Such a class of individuals would be raised up, by female seminaries. And therefore they would be likely to have highly important and happy effects on common schools.

It is believed, that such institutions, would tend to prolong, or perpetuate our excellent government.

An opinion too generally prevails, that our present form of government, though good, cannot be permanent. Other republics have failed, and the historian and philosopher have told us, that nations are like individuals; that at their birth, they receive the seeds of their decline and dissolution. Here deceived by a false analogy, we receive an apt illustration of particular facts, for a general truth. The existence of nations, cannot, in strictness, be compared with the duration of animal life: for by the operation of physical causes, this, after a certain length of time, must cease: but the existence of nations, is pro-

longed by the succession of one generation to another, and
there is no physical cause, to prevent this succession's going on, in a peaceable manner, under a good government,
till the end of time. We must then look to other causes,
than necessity, for the decline and fall of former republics. If we would discover these causes, and seasonably
prevent their operation, then might our latest posterity
enjoy the same happy government, with which we are
blessed, or if but in part, then might the triumph of
tyranny be delayed, and a few more generations be free.

Permit me then to ask the enlightened politician of any
country, whether amidst his researches for these causes, he
cannot discover one, in the neglect, which free governments in common with others, have shown, to whatever
regarded the formation of the female character.

In those great republics, which have fallen of themselves, the loss of republican manners and virtues has been
the invariable precursor of their loss of the republican
form of government. But is it not in the power of our sex,
to give society its tone, both as to manners and morals?
And if such is the extent of female influence, is it wonderful, that republics have failed when they calmly suffered that influence, to become enlisted in favour of
luxuries and follies, wholly incompatible with the existence of freedom?

It may be said, that the depravation of morals and manners, can be traced to the introduction of wealth, as its
cause. But wealth will be introduced; even the iron laws
of Lycurgus could not prevent it. Let us then inquire, if
means may not be devised, to prevent its bringing with it
the destruction of public virtue. May not these means be
found in education? in implanting, in early youth, habits,
that may counteract the temptations, to which, through
the influence of wealth, mature age will be exposed? and
in giving strength and expansion to the mind, that it may
comprehend, and prize those principles, which teach the
rigid performance of duty? Education, it may be said, has
been tried as a preservative of national purity. But was it

applied to every exposed part of the body politic? For if any part has been left within the pestilential atmosphere of wealth, without this preservative, then that part becoming corrupted, would communicate the contagion to the whole; and if so, then has the experiment, whether education may not preserve public virtue, never yet been fairly tried. Such a part has been left in all former experiments. Females have been exposed to the contagion of wealth without the preservative of a good education; and they constitute that part of the body politic, least endowed by nature to resist, most to communicate it. Nay, not merely have they been left without the defence of a good education, but their corruption has been accelerated by a bad one. The character of women of rank and wealth has been, and in the old governments of Europe now is, all that this statement would lead us to expect. Not content with doing nothing to promote their country's welfare, like pampered children, they revel in its prosperity, and scatter it to the winds, with a wanton profusion: and still worse,—they empoison its source, by diffusing a contempt for useful labour. To court pleasure their business,—within her temple, in defiance of the laws of God and man, they have erected the idol fashion, and upon her altar, they sacrifice, with shameless rites, whatever is sacred to virtue or religion. Not the strongest ties of nature, not even maternal love can restrain them! Like the worshipper of Moloch, the mother while yet yearning over the new born babe, tears it from the bosom, which God has swelled with nutrition for its support, and casts it remorseless from her, the victim of her unhallowed devotion!

But while, with an anguished heart, I thus depict the crimes of my sex, let not the other stand by and smile. Reason declares, that you are guiltier than we. You are our natural guardians, our brothers, our fathers, and our rulers. You know that our ductile minds, readily take the impressions of education. Why then have you neglected our education? Why have you looked with lethargic indifference, on circumstances ruinous to the formation of other characters, which you might have controlled?

But it may be said, the observations here made, cannot be applied to any class of females in our country. True, they cannot yet; and if they could, it would be useless to make them; for when the females of any country have become thus debased, then, is that country so corrupted, that nothing, but the awful judgments of heaven, can arrest its career of vice. But it cannot be denied, that our manners are verging towards those described; and the change, though gradual, has not been slow; already do our daughters listen with surprise when we tell them of the republican simplicity of our mothers. But our manners are not as yet so altered, but that throughout our country, they are still marked with republican virtues.

The inquiry, to which these remarks have conducted us is this—What is offered by the plan of female education, here proposed, which may teach, or preserve, among females of wealthy families, that purity of manners, which is allowed to be so essential to national prosperity, and so necessary, to the existence of a republican government.

1. Females, by having their understandings cultivated, their reasoning powers developed and strengthened, may be expected to act more from the dictates of reason, and less from those of fashion and caprice.

2. With minds thus strengthened they would be taught systems of morality, enforced by the sanctions of religion; and they might be expected to acquire juster and more enlarged views of their duty, and stronger and higher motives to its performance.

3. This plan of education, offers all that can be done to preserve female youth from a contempt of useful labour. The pupils would become accustomed to it, in conjunction with the high objects of literature, and the elegant pursuits of the fine arts; and it is to be hoped, that both from habit and association, they might in future life, regard it as respectable.

To this it may be added, that if housewifery could be

raised to a regular art, and taught upon philosophical principles, it would become a higher and more interesting occupation; and ladies of fortune, like wealthy agriculturists, might find, that to regulate their business, was an agreeable employment.

4. The pupils might be expected to acquire a taste for moral and intellectual pleasures, which would buoy them above a passion for show and parade, and which would make them seek to gratify the natural love of superiority, by endeavouring to excel others in intrinsic merit, rather than in the extrinsic frivolities of dress, furniture, and equipage.

5. By being enlightened in moral philosophy, and in that, which teaches the operations of the mind, females would be enabled to perceive the nature and extent, of that influence, which they possess over their children, and the obligation, which this lays them under, to watch the formation of their characters with unceasing vigilance, to become their instructors, to devise plans for their improvement, to weed out the vices from their minds, and to implant and foster the virtues. And surely, there is that in the maternal bosom, which when its pleadings shall be aided by education, will overcome the seductions of wealth, and fashion, and will lead the mother, to seek her happiness in communing with her children, and promoting their welfare, rather than in a heartless intercourse, with the votaries of pleasure: especially, when with an expanded mind, she extends her views to futurity, and sees her care to her offspring rewarded by peace of conscience, the blessings of her family, the prosperity of her country, and finally with happiness beyond the grave.

Thus, laudable objects and employments, would be furnished for the great body of females, who are not kept by poverty from excuses. But among these, as among the other sex, will be found master spirits, who must have preeminence, at whatever price they acquire it. Domestic life cannot hold these because they prefer to be infamous, rather than obscure. To leave such, without any virtuous

road to eminence, is unsafe to the community; for not un-
frequently, are the secret springs of revolution, set in motion by their intrigues. Such aspiring minds, we will regulate, by education, we will remove obstructions to the
course of literature, which has heretofore been their only
honorable way to distinction; and we offer them a new object, worthy of their ambition; to govern, and improve the
seminaries for their sex.

A few words more, and I close my remarks.

In calling on my patriotic countrymen, to effect so noble
an object, the consideration of national glory, should not
be overlooked. Ages have rolled away;—barbarians have
trodden the weaker sex beneath their feet;—tyrants have
robbed us of the present light of heaven, and fain would
take its future also. Nations, calling themselves polite,
have made us the fancied idols of a ridiculous worship,
and we have repaid them with ruin for their folly. But
where is that wise and heroic country, which has considered, that our rights are sacred, though we cannot defend
them? that tho' a weaker, we are an essential part of the
body politic, whose corruption or improvement must effect
the whole? and which, having thus considered, has sought
to give us by education, that rank in the scale of being,
to which our importance entitles us? History shows not
that country. It shows many, whose legislatures have
sought to improve their various vegetable productions, and
their breeds of useful brutes; but none, whose public
councils have made it an object of their deliberations, to
improve the character of their women. Yet though history
lifts not her finger to such an one, anticipation does. She
points to a nation, which, having thrown off the shackles
of authority and precedent, shrinks not from schemes of
improvement, because other nations have never attempted
them; but, which, in its pride of independance, would
rather lead than follow, in the march of human improvement: a nation, wise and magnanimous to plan, enterprising to undertake, and rich in resources to execute. Does
not every American exult that this country is his own?
And who knows how great and good a race of men, may

yet arise from the forming hand of mothers, enlightened by the bounty of that beloved country, to defend her liberties, to plan her future improvement, and to raise her to unparallelled glory.

Document 59

(Plates 28 and 29)

Before and after Boarding School

Here is another example of the genre art of John L. Krimmel (1787–1821), who painted the Fourth of July scene in document 34. This artist was beginning to develop the gift of genial satire when he was accidently drowned at the age of thirty-four, the year after these prints were published. The two scenes supply an independent confirmation for Emma Willard's view in the preceding document that a young woman was likely to return from boarding school "improved in fashionable airs, and expert in manufacturing fashionable toys," but unimproved in mental accomplishment.

These two scenes are also early examples of the new lithographic art as it first appeared in the pages of the *Analectic Magazine* beginning in 1816. The difference in values of the two pictures, the one shaded in mezzotint and the other stressing line, is not explained. The artist or engraver may have decided that line was more effective for communicating the sharp satire of the second picture. In any event, readers of the *Analectic Magazine,* most of them belonging to the educated urban class, received an unusually intimate glimpse into rural family life.

DOCUMENT 60

A National Literature

American writers and critics were divided between English neo-classical preferences and romantic literary nationalism. Of the growing number of literary nationalists since the 1790's—a list which included the names of Thomas Odiorne, Charles Ingersoll, John Knapp, Robert Walsh, Jared Sparks, Edward Channing, Hugh Swinton Legaré, and William Cullen Bryant—James Kirke Paulding (1778–1860), who wrote the next document, was one of the few who seemed to realize that the call to greatness required more of American writers than the mere celebration of native subject matter. Besides freeing oneself from "servile imitation" of foreign tastes, one had to discover "those little peculiarities of thought, feeling, and expression which belong to every nation" and to seek the universal in the "tissue of events."

Above all, he wanted a national literature which would be in harmony with the scientific spirit of the age. In all this, of course, he anticipates Emerson's American Scholar Address. The viewpoint of those who leaned toward English models is best represented in Washington Irving's well-known essay from his Sketchbook, "English Writers on America" (1820).

SOURCE: James Kirke Paulding, "National Literature" (1820), in Salamagundi Papers, Second Series, Vol. IV of his Collected Works (New York: 1835), pp. 265, 269–71.

It has been often observed by such as have attempted to account for the scarcity of romantic fiction among our native writers, that the history of the country affords few materials for such works, and offers little in its traditionary lore to warm the heart or elevate the imagination. The remark has been so often repeated that it is now pretty generally received with perfect docility, as an incontrovertible truth, though it seems to me without the shadow of a foundation.

Wherever there are men, there will be materials for romantic adventure. In the misfortunes that befall them; in the sufferings and vicissitudes which are everywhere the lot of human beings in the struggles to counteract fortune, and in the conflicts of the passions, in every situation of life, he who studies nature and draws his pictures from her rich and inexhaustible sources of variety, will always find enough of those characters and incidents which give relish to works of fancy. The aid of superstition, the agency of ghosts, fairies, goblins, and all that antiquated machinery which till lately was confined to the nursery, is not necessary to excite our wonder or interest our feelings; although it is not the least of incongruities, that in an age which boasts of having by its scientific discoveries dissipated almost all the materials of superstition, some of the most popular fictions should be founded upon a superstition which is now become entirely ridiculous, even among the ignorant.

The best and most perfect works of imagination appear to me to be those which are founded upon a combination of such characters as every generation of men exhibits, and such events as have often taken place in the world, and will again. Such works are only fictions, because the tissue of events which they record never perhaps happened in precisely the same train, and to the same number of persons, as are exhibited and associated in the relation. Real life is fraught with adventures, to which the wildest fictions scarcely afford a parallel; and it has this special advantage over its rival, that these events, however extraordinary, can always be traced to motives, actions and passions, arising out of circumstances no way unnatural, and partaking of no impossible or supernatural agency. . . .

That these materials have as yet been little more than partially interwoven into the few fictions which this country has given birth to, is not owing to their being inapplicable to that purpose, but to another cause entirely. We have been misled by bad models, or the suffrages of docile critics, who have bowed to the influence of rank and fashion, and given testimony in favor of works which their better judgment must have condemned. We have cherished a habit of looking to other nations for examples of every kind, and debased the genius of this new world by making it the ape and the tributary of that of the old. We have imitated where we might often have excelled; we have overlooked our own rich resources, and sponged upon the exhausted treasury of our impoverished neighbors; we were born rich, and yet have all our lives subsisted by borrowing. Hence it has continually occurred, that those who might have gone before had they chosen a new path, have been content to come last, merely by following the old track. Many a genius that could and would have attained an equal height, in some new and unexplored region of fancy, has dwindled into insignificance and contempt by stooping to track some inferior spirit, to whom fashion had assigned a temporary elevation. They ought to be told, that though fashion may give a momentary popularity to works that neither appeal to national attachments, domestic habits, or those feelings which are the same yesterday, today, and forever, and everywhere, still it is not by imitation that they can hope to equal any thing great. . . .

By freeing himself from a habit of servile imitation; by daring to think and feel, and express his feelings; by dwelling on scenes and events connected with our pride and our affections; by indulging in those little peculiarities of thought, feeling, and expression which belong to every nation; by borrowing from nature, and not from those who disfigure or burlesque her—he may and will in time destroy the ascendancy of foreign taste and opinions, and elevate his own in the place of them. These causes lead to the final establishment of a national literature, and give that air and character of originality which it is sure to acquire, unless it is debased and expatriated by a habit of servile imitation. . . . This country is not destined to be always behind in the race of literary glory. The time will assuredly come, when that same freedom of thought and action which has given such a spur to our genius in other respects, will achieve similar wonders in literature. It is then that our early specimens will be sought after with avidity, and that those who led the way in the rugged discouraging path will be honored, as we begin to honor the adventurous spirits who first sought, explored, and cleared this western wilderness.

DOCUMENT 61

Thanatopsis

The call to greatness produced three major writers. Bryant's "Thanatopsis" appeared in 1817, Irving's *Sketchbook* in 1820, and Cooper's *The Spy* in 1821, followed in 1823 by *The Pioneers*. While all four works exploited native materials, none can be said to be "in harmony with the scientific spirit of the age," since they were either retrospective or nature-centered. Cooper came closest to vernacular expression in *The Pioneers*. This work, together with *The Spy* and the *Sketchbook*, became a best-seller. "Thanatopsis" has been chosen to represent the group, however, because of its brevity and, more significantly, because of its anticipation of the American cult of nature, discussed in the next two documents.

The poem is reprinted below in its first published version, preceded by Bryant's own account of the reading which influenced it. He had not then discovered Wordsworth, nor added the Wordsworthian introduction and conclusion. The reader may well wonder what is distinctively American about it . . . or about its treatment of nature. A contemporary pictorial parallel can be found in document 63.

SOURCES: Parke Godwin, A *Biography of William Cullen Bryant* . . . , 2 vols. Vol. I, p. 37. New York: 1883. *North American Review*, Vol. V, pp. 339–40 (1817).

About this time my father brought home, I think from one of his visits to Boston, the "Remains of Henry Kirke White," which had been republished in this country. I read the poems with great eagerness, and so often that I had committed several of them to memory, particularly

the ode to the Rosemary. The melancholy tone which prevails in them deepened the interest with which I read
them, for about that time I had, as young poets are apt to
have, a liking for poetry of a querulous caste. I remember
reading, at this time, that remarkable poem Blair's
"Grave," and dwelling with great satisfaction upon its finer
passages. I had the opportunity of comparing it with a
poem on a kindred subject, also in blank verse, that of
Bishop Porteus on "Death," and of observing how much
the verse of the obscure Scottish minister excelled in originality of thought and vigor of expression that of the English prelate. In my father's library I found a small, thin
volume of the miscellaneous poems of Southey, to which
he had not called my attention, containing some of the
finest of Southey's shorter poems. I read it greedily. Cow-
per's poems had been in my hands from an early age, and I
now passed from his shorter poems, which are generally
mere rhymed prose, to his "Task," the finer passages of
which supplied a form of blank verse that captivated my
admiration.

> ——Yet a few days, and thee,
> The all-beholding sun, shall see no more,
> In all his course; nor yet in the cold ground,
> Where thy pale form was laid, with many tears,
> Nor in th' embrace of ocean shall exist
> Thy image. Earth, that nourished thee, shall claim
> Thy growth, to be resolv'd to earth again;
> And, lost each human trace, surrend'ring up
> Thine individual being, shalt thou go
> To mix forever with the elements,
> To be a brother to th' insensible rock
> And to the sluggish clod, which the rude swain
> Turns with his share, and treads upon. The oak
> Shall send his roots abroad and pierce thy mould.
> Yet not to thy eternal resting place
> Shalt thou retire alone—nor couldst thou wish
> Couch more magnificent. Thou shalt lie down
> With patriarchs of the infant world—with kings

The powerful of the earth—the wise, the good,
Fair forms, and hoary seers of ages past,
All in one mighty sepulchre.—The hills,
Rock-ribb'd and ancient as the sun,—the vales
Stretching in pensive quietness between;
The venerable woods—the floods that move
In majesty,—and the complaining brooks,
That wind among the meads, and make them green,
Are but the solemn decorations all,
Of the great tomb of man.—The golden sun,
The planets, all the infinite host of heaven
Are glowing on the sad abodes of death,
Through the still lapse of ages. All that tread
The globe are but a handful to the tribes
That slumber in its bosom.—Take the wings
Of morning—and the Borean desert pierce—
Or lose thyself in the continuous woods
That veil Oregan, where he hears no sound
Save his own dashings—yet—the dead are there,
And millions in those solitudes, since first
The flight of years began, have laid them down
In their last sleep—the dead reign there alone.—
So shalt thou rest—and what if thou shalt fall
Unnoticed by the living—and no friend
Take note of thy departure? Thousands more
Will share thy destiny.—The tittering world
Dance to the grave. The busy brood of care
Plod on, and each one chases as before
His favourite phantom.—Yet all these shall leave
Their mirth and their employments, and shall come
And make their bed with thee!——

DOCUMENT 62

(PLATE 30)

Sublime Nature

The theme of the return to nature vied with that of
the return to classical antiquity in American cultural
life. Both developments, of course, had roots in Europe. The romantic love of nature had a deeper, more
lasting appeal for Americans, however, because it was
closely tied to nationalism—even more than the Classical
Revival. The main reason for this was the frontier tradition and the myth of America as a second Eden. As
the wilderness retreated before the expanding American civilization, images of the wild came more into
demand, representing both a protest against deleterious
change and a testimonial to America's superiority
over the supposedly effete, artificial European nations.

The special grandeur of America, many Americans
thought, was best expressed by the more awesome aspects of nature: by tempests, towering mountains,
craggy precipices, thundering waterfalls, and other
such works of deity. Therefore, they favored the sublime over the merely picturesque and sentimental,
tame, artificial views of nature which spoke more
loudly to them of Europe and gentility. Lovers of the
sublime had much in common with literary nationalists who deplored our imitativeness and cultural de-
pendency on Europe. The wild landscape depicted in
this document, as an evocation of a scene from Cooper's
The Last of the Mohicans, links sublime nature to
literary nationalism.

DOCUMENT 63

(PLATE 31)

Picturesque Nature

John Hill (1770–1850) and Joshua Shaw (1776–1860) were two recent immigrants from London who in 1820 published a slender volume of aquatints entitled *Picturesque Views of American Scenery,* from which the next document comes. A rather similar volume, *The Hudson River Portfolio,* by another immigrant, William G. Wall, appeared in 1828, anticipating the Hudson River School of landscape painting. The scenes in these volumes, for the most part, present nature in the near vicinity of civilization—nature hedged, trimmed, cultivated, and sentimentalized, as in the scene on Plate 31, which shows a melancholy glimpse of Washington's tomb at Mount Vernon. The astute bookseller, Mason Weems (see doc. 17), did not think that such views would sell very well, and he advised against their publication.

DOCUMENT 64

Who Reads an American Book?

The famous British criticism of American culture which follows typifies much of the criticism which Americans encountered throughout this period in the pages of the *Edinburgh Review* and in the works of such British travelers as Henry Feron and William Faux. The author, Sidney Smith (1771–1845), was ignorant of the more important achievements of the period, as represented here, pages 170 to 261. But so too was the American Robert Walsh, who wrote the supposedly definitive answer to all such criticism in his *Appeal from the Judgments of Great Britain Respecting the United States . . .* (Philadelphia: 1819) without mentioning the work of Dr. Beaumont or Washington Irving or Daniel Raymond and others. A popular satire of British criticism was Paulding's *John Bull in America; or the New Munchausen* (New York: 1825).

Sidney Smith justly attacks the jingoistic quality of American patriotism, but he seems unaware that the intemperate nature of British criticism was partly responsible for it. Sensitive pride, a sense of cultural inferiority since colonial days, and considerable self-righteousness—all associated with the mission into the wilderness to redeem man, "this new man," from wicked old Europe—were the other ingredients.

SOURCE: from Sidney Smith's review of Adam Seybert, *Statistical Annals of the United States of America* (Philadelphia: 1818), in the *Edinburgh Review*, XXXIII, pp. 78–80 (Boston: 1820).

. . . Such is the land of Jonathan—and thus has it been governed. In his honest endeavours to better his situation, and in his manly purpose of resisting injury and insult, we most cordially sympathize. We hope he will always continue to watch and suspect his Government as he now does—remembering, that it is the constant tendency of those entrusted with power, to conceive that they enjoy it by their own merits, and for their own use, and not by delegation, and for the benefit of others. Thus far we are the friends and admirers of Jonathan: But he must not grow vain and ambitious; or allow himself to be dazzled by that galaxy of epithets by which his orators and newspaper scribblers endeavour to persuade their supporters that they are the greatest, the most refined, the most enlightened, and the most moral people upon earth. The effect of this is unspeakably ludicrous on this side of the Atlantic—and, even on the other, we should imagine, must be rather humiliating to the reasonable part of the population. The Americans are a brave, industrious, and acute people; but they have hitherto given no indications of genius, and made no approaches to the heroic, either in their morality or character. They are but a recent offset indeed from England; and should make it their chief boast, for many generations to come, that they are sprung from the same race with Bacon and Shakespeare and Newton. Considering their numbers, indeed, and the favourable circumstances in which they have been placed, they have yet done marvellously little to assert the honour of such a descent, or to show that their English blood has been exalted or refined by their republican training and institutions. Their Franklins and Washingtons, and all the other sages and heroes of their revolution, were born and bred subjects of the King of England,—and not among the freest or most valued of his subjects: And, since the period of their separation, a far greater proportion of their statesmen and artists and political writers have been foreigners, than ever occurred before in the history of any civilized and educated people. During the thirty or forty years of their independence, they have done absolutely nothing for the Sciences, for the Arts, for Literature, or even for the statesman-like studies of Politics or Political

Economy. Confining ourselves to our own country, and to the period that has elapsed since *they* had an independent existence, we would ask, Where are their Foxes, their Burkes, their Sheridans, their Windhams, their Horners, their Wilberforces?—where their Arkwrights, their Watts, their Davys?—their Robertsons, Blairs, Smiths, Stewarts, Paleys and Malthuses?—their Porsons, Parrs, Burneys, or Blomfields?—their Scotts, Campbells, Byrons, Moores, or Crabbes?—their Sidonses, Kembles, Keans, or O'Neils?— their Wilkies, Laurences, Chantrys?—or their parallels to the hundred other names that have spread themselves over the world from our little island in the course of the last thirty years, and blest or delighted mankind by their works, inventions, or examples? In so far as we know, there is no such parallel to be produced from the whole annals of this self-adulating race. In the four quarters of the globe, who reads an American book? or goes to an American play? or looks at an American picture or statue? What does the world yet owe to American physicians or surgeons? What new substances have their chemists discovered? or what old ones have they analyzed? What new constellations have been discovered by the telescopes of Americans?—what have they done in the mathematics? Who drinks out of American glasses? or eats from American plates? or wears American coats or gowns? or sleeps in American blankets?— Finally, under which of the old tyrannical governments of Europe is every sixth man a Slave, whom his fellow-creatures may buy and sell and torture?

When these questions are fairly and favourably answered, their laudatory epithets may be allowed: But, till that can be done, we would seriously advise them to keep clear of superlatives.

Like half a Rainbow rising on yon shore
While its twin partner spans the semi o'er
And makes a perfect whole that need not part
Till time has furnish'd us a nobler art.

PART III

Dispersion, Expansion, and Change

DOCUMENT 65

American Speech: Sectional or National?

It was, of course, both. But until the appearance of
Cooper's *The Pioneers* and Henry Cogswell Knight's
Letters from the South and West, from which the
next selection is taken, the vernacular speech of the
American people had seldom found its way into polite
literature, and even these authors used it patronizingly.
As document 100 suggests, it met strong opposition
from followers of the cultivated European tradition.
Western and southwestern story tellers were to exploit
it more fully in the next period. Significantly, the use
of vernacular speech accompanied the rise of Realism.
Vernacular expression, developing in close organic relationship to experience and environment, reflected a
different way of "seeing" life (as in docs. 101 and
102).

Henry Cogswell Knight (1788–1835), highly sensitive to sectional differences and gifted with what is
surely the most exciting prose style of the period, wrote
its most perceptive social record. It is regrettable that
it cannot be reproduced below in whole, for it deserves
to be better known. Also worth reading today is his
poetical description of college curricula in *The Broken
Harp* (Philadelphia: 1815).

SOURCE: [Henry Cogswell Knight], *Letters from the South
and West,* by Arthur Singleton, pp. 29–30, 81–82, 106–7,
125–27. Boston: 1824.

* * *

Until you leave home, you will not be aware how many
provincial, and fatherless and motherless heathenisms, are
used in daily parle by *some* New Englanders; although

they justly take pride in being more literate than most other states. For ensample:—they use the word *conduct* as a neuter verb; the substantive *progress* as a verb; and stop short at the sign of the infinitive mood, as, she can sing if she chooses to; i. e. to sing. They say, flowers wilt for wither, thus used in Salmagundi; tip up for tilt up, so used in the Pilgrim's Progress; transmogrified, used by Smollet; heft, old Saxon, for weight; serious for religious; rungs for rounds of a ladder; sauce for vegetables; gunning for shooting; tackling for harness; notions for articles; birth for office; scrawls for faggots; fix for fixture; spry for nimble; lengthy for lengthened; lick for strike; hang the horse; had not ought; to convene for to be convenient; complected for complexioned; slump; jounce for jolt; chunky for chubby; slushy for sloppy; smash for quash; and so on. And in pronunciation, they do not aspirate the *h* in many words, as wich for which, were for where, wen for when; and they flatten other words, as na-ter for nat-ure, vir-too for virt-ue, with many more. All such backbiters of the king's English should be eschewed by every scholar, as he would eschew mean company. However, you need not hence conclude all the rest of the states to be perfect in phraseology. The Philadelphians, beside many of the above, have some peculiarities of their own, as:—like I used, for as I used; did not let on, for did not explain; get shut of a thing, for get rid of a thing; durst I go, for may I go? leave me do this, for permit me to do this; little bit of time; this is queer, for this is strange; the dear knows, for the demon knows; and the flat emphasis of *a*, as payer for pa'a; mayer for ma'a. But, at the South, and the West, there may you hear idiomatic vulgarisms rivalling the Eastern; and if I go thither, I will endeavour to turn the tables upon them in these matters.

* * *

The Virginian *phraseology* sounds a little peculiar to a northern ear at times. There is the executive *belittle* for demean, which, however, being an expressive word, the ex-president hath rather *belarged* his fame by adding it to our vocabulary. As the New Englanders guess, so do the Virginians reckon. What in New England is called the husk of corn, in Virginia is called the *shuck*; and what we call cob, they call husk; as also the external envelope of the kernel, which cannot be reduced to meal, and which makes the bran; they also call, what we call the spindle, the tassel. The Virginians use clever for intelligent; whereas we use it for a kind of negative character of weak intellect, but good disposition; the correct meaning is rather with them, than with us, as shrewd, cunning, dexterous. What they call chamber, is the room where the madam sleeps, and is usually *below* stairs; and what we call afternoon, they call evening, making no quarter divisions of the day. *Tote*, a slave word, is much used; implying both sustentation and locomotion, as a slave a log, or a nurse a babe. They say—to grow a crop, for, to raise a crop; he was raised, for, he was educated; mad for angry, as do the Irish; gear for harness; lines for reins; and madam and mistress, instead of our abbreviations. Children learn from the slaves some odd phrases; as, every which way; will you *all* do this? for, will *one* of you do this? and the epithet *mighty* is quite popular with old and young, as, for instance, mighty weak. Nor is their pronunciation without some slight peculiarities, as, stars for stairs, arr for air, bar for bear; and Talliaferro, a surname, of which they had a governor, is pronounced Tollifer.

* * *

The Phraseology in [Kentucky] is sometimes novel. When you arrive at a house, the first inquiry is, where is your plunder? as if you were a bandit; and out is sent a slave to bring in your plunder; i. e. your trunk, or valise. Instead of saying of a promised mother, with Shakespearean delicacy, that she is "nigh fainting under the pleasing punishment, that women bear;" the hint is quite Shakerlike, that she is "about to tumble in pieces." I have often heard the word *human* used here as a noun. The word *great* is sometimes used to signify *little*; as, that lady has a great foot, meaning, without irony, a little foot. Many

from habit, like the Virginians, tuck a *t* at the end of
such words as onct, twict, skifft. They here call a river, a
run; a lot, a section of land; they say to stall, i. e. overload,
a horse; and cupping for milking. In the fields, a kind of
foxtail grass here becomes timothy; and our black-and-
yellow caterpillar is named fever-and-ague. In the garden,
they cultivate their collards, i. e. probably coleworts, and
kashaws; and, at the oven, children wait for their crab-
lanterns, and cobble. Some words are used, even by genteel
people, from their imperfect educations, in a new sense;
and others, by the lower classes in society, pronounced very
uncouthly, as:—to eat a liquid, to quile for to quiet, to
suspicion one, to legerize an account, to prize for to raise
by lever, to fayz for to fix, offer for the candidacy, best
book I ever read after, well liked of, steed too gayly, heap
of times, did done do it, done done did it, painter for
panther, varmont for vermin, contráry, hȳmn, brēēthren,
an oxen, I seen, I brung, exhibitation, schrowd, yearth,
yearn for earn, bresh, hommer, sketes, drap, fotch, mought,
and so forth; which corruptions I have noted for Mr. Pick-
ering's very useful "Vocabulary."

* * *

All proclamations and newspapers [in New Orleans]
are printed with parallel sides, or columns, of English,
French, and some of Spanish. Sunday is the busy holiday,
when the theatre, and the circus, have most spectators, as
then they least value the time. Duels are very fashionable,
if they can contrive an affront; such as:—"How dared you
to spit as I was passing?"—"How dared you to pass as I was
spitting?" or, "You shall not sneeze where I am!" This
would make a pleasant duel. There is a corner called
Cadiz, a rendezvous for assassins, and no inquiry made.
As the good people of New England are scandalized by
their travelling pedlers, so are the Kentuckians dreaded
on account of their swaggering boatmen; and as the Western people call all the Eastern travellers Yankees, so do
the citizens of New-Orleans call all the up-river boatmen
Kentuckians. I would not, because it were unjust, entitle

New-Orleans a pandemonium of devils, a limbo of vanity, or a paradise of fools. But is it not a thoroughfare of speculators, and brief sojourners, going and coming, whence and where, few know, and few care; a place in which, if a man is not fleeced, more or less, it is his own fault? . . . It is common to ask a young gallant, who is about to marry:—"how much?" rather than:—"whom?" And too frequently do insolvent libertines come from the north to the south, to speculate into a lady's heritage. . . . A *bit* is the Pennsylvanian *eleven-pence*, the New York *shilling*, and the New England *nine-pence*. In this city, are hundreds of Eastern merchants; and, notwithstanding the foregoing remarks, many lovers of morality, and reverers of religion.

*   *   *

DOCUMENT 66

Uncle Sam: A Sectional Fable

Henry Cogswell Knight had written a national anthem for the *Port Folio's* 1814 competition in patriotic songs. His and several other entries adapted the tune of an old British drinking song, "Anacreon in Heaven," from which also came the music for Francis Scott Key's "The Star-Spangled Banner."

The War of 1812 produced another permanent symbol of American nationality in the character of Uncle Sam, whose derivation from "Brother Jonathan" is the subject of the next document by James Kirke Paulding. Though written about 1830, the idea for it was projected much earlier in Paulding's best-selling wartime allegory, *The Diverting History of John Bull and Brother Jonathan* (New York and Philadelphia: 1812). By the end of 1813, journalists had given the name of Uncle Sam almost as much currency as that of John Bull. The first cartoons of the familiar figure appeared in 1832.

In the following document, Paulding casts a jaundiced eye at the sectional ambitions of the period, including those of his native New York, the state which gave birth to Uncle Sam. Of special interest is Paulding's attempt, not always successful, to imbue his fable with life by using vernacular speech.

SOURCE: James Kirke Paulding, *The Diverting History of John Bull and Brother Jonathan*, pp. 177–92, *passim*. New York: 1835.

Once upon a time there lived, and lives still, in a country lying far to the west, a famous squire, rich in lands and paper money. Report made him out to be the son of John Bull, who every one knows has children in all parts of the world. But, if the truth were known, I believe he had a great many fathers, though his mother was a very honest woman, for he looked like as many people as there were hairs on his chin. But old Squire Bull had the credit of being his father, and truly there was a great likeness between them. Like Bull, he was somewhat given to boasting, tippling, fighting, and sailing boats; and was apt to hold his neighbours in contempt, dubbing them a pack of snivelling, pitiful rascals, that did not dare to call their souls their own, or look their king in the face, as every cat had a right to do. He took after his father in another respect; that is to say, nobody could tell which he was most fond of, making money like a horse, or spending it like an ass. But for all this he did not so much favour John Bull, but that you could now and then catch an expression in his face that put you in mind of everybody you had ever seen in the world.

John Bull had christened this son of his by the name of Jonathan; but by-and-by, when he became a man grown, being a good hearty fellow, about half horse half alligator, his friends and neighbours gave him the nickname of Uncle Sam; a sure sign that they liked him, for I never knew a respectable nickname given to a scurvy fellow in my life. Be this as it may, his family and all his neighbours at last came to call him nothing else but Uncle Sam; and all his beef, pork, and flour, in fact every thing that belonged to him, was marked with a huge U. S., six inches long.

* * *

By good management and good luck he at last got to have a vast property in lands, which he was every day adding to by buying out the Indians, or taking farms for debts that were owing him. In short, he prospered in all his undertakings, and became, in process of time, a great man among his neighbours. But to my mind he was not above half as clever a fellow as when he was poor. Then he was a jolly, careless, high-minded dog—generous as a prince, and hospitable as a Turk. He would swear a little at times, but he never meant any harm by it. But as he got rich, he set himself to be mighty genteel; aped the manners of all the would-be fashionable stragglers that came that way; never invited anybody to his house except to show off his new finery, and left off all his honest old habits by little and little.

The fact is, and I don't care who knows it, he took to canting, and turned the embroidered side of his jacket outwards, as a Turk does when he goes to court. Many people doubted whether he was any thing the better for this; and, if I must speak my mind, I think he lost more than he gained; for, as respects myself, I had rather a man should swear and drink punch a little, than pick my pocket while he is canting about brotherly love and good-will to all men. If Uncle Sam is angry at this, let him scratch his back and get pleased again.

*   *   *

You must know that as soon as Uncle Sam thought himself able to maintain a family comfortably, he got him a wife, who proved an excellent housekeeper, and in the course of twice as many years his children amounted to four-and-twenty; all jolly, strapping, roystering blades, with the exception of two or three, that were rather stinted in the growth, or, as Uncle Sam used to say in joke, "shrunk in the boiling." These last were rather conceited and jealous, as most little people I believe are.

As fast as these lads grew up, Uncle Sam portioned them off on his farms, which they were to pay for when they were able, at very low prices. They all turned out pretty clever, industrious fellows, with the exception of here and there one who was rather lazy, and got all his work done by negroes. They all differed in some respects; but there was a family likeness among them—all took after the mother, who was a pretty considerable particular talker. One was a famous fellow for cod-fishing; another a great hand at splitting shingles; a third was an amateur of road-making and ditching; a fourth was mighty fond of barbecues, taking after his father in that particular; a fifth dealt largely in wooden bowls and onions; a sixth was a great cultivator of rice and cotton; a seventh was a pretty high-handed fellow, fond of a good horse, and of an independent, open-hearted spirit; and so on. They all lived together like loving brothers, having a rich father who could do what he pleased with his money—that is to say, they were as jealous of each other as two cocks running in the same yard.

If Uncle Sam made a Christmas-present to one, or conferred a particular kindness on another, there was the deuse to pay among the rest. They accused the old man of being more partial to one than the other, and never gave him any rest till he put them all on a level; which he had no sooner done than they, one and all, began to grumble and find fault, saying the poor man was in his dotage, only because he had not given each one a preference over his brother. Uncle Sam sometimes said to himself, "Happy is the man who has nothing to give away, for his children won't quarrel about his estate."

But this was not the worst of it. The old Harry got into them about improving their farms, which they all swore was Uncle Sam's business; he was devouring all the money they could rake and scrape together to pay for the lands he had sold them. They said it was a sin and a shame for him to make them pay every thing, seeing they were his natural born children, entitled to bed, board, education, and an outfit. Besides, the old man was now become so rich he did not know what to do with his money, and it was actually a kindness to rid him of its management in his old age.

Thus these cunning varlets agreed in the propriety of sharing Uncle Sam's money, but they fell out about the manner of dividing it, like a parcel of undutiful rogues as they were. The big fellows argued that they ought to share according to weight, and insisted they should all go down to the mill and be weighed. But the little fellows who had been "shrunk in the boiling" demurred to this, and swore it was all in my eye, Betty Martin.

* * *

But these fine boys had another iron in the fire, which they heated till it was red hot. Quoth one of the cunning varlets, I believe it was the barbecue chap, "Let us set about improving our farms, and make the old boy pay the piper"—upon which they all agreed, and set up a hurrah about internal improvement, which used in old times to be considered improvement of mind and morals, but now means digging ditches, pulling up snags, and making roads through the desert.

Upon this one of them went and set up a loom in his back building, as he said, for the encouragement of domestic industry, and hired other people to come and tend it. When he had done this, he went to Uncle Sam, and insisted he should give him a handful or two of money, to encourage him in such patriotic and praiseworthy undertakings.

"Stop, there, my little fellow," cried the biggest brother of all, who had a fist like a sledge-hammer; "stop, if you please, I have set up my looms at my own expense; and I'll be switch'd if the old man is going to pay you for doing what I have done for myself."

Then another chap of the family set up a blacksmith shop for making hobnails, and made the same claim to touch a few thousands of the old gentleman's money for the encouragement of domestic industry, which about this time began to be very low-spirited, and wanted a little patting.

"Avast, there, you land-lubber," exclaimed one of the brothers, a bold, hearty Jack tar, who had sailed round and round the world, and was a mighty navigator. "Avast, there, none of your fresh water gabble. I should like to know the reason why you should be paid for making hobnails any more than I am for building ships. Avast, there, I say, you lubber, or I'll be foul of your dead-lights."

Next came another brother, who was a great hand at raising sheep, which he called being a wool-grower, to demand that as people could not exist without clothes, Uncle Sam should shell out a few dollars to reward him for being a great public benefactor.

"Fudge!" exclaimed the cotton-growing brother, "where one man is clothed in wool, a thousand wear cotton. Why not encourage me, then, instead of this woolly fellow? Away with your bleating, or I'll be into your mutton before you can say Jack Robinson."

Next came a sober, sedate, economical brother, who had set up a shoe-shop, and wanted Uncle Sam's protection—that is to say, some of his money.

"Rot your sole," cried the high-handed gentleman, who despised hard work, and had rather ride a blood horse than make his own shoes a thousand times. "What are you talking about there? It's mighty natural, to be sure, that you should be asking encouragement for making shoes. If it were horseshoes now, I'd talk to you." So saying, he mounted his horse, and challenged Uncle Sam to run a race for a thousand dollars.

After this, for there was no end of their persecution of the poor old man—after this came another brother, a great mechanical genius, who had invented a machine for peeling apples, and wanted encouragement of Uncle Sam for the great saving of time and labour in making apple-pies.

"Whoo! whoo! whoop!" cried the wild, harem scarem, barbecue boy, one of Uncle Sam's youngest sons, who had just settled a town away off west, and had not yet thrown off his moccasins; "whoop! mister, mind which way you point your rifle there—I can turn a flip-flap somerset, grease your head with bear's meat, and swallow you whole without a pang. You'd better take 'keer how you steer your steamboat, or you'll run foul of a snag."

By-and-by came another of this hopeful family, with a long story of the great advantage Uncle Sam would derive from clearing out a ditch, at his own expense, for the benefit of other people.

Here the great big fellow mentioned before, who was the richest of the brothers, put in his oar and cried out—

"None of that fun, Brother Jonathan; I've done all my own ditching myself, and I'll be tetotally ramswisled if I am going to let daddy pay you for what I did all myself. Dig your own ditches, my boy, as I have done."

Then came a fine fellow, one of the young fry, who wanted to persuade Uncle Sam to pony up for a lane he was about making from his barn to his bog-meadow, which he assured the old man would be a vast public improvement; for that, whereas his carts stuck in the mud now, they would be able to get along like a streak of lightning as soon as the improvement was made.

"Thunder and blarney!" exclaimed three or four of the elder brothers all at once, "haven't we made our own roads at our own cost, and without asking daddy for a cent; and do you think, you snivelling blockhead, we'll stand by and see the old man cheated out of what belongs to us?"

*   *   *

Things went on, getting worse and worse, for some time afterwards. Uncle Sam was almost every day pestered for money to pay for some improvement or other in the boys farms. He kept an account of these, and the amount they would cost, and found that it would take all he was worth in the world, and more besides, to get through with half of them. So one day he put his hands in his breeches pockets, and swore roundly they were a brood of ungrateful rogues, that wanted to get him on the parish, and not another penny would he pony up for man or beast.

This raised a terrible hue and cry among the boys, who threatened to disinherit the old man and set up for themselves.

*   *   *

Not finding any law for this, they determined to get one passed for the purpose; accordingly they went among the people, and told them a hundred cock-and-bull stories about this, that, and the other thing. They swore the land of right belonged to them when they came of age, according to an old settlement, which declared that Uncle Sam's children should all share his estates equally after his death. But they kept the last part to themselves, as you may suppose, and pretended that they had a right to take the old man's property while he was alive. Besides, they would say, the poor old gentleman don't know

Plate 26. *View of the University of Virginia*, "drawn from nature" and lithographed by Edward Sachse, 1856. Courtesy Harry Shaw Newman, The Old Print Shop.

Plate 27, *East Chelmsford in 1825 (Lowell)*, by Benjamin Mather. Plate no. 38 in Wilson Waters, HISTORY OF CHELMSFORD, MASSACHUSETTS (Lowell: 1917). Photo by the Burns Studio.

Plate 28. *Departure for Boarding School*, by John L. Krimmel in the *Analectic Magazine*, Vol. XVI, opp. p. 421 (1820). Photo by the New York State Library.

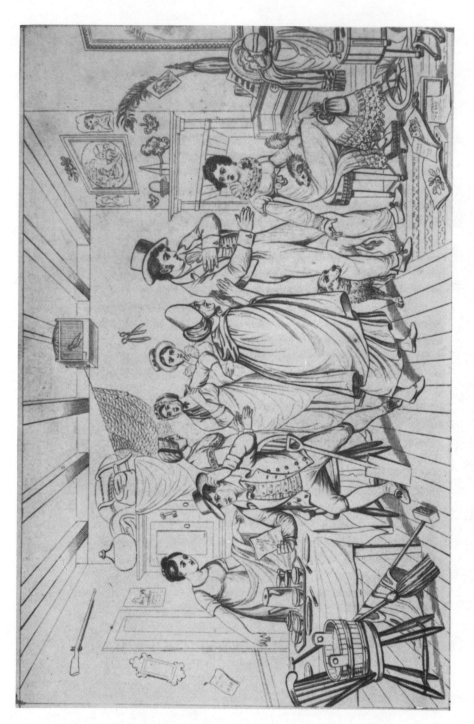

Plate 29. *Return from Boarding School*, by John L. Krimmel in the *Andlectic Magazine*, Vol. XVI, opp. p. 507 (1820). Photo by the New York State Library.

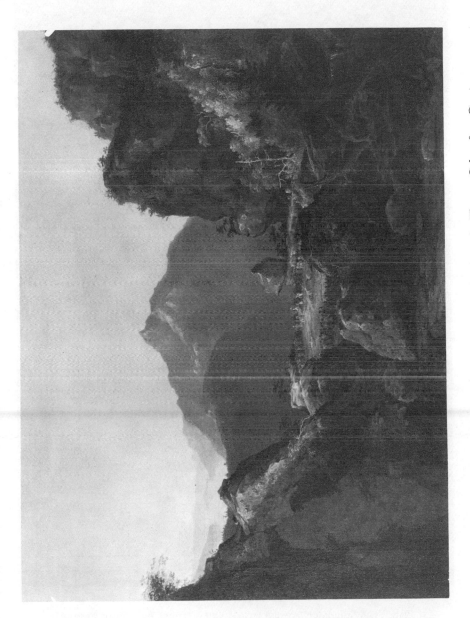

Plate 30. *Landscape*, a scene from The Last of the Mohicans, by Thomas Cole, 1827. Courtesy of the New York State Historical Association, Cooperstown, New York.

Plate 31. *Washington's Sepulchre, Mount Vernon*, from PICTURESQUE
VIEWS OF AMERICAN SCENERY, painted by Joshua Shaw and engraved
by John Hill, Plate II (Philadelphia: 1820). Photo by Alderman
Library, University of Virginia.

Plate 32. *View of the Canal*, by William G. Wall, ca. 1834. From an engraving in the collections of the New York State Library.

Plate 33. A *Kidnapping*, from Jesse Torrey, Jr., A Portraiture of Domestic Slavery in the United States, opp. p. 36 (Philadelphia: 1817). Photo by the Burns Studio.

Plate 34. *The Old Plantation*, anonymous, South Carolina, ca. 1800. From the Abby Aldrich Rockefeller Folk Art Collection, Williamsburg, Virginia.

Plate 35. *Dormitory Built ca. 1825 for Unskilled Mill Operatives at Lowell,* from John P. Coolidge, MILL AND MANSION, *A Study of Architecture and Society in Lowell, Massachusetts, 1820–1865,* fig. 4 (New York: Columbia University Press, 1942).

Plate 36. *Dormitory Built ca. 1825 for Skilled Operatives at Lowell,* from John P. Coolidge, MILL AND MANSION, fig. 9.

Plate 37. *The Foreman's (Paul Moody) House at Lowell*, ca. 1825, from John P. Coolidge, MILL AND MANSION, fig. 13.

Plate 38. *The Resident Manager's (Kirk Boott) House at Lowell*, ca. 1825, from John P. Coolidge, MILL AND MANSION, fig. 14.

Plate 39. *The Union Manufactories of Maryland on Patapsco Falls*, sketched by Maximilian Godefroy, ca. 1812. Courtesy of the Maryland Historical Society.

Plate 40 (above). *The Tea Party*, by Henry Sargent, ca. 1820.
Plate 41 (below). *The Dinner Party*, by Henry Sargent, ca. 1825.
Both courtesy of the Museum of Fine Arts, Boston.

Plate 42. An *Early Mississippi Steamboat*, from David Stevenson, SKETCH OF THE CIVIL ENGINEERING OF NORTH AMERICA, opp. p. 151 (London. 1838).

Plate 43. *Fulton's Clermont*, a contemporary painting. From the Phelps Stokes Collection, New York Public Library.

Plate 44. *The John Stevens' Locomotive and Circular Track at Hoboken, 1825.* Courtesy of the Stevens Institute of Technology. The original model, with four vertical guide posts added, is at the Smithsonian Institution.

Plate 45. *Trevithick's English Locomotive and Railway*, from the Rowlandson drawing of 1808 in the Newcomen Society TRANSACTIONS, Vol. I, Plate XIII (1920-21).

Plate 46. *Evans' Orukter Amphibolos Before Centre Square.* The picture of Evans' dredger comes from THE MECHANIC, p. 193 (Boston: 1834); of Centre Square from WATSON'S ANNALS OF PHILADELPHIA (Philadelphia: 1857). Photo by the Burns Studio.

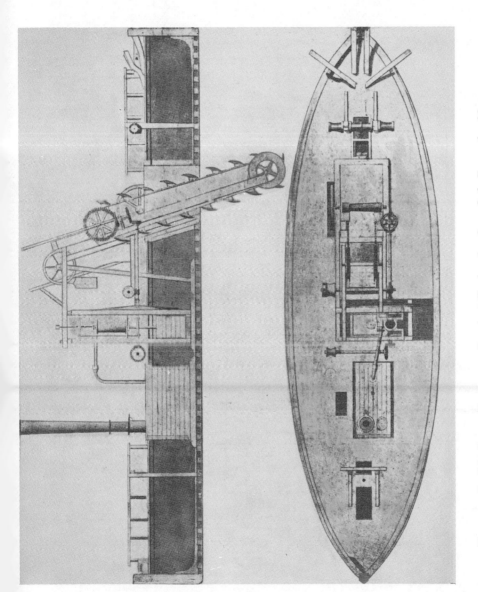

Plate 47. *English Steam Dredger at Deptford Dockyard, 1803–1806. From the Newcomen Society TRANSACTIONS, Vol. III, Plate III (London: 1922–23).*

Plate 48. *View of T. Pope's Flying Lever Bridge,* from Thomas Pope, A TREATISE ON BRIDGE ARCHITECTURE, frontispiece (1811). Photo by the Burns Studio.

Plate 49. *Town's Bridge,* from the *Journal of American Science and Arts,* Vol. III, frontispiece (1821). Photo by Rensselaer Polytechnic Institute.

Plate 50. *The Monumental Church, Richmond, Virginia*, an en-
graving of Robert Mills' original design, ca. 1811. From H. M. Pierce
Gallagher, ROBERT MILLS, ARCHITECT OF THE WASHINGTON MONU-
MENT, 1781–1855, opp. p. 82 (New York: Columbia University
Press, 1935).

Plate 51. *The Monumental Church, Richmond, Virginia*, as actually
built by Robert Mills, ca. 1811–1814. From H. M. Pierce Gallagher,
ROBERT MILLS, ARCHITECT OF THE WASHINGTON MONUMENT, opp.
p. 80.

Plate 52. *Natty Bumppo's Farewell,* an illustration for *The Pioneers* in the PORT FOLIO, Vol. XVII (1824). Photo by the Burns Studio.

Plate 53. *Daniel Boone, 1819,* an engraving of Chester Harding's painting. Courtesy of the Missouri Historical Society.

Plate 54. *George Washington*, by Gilbert Stuart, 1796. Courtesy of
the Pennsylvania Academy of the Fine Arts.

Plate 55. *The Return of Rip Van Winkle*, by John Quidor, 1829. Mellon Collection, courtesy of the National Gallery of Art, Washington, D.C.

Plate 56 (left). *Comedy*, sculptured in wood by William Rush, 1808.
Photo by the Philadelphia Museum of Art, reproduced with the permission of the Edwin Forrest Home, Philadelphia.

Plate 57 (right). *Tragedy*, sculptured in wood by William Rush, 1808.
Photo by the Philadelphia Museum of Art, reproduced with the permission of the Edwin Forrest Home, Philadelphia.

what to do with so much land; half of it lies waste for want of proper attention, and if we only had it, we would make it ten times more valuable, and pay the taxes, which he is exempted from, by virtue of an old charter.

The notion of getting money by taxation is a bait which generally takes with people whose business is law-making, not tax-paying, as I have always heard. So the legislature which governed where Uncle Sam's property lay, rubbed their hands, and were mightily tickled with the notion of being able to squeeze a little money from Uncle Sam's new lands. Perceiving this argument told, the boys hatched another notion, about Uncle Sam receiving all the money for the lands he sold, and then forcing those who bought them to work their fingers to the bone to make themselves whole again, as if this were not the way all over the world.

Uncle Sam defended his bacon to the last, like a stout old hero as he was; but by degrees the influence of these ungrateful rogues prevailed, and a law was passed taking away all his property, dividing it equally among the boys, so that those who were "shrunk in the boiling" got the same portion as the big roystering blades, who, rather than not come in for a slice, consented at last to share and share equally. They were all specially enjoined to take care of Uncle Sam, and see that he wanted for nothing; but the poor old man fared pretty much as people generally do who make over all their property to their children in their life-time.

DOCUMENT 67

Erie Canal: The Meeting of the Waters

The main sectional issue of the period was internal improvements. The next documents, occasioned by a great public celebration in Albany on October 10, 1823, of the junction of the waters of Lake Erie and the Hudson, view this sectional enterprise in quite a different light from that of Paulding. Although William Bayard acknowledges the canal's commercial value to New York, he stresses its contribution toward consolidating the union of states; while William James, a wealthy contractor and grandfather of the novelist and the philosopher, regards it as a great American epic of the chosen people's triumph over sin.

The people of New York were particularly proud that they had succeeded in so vast an undertaking without federal aid. The history of internal improvements, except for the Cumberland Road, completed under federal subsidy through the brilliance of Henry Clay, was marked by a series of presidential vetoes, including Madison's and Monroe's vetoes of bills for the upkeep of the Cumberland Road!

The messages which accompanied these vetoes can be found in Henry Steele Commager, ed., *Documents of American History*. The chief ground given, that of unconstitutionality, would doubtlessly have been considered by Paulding a mere rationalization of sectional jealousy. The most statesmanlike speech in Congress supporting the Erie Canal—little known today, though it was one of the finest addresses of a period noted for political eloquence—was that of Peter Porter of New York in 1810, reprinted in David Hosack, *Memoir of De Witt Clinton*, pp. 359-74 (New York: 1829). The importance to the West of the Cumber-

land Road and the Erie Canal is expressed in James
Hall, *Letters from the West . . . ,* pp. 50–56 (London: 1828).

SOURCE: *Albany Gazette,* October 14, 1823.

Wm. Bayard, Esq. chairman of the New-York committee presented the following address to the committee of the citizens of Albany:

GENTLEMEN:—In behalf of a meeting of the citizens
of New York, convened on the 6th inst. in that city, we
have now the satisfaction of offering to you, their cordial
congratulations on the great and interesting event, which
we are now commemorating.

The completion of more than three hundred miles of
canal in less than seven years, by a state which possessed
a population not much greater than the metropolis of the
British empire—the junction of the waters of our inland
seas with the Atlantic, are facts which will exercise a most
important influence on the prosperity of our state, on the
social and moral character of our people, and on the political power and importance of this nation.

It would be useless to speak at this moment of the advantages of the Great Western Canal: you have the best
proofs of them in joyous acclamation of the freemen who
surround you. But we may be permitted to remark, that
the character and happiness of the United States, are intimately concerned in the extension of agriculture and the
increased productiveness of our soil. The great enterprize
we celebrate, destined as it is to connect the valleys of
the Ohio and the Mohawk, will hereafter create a home-
market for our products, which perhaps the most sanguine amongst us, do not yet fully appreciate. Our canal
is but the commencement of a system of internal improvements, which by the facility of transportation they
will afford, while they lessen the cost, will increase the
amount of our domestic productions. Hereafter our wheat
will compete in the European markets, with that of Poland and Odessa, and a commerce be thus established,

important to the merchant, and beneficial to the agriculturalist.

But we pass over this and every other topic, to address you on one which appeals powerfully to the heart of every American, jealous of the character and permanence of our republican institutions. The Great Western Canal, while it brings distant countries into close contact, and extends the blessings of social intercourse, will unite a large portion of our people in the strong ties of a community of commercial interest, and under God, as we trust, secure and consolidate for ever, the union of these states. Thus our republican institutions will be preserved, the example of a representative government, founded on the people's will, be maintained in its pristine purity—and the once fond wish of the patriot be realized, in the unsullied perpetuity of our constitution.

We beg leave, gentlemen, to felicitate you as citizens of this ancient capital. The canal will pour its fertilizing stream into the bosom of your city, restore it to its wonted prosperity, and add another triumph to the patriotic efforts of its inhabitants.

To which Wm. James, Esq. chairman of the committee replied:

Sir.—It is the distinguishing attribute of man to be excited by what is grand, beautiful, and sublime in nature, or what is great and beneficial in the combinations of intellect and art.

This principle of our nature has congregated the immense number of citizens you now behold, to celebrate the completion of a work which in grandeur of conception, and benefits resulting to the human family, surpass every national improvement that has been attempted in any country; a work that sheds additional lustre on the United States, bearing the stamp of the enterprising spirit, and resolution which declared our independence, and the intelligence and wisdom that cemented the union of different republics by the adoption of the federal constitution; and to find that our feelings and sentiments on this occasion have pervaded the great and wealthy metropolis of the union, greatly enhances the dignity of our *fete*, and increases our pleasure on this joyful day; we therefore most sincerely welcome the honorable committee of our respectable fellow citizens of New York, to partake in our festivities, and cordially reciprocate their congratulations on this great and auspicious occasion. In this grand work, we perceive the strongest cement of our connection, and an immense reciprocal increase of the trade and intercourse of the two cities. If facilities of intercourse be the true cause of the superior intelligence, happiness, and wealth of nations, by what bounds can we circumscribe the blessings and benefits which may be expected to flow from the great canals—That to the north connects us with the Bay of Labrador, and that to the west with the Gulph of Mexico, uniting or intersecting many navigable lakes and rivers, affording the advantages and convenience of marine settlements to the most fertile lands in the world, for many hundred miles from the sea, and thereby giving a solid value to the products of their soil, by enabling them to transport it to the best markets at a trifling expense. Behold the multitude of boats now floating on the canals, pressing from distant interior countries to southern markets with rich and valuable cargoes: if such be the immediate benefits to this and several other states, which will increase with their population, where shall we limit the blessings and advantages which will descend to future generations from the great achievement we this day celebrate. It is the prerogative of man to trace and anticipate effects from causes, and it is peculiarly the happy privilege of Americans to enjoy the blessings of hope and expectation. Reared and educated under systems of government, and institutions created and improved by the people for the benefit of ourselves, and children, affording an equal participation in the blessings of liberty and property to all, our civil and religious institutions based on intelligence and universal education; and with the perpetual example of despotism and wretchedness in the old world, before our eyes, we may look forward with a well founded hope that neither tyrannical aristocracies, or intriguing demagogues can ever succeed in corrupting our citizens, or blighting our liberties, how bright therefore is the prospect, and how cheerful the anticipations we may this day indulge.

After a retrospect of what has passed in our own time, the imagination imperceptibly glides into the vista of futurity, there she can with equal confidence and pleasure perceive how familiar, interesting and easy, the canal will make the intercourse of our citizens, with the many republican states which will soon be established around our immense lakes and rivers in the west, and the inconceivable quantity of products of the earth, that will glide on its surface, to the Atlantic markets. We therefore rejoice this day for the extension of the population, liberty and happiness of man.

Although we have seen or heard of the works on the canals daily, the mind is yet confounded at the magnitude of the undertaking, astonished at the celerity and grandeur of the execution, and so charmed with the glory and benefits it entails on the country, we can scarcely realize its completion.

I confess I enjoyed the grand project at first only in imagination. I hoped it would finally succeed for the honor of the state, and the good of my children and posterity, and at this moment, I feel an indescribable emotion, something like a renewal of life, at partaking in the festivities of this day.

We know that a much longer time has been often exhausted by the cabinets of kings in talking of a trifling national improvement before the work is begun, or in executing 30 miles of a canal, than has transpired since we first heard the idea of uniting lakes Erie and Champlain with the Hudson. How honorable must such a result be, not only to the commissioners, but to the distinguished citizens, and to the legislatures who aroused public attention, and directed the energies of the state to its accomplishment.

Americans ought to rejoice with gratitude to heaven: nothing but the torpid stupidity of atheism can prevent the reflecting mind from perceiving the special interposition of providence, in protecting and advancing our national honor and greatness.

Instruments have always been prepared and qualified for promoting every great enterprize, at a period when only few could believe success possible: This has been the case in every great undertaking or splendid event interesting to our destiny, since the time when the brave and indefatigable Columbus was spending his strength, and for years wasting his exertions among the venal courtiers of Ferdinand and Isabella, until the present day. Was an empire such as ours to be established, the only emigrants fitted to do it were those who abhorred the profligacy, bigotry, and slavery of European governments. Was the time come, that we should assume a rank among the nations of the world, a Washington and others were ready.

The final issue of that tedious conflict for independence is the best comment on these qualifications for the mighty enterprise.—That atchievment and the consequences which have flowed from our republican institutions, have electrified the moral mass in Europe and elsewhere—and with galvanic power, excited the divine principle of freedom, which had been buried under accumulations of superstition, bigotry, and feudal aristocracy for ages, our revolution has changed their motives for warfare, by giving destructive animation to the principles of equal rights, and despotism, which like the curse denounced by God to the serpent, will continue in combat until one or the other shall finally triumph. Was a consolidation of joining states necessary to the future welfare and glory of all: Men endowed with intelligence and influence for perfecting the great object, were on the stage of action. Were the rights of our country to be again defended: Men arose from obscurity to command our few ships of war, who wounded the enemy in the most sensitive part, and others, who commanding our militia, beat and disgraced the greatest captains and veteran armies of Europe. Are the states to be united by stronger ties than that of a national compact: A man possessing

every quality calculated to arrest public attention and confidence, appears with the sublime project of a canal requiring 400 miles of excavation and locks, in direct lines
—that shall unite the Hudson with great lakes and navigable rivers, for more than 4000 miles; thereby uniting
the extremities of the empire by the most durable of all
ligaments, those of interest and easy internal intercourse.

We all remember, and so do our children, the first
promulgation of the mighty project, the influential exertions, the mathematical and scientific calculations, and
the lucid and eloquent arguments and appeals of its distinguished projector, convincing some of its practicability,
and pursuading others by the influence of his well known
character, into a cooperation of the great undertaking. He
had the astonishing success of soon uniting a body of
patriots and statesmen, in and out of our legislature,
whose influence and exertions afforded efficient and
abundant means for beginning and completing the work,
thereby adding true glory to the nation, and justly acquiring the esteem and gratitude of the present and
future generations for themselves.

We this day commence an epoch which posterity will
consecrate to the honor of the distinguished instruments
of Providence who have conceived and promoted a work
equally splendid and beneficial, and which will be a
lasting monument of glory, and a source of wealth to the
state. Gratitude is a pleasing passion, and also an attribute of humanity.—Public rejoicing for national benefits,
when properly conducted, is an appropriate and acceptable demonstration of homage to the creator, and is also
a proper and suitable mode of expressing national gratitude to national benefactors.

We behold the persons of many now among us who
are highly deserving this tribute of respect, and I assure
you, sir, that the citizens of Albany derive the highest
pleasure in seeing among the distinguished committee of
New York, gentlemen who have always added the weight
and influence of most respectable characters, to the cause
of internal improvement, but especially from the satisfac-

tion of beholding among them, the venerable president and the virtuous and enlightened secretary of the meeting whose committee presented the luminous memorial to our legislature which prepared and convinced the public mind for commencing the great work we now celebrate. We again renew our most cordial invitation to the honorable members of the New-York committee, to now unite with us in the festivities of the day, appointed for shewing our respect and esteem to the commissioners who have so successfully conducted the magnificent work to its present issue.

DOCUMENT 68

Song: *The Meeting of the Waters*

The completion of the Erie Canal for through traffic from the Great Lakes to the Atlantic was celebrated in October 1825. For this grand occasion, Samuel Woodworth (1784–1842), a popular poet, playwright, and journalist, wrote the song, "The Meeting of the Waters of Hudson & Erie." Woodworth wrote many other songs during his lifetime, including the sentimental favorite, "The Old Oaken Bucket." His play *The Forest Rose,* written in 1825, created a famous Yankee character, Jonathan Ploughboy, and was one of the longest-lived American plays before the Civil War.

The song below is less interesting for its music, based on a well-known melody of Thomas Moore's, than for its words, which make it a hymn to scientific progress and the canal achievement a sublime national example for Europe to follow in paths not of wealth or empire, but of peace and liberty. The pious faith that material achievement would lead to moral and spiritual ends was not likely, of course, to be challenged by anyone participating in the celebration. It was one of the major creeds of the period, eloquently defended, for example, by Hugh Swinton Legaré in the first document in this volume. Challenges to it were usually covert, as in document 70.

SOURCE: from a contemporary song sheet copyrighted November 1, 1825. Courtesy of the New York State Library.

The Meeting of the Waters
Of Hudson & Erie.

Written by S. Woodworth
Sung by Mr. Keene, at the
GRAND CANAL CELEBRATION.
Respectfully Dedicated to His Excellency
Dewitt Clinton

bloom of that val-ley shall fade from my heart.

u-nion so fruit-ful of glo-ry shall end.

2.
Yet, it is not that Wealth now enriches the scene,
Where the treasures of Art, and of Nature, convene;
'Tis not that this union our coffers may fill—
O! no—it is something more exquisite still.

3.
'Tis, that Genius has triumph'd—and Science prevail'd,
Tho' Prejudice flouted, and Envy assail'd,
It is, that the vassals of Europe may see
The progress of mind, in a land that is free.

4.

All hail! to a project so vast and sublime!
A bond, that can never be sever'd by time,
Now united us still closer—all jealousies cease,
And our hearts, like our waters, are mingled in peace.

DOCUMENT 69

Primitivism and Progress

The fact was that most Americans could address themselves simultaneously to opposing ways of life without sensing any obvious contradiction between them. The reason was not necessarily a compartmentalizing of the mind, though on a deeper, unconscious level this was often true, if unadmitted. On the level of conscious intellect, at least, they resolved the problem by rationalizing that their material civilization was evolving toward moral ends given by nature, influenced in its evolution by nature. They seemed to care mightily about morality in nature as an abstract concept, and considerably less about a poetic harmony with the inner rhythms of nature itself. The contradiction of their position is ably exposed by an English visitor, Basil Hall, who wrote of the two scenes below, "The view from the top of Mount Holyoke, in the State of Massachusetts, is one of the most beautiful in America. I have placed it on the same page with the Erie Canal, to show the contrast between a scene entirely artificial, and one where nature is left to her own devices."* Overt criticism of the "rape of nature" by an aggressive, exploitative civilization came in the next generation with the writings of Emerson and Thoreau. Cooper's character, Natty Bumppo, was, after all, also facing two ways.

* Basil Hall, *Forty Etchings from Sketches Made with the Camera Lucida* London: 1829.

View from Mount Holyoke in Massachusetts.

Western End of the Great Erie Canal.

A *Contrast in Scenes Natural and Artificial*, etched by Basil Hall in his FORTY ETCHINGS FROM SKETCHES MADE WITH THE CAMERA LUCIDA, Plates XI and XII (London: 1829). Photos by the Burns Studio.

Document 70

(Plate 32)

Progress and Primitivism

The same problem is expressed in this document within a single scene, also converging on the cultural meaning of the Erie Canal, but here the sense of tension is more covert. Nature is majestic, wild, and vast; man is small. And yet one feels the impiety of the geometric march of civilization across the ravine with its tumbled, jagged rocks, wind-tossed pines, and, in the foreground, worshiping, silent fishermen waiting for the creaking of the towline and the sound of horses' hooves to pass. The artist is William G. Wall (1782–1864), a naturalized citizen from England who shared with John Hill and Joshua Shaw (see doc. 63) a knowledge of the windswept landscapes of Constable and the "castigated purity" of Girtin which they translated into that drama of the disappearing wilderness called the "picturesque."

DOCUMENT 71

The American Colonization Society

Another sectional issue, slavery, became increasingly prominent as the nation expanded westward and the South "withdrew" into cotton capitalism. In 1819, Missouri's petition for statehood raised the question of the legal status of slavery in all the territory west of the Mississippi. Missouri was finally, in 1820, admitted as a slave state, Maine as a free state, and slavery excluded from the Louisiana Purchase north of the line 36°30′.

Documents relating to the Missouri Compromise are well known. Less well known are those surrounding the American Colonization Society, founded in 1817 to help freed Negroes emigrate to Africa or elsewhere. The tone of moderation which prevailed in both instances was possible only because of the strength of national feeling. In evading the question of a gradual emancipation of slaves, as the following documents show, members of the Society sought to salve their consciences by recourse to lesser measures which would yet be in harmony with the nation's reforming sense of mission. The private views of the Northerner who reported these deliberations are expressed in a succeeding document whose tone is quite inconsistent with that of most of the members below.

SOURCE: Jesse Torrey, Jr., *A Portraiture of Domestic Slavery in the United States* . . . , pp. 85–90, 93–94. Philadelphia: 1817.

Since the original of the Portraiture of Slavery was composed, a highly respectable meeting, consisting of a considerable number of the members of our national legislature, with many benevolent and intelligent citizens of the District of Columbia, has been held in the city of Washington, (on the 21st Dec. ult.) for the purpose, as expressed by the gentleman who presided as chairman, (Mr. Clay,) *"of considering the propriety and practicability of colonizing the free" people "of colour in the United States, and of forming an asylum in relation to that object."*

As the proceedings of this meeting indicate a flattering prospect of the consummation of a measure, on which I had recorded my sentiments, and hope of its adoption, several weeks previous to the time that the meeting was announced, it is deemed useful and appropriate to annex a sketch of their deliberations, as published in the National Intelligencer.

Extracts from the speech of Mr. Clay, (on taking the chair.)

"That class of the mixt population of our country was peculiarly situated. They neither enjoyed the immunities of freemen, nor were they subject to the incapacities of slaves, but partook in some degree of the qualities of both. From their condition, and the unconquerable prejudices resulting from their colour, they never could amalgamate with the free whites of this country. It was desirable, therefore, as it respected them, and the residue of the population of the country, to drain them off. Various schemes of colonization had been thought of, and a part of our own continent, it was supposed by some, might furnish a suitable establishment for them. But for his part, Mr. C. said, he had a decided preference for some part of the coast of Africa. There ample provision might be made for the colony itself, and it might be rendered instrumental to the introduction, into that extensive quarter of the globe, of the arts, civilization and christianity. There was a peculiar, a moral fitness in restoring them to the land of their fathers. And if, instead of the evils and sufferings which we had been the innocent cause of inflicting upon the inhabitants of Africa, we can transmit to her the blessing of our arts,

our civilization, and our religion, may we not hope that
America will extinguish a great portion of that moral debt
which she has contracted to that unfortunate continent?
Can there be a nobler cause than that which, whilst it
proposes, &c. contemplates the spreading of the arts of
civilized life, and the possible redemption from ignorance and barbarism of a benighted quarter of the globe?

"It was proper and necessary distinctly to state, that
he understood it constituted no part of the object of this
meeting to touch or agitate in the slightest degree, a
delicate question connected with another portion of the
coloured population of our country. It was not proposed
to deliberate upon, or consider at all, any question of
emancipation, or that was connected with the abolition
of slavery. It was upon that condition alone, he was sure,
that many gentlemen from the south and the west, whom
he saw present, had attended, or could be expected to
co-operate. It was upon that condition, only, that he
had himself attended."

Extracts from the speech of Elias B. Caldwell, Esq. of
the District of Columbia.

"The more you improve the condition of these people,
the more you cultivate their minds, the more miserable
you make them in their present state. You give them a
higher relish for those privileges which they can never
attain, and turn what we intend for a blessing into a
curse. No, if they must remain in their present situation,
keep them in the lowest state of degradation and ignorance. The nearer you bring them to the condition of
brutes, the better chance do you give them of possessing
their apathy. Surely, Americans ought to be the last people
on earth, to advocate such slavish doctrines, to cry peace
and contentment to those who are deprived of the privileges of civil liberty. They who have so largely partaken of
its blessings—who knows so well how to estimate its value,
ought to be among the foremost to extend it to others."

These sentiments . . . clash diametrically with those
which I had previously advanced . . . , on the subject of
extending mental cultivation to the African race in this

country. And notwithstanding I have no inclination to retract the sentiments which I have heretofore had occasion to express, concerning the practical benevolence and ardent zeal of Mr. Caldwell in the cause of religion and human happiness; yet, it is out of my power to unite with him in his opinion, of the utility of subjecting *men* of any colour, or any situation whatever, to *"the lowest state of degradation and ignorance,"* and, as near as possible, *"to the condition of brutes."* Right education and knowledge, should teach the legitimate slave fortitude, and the advantages of submission, duty, and fidelity; and should elevate the free man of whatever colour, above the unhallowed crime of despising himself for its having been ordained this or that tint, or for its being obnoxious to those who have been created with a different colour, or with none at all. Ask Capt. Paul Cuffee, Prince Saunders, and many other well educated and worthy persons of African extraction, whether they hate themselves, or whether any body else possessing common sense, hates them, because they cannot *repeal* the laws of nature; or because there is a political and physical propriety in their being considered as foreigners and aliens in *our* country.

Mr. Caldwell, having considered the various positions in which it had been respectively proposed to establish the colony, and expressing his preference of Africa, enlarged upon the greater importance of selecting that quarter of the globe, "in the belief and hope of thereby introducing civilization and the christian religion, &c." correspondent to the sentiments of Mr. Clay. "The great movements (said he) and mighty efforts in the moral and religious world, seem to indicate some great design of Providence on the eve of accomplishment. The unexampled and astonishing success attending the various and numerous plans which have been devised and which are now in operation in different parts of the world, and the union and harmony with which christians of different denominations unite in promoting these plans, clearly indicate a Divine Hand in their direction. Nay, sir, the subject on which we are now deliberating has been brought to public view, nearly about the same time in different parts of our country. In new Jersey, New York, Indiana, Tennessee, Virginia, and perhaps other places not known to me, the public attention seems to have been awakened, as from slumber, to this subject."

Mr. Caldwell remarked, that "it is a great national object, and ought to [be] supported by the public purse. And that, as had been justly observed by the honourable gentleman in the chair, there ought to be a national atonement for the wrongs and injuries which Africa had suffered." He said that "as a nation, we cannot rid ourselves entirely from the disgrace attending the iniquitous slave traffic formerly pursued by this country, until we, as a nation, have made every reparation in our power." He observed, that the example of our own ancestors, braving the various dangers and hardships of their early emigration and settlement upon these shores; and the prospect of the enjoyment of civil rights and a state of equality, ought to encourage and influence these people to comply cheerfully with the proposed plan of colonization.

The question being stated by the chairman, on agreeing to the preamble and resolutions offered by Mr. Caldwell for forming an association to accomplish the object of the meeting:

"Mr. John Randolph (of Roanoke) rose and said, that it had been properly observed, by the chairman as well as by the gentleman from this district, that there was nothing in the proposition submitted to consideration which in the smallest degree touches another very important and delicate question, which ought to be left as much out of view as possible, (Negro Slavery.)

"There was no fear, Mr. R. said, that this proposition would alarm the slave holders; they had been accustomed to think seriously of the subject. There was a popular work on agriculture, by John Taylor of Caroline, which was widely circulated, and much confided in, in Virginia. In that book, much read because coming from a practical man, this description of people were pointed out as a great evil. They had indeed been held up as the greater bug bear to every man who feels an inclination to emancipate his slaves, not to create in the bosom of his country so great a nuisance. If a place could be provided for their reception, and a mode of sending them hence, there were hundreds, nay thousands of citizens, who would, by manumitting their slaves, relieve themselves from the cares attendant on their possession. The great slave holder, Mr. R. said was frequently a mere sentry at his own door—bound to stay on his plantation to see that his slaves were properly treated, &c. Mr. R. concluded by saying, that he had thought it necessary to make these remarks, being a slave holder himself, to shew that, so far from being connected with abolition of slavery, the measure proposed would prove one of the greatest securities to enable the master to keep in possession his own property."

Extracts from the Speech of Mr. Wright.

"Mr. Robert Wright (of Md.) said he could not withhold his approbation of a measure, that had for its object the amelioration of the lot of any portion of the human race, particularly of the free people of colour, whose degraded state robs them of the happiness of self government, so dear to the American people. And, said he, as I discover the most delicate regard to the rights of property, I shall with great pleasure lend my aid to restore this unfortunate people to the enjoyment of their liberty, but I fear gentlemen are too sanguine in their expectation, that they would be willing to abandon the land of their nativity, so dear to man. However, I have no indisposition to give them that election by furnishing all the means contemplated by the honourable and benevolent propositions submitted to our consideration."

"Nothing would have a stronger tendency to effect the contemplated relief of the free people of colour, than some efficient laws to secure the restoration of those not entitled to liberty, to their masters, whose rights ought to be protected by law, and who, without such law, would be certainly sacrificed by the transportation of the free blacks with whom they would most certainly mix for that purpose. However, I feel no hesitation in saying, I should be happy to see some plan for the gradual abolition of slavery, that would prepare the rising generation for that state, and remunerate the master out of the funds of the nation, amply abundant for that purpose, without being felt by the people of America."

It is a strong presumptive evidence in favour of the rationality of a moral proposition, when it emanates from several sources perfectly distinct and remote from each other. The sentiments of Mr. Wright on the propriety of adopting some plan for the gradual abolition of slavery, &c. and remunerate the master out of the funds of the nation, &c. are so perfectly analogous to those which I had adopted and recorded . . . fifteen days previous to the meeting at Washington, that my confidence in their correctness, and hope of their favourable reception by the citizens in general of the United States, is greatly strengthened; particularly as Mr. Wright is one of the representatives of a large state in which slavery prevails, and is himself probably a possessor of slaves.

The preamble and resolutions having been unanimously adopted by the meeting, committees were appointed to draught articles of association, &c.

The following are the two first articles of the constitution:—

"Article I.—The Society shall be called, "The American Society for Colonizing the Free People of Colour of the United States."

"Article II.—The object to which its attention is to be exclusively directed, is to promote and execute a plan for colonizing (with their consent) the free people of colour, residing in our country, in Africa, or such other places as Congress shall deem most expedient."

In pursuance of this object, a board of managers have been organized; of which Bushrod Washington, one of the judges of the supreme court of the United States, has been appointed president. This body have submitted their views to the Congress, by a memorial. [The memorial is then presented]. I will conclude for the present, with a transcript of the proceedings of a meeting of the free coloured people at Richmond, (Virg.) which have come to hand (through the "Freeman's Journal,") just in time for insertion, before this work is dismissed from the press.—They are similar to those of a similar meeting at Georgetown several weeks ago:

RICHMOND, Jan. 28.

MEETING OF FREE PEOPLE OF COLOUR.

At a meeting of a respectable portion of the Free People of Colour, of the city of Richmond, on Friday, the 24th of January, 1817, William Bowler was appointed Chairman, Ephraim Speed, Moderator, and Lantey Crow, Secretary.

The following Preamble and Resolution was read, unanimously adopted, and ordered to be printed:

Whereas, A Society has been formed at the seat of Government, for the purpose of "colonizing (with their own consent,) the Free People of Colour of the United States;" therefore, we the Free People of Colour of the city of Richmond, have thought it adviseable to assemble together, under the sanction of authority, for the purpose of making a public expression of our sentiments on a question in which we are so deeply interested: we perfectly agree with the Society, that it is not only proper, but would ultimately tend to the benefit and advantage of a great portion of our suffering fellow-creatures, to be colonized: but while we thus express our entire approbation of a measure, laudable in its purposes and beneficent in its designs, it may not be improper in us to say, we prefer being colonized in the most remote corner of the land of our nativity, to being exiled to a foreign country.*

* Several free persons of colour, of both sexes, and all a little shaded with a yellowish tint, being employed as servants in the house in which I lodge, I inquired of two of the females, a few days ago, whether they would like to go to Africa, as it was the country of their forefathers. One of them expressed great repugnance at going there, and the other said her fathers did not come from Africa, "and (said she) if they (the Americans) did

And whereas, The President and Board of Managers of the said Society, have been pleased to leave it to the entire discretion of Congress to provide a suitable place for carrying their laudable intentions into effect—

Be it therefore resolved, That we respectfully submit to the wisdom of Congress, whether it would not be an act of charity to grant us a small portion of their territory, either on the Missouri river, or any place that may seem to them most conducive to the public good, and our future welfare; subject, however, to such rules and regulations as the government of the United States may think proper to adopt.

W. BOWLER, *Chairman.*

EPHRAIM SPEED, *Moderator.*

LANTEY CROW, *Secretary.*

The following article from the New York Columbian, may, perhaps, throw a little additional light on this subject:—

"NECESSITY OF A COLONY OF FREE BLACKS– Superseded.

We gave an abstract of the constitution of Hayti some weeks ago; and out of compassion, &c. we again publish the 44th clause, which shows a land of promise nearer our doors than Sierra Leone.

44. "Every African, Indian, and their descendants, born in the colonies of foreign countries, who shall come to reside in the Republic, shall be recognized as Haytians, but shall not enjoy the rights of citizenship until after a year's residence."

The same constitution that excludes the white man, invites the black; and, gentlemen from Port au Prince have assured us, that President Petion gives a marked welcome to the Free Blacks from the United States who settle in Hayti."

---

not want us, they had no need to have brought us away; after they've brought us here, and made us work hard, and *disfigured the colour,* I don't think it would be fair to send us back again."

DOCUMENT 72

(PLATE 33)

Slavery: A Northern View

Here, the artist depicts a brutal kidnapping of a freed slave, the immoral treachery of the deed etched in black against a background of sunny skies and fertile fields, contrasting the evil of man with the innocence of nature which is the true heritage of the Republic. The author of the work in which this scene appears, Jesse Torrey, Jr. (1787–1834?), had come to Washington to secure the release of free Negroes kidnapped into · slavery, a mission in which he received legal assistance from Francis Scott Key, who wrote "The Star Spangled Banner." In an earlier work, *The Intellectual Torch*, Torrey proposed a plan for establishing free public libraries.

DOCUMENT 73

(PLATE 34)

Slavery: A Southern View

In sharp contrast to the preceding document, the anonymous artist of this scene has chosen to stress the contentment of the Negro in slavery. This slave group on a South Carolina plantation are engaged in a traditional African folk dance, accompanied by tambour, banjo, and pipe. This emphasis on the survival of African culture is quite in harmony with the objectives of the American Colonization Society but inconsistent with the statements to a member of that Society (see doc. 71) by Negroes who considered themselves Americans and did not wish to be colonized. One can only conclude that, on the level of public discussion at least, whites have agreed to submerge the problem.

DOCUMENT 74

The Modern Factory Comes to America

The shift from commerce to manufacturing after the War of 1812, as the next document shows, introduced a new sectional issue: the protective tariff. But it was not yet in this period the hot issue it was to become in 1828, when John C. Calhoun, who had earlier represented the South's hope of itself embarking upon manufacturing, and Daniel Webster, earlier a representative of the still-dominant New England commercial interest, reversed positions. Their eloquent justifications have often been reprinted.

But the controversy over the protective tariff was symptomatic of a much larger issue which touched the nerve of national feeling: whether the new factory system imported from Europe would corrupt the morals of this virtuous agrarian republic or lead it into a new era of humane progress and prosperity. Nathan Appleton (1779–1861), one of the chief actors in the enterprise at Waltham and Lowell, Massachusetts, below recounts the efforts of himself and his associates to adapt large-scale manufacturing to American conditions. He was convinced of their success in converting the factory system into an instrument of national reform.

Documents 56 and 75–78 will suggest the essentially undemocratic nature of their social arrangements. The leadership of this period was paternalistic and patrician rather than democratic in the popular sense, and the industrial pioneers shared much in common with the paternalistic leadership of De Witt Clinton in New York, Thomas Jefferson at the University of Virginia, and Robert Dale Owen at New Harmony, Indiana. The common man had not yet discovered his own power for winning better working conditions, free public education, and a broader suffrage.

The problem of social and political leadership paralleled that of leadership in the arts, torn between the example of Europe and the drift of American experience.

SOURCE: Nathan Appleton, *Introduction of the Power Loom and the Origin of Lowell,* pp. 7–16, 32. Lowell, Mass.: 1858.

My connection with the Cotton Manufacture takes date from the year 1811, when I met my friend Mr. Francis C. Lowell, at Edinburgh, where he had been passing some time with his family. We had frequent conversations on the subject of the Cotton Manufacture, and he informed me that he had determined, before his return to America, to visit Manchester, for the purpose of obtaining all possible information on the subject, with a view to the introduction of the improved manufacture in the United States. I urged him to do so, and promised him my co-operation. He returned in 1813. He and Mr. Patrick T. Jackson, came to me one day on the Boston exchange, and stated that they had determined to establish a Cotton manufactory, that they had purchased a water power in Waltham, (Bemis's paper mill,) and that they had obtained an act of incorporation, and Mr. Jackson had agreed to give up all other business and take the management of the concern.

The capital authorized by the charter was four hundred thousand dollars, but it was only intended to raise one hundred thousand, until the experiment should be fairly tried. Of this sum Mr. Lowell and Mr. Jackson, with his brothers, subscribed the greater part. They proposed to me that I should take ten thousand of this subscription. I told them that theoretically I thought the business ought to succeed, but all which I had seen of its practical operation was unfavorable; I, however, was willing to take five thousand dollars of the stock, in order to see the experiment fairly tried, as I knew it would be under the management of Mr. Jackson; and I should make no complaint under these circumstances, if it proved a total loss. My proposition was agreed to, and this was the commencement of my interest in the cotton manufacture.

On the organization of the Company I was chosen one of the Directors, and by constant communication with Messrs. Lowell and Jackson, was familiar with the progress of the concern.

The first measure was to secure the services of Paul Moody, of Amesbury, whose skill as a mechanic was well known, and whose success fully justified the choice.

The power loom was at this time being introduced in England, but its construction was kept very secret, and after many failures, public opinion was not favorable to its success. Mr. Lowell had obtained all the information which was practicable about it, and was determined to perfect it himself. He was for some months experimenting at a store in Broad street, employing a man to turn a crank. It was not until the new building at Waltham was completed, and other machinery was running, that the first loom was ready for trial. Many little matters were to be overcome or adjusted, before it would work perfectly. Mr. Lowell said to me that he did not wish me to see it until it was complete, of which he would give me notice. At length the time arrived. He invited me to go out with him and see the loom operate. I well recollect the state of admiration and satisfaction with which we sat by the hour, watching the beautiful movement of this new and wonderful machine, destined as it evidently was, to change the character of all textile industry. This was in the autumn of 1814.

Mr. Lowell's loom was different in several particulars from the English loom, which was afterwards made public. The principal movement was by a cam, revolving with an eccentric motion, which has since given place to the crank motion, now universally used; some other minor improvements have since been introduced, mostly tending to give it increased speed.

The introduction of the power loom made several other changes necessary in the process of weaving. The first was in the dressing, for which Mr. Horrocks of Stockport, had a patent, and of which Mr. Lowell obtained a drawing. On putting it in operation, an essential improvement was made, by which its efficiency was more than doubled. This Waltham dressing machine continues in use, with little change from that time. The stop motion, for winding on the beams for dressing, was original with this Company.

The greatest improvement was in the double speeder. The original fly-frame introduced in England, was without any fixed principle for regulating the changing movements necessary in the process of filling a spool. Mr. Lowell undertook to make the numerous mathematical calculations necessary to give accuracy to these complicated movements, which occupied him constantly for more than a week. Mr. Moody carried them into effect by constructing the machinery in conformity. Several trials at law were made under this patent, involving with other questions, one, whether a mathematical calculation could be the subject of a patent. The last great improvements consisted in a more slack spinning on throstle spindles, and the spinning of filling directly on the cops, without the process of winding. A pleasant anecdote is connected with this last invention. Mr. Shepherd, of Taunton, had a patent for a winding machine, which was considered the best extant. Mr. Lowell was chaffering with him about purchasing the right of using them on a large scale, at some reduction from the price named. Mr. Shepherd refused, saying "you must have them, you cannot do without them, as you know, Mr. Moody." Mr. Moody replied—"I am just thinking that I can spin the cops direct upon the bobbin." "You be hanged," said Mr. Shepherd. "Well, I accept your offer." "No," said Mr. Lowell, "it is too late."

From the first starting of the first power loom, there was no hesitation or doubt about the success of this manufacture. The full capital of four hundred thousand dollars was soon filled up and expended. An addition of two hundred thousand was afterwards made, by the purchase of the place below in Watertown.

After the peace in 1815, I formed a new copartnership with Mr. Benjamin C. Ward. I put in the capital for the purpose of importing British goods, with the understanding that I was not to perform any part of the labor of carrying on the business. I was content with a moderate fortune, but not willing to disconnect myself entirely from business. An accidental circumstance occasioned the continuance of this copartnership until 1830.

At the time when the Waltham Company first began to produce cloth there was but one place in Boston at which domestic goods were sold. This was at a shop in Cornhill kept by Mr. Isaac Bowers, or rather by Mrs. Bowers. As there was at this time only one loom in operation, the quantity accumulating was not very great. However, Mr. Lowell said to me one day that there was one difficulty which he had not apprehended, the goods would not sell. We went together to see Mrs. Bowers. She said every body praised the goods, and no objection was made to the price, but still they made no sales. I told Mr. Lowell, the next time they sent a parcel of the goods to town, to send them to the store of B. C. Ward & Co., and I would see what could be done. The article first made at Waltham, was precisely the article of which a large portion of the manufacture of the country has continued to consist; a heavy sheeting of No. 14 yarn, 37 inches wide, 44 picks to the inch, and weighing something less than three yards to the pound.

That it was so well suited to the public demand, was matter of accident. At that time it was supposed no quantity of cottons could be sold without being bleached; and the idea was to imitate the yard wide goods of India, with which the country was then largely supplied. Mr. Lowell informed me that he would be satisfied with twenty-five cents the yard for the goods, although the nominal price was higher. I soon found a purchaser in Mr. Forsaith, an auctioneer, who sold them at auction at once, at something over thirty cents. We continued to sell them at auction with little variation of the price. This circumstance led to B. C. Ward & Co. becoming permanently the selling agents. In the first instance I found an interesting and

agreeable occupation in paying attention to the sales, and
made up the first account with a charge of one per cent
commission, not as an adequate mercantile commission,
but satisfactory under the circumstances. This rate of commission was continued, and finally became the established
rate, under the great increase of the manufacture. Thus,
what was at the commencement rather unreasonably low,
became when the amount of annual sale concentrated in
single houses amounted to millions of dollars, a desirable
and profitable business.

Under the influence of the war of 1812, the manufacture of cotton had greatly increased, especially in Rhode
Island, but in a very imperfect manner. The effect of the
peace of 1815 was ruinous to these manufacturers.

In 1816 a new tariff was to be made. The Rhode Island
manufacturers were clamorous for a very high specific
duty. Mr. Lowell was at Washington, for a considerable
time, during the session of Congress. His views on the tariff
were much more moderate, and he finally brought Mr.
Lowndes and Mr. Calhoun, to support the minimum of
6¼ cents the square yard, which was carried.

In June 1816, Mr. Lowell invited me to accompany him
in making a visit to Rhode Island, with a view of seeing
the actual state of the manufacture. I was very happy to
accept his proposition. At this time the success of the
power loom, at Waltham, was no longer matter of speculation or opinion: it was a settled fact. We proceeded to
Pawtucket. We called on Mr. Wilkinson, the maker of
machinery. He took us into his establishment—a large one;
all was silent, not a wheel in motion, not a man to be seen.
He informed us that there was not a spindle running in
Pawtucket, except a few in Slater's old mill, making yarns.
All was dead and still. In reply to questions from Mr.
Lowell, he stated, that during the war the profits of manufacturing were so great, that the inquiry never was made
whether any improvement could be made in machinery,
but how soon it could be turned out. We saw several
manufacturers; they were all sad and despairing. Mr. Low-

ell endeavored to assure them that the introduction of the power loom would put a new face upon the manufacture. They were incredulous;—it might be so, but they were not disposed to believe it. We proceeded to Providence, and returned by way of Taunton. We saw, at the factory of Mr. Shepherd, an attempt to establish a vertical power loom, which did not promise success.

By degrees the manufacturers woke up to the fact, that the power loom was an instrument which changed the whole character of the manufacture; and that by adopting the other improvements which had been made in machinery, the tariff of 1816 was sufficiently protective.

Mr. Lowell adopted an entirely new arrangement, in order to save labor, in passing from one process to another; and he is unquestionably entitled to the credit of being the first person who arranged all the processes for the conversion of cotton into cloth, within the walls of the same building. It is remarkable how few changes have since been made from the arrangements established by him, in the first mill built at Waltham. It is also remarkable, how accurate were his calculations, as to the expense at which goods could be made. He used to say, that the only circumstance which made him distrust his own calculations, was, that he could bring them to no other result but one which was too favorable to be credible. His calculations, however, did not lead him so far as to imagine that the same goods which were then selling at thirty cents a yard, would ever be sold at six cents, and without a loss to the manufacturer, as has since been done in 1843, when cotton was about five or six cents a pound. His care was especially devoted to arrangements for the moral character of the operatives employed. He died in 1817, at the early age of 42, beloved and respected by all who knew him. He is entitled to the credit of having introduced the new system in the cotton manufacture, under which it has grown up so rapidly. For, although Messrs. Jackson and Moody were men of unsurpassed talent and energy in their way, it was Mr. Lowell who was the informing soul, which gave direction and form to the whole proceeding.

The introduction of the cotton manufacture in this country, on a large scale, was a new idea. What would be its effect on the character of our population was a matter of deep interest. The operatives in the manufacturing cities of Europe, were notoriously of the lowest character, for intelligence and morals. The question therefore arose, and was deeply considered, whether this degradation was the result of the peculiar occupation, or of other and distinct causes. We could not perceive why this peculiar description of labor should vary in its effects upon character from all other occupation.

There was little demand for female labor, as household manufacture was superseded by the improvements in machinery. Here was in New England a fund of labor, well educated and virtuous. It was not perceived how a profitable employment has any tendency to deteriorate the character. The most efficient guards were adopted in establishing boarding houses, at the cost of the Company, under the charge of respectable women with every provision for religious worship. Under these circumstances, the daughters of respectable farmers were readily induced to come into these mills for a temporary period.

The contrast in the character of our manufacturing population compared with that of Europe, has been the admiration of the most intelligent strangers who have visited us. The effect has been to more than double the wages of that description of labor from what they were before the introduction of this manufacture. This has been, in some measure, counteracted, for the last few years, by the free trade policy of the government; a policy, which fully carried out, will reduce the value of labor with us, to an equality with that of Europe.

*   *   *

It was the Americans who first introduced the manufacture of heavy goods by the application of the least amount of labor to the greatest quantity of raw material, thus producing a description of goods cheaper to the consumer than any heretofore existing. This system the English have been obliged to follow, and have even adopted our name of domestics, whilst they have the advantage of using the cheaper cotton of India, which the Americans have not yet done, but which they will surely find themselves compelled to do.

In 1818, Mr. Calhoun visited the establishment at Waltham, with the apparent satisfaction of having himself contributed to its success. It is lamentable to think that in 1832, under the alluring vision of a separate Southern confederacy, he should have become the active enemy of the manufacture which was doing so much for the interest of the planters, and that the influence of his name has continued to keep them in that error.

*   *   *

DOCUMENTS 75–78

(PLATES 35, 36, 37 AND 38)

Mill and Mansion

Lowell was projected as a model factory town in order to counter agrarian fears that manufacturing on a large scale in America would produce hideous industrial slums like those of Durham and Dunbar near Liverpool in England. During the early years of its existence, before the advent of cheap immigrant labor and sweat-shop conditions, Lowell became one of the showplaces of the nation, visited by distinguished people from home and abroad. President Jackson, for example, gave it his blessing. Colonel Davy Crockett wrote of his visit in 1835, "I could not help reflecting on the difference of conditions between these females, thus employed, and those of other populous countries, where the female character is degraded to abject slavery. Here were thousands, useful to others, and enjoying all the blessings of freedom, with the prospect before them of future comfort and respectability. . . . I regret that more of our southern and western men do not go there, as it would help much to do away with their prejudices against these manufactories."*

Few visitors noted, however, the high degree of regimentation in the lives of these female operatives or the essentially undemocratic nature of this paternalistic community suggested by the photos. Unskilled operatives were lodged in frame houses (doc. 75), skilled operatives in brick dormitories (doc. 76); while Paul Moody, the inventive genius of the company, occupied the large colonial homestead shown in document 77 and Kirk Boott, the resident manager and chief architect

* The quotation above is from An Account of Col. Crockett's Tour to the North and Down East. Philadelphia: 1835.

of Lowell, lived in an outlying mansion house (doc. 78). The dualism in Boott's planning of the town (see again doc. 56) was carried into the construction of his house when he appended a Greek facade and cornices to a Georgian dwelling unit.

DOCUMENT 79

(PLATE 39)

Mill and Mess

The idealistic example of the projectors of Lowell was not followed everywhere in the United States, as this view of the Union Textile Manufactories in Maryland shows. Indeed, William A. Sullivan in his book *The Industrial Worker in Pennsylvania, 1800–1840* (Harrisburg: 1955) has emphasized the element of economic exploitation in that part of the country during the early years of the Industrial Revolution.

The picture stresses confusion and squalor, the extended riverside slum clustering about the base of the mills like the huts of serfs around some towering feudal castle. One suspects that working conditions at these mills were very bad. Yet the picture was commissioned as company propaganda, projecting to the public what we would call today "a corporate image." Perhaps the riverside slum has no connection with the mills. Perhaps it was considered "picturesque" and made the picture more interesting to romantic lovers of the picturesque.

DOCUMENTS 80–81

(PLATES 40 AND 41) ·

High Life in Boston

Insofar as their subject matter is concerned, these scenes can be bracketed with the genre pictures of farm life in document 59. They treat a common theme: the effect of material prosperity on the social classes—but with what a difference of intention and tone! The people depicted here represent gentility and refinement as well as wealth. If some of them, like the Cabots and the Lowells, have invested money in the new textile manufactories, they nevertheless are members of old ruling families.

In any event, the artist, Henry Sargent (1770–1845), treats them with respect. They hardly come to life at all, captured in stiff, stylized poses and speaking, we may imagine, in the hushed tones of a Henry James novel. The artist's main interest, however, centers on the play of light and shadow and especially the architectonic composition of the Federal style interiors. Except for a certain Continental splendor in the drapes and rich carpeting, the grandiose Empire style of Napoleon emulated by the emerging Caesars of commerce and industry has not yet reached these interiors.

DOCUMENT 82

The Fulton Monopoly

The next few documents on the steam engine and
steamboat illustrate the tensions introduced into American life by the Industrial Revolution. There was a
direct connection between technological innovation, the
material expansion of the country, the release of com-
petitive energies, and the apocalyptic images found in
documents 15–24. Such inventors of the period as Eli
Whitney and Robert Fulton, though supposedly protected by patent law, became desperately engaged in
long, expensive litigation with competitors, who, as we
say, knew a good thing when they saw it.

The monopoly of steamboat navigation granted to
Robert Fulton (1765–1815) by New York was broken
in 1824 by John Marshall's important decision in the
case of Gibbons *vs.* Ogden, reprinted in Henry Steele
Commager, ed., *Documents of American History.* This
decision, based upon a loose construction of the commerce clause in the Constitution, was preceded by a
long litigation, of which Fulton's public letter to Aaron
Ogden in 1813, reprinted below, is a product. Though
Fulton played a paternalistic role in steamboat development, he makes here no such profession of public morality as that claimed by the promoters at Waltham
and Lowell; yet one gains from him an impression of
broader mental horizons. How is this, and what does
it mean?

SOURCE: *Robert Fulton to Aaron Ogden, Esq.,* pp. 1–7. New
York: 1813.

Sir,

Studiously occupied on a new invention which presents
a prospect of great national utility, and relying on the dig-

nified integrity of a Legislature, distinguished for the patronage and protection it gives to useful improvements; I
have not attended at Albany to guard from your address
and industry, the rights granted to Livingston and Fulton,
and which I hope every upright and liberal mind will acknowledge, they have faithfully and honorably earned.

But by letters, received from Albany, I am informed,
that in your address to the committee, among other things
attempting to prove that I am not the inventor of Steam
Boats, you exhibited Charnock's work on naval architecture, to shew that I have quoted him in my patent, and
thereby you endeavored to make an impression, that I had
patented the experiments on the resistence of bodies
moving through water, *as my own*. If, Sir, you have done
so before the honorable committee, and they and the audience know it, then you have done it, knowing it to be
false; for you made a like attempt before a committee at
Trenton, in February last, at which time I presented to
you and the committee the drawing from my patent, and
quotations from said work, at the bottom of which, I gave
the author credit for the information I received, in the
following words: "This table of the resistance of bodies
moved through water, is taken from experiments made in
England by a society for the encouragement of naval architecture, between the years 1793 and 1798." This fact you
knew at Trenton, and there acknowledged that I had not
attempted to patent the experiments of others, but only
used them as a means for demonstrating principles. Hence
if at Albany you have impressed the committee with a belief, that I could be so base as to pirate the labors of others,
and present them to my liberal countrymen as my own,
you have done an unjust and ungenerous deed, which
would make the cheek of rigid honor blush: I say, if you
have done so,—for I place it on the conjunction *if*—you
have departed from that noble candor, that respect for
truth, which marks the moral man and man of honor,—
and you have attempted to destroy my character for
honesty, by depicting me as guilty of perjury: For in obtaining my patent, I swore that I believed myself the orig-

inal discoverer and inventor of the thing patented. To a
man who loves his country, and whose greatest pleasure is
to merit the esteem of his countrymen, this is too serious
a charge to remain without refutation.

That a patent may be taken according to law, it must
be so explained, that a person skilled in an art which most
resembles it, could from the specification, drawings or
models, make the machine. Therefore I drew from those
tables such conclusions as in my opinion would shew to
other persons how the calculations should be made, to ascertain as near as possible the resistance of any given boat,
while running from one to six or more miles an hour,
and from her resistance also shew, what should be the
power of the steam engine to drive her the required velocity, then shew what should be the size of the wheel
boards, which take the purchase on the water, and their
speed compared to the speed of the boat, all of which
were necessary to be ascertained, selected and combined
before any one could originate a useful steam-boat; and
it was for want of such selection and just combination of
first principles, founded on the laws of nature, that every
attempt at constructing useful steam-boats, *previous to
mine, failed.* But now that they are discovered and carried
into practice on the great scale, you and Mr. Dodd can
copy them, and have copied them exact: this is proved
by the affidavits of many experienced and respectable engineers, and will be acknowledged by every one who has
the least information on mechanical combinations, yet
neither you or Mr. Dodd, possessed as you are of Charnock's book, now know the principles which originated
and govern the construction of steam-boats, nor can you
find them in that book or any other.

But as you have looked much into books, models and
abortive experiments, to prove Steam Boats an old invention, can you shew any publication, model or work, that
distinctly points out what the power of the engine must be
to drive the boat the required velocity? or any work that
distinctly shews the best mode for taking the purchase on
the water, whether by oars, paddles, shulls, endless chains,

ducks' feet, valves or wheels? or what should be the size of the paddle-boards and their velocity? No, Sir, *you cannot* —these indispensible first principles are no where to be found, except in my patent; they are the discovery, the invention, which caused success. Previous to my experiments, all was doubt and conjecture; no one could tell the requisite power of the engine; no one had determined the best mode for taking the purchase on the water, or the powers and velocities of the component parts. If they had, why did you not avail yourself of them, and construct a useful steam-boat ten years ago? If those proportions and powers, which are now demonstrated by actual practice in my boats on the great scale, and where every intelligent blacksmith and carpenter can go and measure them, copy them, and make a successful steam-boat, were formerly known, how is it that Mr. *Stevens,* Chancellor *Livingston,* Mr. *Rumsey,* Mr. *Fitch,* Lord Stanhope and Oliver Evans, could not find them in twenty years labor, and at the expence of 100,000 dollars? Why were not steam-boats made ten years ago, for Charnock's book has been published fifteen years? And here let me present to you a curious fact: The experiments in that book were in great part conducted by Lord Stanhope, who himself since failed in his experiments on steam-boats; and if you have not yet so far affected my character for truth, that my countrymen will cease to believe me, I will state another fact—he, Lord Stanhope, in October, 1806, told me in London, that I could not construct a successful steam-boat on the principles and combinations I proposed, and which I now practice with complete success; consequently that book does not shew how to construct a steam-boat, any more than the multiplication table shews how to calculate an eclipse —yet the multiplication table is useful to those who know how to apply it to that purpose. But now that I have succeeded, contrary to all public belief, though as you say without the merit of invention, you collect a basket of scraps, conjectures, and abortive essays, out of which by a kind of magical sophistry, you attempt to place before a discerning committee a successful steam-boat of some

twenty years old. Suppose you were to collect a basket of
old ballads and bad verse without ideas, but rhyming and
containing the twenty-four letters of the alphabet, could
you not, from those parts used by Pope, prove that he did
not conceive or invent the Dunciad, or Essay on Man and
Criticism? Or could you or Mr. Dodd have got his manuscript, and put the strokes on his *Tees,* might you not
insist that you had made an important improvement, then
print and sell the poems as your own? For such is exactly
the kind of improvements you and Mr. Dodd have made
on steam-boats. But there is not so much to be made by
such improvements on poetry, as by moving parallel links
from one part of a steam-engine to another; hence avarice
suffers poets, particularly bad ones, to be tranquil; nor does
it interfere with unsuccessful mechanicians; it is only the
successful artists, they who really benefit their country,
that are fit subjects for plunder.—Cupidity never en-
croached on *Fitch,* or *Rumsey,* or on *Lord Stanhope;* they
were not so fortunate as to succeed and exhibit profits; it
even left tranquility to me in 1807 and 1808; in those years
the permanent success was not fully established, nor the
profits visible; but in 1809 they were; then envy and avarice
combined—to destroy the inventor. Yet with these facts,
known to every candid man in this state, you say steam-
boats are an old invention, and you have purchased from
Fitch's heirs all their right to his invention; but his heirs
however had no right, for his patent had expired five years
before you purchased, and his invention, if good for any
thing, is public property; but now that you have purchased
Fitch's invention, as you say, for a valuable consideration—
but as it is believed at Trenton, for a mere nominal sum,
that you might possess a phantom to frighten me, or to perform in your exhibitions to the public. Why have you not
built your boat like his, with paddles behind and chain
communications? It must be that you had not so much
confidence in his invention as in mine, and for the good
reason, that he failed, but I had succeeded. And now, Sir,
permit me to make a remark on your logic. You say Fitch
is an inventor; that his invention merits protection; yet you

do not use any one part of it. There is no part of his invention in your boat Sea-Horse. Mr. Daniel D. Dodd is also an inventor, as you say, of one link in your great chain of argument; and yet Fulton, who investigated and combined just principles, coustructed and gave to the world steam-boats, at the time the world had not one steam-boat, and the project was deemed visionary—this Fulton, according to your logic, is an impostor, and no inventor.— Why, Sir, there is something so flimsy, and totally ignorant of mechanical combination, and inventor's rights, in all these your assertions, that it is an insult on common sense to state them to any man who has the least penetration.

Having said so much, I have sent to Albany a copy of that part of my patent which contains extracts from Charnock's tables, it is attested by the clerk of the court to be a true copy. I have also sent a true copy of Fitch's patent, to show how much unlike it is to my boats, and the one you have copied from me; and I have sent the certificates of two experienced English engineers, who are now engaged, in Talman & Ward's manufactory, in the Bowery, who state that the links claimed by Mr. Dodd as his invention, and an important improvement, have been to all Boulton & Watt's engines for fourteen years. When I put these links in my patent, I did not patent them exclusively for all kinds of machinery, nor did I patent the steam engine, nor Charnock's tables; I made use of all these parts to express my ideas of a whole combination, new in mechanics, producing a new and desired effect, giving them their powers and proportions indispensible to their present success in constructing steam-boats; and these principles, those powers and parts which I combined for steam-boats, and which never before had been brought together in any steam-boat, I patented for that purpose and no other; as every artist, who invents a new and useful machine, must compose it of known parts of *other* machines. So in patent medicines, Lee's billious pills: he did not invent their elements, but combined certain ingredients in certain proportions to make a useful medicine, in which the just proportions are absolutely necessary and part of the invention—as in mechanics, the discovery of the proportion of the parts which produce the desired effect, make part of the invention.

As you have been heard before the committee and a crowded house in pleading your own cause, in your own way, carefully using only such arguments as you hoped would destroy me, I have thus sought the indulgence of a generous public, to hear my statement of facts, none of which you can disprove. And now, sir, I leave your merits and mine to the honest and noble feelings of the penetrating Gentlemen of this truly great and honorable State: They cannot be mistaken in your view: it is to seize on the property of mind, the fruit of ten years of my ardent studies and labor, and apply it to your own use, thereby destroying for ever all confidence in contracts with this state, and placing the property of inventors in a position so insecure, as to destroy every mental exertion.

DOCUMENT 83

Steamboat Litigation and Explosions

The following documents form a unit. The first two
are letters by Oliver Evans to a congressman expressing
hostility to the Fulton steamboat monopoly, especially
since Evans considered that he had improved notably
on English designs. This appeal to national pride had
little persuasive effect. Several years later, in a public
announcement, Aaron Ogden, who succeeded to Fulton's monopoly, claimed greater safety for the operation of his English low-pressure Boulton and Watts
engine in his vessel *Sea-Horse* than for Evans' high-
pressure engines (see doc. 84). Evans' response to
Ogden is contained in the third letter below. Meanwhile, the large number of steamboat explosions involving engines of both types provoked public alarm,
an expression of which appears in the editorial from
the Philadelphia *Aurora*, June 4, 1817. The last
document of this unit is part of an official report by a
Philadelphia committee of inquiry which investigated
steamboat explosions. The report is dated July 1817.

SOURCE: Greville and Dorothy Bathe, *Oliver Evans: A Chronicle
of Early American Engineering*, pp. 178–79, 252–53, 255–56.
Philadelphia: Historical Society of Pennsylvania, 1935.

To The Honble Timo. Pitkin.
Mars Works Phila. Dec. 21, 1811

*   *   *

I am alarmed in reading that there is a bill before Congress for the Relief of Robt. Fulton and others having
been informed that he intended applying to Congress to
make his patent good for steam boats which if done may

take away from me half of my Patent right for Steam Engines of my invention invented and perfected for the express purpose of Steam Boats and Steam waggons as my Patent specification will show and I exhibited a steam boat and steam waggon in the year 1804 in the Delaware and on Market Street to thousands of spectators before Fulton ever done anything of the kind I never conceived that I had a right to a patent for a steam boat after Franklin had proposed it and several had attempted it and I actually exhibited it and patented it. My object was to show that my engine ten times as powerful as those that had been tried would succeed perfectly even supposing theirs would not and with a clumpy flat of great weight and a small engine I left every vessel under sail half way and with an engine 5 or 6 horse power I moved a Waggon burdened equal to 200 bbls flour. [See doc. 48–Ed.] These experiments were tempery under great disadvantages and I thought sufficient to convince the most doubtful.

I conceive Congress by the Constitution have power to grant exclusive rights for limited times to the Original Inventors only for their respective inventions and improvements. This Fulton company have under the patent law if he has originally invented anything an improvement on steam boats which I never have yet learned he has done.

I do not believe Congress ever will pass any act knowingly that will grant away to others the rights secured to patentees for the use of their inventions or improvements yet I would think it my duty to present a memorial to Congress praying that my right to apply my engine to boats as secured to me by Patent should be guarded if I was certain that Mr. Fulton has so applied. Therefore I will thank you much to enclose to me a printed copy of the bill for his relief.

It would be great injury to the public to deprive them of the use of my Engine for boats I am making them for that use have 3 engaged and expect to engage the 4th in a few days.

It is 36 years since I discovered the powerful principles

of my engines and 30 years at least since I began to try to induce people to apply them to boats on the western waters not being able to do it myself they are now going rapidly into use and I would be sorry to be stopped in my progress.

Honble Sir your obet svt.
Oliver Evans

To the Same
Mars Works Phila. Dec. 27, 1811

* * *

I have been alarmed at reports that Congress were likely to pass a law favorable to a powerful Co. engaged in Steam Boats to the exclusion of others who may have invented and patented improvements to be applied to steam Boats. As I myself have done 36 years ago and have been engaged for 30 years endeavoring to get them applied to boats. I mean my steam engine *ten times as powerful as the British Engine* therefore more suitable for Boats and land Carriages. I verily believe Congress could not do a thing to impede the progress of the useful art more than to impede the progress of my engine to use in propelling boats I send you an extract from a letter from Isaac Sandford, chief artist of the Middletown Manufactory who has been in England 13 years and seen all the best engines there.

'Middletown 16 June 1811 as to the Engine we had from you it continues to perform with increasing credit and thus far exceeds anything of the kind I ever see, it is my opinion that it will continue to be superior to all other modes of constructing Steam Engines, as to all former constructions for that purpose they are so far inferior (in my opinion) that I would not take them as a gift, could I obtain yours at your price.'

Therefore I have prepared a Memorial to Congress, sent to the care of the Honble Adam Seybert. I will thank you to call on him and see it and encourage its being presented and read in Congress.

I am engaged to make three Steam Engines for boats have one nearly finished for Boston and if I should be arrested, it will be a great injury not only to me but to the United States, for I am confident that my engines will excell more for boats, than it has for mills and no man after seeing one of my steam mills work, will think of getting an English engine for that purpose, I will thank you to confer with the Honble. J. Quinsey he will perhaps defend his Constitutients in Boston, who have engaged me to make two Steam engines for Boats.

Sir, Your Obet

Huml Servt.

Oliver Evans.

To Aaron Ogden, Esq.

Sir—Are you indeed a member of that company or association, which set on foot and got up a chain of communication by steam boats and stages, between the cities of Philadelphia and New York, and who contracted with the proprietors of the steam boat Etna to form the first main link, to transport the passengers from Philadelphia to Bristol, and the return on the same route? As you have said you are a member of that association, in your answers to the queries of A Citizen in the Aurora, I must believe it; but permit me to entertain some doubts on another assertion of yours—that is—you say, you have "come innocently into the Delaware with the steam boat Sea-Horse". I very much mistake the meaning of the vulgar tongue, if you are innocent of a mistake in this particular. To do a thing innocently is to intend neither hurt nor harm, to any body; and if you are already a member of the association for the purposes above expressed, I should like to know how you can make out, that acting in direct violation of a contract, is to be reconciled with innocence? I am always apprehensive that my ideas are not expressed as clearly as I understand them myself, so I shall endeavor to place the matter in another set of terms. The aforesaid company contracted with the owners of the steam boat Etna to carry the passengers on the Delaware part of the passage, to and from Philadelphia and New York; you were one of the company who made this contract, for so you say yourself; but although you are a party to this contract, you bring the steam boat Sea horse into the Delaware to perform that very service which you (as a member of the company) had contracted with the Etna to do—and you say this is innocent. You remind me of the fable of the mother, the boy, and the cat. The boy had tied the cat by the tail and suspended by a line, and was beating the poor animal to death: a by-stander observed, to the boy's mother, that he should be reproved for his cruelty—"Reproved, indeed, said this exemplary mother, the sweet innocent, he is only making a little innocent sport for himself".

I recollect, sir, a little more innocent sport of yours, at Trenton, with the late lamented Fulton; that was another of your innocent amusements. There is a strong propensity among people who are not provided with head furniture of their own, to make free with the furniture of other men's brains:—perhaps, this habit is also innocent.

You say, moreover, that the "Etna is worked by an high steam boiler; that it is a boat in which there is no safety on board, in case the boiler should happen to explode;" I suppose this is all innocence too; sweet innocence! You are reported to be the very same Aaron Ogden, who was once governor of the respectable state of Jersey. You were also, it is reported, concerned with Mr. Daniel Dod in planning and constructing the Atalanta steam boat, and the Powhatan steam boat, and now you come innocently into the Delaware with the Sea horse steam boat; and it is you who talk of exploding of boilers; you have had experience indeed, I wish I could say innocently; for in the two first named steam boats, the boilers exploded, I say the boilers of the two steam boats Atalanta and Powhatan exploded, and did cruel mischief. Like mother of the boy who tortured the cat—you cannot surely say this was innocently done.

As you have gone so far in your innocent way, permit me to proceed a little further. I make no such pretensions to innocence as you seem to think necessary; I am a plain mechanical minded man, and as I do not depend upon other men's brains, I usually understand what I am about.

How and through what cause did it happen, that so many people were killed and tortured on board the two boats Atalanta and Powhatan, in which you had the innocent concern? Did it not arise out of your attempt to use my patent principles in the application of high pressure steam, and your ignorance of the principle of application; here I suppose you will plead innocence; how could you know what you did not know? How could you construct your boilers, or construct a safety valve, if you did not know the principle? You have a right to plead innocence of this knowledge; but your innocence was very unfortunate for those who lost their lives by it.

What new knowledge have you acquired in steam engine building, since you built the Atalanta and the Powhatan, both of which exploded. If you are innocent of any new knowledge, how shall the public think themselves more safe in the Sea-horse, built by the same persons.

About seventy engines on the same construction as that of the Etna are now in operation; not one of them has ever exploded. I say and defy contradiction, that of all the engines constructed on my improved form and principles, such as the Etna is, not one accident has ever befallen a human being.

Yet you, on whose two boats several people were killed, came forward and say you do it innocently too, to impress the public with an opinion, that where there never has been nor can be an injury, there is great danger—and where many lives have been lost, there is no danger at all.— Sweet innocence.—Good bye! Innocence, you will probably hear again from

August 8, 1817.   OLIVER EVANS.

STEAM BOATS: AN EDITORIAL

A Correspondent is alarmed at the prevailing rumour of the danger of Steam Boats!—And it would indeed be a cause of everlasting regret, if this most delightful means of travelling, so superior to every other for expedition and convenience, should fall into discredit by reason of any unfortunate event. But several recent instances of the destruction by fire and the explosion of the boilers, have given just cause of alarm. On the Mississippi the Steam Boat Oliver Evans, lately exploded and scattered such abundance of boiling water, that eleven persons were scalded to death and many others dangerously wounded. We have also an account of the bursting the boiler of a Boat in England, which destroyed many people on board and wounded many others. Is it not therefore an important question for the consideration of our Citizens—whether some of the Steamboats belonging to this City are not of similar construction, and therefore liable to like accidents? Must we wait for the sacrifice of many valuable lives before one single precaution is taken to guard our wives, children and friends, from so dreadful a calamity? It may be premature for the Legislature of the State, or our Corporation, to interpose their authority, before the danger should be ascertained by the investigation of judicious men, who understand the principles of their construction;—it has been therefore suggested by some intelligent persons, that the Citizens of Philadelphia should assemble in town meeting, and appoint a committee of twenty or more disinterested persons, distinguished for their character, talents and mechanical genius, who thoroughly comprehending the nature of the Steam Boat Machinery, may, with the permission of the respective owners, inspect the works and publish their sentiments on the occasion.—A publication on this subject, under the sanction of their names, might remove or confirm the prevailing doubts and apprehensions of danger, and guide the public mind to a correct opinion. When a perpetual motion has been thought sufficiently important for such a

measure, will our citizens neglect a similar provision for
the public security?

And I also trust the owners and inventors of the Boats
in question, will not disapprove a proceeding which, if
our Steam Boats are really safe, would effectually serve to
remove apprehensions unfavorable to their interest.

A COMMITTEE REPORT

* * *

As far as the knowledge of the undersigned extends,
all explosions that have taken place, where the engines
have been worked at seven pounds and below, have done
no injury to the passengers. It is the boilers that have
been made to bear a higher pressure than seven pounds
to the inch, which have proved so fatal; but had the owners known their strength, and been provided with safety
valves properly adjusted, no explosions would have taken
place, unless they had been constructed like the two on
the Mississippi, which have produced such disastrous consequences. This form of boiler should certainly be
abandoned; no safety valve nor any precaution would
make them secure. These boilers are cylindrical, and have
flues passing through their centres. The misfortune has
not happened by the bursting of the boilers; but has
been occasioned by the flue, where the fire is built, being
heated to such a degree, when the water has been suffered to get too low, as to collapse and make an opening
for the steam and water to rush out. This was the case
with the Washington and Constitution. At the Pittsburgh nail factory, where Evans's most improved boilers
had been used for a number of years, it was apprehended
it was time to replace them, and while new boilers were
making, one exploded while the steam was at sixty
pounds. When examined, it was found that a piece was
blown out at the top, about four by six inches. It removed a few bricks, but occasioned no mischief. It was
found that the thickness of the iron was reduced by cor-
rosion to less than one sixteenth of an inch, (when new it

was five sixteenths) at the spot where the explosion took place. The undersigned has not been informed particularly, as to the other disastrous explosions, but he believes, several have taken place as low as twelve or fifteen pounds pressure, and that such ought to be considered as high pressure engines.

Yours, respectfully,

Roberts Vaux, Esq.   JACOB PERKINS.
Chairman of the Select Committee of
Councils on the subject of Steam Boats.

DOCUMENT 84

Two Major Styles in Steam Engine Design

The functional differences between the English low-pressure Boulton and Watts engines and the American high-pressure engines designed by Oliver Evans are shown below. The low-pressure engines were introduced by Robert Fulton for operation on relatively calm Eastern waters and rivers, while the high-pressure engines were in great demand on the more turbulent, fast-moving Western waters. The low-pressure engine was bulkier and required a large condenser, pictured at the extreme right of the first diagram. The second

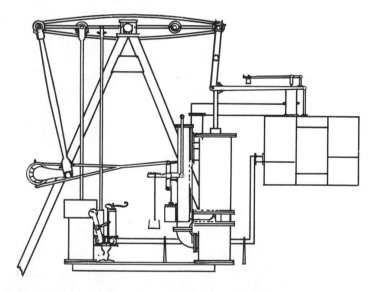

Eastern-Type Low-Pressure Steamboat Engine, from J. B. Marestier, Mémoire sur les Bateaux à Vapeur, Appendix (Paris: 1824). Photo by the Burns Studio.

diagram represents Captain Shreve's innovation of a
direct drive between the piston of a high-pressure
engine and the paddle wheel on the stern of his Western steamboats (see also doc. 85). This is not to say
that low-pressure engines were not in use on the Mississippi, however; nor that rear paddle wheels were more
characteristic than side paddles. Actually, the diagram
of the low-pressure engine below happens to have been
taken from a Western steamer. There is also some
doubt whether Captain Shreve's boat *The Washington*
had a rear paddle as pictured in document 20. A number of his other boats did.

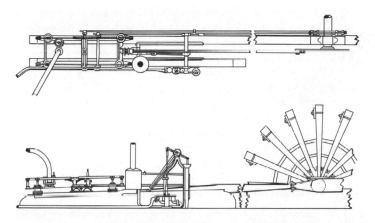

Western-Type High-Pressure Steamboat Engine, from P. R.
Hodge, THE STEAM ENGINE (New York: 1840). Photo by the
Burns Studio.

DOCUMENT 85

(PLATES 42 AND 43)

Two Major Styles in Steamboat Design

The picture at the top presents the typical Mississippi steamboat. It is a double-decker. The dual smokestacks suggest that it also has a double engine with separate drives for each paddle wheel. The boiler and engine are located on the main deck. When the furnace doors are open, the glare of the fires makes the boat appear from the bow like some fire-eating monster. The only major stylistic changes until after the Civil War will be in the direction of greater luxury: the addition of gilding to top the chimneys and decorate the paddle boxes, of fancy glass and gingerbread for the pilothouse and cabins, ornamented railings for the texas and hurricane decks, and, especially, richer appointments for the cabin interiors. This Western style will soon be imitated on Eastern waters.

The design with which Robert Fulton began on the Hudson is seen in the lower picture. This boat has a deeper draft to accommodate the engine below deck. The hull is patterned after traditional oceangoing hulls. The inventor has not yet provided adequate provision for his passengers on the deck. The canopy is designed more for a brief pleasure outing than for long overnight journeys in indifferent weather. During the initial flurry of alarm occasioned by steamboat explosions, Fulton's Hudson River steamers will pull behind them small trailers, or rafts, for their more nervous passengers.

DOCUMENT 86

Styles of Promotion in Technology and Industry

The following group of documents also forms a unit. The great problem of early American inventors was to raise money for the construction and testing of their inventions and then to create a public climate of interest for their reception and sale. Sometimes public acceptance followed quickly upon a successful demonstration, as with "Fulton's Folly"; other times, as with rail locomotion, it was long delayed. When John Stevens failed to interest the public in his railroad (see doc. 87), he sought the patronage of wealthy individuals. But these were reluctant to risk their money without the guarantee of a sure return. The letter of Francis C. Lowell, below, suggests that however benevolent and public spirited the industrialists at Waltham and Lowell were, they had a sound business instinct.

One way of enlisting public interest was to demonstrate the superiority of an American invention like Evans' high-pressure engine to its English counterpart. Documents 87–92 contain a number of pictures comparing English and American inventions. Evans' dredger, for example, was much cruder, but more adaptable than the English dredger in document 89.

SOURCES: "To the Public," an advertisement in *Relf's Philadelphia Gazette*, July 13, 1805. "Steam Engine," an advertisement in Poulson's *American Daily Advertiser*, December 25, 1818. John Stevens letter, a manuscript owned by Mr. John F. Fleming, New York City, published with his permission. Francis C. Lowell letter, pp. 7–8 of Jonathan T. Lincoln, "Beginnings of the Machine Age in New England: Documents Relating to the Introduction of the Power Loom," *Bulletin of the Business Historical Society*, Vol. XII, pp. 6–13 (October 1933).

To The Public

In my first attempt to move the Orukter Amphibolos, or Amphibious Digger to the water by the power of Steam, the wheels and axletrees proved insufficient to bear so great a burthen, and having previously obtained the permission of the Board of Health, (for whom this machine is constructed) to gratify the citizens of Philadelphia by the sight of this mechanical curiosity on the supposition that it may lead to useful improvements.

The workmen who had constructed it, voluntarily offered their labour to make without wages, other wheels and axletrees of sufficient strength, and to receive as their reward one half of the sum that may be received from a generous public for the sight thereof, the other half to be at the disposal of the inventor, who pledges himself that it shall be applied to defray the expense of other new and useful inventions, which he has already conceived and arranged in his mind, and which he will put in operation only, when the money arising from the inventions he has already made, will defray the expense.

The above machine is now to be seen moving round the Centre Square at the expense of the workmen, who expect 25 cents from every generous person who may come to see its operation; but all are invited to come and view it, as well those who cannot as those who can conveniently spare the money.

Oliver Evans.

STEAM ENGINE.

On Saturday, Dec. 26th at 7 o'clock in the evening, Dr. Thomas P. Jones, will deliver a Lecture on the Steam Engine, in one of the lower rooms of the Washington Hall.

Two complete Models will be exhibited at work, one of them a perfect Bolton and Watt's (or low pressure) Engine; the other a high pressure Engine, as constructed by Oliver Evans, and their comparative merits will be discussed.

The internal structure, and mode of operation of this interesting machine, will be familiarly explained, by the aid of Philosophical apparatus and transparencies.

Tickets at 1 dollar each, admitting a Lady or Gentleman, may be had at the Bookstores of Mr. Small, No. 112 Chesnut street, and Mr. Webster No 24 south Eighth street, or at the Hall on the Evening of Lecturing.

The Lecture will be repeated on Monday evening.

To the Hon: John Jay, Esquire
Hoboken June 28th, 1819.

Dear Sir,

Excuse the trouble I give you in perusing the following details—A short time before the termination of the late war, at my solicitation, an act passed the legislature of New Jersey incorporating a Company for forming a Rail-Road from the River Delaware near Trenton to the River Raritan at or near New Brunswick—Had the war continued there is no doubt this act would have been carried into immediate effect—Since this period nothing has been done—I am now however desirous of opening a subscription for the purpose, but am apprehensive the novelty of the undertaken may deter individuals from risking their property on an untried project.—To afford therefore an occular demonstration of the feasibility of the plan, I wish to form a Rail-Road exactly similar to the one intended, extending a short distance, near the Ferry House and Hotel at Hoboken—On this rail-road will be placed a carriage to be propelled by means of steam, to which will be attached one or more pleasure carriages—The pleasantness and novelty of this mode of conveyance will, of course, attract company from New York—and would, I presume, soon more than indemnify me for the expense incurred in its erection.

But this, however flattering the prospect of emolument may be, is, by no means, the main object in view.—Such an experiment would, at once, inspire confidence in the practicability of the projected Rail-road above mentioned, and do away all difficulty in obtaining subscriptions.

To give you some idea of the vast extent of the field my project would ultimately embrace, I take the liberty of enclosing some "Hints on the expediency of a Rail-Road from Philadelphia to Pittsburg," also "Documents," etc.

From these details you will perceive what importance I attach to the business of bringing Rail-Roads into general use throughout the United States.—And, I flatter myself, that you cannot fail to be impressed with similar sentiments—All that is wanting to make such an impression general, is merely to exhibit to public view an exact specimen of the contemplated improvement in actual operation.—To accomplish this I am unable, at present, to command the requisite funds.

To come then immediately to the point—I wish to borrow about $2,500—as a security for the payment of which, I would give a further mortgage to you on the property at Wehaken already mortgaged to you for $5,000 —The property is amply sufficient in value, and has no other encumbrance on it.

> With Sentiments of the highest
> Esteem and Regard,
> I am, Dear Sir,
> Most Respectfully
> Your Obed. Serv.
> John Stevens

To Mr David Greenough

June 9th. 1816

Dear Sir

The original proposal which I made to you and to which you acceded, was that we might see your machinery and copy from it as far as we pleased provided we would permit you to have the use of our patent Looms and warping machine and permit you to copy our Dressing machine. The Quill winder I stated to you did not belong to us and we could sell you no rights about it—it having been in part copied from one of Mr Stowells which would not work but which we had patented. This bargain I consider totally distinct from the other & I refused to go to Lancaster to even look at your machinery till you agreed to it. You then proposed to me the day we went to Waltham that we should make for you and you for us and in this proposal the said bargain was made we were to receive your frame at $900. and deliver you our machinery $90 per loom for 8 looms a Dressing machine like the old one for $500. with any addition it might cost to make it like the new one if that should be preferred, A Warping machine like our last at 250$ and one of the Quill winder for 175$ you paying also for Stowells Patent.

I have asked Mr Moody why his prices are so much higher than the prices just named. He says he still expects to build at their prices for our new manufactory taking time and doing all parts of the work by the job. But that even then he would not undertake to build for any one else at them prices because the expence of putting things together the use of the shop & tools and files, with numberless other little expences not included in any contract is considerable. But that in making the estimate to you he considered that he must build the machines mostly by the day and in a limited time. And so far from considering it any profit to us to supply you at the prices named we should much prefer not doing so, but to have you build your own and we will afford you every facility. As to your frame at 900 dollars we should prefer having it if we can receive it as soon as you named, if not should prefer not to take it. Mr Moody's calculation for a new frame like yours with some saving in the gearing is 600 dollars. The object in taking yours is to have one in the shop to copy from which we think will save us the 300$ difference. It is perfectly indifferent to us whether you relinquish this bargain or not if you think our prices too high build for yourselves or if you think the price of your frame too low keep it. I wish however you will let us know what you determine on immediately. You must understand however that our prices do not include yarn beams either for the looms the dressing machine or the warping machine nor Quills, reeds, shuttles, nor harness for the looms. That if you take the new dressing machine the price of that cannot be estimated till we have finished the one we are now making. We will make the yarn beams for you and charge only the expence and we will get the Quills and shuttles made for you. The reeds you can get better for yourselves. As soon as you decide let us know and we will commence the warping machine immediately which you will need for a fortnight before you have any occasion for the Dressing Machine. As to covering the spring rollers and many other little things we do not expect on either side any difficulties for such trifles, but mean on our part to spare no pains to get you properly under way and give you all proper directions for that purpose & we expect the same in return.

Yrs
Sg^d Francis C. Lowell

It is very uncertain when our new dressing machine will be finished probably it will be 5 or 6 weeks first as it is a new thing. If on seeing the new dressing machine you prefer the old one you can probably have that immediately.

DOCUMENT 87

(PLATES 44 AND 45)

An American and English Locomotive
on Exhibit

John Stevens' American locomotive in the first picture is as rustic as the Hoboken meadow where it is being exhibited. It runs on a cog railway, for the "T" rail has not yet been developed, holding precariously to the track without guide wheels, its four large wagon wheels fixed rigidly to the wooden frame. Stevens later added four guide posts of wood to keep it on the track. Although he hoped to raise money for further experimentation by this kind of public exhibition, the few spectators sitting on the bank in the distance seem more like invited guests, possibly friends and relatives, than like avidly interested patrons who had paid their admission fee.

Whether this is true or not, it can at least be said that Stevens did not have to build a wooden blind around his track to screen out the potential throng of non-payers as did the English inventor Richard Trevithick in the second scene. The latter's locomotive is more sophisticated, pictured here at a much later stage of development, although Trevithick's exhibition took place some fifteen years before that of Stevens. The carriage which follows the locomotive, however, shows little advance in its styling over a horse-drawn carriage. Its elegantly molded shell is in sharp contrast to the rugged frame-design of Stevens' locomotive, but very similar to the stylized English steam carriage in the document which follows.

DOCUMENT 88

Gurney's Steam Carriage

That style is very much a matter of one's cultural
environment is evidenced in this sketch of the Englishman Samuel Gurney's steam carriage. Gurney has
accentuated tradition, and particularly English upper-
class tradition, complete with top-hatted footman-driver,
two-toned paneling and a coat of arms for the coach
body, and decorative flourishes throughout. In the
domain of ideas, however, Gurney's carriage is a bold
anticipation by many, many years of the invention of
the automobile. Stylistically, one might compare this
design to Benjamin Latrobe's Grecian temple pump
house at Centre Square, which is also a ludicrous yok-
ing of the old and new (see doc. 35) and which represents the cultural conservatism of those Americans,
especially of the educated class along the Eastern seaboard, who were influenced by the inherited traditions
of England and Europe. Americans as a whole, however, were less bound by tradition and pioneered in new
industrial forms and techniques if not in first principles and great creative ideas.

Gurney's Steam Carriage, ca. 1827, from the ARCANA OF SCIENCE AND ART, opp. P. 54 (London: 3rd ed., 1828). Photo by the Burns Studio.

DOCUMENT 89

(PLATES 46 AND 47)

An American and English Steam Dredge

Oliver Evans equipped his dredge with wheels and
a paddle in order to deliver it under its own power from
his machine shop in Philadelphia to the city docks on
the Delaware. After several days of circling Centre
Square Waterworks on exhibition, the awkward machine was driven to the Schuylkill River at the upper
end of Market Street, where Evans transferred the belt
drive from the wheels to the simple paddle and let
the water float off the underframe. A long oar provided
a temporary rudder. The dredging mechanism itself does
not appear in the picture, an early illustration sketched
almost thirty years after the 1805 event. The drawing
is also defective in omitting a steering device for the
wheels and in locating the paddle-wheel shaft in a position which would fall below the water line. An
authentic 1933 reconstruction of Evans' dredger can be
seen in the Newcomen Society *Transactions*, Vol. XIV,
plate XI (London: 1933–34).

The 1806 English dredge follows conventional ship
lines and is designed for single-purpose duty. It is a
more graceful, sophisticated design than that of Evans.
The dredging shafts with their bucket chains, however,
were very similar. Evans' shaft was lowered into the
water by means of a chain attached to the digging end.
The British craft apparently employed some kind of
balance-and-wheel control for this purpose.

DOCUMENT 90

The Design of American and British Ploughs (Plows)

Because Americans commonly believed with Jefferson that the principles and the practice of virtue inhered in utility, they had a special feeling for the useful arts which they often communicated to their designs. Thus, James Fenimore Cooper wrote in his *Notions of the Americans* (1828), "I have seen more beautiful, graceful, and convenient ploughs in positive use here, than are probably to be found in the whole of Europe united. In this single fact," he added, "may be traced the history of the character of the people and the germ of their future greatness."

The author of the following essay provides the reader a basis for comparing English and American plows, for he included the drawings of both which appear in documents 91–92. He overlooked, however, the noted Jethro Wood plow of 1819 which used standardized, interchangeable parts, and a picture of this has been added. The reader may feel that the design of these American plows has something in common with the picture of the Western steamboat (doc. 85) and the portraits of Daniel Boone and Natty Bumppo (docs. 101 and 102).

On the other hand, the writer below imputes national differences in design more to stubborn differences of physical terrain than to national character or to aesthetic attitudes toward the useful arts. This in itself need not trouble the reader. It has been argued that we Americans have been too slow to recognize artistic merit in humble things and too apologetic about our most important contributions to art because we have applied to them false, inappropriate European standards.

SOURCE: "The Plough," *The American Journal of Improvements in the Useful Arts, and Mirror of the Patent Office,* Vol. I, pp. 129–33 (1828).

This useful instrument of husbandry, doubtless, had its origin in the earliest times—earlier than the date of any history extant; and yet it seems to be so essentially connected with some degree of civilization, that it must have originated with it. This remark is confirmed by the fact, that the plough has never been found with any of the savage tribes; and among the partially civilized, it has been found to have had a rudeness of form, proportionate to their nearness to the point, from which they started.

In the highly cultivated countries of Europe, much attention has been given, in the last age, and in the present, to the improvement of this valuable machine, especially since the introduction of agricultural chemistry; by which, not only new methods of manuring land have been discovered, but also the nature of different soils, and the difference of treatment which they require. On the benefits of ploughing, generally speaking, there is no difference of opinion; but on the time, the depth, the frequency of ploughing, there is much variety among practical farmers; while all agree in the general position, that these things are to be regulated by the nature of the soil, and by the crops which are to be put upon it. Equally various are the opinions of farmers, as to the best forms and kinds of ploughs, suited to their different purposes. And it is not a little wonderful, that a machine which has been subjected to so much experience, and to which so much attention of the most ingenious men has been given, should yet remain in a state of so much supposed imperfection.

The state of the case is nearly the same in this country as in England. There have been about one hundred patents for improvements upon the plough, in the United States, since the establishment of the Patent Office; probably more than has been taken out in England, in the same period—certainly a greater number in the last twenty years; and yet it would be hazardous to decide as to the best forms in use. It seems, however, to be generally admitted, that the principles on which Davis' and McCormick's ploughs are constructed, are among the best; although they are not universally admitted to have been the originators of these principles. After all, there is something, not only in the use, but in the forms of construction, and adaption, which must be regulated by the sound discretion and long experience of practical farmers.

* * *

One of the leading questions in England, respecting the most useful forms of the plough, lies between the wheel plough, and the plain plough; sometimes called, by way of distinction from the wheel plough, the swing plough, and the foot plough; and it is obvious, that each kind has the advantage, for some purposes. For instance, if the object be to throw up a thin uniform furrow-slice; or, if the object be paring and burning, the wheel plough has greatly the advantage. But if the land be stony and uneven, the wheel plough cannot be used with good effect. Hence, the roughness of surface, and the stony lands, of most parts of the older settlements of this country, are among the reasons why the wheel plough is so little used by our cultivators, rather than want of attention to the instrument itself. Without any other observation, than barely an inspection of the many models in the Patent Office, it will be apparent, that very much attention has been bestowed, and that a great variety of opinions have been entertained upon this subject. Improvements have been made, no doubt; the value of them, however, must be made out by their practical utility.

* * *

A point of the first importance, is to form the breast of the plough, so as to give the least resistance, and at the same time, clear itself of all roots, grass, and the adhesive parts of the soil. The plough presented by President Jefferson, to the English Board of Agriculture, was formed on the idea, that as the bottom of the furrow is flat, the breast should be flat also, so that there should be no tendency of the furrow-slice to sink into any concavity of the breast, or to have to force itself against any hard angle. "The objection to so much concavity, or flatness in the forepart of the breast," says an English writer, "as appears in that supplied by the American President, is that of the loose earth of the furrow loading there, which in some cases it is very apt to do." This plough of Mr. Jefferson, however, stands among the evidences of the variety of his talents, and the minuteness of his observation.

The fair conclusion is, that the breast should neither be too flat, nor too full; as in one case, the plough will not clear itself well; in the other it will give too much resistance, and increase the labor of the team. It is almost impossible to convey a precise idea of the whole sweep of that part of a plough, called the breast, without reference to a drawing, since there is such a variety of forms in use; and since some persons would include more in what they would call the breast of the plough, than others. We think the most perfect turn of this part of the plough, is that of a segment of an ellipsis, beginning a little back of the point, and sweeping round till it meets the beam.

The next point of importance is, the mould-board, or side-board, as it is sometimes called. We use the English terms; as it is from them we derive both the name and the thing.

The mould-board should have neither too much, nor too little twist, or curvature. If it has too much, it will cramp the furrow-slice, and create resistance; if it has too little, it will not turn it over handsomely; if it has too much length, it will give the more friction, and make the plough run heavily; if it has too little length, the plough will run unsteadily, and the furrow-slice will be apt to break and fall over irregularly; if it has too little breadth, it will curl the furrow-slice too soon; if it has too much breadth, it will not turn it over at all. So that it will readily be seen, that the same breadth or depth of mould-board, will not answer equally well, both for deep and shallow ploughing. To remedy this defect, and make the same plough serve for both deep and shallow ploughing, the English have contrived to have what they call a moveable mould-board, so fixed as to accommodate itself to different kinds of work.

The double mould-board plough is an English invention, well known in some parts of this country; and indeed, a supposed improvement of it has been patented here.

The handles, or stilts, as they are sometimes called, are much varied among plough makers, according to the judgment, or perhaps whim, of the artist, or the employer. It is obvious, that the slant of them, must be in proportion to the length; and yet if they are too long, they render the plough cumbersome, and throw the holder too far from the body of it. On the other hand, if they are too short, the plough is thereby rendered stiff, and the lever purchase of the handles is lost; so that it becomes harder for the team, besides the holder's not having the power to guage the cut of the plough.

One more remark shall suffice. This respects the length of the beam, nib, or neap. It should have a length in proportion to the size, it is said; but this is the question. Certainly the neap of the plough is too short in many instances among the farmers. The advantage of a long neap, (not too long) is that it brings the draft more in a line with the cut of the plough, and of course, increases the power of the team, and gives a more steady and uniform motion of the plough itself.

The double furrow plough is an English invention, the object of which, is to save labor. The principal objection to it is, that it does not do its work so well as the single plough. The saving of labor, lies in these two particulars—that one hand will hold it; and that it does not require a double strength of team.

The English farmers make more use of the coulter,

than the American; although of late years with us, the use of the coulter has very much increased. There are two ways of fitting them on—one, to fasten the coulter firmly in the beam, leaving a clear distance between the share and the point of the coulter—the other to lock the lower end of the coulter into the share. Sometimes, the plough point is made to the coulter, and the share is locked into the coulter. This, however, is the weakest kind of coulter plough. Where the object is strength to cut roots, &c. the coulter which locks into the share, is the most powerful.

The hoe and shovel plough, of which there are a great variety in England, and in this country, are very useful in the cultivation of corn and other crops. We should be glad to see them introduced more generally, especially in those parts where they are in the habit of hoing over the ground, at a great loss of labor.

We shall give a variety of drawings, both of English and American ploughs, without specifications of them. The forms themselves will show the improvements and the present state of that instrument, in both countries.

DOCUMENT 91

Representative American Plows

The two plows pictured at the top are the famous Jethro Wood plow, seen from two sides; the two at the bottom, two different versions of the Davis plow mentioned in the preceding document. In referring to these plows, let us retain the terminology of the author of the preceding document. Let the first side view of the Wood plow be our example. Then the plow's "blade" is the entire cutting instrument which reminds one in shape of the forked stick used by primitive man for plowing. The blade's "breast" is the profile curve of its leading edge, extending from the extreme point to its juncture with the "beam, nib, or neap." The "beam," of course, is the forward extending top rib to which the horses are hitched by means of traces and whippletree. The "share" of the blade is the lower portion of the blade (B), which, because it includes the penetrating point of the blade, must be made of the toughest material possible so as not to break off on stones, clay, or thick sod. Wood has cast this piece separately so that it might be easily replaced in the event of breakage. The "mould-board," or "side-board," the upper, outward-curving part of the blade (A), was originally made of wood, but Jethro Wood has also cast this in iron to give it additional strength for turning the furrow and also to make it self-cleaning (steel was not yet known). The plow's "stilts," or "handles," are readily identified. The "coulter," however, is not included in this plow. The coulter is a knife or wheel extending downward from the beam in advance of the plowshare for the purpose of cutting through roots or unusually thick sod in order to ease the penetration of the share. The reader is now in a better position to assess the correctness of our author's views in the preceding document.

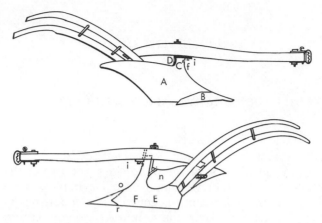

The American "Jethro Wood" Plow, 1819. Courtesy of the Division of Agriculture and Forest Products, Smithsonian Institution.

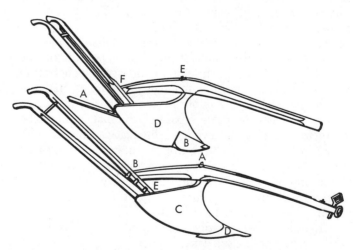

The American "Davis" Plow, ca. 1825, from THE AMERICAN JOURNAL OF IMPROVEMENTS IN THE USEFUL ARTS, AND MIRROR OF THE PATENT OFFICE, Vol. I (1828). Photo by the Burns Studio.

Representative English Ploughs

The first thing to note about the English ploughs is that they are more intricate and varied in design than the American—even ugly, since their lines are so broken up by such additional features as balancing wheels, coulters, and double blades. They are so intricate, indeed, that the principle of standard, interchangeable parts would hardly work at all. They are "sophisticated," a favorite word of opprobrium in early America, though one feels in them the same sensitive adaptation to peculiar English conditions that has been applauded in American vernacular design. The American instruments suggest the clean, uniform sweep of large open fields and prairies, while the English ploughs seem designed to grub in cramped little corners. Their shares, incidentally, even with protecting coulters, would seem to be particularly vulnerable and difficult to replace, except with a new plough. It is difficult to judge, without practical experience, the relative effectiveness of the various beams and handles as compared to American plows. Aesthetically, they are less pleasing. But, then, aesthetic considerations expended on instruments of manual labor are less to be expected of a stratified, class-conscious society for whom cultivation of the arts is reserved to the elite—or is this final judgment also a brash Americanism? For enlightenment on this problem of evaluation, one might read John D. Nef's *The Cultural Foundations of Industrial Civilization* (Cambridge, England: 1958), an American Catholic's appreciation of Europe's cultural heritage.

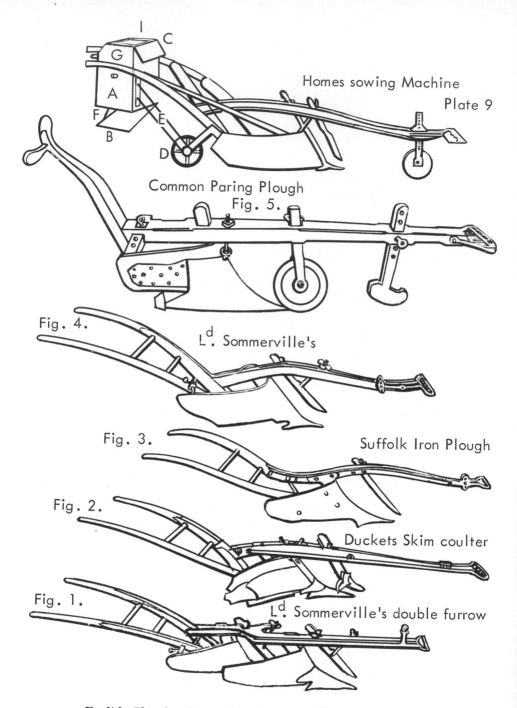

Homes sowing Machine

Plate 9

Common Paring Plough
Fig. 5.

Fig. 4.

Lᵈ. Sommerville's

Fig. 3.

Suffolk Iron Plough

Fig. 2.

Duckets Skim coulter

Fig. 1.

Lᵈ. Sommerville's double furrow

English Ploughs. From THE AMERICAN JOURNAL OF IMPROVE-
MENTS IN THE USEFUL ARTS, AND MIRROR OF THE PATENT
OFFICE, Vol. I, Plate 9 (1828). Photo by the Burns Studio.

DOCUMENT 93

The Flying Pendent Lever Bridge: A Poem

A "case study" of three bridges of the period will illustrate the problem of vernacular art, particularly in building and industrial design.

The main problem seems to be this: that the connection between thinking and doing must be so organically intimate, so instinctive, as almost to preclude theory. We have thus produced few theoretical scientists of first rank, but many practical geniuses; while in the arts, and especially literature, two rather distinct traditions have emerged, the one emphasizing the formal, cerebral approach to experience and the other the sensory apprehension of experience. Vernacular expression belongs to the latter.

The author of the following poem, Thomas Pope, a landscape gardener as well as bridge builder, seems to have been a first rate theorist. His prose exposition of structural stresses and strength of materials for his pendent lever bridge is too technical to include here. His poem renders the same ideas in a form easily understood by the layman, fusing abstruse theory to sensate experience. Yet neither his bridge (see doc. 94) nor his language in the poem below can be called true vernacular creations. The heroic couplet form has more in common with English how-to-do-it poems of the eighteenth century than with the shape of Western steamboats or characters like Natty Bumppo. The only familiar folk notes struck are his contempt for pedants and scholars and his sense of serving the national mission.

SOURCE: Thomas Pope, A *Treatise on Bridge Architecture*, pp. 281–88. New York: 1811.

Let the broad arc the spacious HUDSON stride,
And span COLUMBIA'S rivers far more wide;
Convince the world AMERICA begins
To foster Arts, the ancient work of kings.
Stupendous plan! which none before e'er found,
That half an arc should stand upon the ground,
Without support while building, or a rest;
This caus'd the theorist's rage and sceptic's jest.
Like half a rainbow rising on one shore,
While its twin partner spans the semi o'er,
And makes a perfect whole, that need not part,
Till time has furnish'd us a nobler art.
　　The muse with humble flight will now unfold
The myst'ries of a work that ne'er was told;
Delineate the plan by simple rules,
That those who can't believe may prove they're fools.
One single arc, whate'er the span may be,
Of river, lake, or swamp, or arm of sea,
Is all it needs, so wond'rous is it plann'd,
To form a spacious Bridge from land to land.
The towering poles of navies in full sail
May pass this arc in e'er so brisk a gale,
And ships at anchor ride beneath the arm,
Or moor to shelter'd wharf, secure from harm.
Thus navigation chastely is preserved,
And sons of commerce lose not their reward.
The butment's built of stone, where stone is found,
For nought can last so long or keep so sound;
But if the place should timber only grant,
Then stone and iron the builder will not want.
The length of butment's not, as men have told,
So long to cut a city in two-fold;
For rivers North and East may have a Bridge,
And streets call'd South and West may bound their ridge.
If half the arc a thousand feet demand,
One hundred is enough upon the land,
To form the butment and the steelyard's prop,
Which balances the power, lest it should drop.
This butment must more gravity possess

Than flying arm by weight can furnish stress;
Consolidation of a mass of stone,
Or towers erect, like those which China own;
But best when butments form a group of stores,
To house the treasure brought from distant shores:
The rent they furnish pays the building's cost,
Which in all other Bridges must be lost.
The stones that first compose the fulcrum's base
Are large and massy, but of even face,
Well bonded by their square and equal form,
So closely plac'd to leave no room for worm,
Or spurious matter of a worthless kind,
That oft is fill'd, in walls, in hopes to bind
The unconnected parts, which ne'er did rest;
These make but cobweb-structures at the best.
The mortar all is ground within a mill;
The only labour is the hods to fill;
One horse and boy for twenty men provide
With cement better made, more cheap beside.
The arms of Bridge are built of stone or wood,
But iron, cast, would furnish twice the good;
Its extra beauty and its lesser weight
Confound the pride and ignorance of the *great*.
Combining levers stretch from shore to shore,
And span the foaming flood ne'er span'd before;
By logs of timber plac'd at angles right
The bold formation is made strong and tight;
Each semi arc is built from off the top,
Without the help of scaffold, pier, or prop;
By skids and cranes each part is lower'd down,
And on the timber's end-grain rests so sound,
That all the force of weight can ne'er divide
Each tabled timber from its partner's side:
And, lest the end-grain should not stand the test,
A sheet of iron 's plac'd between each rest,
That no compression or indention can
Make an impression to defeat the plan.
    The usual mode of building house or ships,
Of framing Bridges, tables, purlins, hips,

'Tis end to side-grain by the ancients plann'd,
On which their ponderous loads were made to stand;
And all the Bridges that were ever built
Repos'd their weight on ceintre, pier, or stilt.
Not so the Bridge the author has to boast;
His plan is sure to save such needless cost;
A ladder on each side is lower'd down,
And shifted from the fulcrum to the crown;
Two men on each descend to drive the bolts,
Wedge fast the trunnels or set taught the nuts,
Or line with boards the parabolic form,
Expos'd to weather and the furious storm.
The lateral shape of Bridge resists the wind,
By concave circle throws its force behind;
The butment on each shore receives the charge,
Repels with weight the pressure by, and large.
If shores supply with rock to build upon,
The builder then hath an advantage won,
By which he saves the cost that oft ensues
In sinking coffers, caissons, or mud pews.
But should some softer strata heave in sight,
The consequences will be truly light,
As nothing is more easy to provide
Than concave circle on the under side,
By which the pressure will combine to force
The neighbouring infirm strata much more close;
Its watery particles must soon escape,
And force the solid grains into a heap,
By which the massy butment rests secure,
And through its firm foundation must endure.
Not so the tottering piles of ancient day;
When prest by weight they quickly slide away,
Wreck, from the centre to the structure's base,
And all its bond and beauty soon deface.
   When Time, with hungry teeth, has wrought decay,
Then what will sceptics be dispos'd to say?
Why, "down the Bridge must fall, without repair,
"And all the author's pleadings will be air."
Not so, he's better arm'd than you expect,

For nought can bring to ruin but neglect;
A mean 's provided, which can never fail,
To keep up strength whate'er the Bridge may ail:
Each log of wood, where'er its station be,
Is safely shifted for a sounder tree,
With greater ease remov'd than heretofore
A piece could be repair'd in an old floor.
For lasting age this Bridge will far exceed
All others ever built; they rot with speed.
'But how to reconcile these novel truths
'With what the *Doctors* teach their college youths
'Is hard for us (say some) to understand,
'How timber Bridges can fly off the land,
'Without a prop or scaffold from the strand,
'And meet to join in centre hand in hand,
'Is truly strange and marvellous to me,
'And, till I see it, never can it be!"
    Yes, teachers many have their pupils taught
That nothing strange or new can e'er be brought,
But what in ancient times were known or wrought,
So narrow and so mean their scanty thought.
But, base that works of art should judged be
By fools in skill, who have no eyes to see;
Who ne'er by arduous thought, or stretch of mind,
Trac'd causes old, some new effects to find;
Whose stupid life to man was ne'er of good,
Except it were to eat another's food;
And numerous is this tribe, that gain a name,
But not by works of skill, deserving Fame.
    Yet, science has her sons in every age,
Her babes of skill, her striplings, and the sage,
And daughters too, on which her hand bestows
Sublime discernments, that no stranger knows;
Though bastards oft intrude and steal the bread
With which the sons of merit should be fed,
Array themselves in ep'lettes, swords and gowns,
And strut about like showmen's drest-up hounds;
And if you ask them a new work to view,
'Oh, sir! say they, it never can be true;

'Besides, I have no time to spare, to look
'At schemes like these; they 're not within my book.
But science owns not such a gaudy train,
Who can on sons of genius pour disdain,
Nor *quack philosophers*, who durst decide
On works of merit they have never tried,
Nor half-taught theorists, of whatever name,
Who seek by others' skill to gather fame;
Nor wanton sceptics, who can dare condemn
More worthy works than ever fell to them.
Methinks the sons of art would be too blest
Were there not men like these to prove their pest.
    What! though this Bridge surpass all else before,
Should it be disbelieved e'er the more,
What finite man, to whom all skill was given,
That none beside should read the starry heav'n,
Or find a plan by which to pass the deep,
While blockheads and their follies rest in sleep;
Descry a continent, find out a land,
Mark out a shoal, make known where lies quicksand,
Or trace the magnet which to poles directs,
And, with the quadrant, all mistake corrects;
Or cast great guns, whose thunders loudly roar,
Or make silk cars, philosophers to soar,
Or Drake's dread fireships, that no quarters give,
But blast in sunder all, that none survive
To tell the dismal tale of dire despair,
That ship, and guns, and men, are blown in air;
Or excavate the earth, to float a bark,
To carry goods through rocks and mountains dark,
Propel a boat by steam, 'gainst wind and tides,
That in a calm by others swiftly slides;
That travels night and day, like a stage coach,
Which at the usual time make its approach:
Or make sweet sounds to soothe some savage breast,
Or link such words as poets deem the best,
Or carve some marble that shall stamp renown,
Or paint some golden scene that fame shall crown,
Or build this flying Bridge, the author's boast,

Or thousand other schemes now gone and past,
Or thousand things to come, that none e'er knew,
As time rolls on, invention shall prove true:
If these were all design'd for one man's work,
The other sons of art in caves might lurk,
And mourn their useless state, as lost to fame,
Compell'd to live and die without a name.
ARCHIMEDES foretold the lever's power,
How he could with a pole upset a tower,
Or raise the globe, if fulcrum were but strong,
Sufficient for to rest his lever on.
The author's Bridge shall surely rise to fame,
In spite of envy's efforts, power, or claim,
And men of liberal science own its worth,
Respect his name and cultivate its growth.

T. POPE.

DOCUMENT 94

(PLATE 48)

View of the Flying Pendent Lever Bridge

This visionary drawing of Pope's bridge emphasizes
the daring of his conception, the breath-taking beauty
of the slender suspension, heralding a new age of
progress and joining the old and the new in aesthetic
harmony. Sailing vessels ply the same waters with
steamboats. The oriental towers at the right seem both
modern and ancient. It is a glorious day for America.

Many years later, another poet, Hart Crane, attempted to create a meaningful, affirmative integration
of American life through the symbolism of another
bridge, the Brooklyn Bridge. He failed.

DOCUMENT 95

The Lattice-truss Wooden Bridge: A Treatise

In document 96 the reader will recognize the familiar
New England covered bridge, but he will perhaps be
surprised to learn that it was a product of careful
thought. Ithiel Town (1784–1844), Connecticut-born
and professionally trained as an architect under the
carpenter-builder Asher Benjamin of Boston, exerted
a considerable influence in bringing professional com-
petence and order to American building art. His firm
of Town and Davis received a magnificent tribute for
their virtual mass production of Classical Revival
buildings in a large canvas painted by Thomas Cole
called "The Architect's Dream" (1840), which showed
Town reclining on a pedestal in front of the massed
glory of Greece and Rome.

Town's lattice-truss, described below, followed classical principles of simplicity and strength. Though it
has acquired since a rustic, vernacular association, it
should be compared, for example, with the ranging
colonnaded Greek dormitories of the University of
Virginia (doc. 55) rather than with, let us say, the
homey farmhouse artifacts in document 59.

Like Thomas Pope, Town was conscious of making
a patriotic contribution, and he contrasted American
and European experiences in bridge building.

SOURCE: Ithiel Town, *Description of Ithiel Town's Improvement in the Construction of Wood and Iron Bridges* (1821), as
reprinted in *The American Journal of Science and Arts*, Vol. III,
pp. 158–61, 164–65 (1821).

To establish a general mode of constructing wooden
and iron Bridges, and which mode of construction shall,

at the same time, be the most simple, permanent, and economical, both in erecting and repairing, has been, for a long time, a desideratum of great importance to a country so extensive, and interspersed with so many wild and majestic rivers as ours is. It has been too much the custom for architects and builders to pile together materials, each according to his own ideas of the scientific principles and practice of Bridge-building, and the result has been, 1st. That nearly as many modes of construction have been adopted as there have been bridges built. 2d. That many have answered no purpose at all, and others but very poorly and for a short time, while most of the best ones have cost a sum which deters and puts it out of the power of probably five-sixths of those interested in ferries, to substitute bridges, which would obviate the many dangers and delays incident to them.

That architects and builders adhere to their own ideas in the construction of not only bridges, but of buildings, is almost universally true; they are obstinately opposed to the adoption of any other mode than their own, consequently it is as true, and it is seen to be so, throughout the country, (and it is much to be regretted,) that in very few instances, either in erecting bridges or buildings, there is any model either uniform, or, in general, very good. But in bridges and public buildings, it would seem, something better might be expected, if men scientifically and practically acquainted with such subjects, would step forward, in a disinterested manner, and determine between principles which are philosophical, and those which are not, and between modes of execution which are founded in practice and experience, and those which are founded in ignorance and inexperience; and in matters of taste, if they would determine in favour of classic and well established taste, and that which is the offspring of unimproved minds and whimsical fancies, which are ever upon the rack to establish new things, the creation of their own imaginations; and which are therefore sure to be wrong for this good reason, that their authors are so.

Perhaps the following proposition comprises what is the

most important to be determined with regard to a general system of Bridge-Building, viz.

By what construction or arrangement will the least quantity of materials, and cost of labor, erect a bridge of any practicable span or opening between piers or abutments, to be the strongest and most permanent, and to admit of the easiest repair?

In giving the best answer to this proposition, which I am capable of, after a number of years' attention to the theory and practice of this subject, I shall refer to the plates accompanying this article. The mode of construction is so simple and plain to inspection, as to require little explanation of them.

Figure 1, is an elevation of one of the trusses of a bridge; one, two, or three of those trusses placed vertically upon piers, are to be considered as the support of the bridge, and are to be of a height, at least, sufficient to admit a waggon to pass under the upper beams, which lie horizontally upon the top string-piece of the side trusses; and on these same side-string-pieces rest the feet of rafters, which form a roof to shingle upon. In this case, a middle truss is used, which will always be necessary in bridges of considerable width; the height of it will be as much greater than the side ones as the height or pitch of the roof. The height of the trusses must be equal to the whole height of the bridge required, and is to be an exact continuation of the work represented in Fig. 1.

The height of the trusses is to be proportioned to the width of the openings between the piers or abutments, and may be about one-tenth of the openings, when the piers are fifteen feet or more apart—a less span requiring about the same height, for the reasons before stated.

The diagonal bearing of these trusses, is composed of sawed plank ten or eleven inches wide, and from three to three and a half inches thick; it may be sawed from any timber that will last well, when kept dry. White pine and spruce are probably the best kinds of timber for the purpose, on account of their lightness, and their not being so subject to spring or warp as white oak.

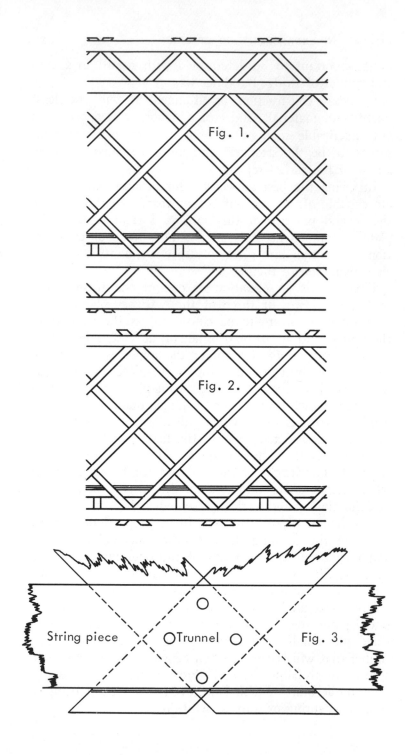

Fig. 1.

Fig. 2.

String piece   Trunnel   Fig. 3.

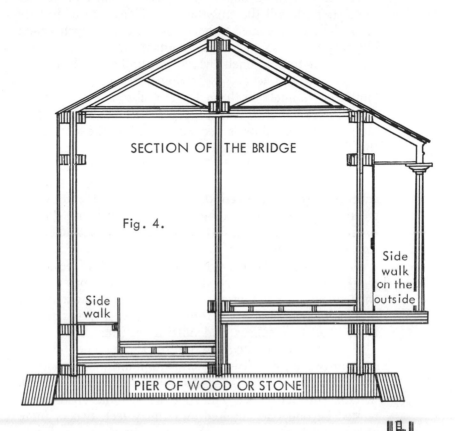

SECTION OF THE BRIDGE

Fig. 4.

Side walk

Side walk on the outside

PIER OF WOOD OR STONE

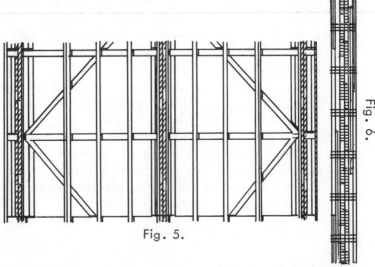

Fig. 5.

Fig. 6.

The nearer those braces are placed to each other, the
more strength will the truss have, and in no case are they
to be halved or gained, where they intersect each other;
but they are to stand in close contact, depending entirely
on three or four trunnels, which go through each joint or
intersection, and where the string-pieces pass over these
joints the trunnels go through them also, and are each of
them wedged at each end to keep the timber in close contact; a chain or clamp is necessary to bring the work tight
together.

The trunnels may be made of white oak, one and a half
inches in diameter. They are made very cheaply and ex-
cellently, by being rived out square, and driven, while
green or wet, through a tube fitted to a block and ground
to an edge at the top end; they are then to be seasoned before they are used.

The string-pieces are composed of two thicknesses of
plank, of about the same dimensions as the braces, and
they are so put together as to break joints as shewn at Fig.
6. This renders long hewn timber unnecessary, as also any
labor in making splices, and putting on iron work.

For any span or opening not exceeding one hundred
and thirty feet, one string-piece at top and one at bottom
of each truss, if of a good proportion and well secured,
will be sufficient, (see Fig. 2.;) but as the span is extended beyond one hundred and thirty feet, two or more
at top and bottom would be required as shown in Fig. 1
where two string-pieces run over the two upper and lower
series of joints or intersections of the braces, and in wide
spans the floor-beams may be placed on the second string-
piece as shown at Fig. 1.

Fig. 3, shows on a larger scale how each joint is secured,
by which it is seen that the trunnels take hold of the
whole thickness of each piece.

Fig. 4, is a section of a bridge of this construction, and
shows the manner in which the braces and string-pieces
come together, and also the manner of making the floor of
the bridge, and of putting beams and braces over head,
which are to be connected with the middle truss for the

purpose of bracing the bridge against lateral rack or motion. Very flat pitched roofs will be preferable, as it will, in that case, be a greater support to the upper part of the bridge.

Fig. 5, is the floor or plan of the bridge, showing the mode of bracing and the floor-joist.

Fig. 6, is a view of the bottom or top edge of the string-pieces, and shows how the joints are broke in using the plank, and also how the trunnels are distributed.

This mode of construction will have the same advantages in iron as in wood, and some in cast-iron which wood has not, viz. that of reducing the braces in size between the joints and of casting flaunches to them where they intersect, thereby making it unnecessary to have more than one bolt and nut to each joint or intersection.

When it is considered that bridges, covered from the weather, will last seven or eight times as long as those not covered, and that the cheapness of this mode will admit of its being generally adopted, with openings or spans between piers composed of piles, and at a distance of one hundred and twenty to one hundred and sixty feet apart, then the construction of long bridges over mud bottomed rivers, like those at Washington, Boston, Norfolk, Charleston, &c. will be perceived to be of great importance, especially as the common mode of piling is so exposed to freshets, uncommon tides, drift-wood, and ice, as not to insure safety or economy in covering them, and consequently continual repairs, and often rebuilding them, become necessary. There is very little, if any, doubt, that one half of the expense, computing stock, and interest, that would be required to keep up, for one hundred years, one of the common pile bridges, like those at Boston, would be sufficient to maintain one built in this new mode, keep it covered, and have all or nearly all the piers built with stone at the end of the one hundred years. If this be the case, it would be great economy to commence rebuilding, by degrees, in this manner. The saving, in the one article of floor planks, if kept dry, would be very great, as by being so much wet they rot and wear out in about half the time.

* * *

I shall conclude this article by a few ideas, taken from the celebrated Robert Fulton's treatise on canal navigation, page 117, and subsequent pages.

In England, the attention of engineers has of late years been much engaged on bridges of iron. These bridges, as experience produces courage, are progressively enlarging their dimensions, nor should I be surprised if genius should in time, produce the mechanic rainbow of one thousand feet over wide and rapid rivers. In crossing the rivers in such countries as Russia and America, an extensive arch seems to be a consideration of the first importance, as the rivers or even rivulets, in time of rain, suddenly swell to a great height, and in the spring, on breaking up of the ice, the immense quantity which is borne down with a rapid stream would, if interrupted by small arches and piers, collect to such a weight as ultimately to bear away the whole. It is therefore necessary that, in such situations, an arch should be extended as far as possible, and so high as to suffer every thing to pass through, or the inhabitants must, without some other expedient, submit their passage to the casualities of the weather.

The important objection to bridges of wood is their rapid decay, and this objection is certainly well founded when particular situations are alluded to where timber is scarce and consequently expensive. But in such countries as America where wood is abundant, I conceive it will be a fair criterion to judge of their application by calculating on the expense of a bridge of stone, and one of wood, and then compare the interest of the principal saved in adopting the wood bridge, with the expense of its annual repairs.

I have before exhibited the necessity of constructing bridges in America of an extensive span or arch, in order to suffer the ice and collected waters to pass without interruption: and for this purpose it must be observed that a wood arch may be formed of a much greater length or span than it is possible to erect one of stone; hence wooden bridges are applicable to many situations where accumulated waters bearing down trees and fields of ice, would tear a bridge of stone from its foundation.

It therefore becomes of importance to render bridges of wood as permanent as the nature of the material will admit.

Hitherto, in bridges not covered from the weather, the immense quantity of mortices and tenons, which, however well done, will admit air and wet, and consequently tend to expedite the decay of the weak parts, has been a material error in constructing bridges of wood.

But to render wood bridges of much more importance than they have hitherto been considered, first from their extensive span; secondly from their durability; two things must be considered, first that the wood works should stand clear of the stream in every part, by which it never would have any other weight to sustain than that of the usual carriages, secondly that it will be so combined as to exclude as much as possible the air and rain.

When the true principle of building bridges of wood is discovered, their progressive extension is as reasonable as the increased dimensions of shipping; which, in early ages, was deemed a great work if they amounted to one hundred tons burthen; but time and experience have extended the art of ship-building to two thousand tons, and in the combination and arrangement of the various and complicated parts, there certainly is more genius and labour required than in erecting a bridge of five hundred or one thousand feet span: but the great demand for shipping has rendered their formation familiar, and their increased bulk has gradually grown upon our senses. But had a man, in the infancy of naval architecture, hinted at a vessel of two thousand tons, I am inclined to think his cotemporary artists would have branded him as a madman.

DOCUMENT 96

(PLATE 49)

View of the Lattice-truss Wooden Bridge

If the picture of Pope's cantilever bridge in document 94 is a hymn to hope and futurity, this scene of Town's bridge represents the more prosaic reality of American life. Quite as much stress has been placed upon the details of landscape as on the bridge, which tends to merge into the background. Pope's poetic sails have been replaced in the foreground by a rowboat. It is a quiet, restful scene, undisturbed by the yearning strain of progress. Town's bridge is an accomplished *fact;* Pope's an unproven dream.

Document 97

The Arch-truss Bridge: A Narrative

Theodore Burr (1771–1822), author of the next document and a relative of Aaron Burr, was one of the practical bridge builders mentioned by Town who experimented with various modes of construction, among them the combined arch-and-truss bridge about which he writes below. No theorist, Burr nevertheless considered himself a sound, experienced builder, having had numerous successes before he undertook the McCall's Ferry-Bridge. He undoubtedly fulfills the requirements of the vernacular tradition. But it took the theorist Ithiel Town to free the truss from its unnecessary dependence on the arch.

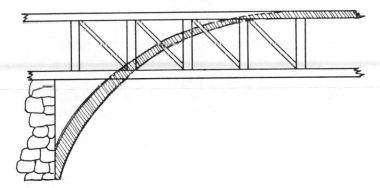

The Arch Truss. Drawing by C.L.S.

The narrative which follows creates the impression of another success—hard-won, to be sure, with a democracy of amateur helpers, a daring fortified by alcohol, and considerable luck, but a success nonetheless. Two years later ice destroyed the bridge, and it was never replaced. If this statement seems unfair to Burr in view of the great probability that some of Town's covered bridges must also have been soon destroyed by flood or ice, it should be judged against the boastful tone of Burr's narrative and the publicity given it.

SOURCE: *Niles' Weekly Register*, Vol. IX, pp. 200–2. (1815–16).

Theodore Burr to Reuben Field, bridge-builder, Waterford, New York.

Harrisburg, Feb. 26, 1815

Dear Sir—I can now inform you, with a considerable degree of satisfaction, that I have at length succeeded in getting up the long arch at McCall's ferry. This arch is without doubt the greatest in the world. Its length, between the abutment and pier, is three hundred and sixty feet four inches, the chord line of the arch, three hundred and sixty-seven feet. The width of the main part of the bridge is thirty-two feet; the wings of the pier spread eleven feet eight inches on each side, which makes a base of fifty-five feet four inches. At the abutment, the wings spread seventeen feet each, which makes a base of sixty-six feet. The altitude or rise of the arch is thirty-one feet. The arch is double, and the two segments are combined by king-posts seven feet in length between the shoulders, and are united to the arch by lock-work. Between the king-posts are truss-braces and counteracting braces. The arch stands firm and remarkably easy, without the least struggling in any part of the work.

It will be difficult to convey to you, by the description, the process by which we finally succeeded in surmounting the almost unconquerable difficulties opposed to its erection, not only by nature, but by all the elements combined.

In the first place, we raised it on floats lying in the water, ranged along the shore nearly a quarter of a mile below the abutment. The floats were placed at proper distances, with their ends to the shore, and on each of them were raised two bents or frames, varying in height to correspond with the curve of the arch. This made sixteen bents, on which the grand and enormous structure was raised, amidst tremendous storms and tempests, accompanied with floods and whirls and the bursting of waters. The scene at times was truly terrific. Frequently in the darkest nights we were under the necessity of going between the floats, and from one to the other, on small timbers, over a depth of one hundred feet water, in order either to shorten or lengthen out the ropes by which they were fastened, and to brace off or haul in the floats, as the water rose or fell. It took $1500 worth of ropes to stay the works against the flood and storms that we often had to contend with; and you must understand that storms of wind are much more frequent and tremendous at this place, than almost any other, owing to the great height of the mountains which closely border the river on each side.

From the time we commenced till we got the arch on the floats was ten weeks; during the whole of which time the water was never stationary, but continually either rising or falling. At one time it was twenty feet above common low-water mark; but in general it rose and fell from ten to twelve feet.

You will now observe that the arch stood lengthways up and down the river, along a shore of huge and uneven points and projections of rocks, which kept us always in jeopardy, in consequence of the rising and falling of the water, as I before observed. On the 17th of December, we had the whole in readiness to move up to the abutment, and on the same day the anchor-ice began to run a little. The next (which was the day we had fixed upon to move the arch to its place) the ice ran in still greater quantities, and about one o'clock it stopped for the space of about half a mile, and began to crowd the floats. It continued to move for more than one hundred miles above, where the river is from one and an half to two miles wide; whereas at this place you will observe it is only six hundred and nine feet in high water; and in low water the whole river runs in the space of three hundred and forty-eight feet. In this state it has been sounded by doctors *Preston, Marshall* and *Baley,* gentlemen interested in the bridge, and ascertained to be one hundred and fifty feet in depth; and it will perhaps not be improper to observe here, that taking a view of the great expert of country through which the Susquehanna runs, the number of great and almost innumerable smaller streams that empty into in it in its course, there is in all probability running in this space of three hundred and forty eight, and under the long arch, at least fifteen times the quantity of water that passes under the Union Bridge at Waterford.

The ice continued to run during the 9th, 10th and 11th, and pressed so hard against the floats that it raised up the outer ends of some two feet, others three feet; some less and some none at all; so that the scaffolding began to stand in all directions, the braces breaking and bursting out the spikes and bolts and the arch careening heavy towards the shore, touching only here and there upon the timbers which supported it; but as yet it had sustained no injury. The only chance of saving it now depended on the ice either becoming strong enough to support it, or gradually melting away so as to go off easy, without tearing the whole with it. I determined upon trying it on the ice, and on the 12th we fixed our capstan on the ice, and fastened ropes to it and to the arch to sustain it from falling, and also put some braces between it and the rocks on the shore.

From this time till Christmas we could do but little, in consequence of a thaw which took all the ice out of the river except about half a mile that first stopped; which we also expected would go, but it did not. Soon after, the weather became severe and hove in a mountain of ice upon us, the average height of which, for about a mile above and below us, was ten feet above the surface of the water at the shores. It did not, however, effect our works so much as might have been expected. The outer ends of the floats had settled down about a foot by the thaw; but this hove them up something worse than they were at first. At the same time the whole body of ice moved down, from twenty-five to thirty feet, which bore so hard against the floats, that they pressed so hard against the rocks, that it broke and mashed more than half of them to pieces. Still the arch remained unhurt and the scaffolding stood beyond expectation.

On the 28th we commenced leveling the ice, in order to take the scaffolding and arch off the floats on to it. I had 18 men employed at that business; and I presume that on an average they were in, up to their arms, forty times each in one day. But it will be necessary to explain to you the nature of the ice here: It is made up of floating ice from one-fourth inch to two inches thick. It forms from fifty to two hundred and fifty miles above the bridge, where the water is not very rapid but very wide; and in some winters runs constantly, for three or four weeks, without stopping. From the head of Turkeyhill falls to within three-fourths of a mile of the bridge, a distance of about fifteen miles, there is almost one continued fall, the bed of the river abounding with rocks that break the ice very fine. The river being so long and wide above, there is an immense quantity of this ice formed, and so very narrow at the bridge, that there it becomes an immense mass of from twelve to fifteen feet deep, before it stops. When this takes place, all the ice from above drives beneath into the deep water, until it becomes from sixty to eighty feet deep; and you may, by digging down three feet, take a pole sixty feet long, and with the strength of your hands run it down the whole length, and find no termination of what is called the mush ice.

On the 29th, we began to bridge a space of about fifty feet from the floats, which was soft, in order to move the arch sideways to where the ice was stronger. It took us from the 29th to the 8th of January to prepare one-half of the arch for moving. This was Sunday; and by evening we had eight capstans, with each a double-fold tackel fast to it, and with the assistance of about fifty citizens of the vicinity we made a move of four feet.

On the morning of the 9th, we fourfolded all the capstans, except one, and moved the one-half of the arch off sideways, forty-six feet, on to the runners one hundred and eighty-five feet long. On the 10th, we fixed the cross-runners (upon which we moved it sideways) on to the runners that extended lengthways with the arch, and confined all tight together. On the 12th, in the forenoon, it rained; in the afternoon we levelled the ice for a road, before it would freeze again. The 13th, we moved the arch seventy-seven feet; the weather soft. 14th, we made some rollers; the weather still soft but snowing. 15th, had but few hands; moved the arch fifty feet, 16th, we introduced the rollers every where, and moved the arch 217 feet in three hours. 17th, made a move of upwards of 300 feet. 18th and 19th, got up the one half of the arch.

We now commenced upon the other half, which we fitted and got up in eight days. Now we wheeled to the right and left, one half of the arch to the abutment, and the other half to the pier; fitted the buts to their places; cut off the scaffold-posts at bottom, some more some less, from one to twelve inches, so as to bring the whole arch to its perfect height and curve, and then united the centre. On Monday, the 30th, about 9 o'clock at night, we had the arch every where keyed up, and on Tuesday morning it stood of itself. Along the middle way of the arch the scaffolding had fallen away six or seven inches; but less and less towards the abutment and pier. To have an idea of the cause of this, you must understand, that there is a regular ebbing and flowing in the river at this place, once in twenty-four hours, of from two to four feet, which has a proportionate effect on the ice, causing it to rise and fall from fifteen inches to two feet, which at the same time is continually working itself down stream, slowly and imperceptibly to the eye.

On Tuesday morning, as I observed, the arch supported itself. We examined every part of it, drove some keys, and made every thing tight as possible. In the afternoon, we began to cut away the scaffolding, and got down two-thirds of it before dark; then stopped an hour for refreshment, and, before we began again, had two large fires made, on each side, about sixty feet from the abutment or shore. We then set to cutting down the remaining part of the scaffolding, which was completed about half past 8 o'clock. The whole now exhibited the grandest spectacle I ever saw. Aided by the light of the fires, we could plainly see the shore, and the arch rising from the abutment and extending itself west out of sight. It was a joyful moment to my brave fellows; and you may well suppose they gave way to the impulse, in loud and repeated hurras. The next day was set apart as a day of rejoicing.

The centre of the arch is sixty-one feet from common low water to the lower, and seventy feet four inches to the upper segment, and fifty-two and sixty-one feet four inches from the surface of the ice when it was put on. During the whole of this struggle, the humane feelings and kind disposition of the inhabitants, for twelve to fourteen miles distance, on both sides the river, were manifested to a degree that I believe was scarcely ever equalled. They voluntarily assisted from day to day; so that from the 8th of January to the 1st February, I had of this class from forty to one hundred and twenty men every day; and none ever discovered more zeal, or behaved with more order and decorum, in any service, where the most exact discipline was rigorously enforced. They came early, staid till dark, and returned home after night. Some attended every day; whilst others at times would ride day and night to notify and bring on troops. One day we could call on Lancaster co. the next on York, and sometimes on both in the same day, and for the most part we did not want for men. To move an arch of such an enormous weight, fifty and sixty feet in the air, was no small business; and, had it not been for the friendship of these people, I almost doubt whether I should ever have effected the object.

What is perhaps remarkable, is the fact, that (although liquor was handed round in great abundance) there were but two persons, during the whole time, that were the least intoxicated. And what is still more remarkable, there was but one man that was injured; that was *Augustus Stoughton.* He fell fifty-four feet, hit on the braces twice, then into the water. He in a few days was again at work; and no other person hurt.

On the whole, we were from the 1st of October till the 1st of February, in doing what might have been done in four weeks of steady weather, without floods.

It is a long arch, and you have a long letter; yet it does not explain to you one-half the difficulties we had to encounter, in getting it to its destined place.

I am, sir, respectfully, yours.

THEODORE BURR.

DOCUMENT 98

Gentleman-Architects and Carpenter-Builders

A new era is always announced by conflicting styles
and traditions, whether in building bridges or constructing a poem. Here Benjamin Latrobe urges his
young disciple, Robert Mills, to adopt a professional
mode of architecture in defiance of the gentleman-
architects and carpenter-builders who dominated the
American architectural scene. That Mills was not
always able to follow this advice is indicated by the
contrast between his original design for the Monumental
Church and the design which the Church committee
finally accepted (doc. 99).

The problem was more complicated than Latrobe
realized. Latrobe thought of himself as the professional man of the future and of carpenter-builders as
survivors of the colonial past. On the other hand, a
thesis of this book has been that the leadership of rough,
practical men came in with the new age of competition.
To complicate matters still further, a commonly accepted scholarly viewpoint is that Latrobe represented
the old cultivated tradition of Europe, while the breed
of carpenters, mechanics, and tinkerers belonged to a
new vernacular tradition out of which were to come
more advanced technical and structural changes.

SOURCE: Talbot Hamlin, *Benjamin Henry Latrobe*, pp. 586–91.
New York: Oxford University Press, 1955.

Washington, July 12th, 1806

* * *

The profession of architecture has been hitherto in the
hands of two sorts of men. The first,—of those, who from
travelling or from books have acquired some knowledge

of the theory of the art,—but know nothing of its practice:
—the second—of those who know nothing but the practice,—and whose early life being spent in labor, & in the
habits of a laborious life,—have had no opportunity of acquiring the theory. The complaisance of these two sets of
men to each other, renders it difficult for the Architect
to get in between them, for the Building mechanic find[s]
his account in the ignorance of the *Gentleman-architect*;
—as the latter does in the submissive deportment which
interest dictates to the former.—

It is therefore with sincere regret that I have observed your talents and information thrown into a sort of
scramble between the two parties,—in the designs of the
churches you have given to the congregations at Charleston. You remember the faults I pointed out to you at an
early period of your studies in my office especially in the
round church.—You corrected them. Your design had besides very great & intrinsic merits of its own.—What has
been the event.—Of all those who have contributed their
ideas to that church you have been considered as the most
ignorant. You have not even been permitted to correct
your own errors, and in other points you have been overruled so far as to have [been] obliged to admit into your
plan absolute absurdities,—such as, for instance the Gallery within the cupola, which may probably be the cause
why within an interior circle of a certain diameter in the
Center of the Church the preacher's voice is said to be not
perfectly heard.—

Such a situation is degrading and would not be submitted to by any other member of a liberal Profession, &
scarcely by a Mechanic whose necessities were not greater
than his pride.—In our country indeed the profession of
an Architect is in a great measure new. The building
artisans, especially the Carpenters have been sufficiently
informed to get through the business & supply the orders of a young country. Out of this state of infancy we
are now emerging,—& it is necessary that those who have
devoted their best Years & a very considerable expenditure to the attainment of that variety of knowledge which

an Architect ought to possess,—should take their legitimate rank themselves, or not venture into that Ocean of
contact with all above & all below them into which a mistaken complaisance will throw them, but adopt some
other profession sanctioned by the habits & opinions of
the country.—

It will be answered,—"If you are paid for your designs &
directions, he that expends his money on the building
has an undoubted right to build what he pleases."—If
you are paid!!—I ask in the first place are you paid?—
No! The custom of all Europe has decided that 5 p Cent
on the cost of a building, with all personal expenses incurred, shall be the pay of the Architect.—This is just as
much as is charged by a Merchant for the transaction of
business,—expedited often in a few minutes by the labor
of a Clerk: while the Architect must watch the daily
progress of the work perhaps for Years, pay all his Clerk
hire, & repay to himself the expense of an education
greatly more costly than that of a merchant.—But it was
not my intention to enter at present into the question of
compensation, for in your case, I believe that you have
neither asked nor received anything but have given your
advice, pour l'amour de dieu.—The question is in how
far you ought to permit yourself to be overruled in your
opinion by your employers,—and in order to answer it,—I
have neither leisure, nor inclination to go into a methodical disquisition,—but shall in a desultory manner proceed
to the end of my letter which as it is dictated only by
friendship, will not be received by you, as a regular treatise of the *Ethics* of our profession,—but as a proof of my
good will.—

If the most distinguished lawyer of our city,—Mr. Rawle
for instance, or Mr. Wm L. Smith of South Carolina,
were consulted as to the division, settlement, or alienation
of a large Estate,—he would be informed by the parties
concerned,—*what it was, that they actual[ly] wanted,*—the
titles would be put into his hands, the shares, as to their
amount and locality perhaps, exactly defined,—& the draft-
ing of the instrument then would be committed to him.

—As soon as the *draft* of the instrument were prepared; the parties would be called together, its nature, obligations, covenants, & general tendencies would be fully explained. In examining this draft, it would very probably occur, that some intelligent person would discover that the intention of the parties had been mistaken,—that the operation of the arrangement would be different perhaps than was expected, or that improvements in the settlements might be made. The lawyer consulted would not hesitate, to redraw, to change his disposition, untill all parties were satisfied.—But if on hearing the deed read,—any one of the party were to attempt to correct the technical phraseology,—the *terms* of the conveyance,—or to produce the opinions of the physician next door, or of the planter five miles off,—or of some wonderfully ingenious young Lady, or some person of surprizing *natural legal* talents from the backwoods, as to the form of the deed, its construction, or its alteration,—you would certainly hear no more from Mr. Rawle or Mr. Smith, excepting as to the amount of his charge for trouble already incurred.

In exactly this situation is an architect who is consulted on a public work.—He should be first informed *what it is that is wanted*,—what expense might be contemplated by his design,—what are the particular views of the persons who have the management of the money devoted to the Work.—

There will be on the part of a sensible & good tempered Man,—no objection to any reasonable extent of revision, or rerevision of a first design. Enlargement, contraction, alteration of arrangement, of construction & of decoration may be made by a Man of talents in almost infinite variety, & suggestions from unprofessional Men politely & kindly made are always acceptable.—But no honest man will for a moment listen to the proposal that he shall lend his name to the contrivances of Whim or of ignorance,—or under the pretence of a cheap, give to the public a bad work.—there is, as in most proverbs, a vast deal of good sense in the old Latin proverb . . . in sua

arte credendum. We allow full faith to our plainest mechanics in their particular callings. No man thinks himself
capable of instructing his shoemaker, or his tailor. Indeed
we swallow what the physician orders with our eyes shut,
& sign the deed the Lawyer lays before us with very little
enquiry.—But every gentleman can build a house, a prison
or a city.—This appears extraordinary;—for when a Gentleman sets about the work, he has the interests of all those
he employs in array against his fortune, without any protection in his own knowledge. The mechanical arts employed in the erection of a capital building are more than
20. Of these every architect has a competent knowledge,
so as to judge of the quality as well as of the value, & the
amount of the work, but it is at least 20 to one, against
the *Gentleman* who trusts only himself, that he will lose
5 p Cent at least.

Then as to the arrangement. Every architect who has
been regularly educated knows what has been done before in the same line. This knowledge he necessarily ac-
quires in the office in which he studies not only from the
books, and designs which he finds there, but in the instructions, & *actual practice* of his principal, provided he
[be] a man of intelligence, candor, and of business.

You are, on the subject of the difference between the
professional & regular mode of conducting your works, as
well as small buildings,—and the desultory guessing manner in which they are otherwise managed,—too well informed by experience, to render it necessary for me to
proceed further on this head.—I will now give you with my
accustomed frankness, my opinion of the conduct you
should pursue in respect to the proposed peni[tent]iary
house.—

1. In the first place,—*do nothing gratuitously*. The state
of Carolina are infinitely better able to pay you well,
[than] you are to subscribe your time & your talents,—
which is your subsistence towards the *annual revenue* of
the State:—for this is the actual effect of gratuitous professional services.—As far as you have hitherto promoted
the very laudable design of the Government by exhibit-

ing the practicability of such a building as will be necessary, if the penitentiary law be enacted you have done
well. For many people despair of the *end,* unless they see
the *means.* But further you ought not to go without a
very clear understanding as to what is to be the reward
of your labor.—You know too well the course of my professional transactions to suppose that this advice is the
result of a mercenary disposition. The gratuitous services
on a very great scale which I have given to *unendowed*
public institutions for the promotion of religious, or lit-
terary objects are well known to you, for you have had
your share of the labors. But when a rich state is about to
execute a project, from which great public benefit is expected to result, compensation to those who assist in effecting that object is a thing so much of course,—that all
I have said would appear superfluous,—if the example of
the *donation* of time & talent, & expense had not in many
instances been set by yourself. Some years ago I resided
in Virginia. [Here he narrates the account of his finan-
cially disastrous experience as architect of the Virginia
penitentiary. He continues:] My subsequent experience
of what is to be expected from public bodies has not differed from that which I gained from Virginia.—You must
take it for granted that no *liberality,* that is, *voluntary
reward* is ever to be expected from a public body. Individuals, responsible only to themselves in the expenditure of their money, are often generous,—& reward handsomely, independently of stipulation; but a number of
the same individuals, meeting as guardians of the public
money, feel in the first place, the necessity of pleasing
their constituents,—& in the second that of involving
themselves in no unnecessary responsibility.—And if at a
public board, one or more individuals are willing at all
hazards to act as they would in their own case, it is ten to
one but they are a minority.

To balance this want of liberality in public boards, they
have this advantage to offer over individual employment,
—that when a bargain is made, for a salary, or a commis-

sion, it is always rigidly adhered to,—provided it be in writing, & *clearly expressed,* for every ambiguity will always be interpreted for the public, and against the individual.—

In settling what shall be your compensation,—on the presumption of your being employed, I would by all means advise you, to prefer a salary to a commission. It will be both more certain to you, & more satisfactory to your employers.—

2. Take care that before the work begin, the plan is *perfectly understood,* and stipulate that no alteration, but by mutual discussion & agreement shall be made.—

3. Stipulate for the following points,—all of which are most essential:—

No workman shall be employed to whom you object.—

No workman shall be allowed to apply to the *board,* or *individual* to whom the state may delegate the management of the erection of the Work but through you.—

No account shall be paid, unsanctioned by your signature.—

With these powers you will have the mastery of all the operation, and you may do then justice to yourself & to the public, and as no money will pass through your hands, —you will not labor under the temptation, the power, nor the suspicion of violating any point of *pecuniary morality,* —that virtue, which like chastity in women, is in the general opinion supposed to be superior to all others, & almost to render them unnecessary.

4. I fear you have already committed one blunder,— that of leaving your drawings in the hands of the public. —Of the honor, & the gentlemanly feeling of the Governor, far be [it] from me to suggest the slightest suspicion. But his very admiration of your design will produce its exhibition, and as the *principles* of the plan, are the great merit of it,—and these strike at *one view,* you have armed all those who see it, or who hear it described with the weapons of competition against you.—But this is not now to be remedied.

My time will not permit me to say more to you at present. In the conduct of the work should my experience be of any service to you, you will know how freely you may use it.—

* * *

Document 99

(Plates 50 and 51)

The Monumental Church

Benjamin Latrobe and his pupil Robert Mills tried to develop an American style of architecture within a classical framework, locating their Americanism chiefly in a useful, rational disposition of space. Neither was as imitative as Jefferson. To Latrobe, nothing was beautiful which appeared useless or unnecessary, while Mills once wrote, "Go not to the old world for your examples. . . . It is our destiny to lead, not to be led." These views of Mills' Monumental Church show something of his experimentalism, but also his uncertainty. He thought, for example, that an American church should have a spire; yet the spire which he proposed in his original design seems almost an afterthought, poorly integrated structurally with the rest and incongruous in juxtaposition with the dome. Mills has succeeded best in his exposition of space. The deep entrance into a holy place has solemn validity. The hexagonal or octagonal block serves an important functional need in that it provides the shell for an amphitheatre within. Mills was one of the fathers of the amphitheatre church.

DOCUMENT 100

Authorship and Fashions

Surgeon, scientist, editor, poet, James Gates Percival (1795–1856) led a troubled existence trying to find a career in a society which did not take kindly to neurotic, morbid personalities. He had enjoyed a brief day of fame with the publication in 1821 of his first volume of poetry, *Clio*, a rather romantic, Poe-like work. Below he records, with a frankness again like Poe, since he was writing to a comparative stranger, his contempt for the vulgar society which failed to appreciate his rare talent but idolized James Fenimore Cooper. His letter was written to a clergyman, James Lawrence Yvonnet.

The main difficulty with Percival's poetry was not that it was too advanced but that it lacked vitality. His was a pallid, esoteric romanticism, though he claimed to prefer the strong passions and vivid imagery of the early Elizabethans to the classical propriety of Pope and Campbell which his class admired. His stand against vernacular expression, like that of Benjamin Latrobe in the preceding document, can be taken as a defense of refined standards by the cultivated elite. It is a pity that he could not summon as much vitality to his poetry as to his prose.

SOURCE: from two letters to James Lawrence Yvonnet dated June 11, 1822, and July 18, 1823, in Julius H. Ward, *The Life and Letters of James Gates Percival*, pp. 95–99, 170–72. Boston: 1866.

DEAR SIR,—

I received a letter from you directed to me at Charleston a few days since. It remained a long time in that office, and was then forwarded to me. You must therefore excuse me for not answering you earlier. Besides, I am no correspondent. I never kept up a regular correspondence in my life. I shall therefore perhaps disappoint you before long. I returned here in April, and, like a fool, concluded to try authorship as a profession. I therefore hired a pleasant little house to myself, just out of town. But I have found that I cannot live alone. With the exception of one or two young men, I have not the slightest vestige of society. In fact, I have nothing here to excite me. I am as completely without immediate motive as a snail in his shell. I am utterly disgusted with authorship. I shall in the course of this month publish a second and last number of Clio, and then I am determined never to write another line of poetry. I shall then engage in my profession and in good earnest, and raise a battering-ram against error wherever I find it. I want something to act as a constant powerful excitement upon me, and I think if I can get a swarm around my ears I shall have something to keep me awake.

I know of no more contemptible being than an author who writes for money. He converts the only shrine where mind can find a sure asylum into a huckster's shop. He makes the last and best gift to man—language—the miserable means of supplying his miserable wants. If I must labor for subsistence, I will not labor with my pen, particularly when I am paid at a meaner rate than a shoeblack. I have succeeded in causing something of a stir in the papers at least, but the last echoes have died away, and now the whole of it appears puff, puff. I find myself as unnoticed as the most abject would desire to be. I shall leave here as soon as I have finished Clio and can get away.

Cities are truly the great and foul ulcers of society, but they are the only places where one like me can find his excitement or reward, and they are the best places for disappointed hope to die in, unnoticed and unknown. St. Pierre says cities are the best refuge of the unfortunate, the place where they can best hide themselves. I once had something at stake in Philadelphia; I think I

shall renew my stake there and fight it out or die. I am
sometimes lost when I think of the powerful influence of
external excitement. I am a trunk without it.

Perhaps I do not say too much when I assert that I
have gained more reputation as a poet than any American before me; and after all, what is it? Wretched illusion. They may talk of the pleasure of writing and musing and imagining. But were we made to be dreamers? I
have as comfortably despicable an opinion of the mass
of men as heart could wish, but yet I do not like to give
up the opinion that there are some gods and even angels
among them; but the charm of life is broken with me; the
veil that looks so beautiful around us has been torn in
pieces; and after all, I find the best of them are not much
better than I am, and I am poor enough, heaven knows.
Some are mad after books; they study their health out
and find it trash. Two or three clear turns of the eye will
tell them as much as an age of mere reading; and half of
written knowledge is very good to keep children out of
mischief,—most of the rest ought to be burnt up. I have
added to the mountain of books and the myriad of authors. But I sometimes think I had better be annihilated,
books and all, than be the means of making fools gape
and girls cry as I perhaps may. There are religious mad-
men,—mad after heaven or mad with fear of hell,—and
what a profitable thing it is to feel these hopes and cherish
these fears. A young lady whom I once taught, and loved
too, to whom I was so devoted that I am ashamed of it,
and who, I am bold to say, owes the best part of her mind
to me, has lately, I understand, been engaged to a young
Episcopal clergyman,—so the black coat ran away with
beauty. They make the devotees; they connect the love
of God with the love of themselves, worm themselves into
the affections by a sort of religious courtship, and finally
steal them away from those frank and open and high-
toned spirits who disdain to offer anything but their own
naked merit. After all, what a silly thing it is to regret a
woman!—dear sensibility, oh, la! those sighs, and tears,
and glances, and whispers, that cheek of roses, and bosom

of heaped-up lilies, and eye of diamond, and breath like the perfume of Arabia, what nonsense and what stark lies, too, it begets at the pure effervescence of a heavenly spirit, and ends in—the straw! Why should young ladies be so anxious to [be married]? Every one wants a husband, and sets her cap for him as nicely as decency will allow, and sometimes more so. We call them, too,—angels,—but they are too heavy to fly. A little dress, and a little lisping and music and drawing, perhaps a blue stocking filled full of title-pages and technics. Is that unfair?

I am disgusted with all *prestiges*. The talk about liberty is abhorrent to me. I believe there is as much of general liberty here as elsewhere, and that our populace is as enlightened as any; and yet to see how they are yoked, and swayed, and pulled along by the nose, by boy demagogues, —really one would almost forswear his species. They make a great parade of liberty at the South, but it is nothing but the liberty of driving negroes and playing the fool with their earnings. And what was the liberty of Greece and Rome? An immense gang of slaves and a few self-styled republicans, who flattered each other when they saw fit, and murdered each other when they had a mind to,— rich men who outbid each other at the auction of office and votes, which had each their petty price. I, like a thousand others, have talked big about these things, and yet they are, after all, *vox* ——. When a man has got a heap of dollars and a great house he has done something, and yet the getting is all the good about it. As for reading and study it serves to kill time,—a hard task. Talking answers for newspapers, because we can then measure existence by the exertion of mental power. I am very much inclined to think that one had better be lashed through life by a cat-o'-nine-tails than be a rich man at his ease.

* * *

I have heard of Gotham,* but have not seen it. I am glad they have rubbed up Cooper. Perhaps you don't feel

* A volume, "Gotham and the Gothamites,—a Medley," in which the publishers, authors, and wits of New York in those days were severely and personally satirized.—Ed.

about him as I do. I can consider him nothing more than
a literary *parasitic animal* (naturalists give that title to
the creeping things that inhabit the outside of our cra-
niums). What a thing that Pioneers is, with its most
exalted character making *Virginia fence* on his way home
from a bush tavern, after attending divine service on
Christmas Eve, gloriously in the spirit, or rather the spirit
in him; and that Ben Pump, soberly measuring out whole
fathoms of sea-slang, and old Jamaica by the gallon; and
Remarkable, with her sweet tooth, and old Natty Bum!
Ho! and [behold] High-Dutchers and Low-Dutchers and
Mounsheers and Mohegans and Bay State, and Var-
mounters all to show what a great linguist he was. I have
forgot Cuffee, *pop up gobbler*. Now all this is wretched,
not a whit above Coleman's broad grins and [. . .]
pokers. It might do well enough to amuse the select society of a barber's shop or a porter-house. But to have the
author step forward on such stilts and claim to be the
lion of our national literature, and fall to roaring himself
and set all his jackals howling (S——, C——, & Co.) to put
better folks out of countenance,—why, it is pitiful, 't is
wondrous pitiful, at least for the country that not only
suffers it, but encourages it.

As for myself, I say nothing. I have written what I have
written. Let others judge. They call me vain. Perhaps I
have been so. If so, I will correct myself. But it was merely
the innocent vanity of exhilaration. It was but the natural
consequence of rising from the lowest state of depression,
and finding myself on an eminence where I was looked at
by my whole country, and seen too across the Atlantic,
even from proud Augusta, if not Edina. It is a wonder
that I was not thrown into *a vertigo of vanity*. As it is, it
has cost me my most valued friend.

I will tell you one thing *sub rosa*. Morse's picture of
Congress Hall, (have you seen it? if not it is too late now,)
that picture has cost him one hundred and ten dollars to
exhibit it in New York. Tell it not in Gath! He labored
at it eighteen months, and spent many hundred dollars
in its execution; and now he has to pay the public for

looking at it, "largess, largess." Allston says it is a master-
piece of coloring and perspective. Who would write or
paint any good thing for such a *fashionable vulgar* as
ours? For my part, I am tired of patting the dogs. I will
now turn to kicking them. I believe they will use me better then. If some sign-painter had only painted Nettleton
preaching up an awakening, and sent it about the country, he would have filled his pockets with it, and so would
Morse too. If I, instead of writing my present poetry, had
written a heavy blank-verse melody on justification by
faith alone (like Wilcox's Age of Benevolence, which went
off like shot), or if I had written a long, dirty, draggling
tale, I should have made my fortune. I should not have
been as I am now, a good deal worse than nothing. But
I must stop these complaints, and be a man. Let me
only mount my Rosinante, and then Richard's himself
again.

* * *

I imagine, if you can read this letter, you will be, by
this time, heartily tired of it. I assure you, I remember
our slight acquaintance with no little satisfaction. As for
my health, it is not to be spoken of. It is a good maxim
not to speak evil of the dead.

Yours respectfully,
JAMES G. PERCIVAL.

DOCUMENT 101

(PLATE 52)

The New Fashion in Heroes: Natty Bumppo

James Gates Percival's contempt for Cooper's work was not shared by his countrymen. Even polite magazines like the *Port Folio*, in which this earliest known picture of Cooper's hero appeared, had to maintain a deferential attitude toward the new literary fashion. This scene from *The Pioneers* honors one of the homeliest heroes ever to be received into the hearts of the American reading public, a hero physically unattractive, aging, uncouth in dress and often in speech. His chief appeal was to the American love for virtuous, manly conduct, of which his humble appearance and forest associations were recommendations rather than otherwise because affectation in dress and manner suggested a corrupt European aristocracy. Natty Bumppo was conceived as the archetypal new man of the West sprung from the virgin soil to bring about, somehow, the redemption of the effete Old World. Actually, however, Cooper's own sympathies were divided between Natty Bumppo and the civilized gentleman who faces him. Like so many Americans of his generation, Cooper faced in two different directions, unable to resolve his dilemma, the "complex fate" of being an American, moored between two worlds.

SOURCE: "Natty Bumppo's Farewell," a scene from *The Pioneers* in the *Port Folio*, Vol. XVII (1824). Photo by the Burns Studio.

DOCUMENT 102

(PLATE 53)

The New Fashion in Heroes: Daniel Boone

Daniel Boone and Davy Crockett were also popular
heroes of the new folklore. It is difficult to believe that
Cooper did not have Daniel Boone in mind when he
created Leatherstocking or that the picture of Natty
Bumppo was not influenced by Chester Harding's painting of Daniel Boone in 1819, the year before the
great pioneer's death at eighty-five. Both are depicted as
hunters, though Natty's dog and long rifle have been
relegated to the background (see doc. 101). Both followed similar life careers, both retiring before the advance of the civilization for which, ironically, they had
helped to blaze a trail. Both lived long, adventurous
lives, dying beyond the last outposts of settlement on the
edge of the prairies. Both, finally, found a greater bond
of friendship and trust among Indians than among
civilized Americans, who frequently betrayed them. In
the legend, however, Natty Bumppo would have nothing to do with the ownership of property. In fact, Daniel
Boone was a famous land speculator, most of his problems and many of his betrayals deriving from that
interest. Differences between fact and legend are quite
as significant cultural indices as similarities.

DOCUMENT 103

(PLATE 54)

An Old-fashioned Hero: George Washington

    It was not a matter of replacing one kind of national hero with another, for the old heroes of the American Revolution competed on at least equal terms with the new crop of heroes. One has only to mention the immense popularity in this period of William Wirt's biography of Patrick Henry or of Parson Weems' *George Washington*. The important difference is the change in style by which the heroes were rendered, seen in the difference between Stuart's painting of Washington here and Chester Harding's portrayal of Daniel Boone in the preceding document. And these are not isolated examples or matters of individual temperament in the artists merely, but manifestations of a cultural tendency. The new heroes are more rough-hewn and natural, particularly if they come from the West. Thomas Birch's painting of Stephen Decatur, for instance, is more traditional than the Samuel Waldo painting of Andrew Jackson. The new Western hero, forerunner of the cowboy hero in more recent times, *evoked a different response*. Of course, the background and training of the artist are not lacking in importance. Gilbert Stuart followed the London school; Chester Harding painted differently after he studied in London. But this, too, is very much a matter of culture.

DOCUMENT 104

The Old Order Passeth

James Gates Percival's distrust of cities echoed Jeffersonian agrarian fears. Toward the end of the period, as evidenced by the constitutional reforms extending the suffrage in New York, the urban proletariat was beginning to challenge patrician leadership by the landed gentry. In behalf of the landed interest Chancellor James Kent (1763–1847), whose *Commentaries on American Law* helped to separate the principles of American jurisprudence from those of Europe, spoke out in the New York Constitutional Convention of 1821 against the rising democratic tide.

His views combine a lament for a way of life that was passing with a criticism of the changes taking place, and apocalyptic fears (see again docs. 15–24) for the nation's future. "We stand," Kent said, "this moment, on the brink of fate, on the very edge of the precipice. If we let go our present hold . . . , we commit our proudest hopes and our most precious interests to the waves." He feared that the United States would go the way of wicked old Europe. His speech also once again reflects a rather common American emotional tendency to live from crisis to crisis.

SOURCE: *Reports of the Proceedings and Debates of the Convention of 1821*, edited by Nathaniel H. Carter, William L. Stone, and Marcus T. C. Gould, pp. 219–22. Albany: 1821.

I am in favor of the amendment which has been submitted by my honourable colleague from Albany; and I must beg leave to trespass for a few moments upon the patience of the committee, while I state the reasons which have induced me to wish, that the senate should continue, as heretofore, the representative of the landed interest, and exempted from the control of universal suffrage. I hope what I may have to say will be kindly received, for it will be well intended. But, if I thought otherwise, I should still prefer to hazard the loss of the little popularity which I might have in this house, or out of it, than to hazard the loss of the approbation of my own conscience.

I have reflected upon the report of the select committee with attention and with anxiety. We appear to be disregarding the principles of the constitution, under which we have so long and so happily lived, and to be changing some of its essential institutions. I cannot but think that the considerate men who have studied the history of republics, or are read in lessons of experience, must look with concern upon our apparent disposition to vibrate from a well balanced government, to the extremes of the democratic doctrines. Such a broad proposition as that contained in the report, at the distance of ten years past, would have struck the public mind with astonishment and terror. So rapid has been the career of our vibration.

Let us recall our attention, for a moment, to our past history.

This state has existed for forty-four years under our present constitution, which was formed by those illustrious sages and patriots who adorned the revolution. It has wonderfully fulfilled all the great ends of civil government. During that long period, we have enjoyed in an eminent degree, the blessings of civil and religious liberty. We have had our lives, our privileges, and our property, protected. We have had a succession of wise and temperate legislatures. The code of our statute law has been again and again revised and corrected, and it may proudly bear a comparison with that of any other people. We have had, during that period, (though I am, perhaps, not the fittest person to say it) a regular, stable, honest, and enlightened administration of justice. All the peaceable pursuits of industry, and all the important interests of education and science, have been fostered and encouraged. We have trebled our numbers within the last twenty-five years, have displayed mighty resources, and have made unexampled progress in the career of prosperity and greatness.

Our financial credit stands at an enviable height; and we are now successfully engaged in connecting the great lakes with the ocean by stupendous canals, which excite the admiration of our neighbours, and will make a conspicuous figure even upon the map of the United States.

These are some of the fruits of our present government; and yet we seem to be dissatisfied with our condition, and we are engaged in the bold and hazardous experiment of remoddelling the constitution. Is it not fit and discreet: I speak as to wise men; is it not fit and proper that we should pause in our career, and reflect well on the immensity of the innovation in contemplation? Discontent in the midst of so much prosperity, and with such abundant means of happiness, looks like ingratitude, and as if we were disposed to arraign the goodness of Providence. Do we not expose ourselves to the danger of being deprived of the blessings we have enjoyed?—When the husbandman has gathered in his harvest, and has filled his barns and his graneries with the fruits of his industry, if he should then become discontented and unthankful, would he not have reason to apprehend, that the Lord of the harvest might come in his wrath, and with his lightening destroy them?

The senate has hitherto been elected by the farmers of the state—by the free and independent lords of the soil, worth at least $250 in freehold estate, over and above all debts charged thereon. The governor has been chosen by the same electors, and we have hitherto elected citizens of elevated rank and character. Our assembly has been chosen by freeholders, possessing a freehold of the value of $50 or by persons renting a tenement of the yearly value of $5, and who have been rated and actually paid taxes to the state. By the report before us, we propose to annihilate, at one stroke, all those property distinctions and to bow before the idol of universal suffrage. That extreme democratic principle, when applied to the legislative and executive departments of government, has been regarded with terror, by the wise men of every age, because in every European republic, ancient and modern, in which it has been tried, it has terminated disastrously, and been productive of corruption, injustice, violence, and tyranny. And dare we flatter ourselves that we are a peculiar people, who can run the career of history, exempted from the passions which have disturbed and corrupted the rest of mankind? If we are like other races of men, with similar follies and vices, then I greatly fear that our posterity will have reason to deplore in sackcloth and ashes, the delusion of the day.

It is not my purpose at present to interfere with the report of the committee, so far as respects the qualifications of electors for governor and members of assembly. I shall feel grateful if we may be permitted to retain the stability and security of a senate, bottomed upon the freehold property of the state. Such a body, so constituted, may prove a sheet anchor amidst the future factions and storms of the republic. The great leading and governing interest of this state, is, at present, the agricultural; and what madness would it be to commit that interest to the winds. The great body of the people, are now the owners and actual cultivators of the soil. With that wholesome population we always expect to find moderation, frugality, order, honesty, and a due sense of independence, liberty, and justice. It is impossible that any people can lose their liberties by internal fraud or violence, so long as the country is parcelled out among freeholders of moderate possessions, and those freeholders have a sure and efficient control in the affairs of the government. Their habits, sympathies, and employments, necessarily inspire them with a correct spirit of freedom and justice; they are the safest guardians of property and the laws: We certainly cannot too highly appreciate the value of the agricultural interest: It is the foundation of national wealth and power. According to the opinion of her ablest political economists, it is the surplus produce of the agriculture of England, that enables her to support her vast body of manufacturers, her formidable fleets and armies, and the crowds of persons engaged in the liberal professions, and the cultivation of the various arts.

Now, sir, I wish to preserve our senate as the representative of the landed interest. I wish those who have an interest in the soil, to retain the exclusive possession of a branch in the legislature, as a strong hold in which they may find safety through all the vicissitudes which the state may be destined, in the course of Providence, to experience. I wish them to be always enabled to say that their freeholds cannot be taxed without their consent. The men of no property, together with the crowds of dependants connected with great manufacturing and commercial establishments, and the motley and undefinable population of crowded ports, may, perhaps, at some future day, under skilful management, predominate in the assembly, and yet we should be perfectly safe if no laws could pass without the free consent of the owners of the soil. That security we at present enjoy; and it is that security which I wish to retain.

The apprehended danger from the experiment of universal suffrage applied to the whole legislative department, is no dream of the imagination. It is too mighty an excitement for the moral constitution of men to endure. The tendency of universal suffrage, is to jeopardize the rights of property, and the principles of liberty. There is a constant tendency in human society, and the history of every age proves it; there is a tendency in the poor to covet and to share the plunder of the rich; in the debtor to relax or avoid the obligation of contracts; in the majority to tyranize over the minority, and trample down their rights; in the indolent and the profligate, to cast the whole burthens of society upon the industrious and the virtuous; and *there is a tendency in ambitious and wicked men, to inflame these combustible materials.* It requires a vigilant government, and a firm administration of justice, to counteract that tendency. Thou shalt not covet; thou shalt not steal; are divine injunctions induced by this miserable depravity of our nature. Who can undertake to calculate with any precision, how many millions of people, this great state will contain in the course of this and the next century, and who can estimate the future extent and magnitude of our commercial ports? The disproportion between the men of property, and the men of no property, will be in every society in a ratio to its commerce, wealth, and population. We are no longer to remain plain and simple republics of farmers, like the New-England colonists, or the Dutch settlements on the Hudson. We are fast becoming a great nation, with great commerce, manufactures, population, wealth, luxuries, and with the vices and miseries that they engender. One seventh of the population of the city of Paris at this day subsists on charity, and one third of the inhabitants of that city die in the hospitals; what would become of such a city with universal suffrage? France has upwards of four, and England upwards of five millions of manufacturing and commercial labourers without property. Could these kingdoms sustain the weight of universal suffrage? The radicals in England, with the force of that mighty engine, would at once sweep away the property, the laws, and the liberties of that island like a deluge.

The growth of the city of New-York is enough to startle and awaken those who are pursuing the *ignis fatuus* of universal suffrage.

In 1773 it had   21,000 souls.
    1806 „ „   76,000 do.
    1801 „ „   60,000 do.
    1820 „ „ 123,000 do.

It is rapidly swelling into the unwieldly population, and with the burdensome pauperism, of an European metropolis. New-York is destined to become the future London of America; and in less than a century, that city, with the operation of universal suffrage, and under skilful direction, will govern this state.

The notion that every man that works a day on the road, or serves an idle hour in the militia, is entitled as of right to an equal participation in the whole power of the government, is most unreasonable, and has no foundation in justice. We had better at once discard from the report such a nominal test of merit. If such persons have an equal share in one branch of the legislature, it is surely as much as they can in justice or policy demand. Society is an association for the protection of property as well as of life, and the individual who contributes only one cent to the common stock, ought not to have the same power and influence in directing the property concerns of the partnership, as he who contributes his thousands. He will not have the same inducements to care, and diligence, and fidelity. His inducements and his temptation would be to divide the whole capital upon the principles of an agrarian law.

Liberty, rightly understood, is an inestimable blessing, but liberty without wisdom, and without justice, is no better than wild and savage licentiousness. The danger which we have hereafter to apprehend, is not the want, but the abuse, of liberty. We have to apprehend the oppression of minorities, and a disposition to encroach on private right—to disturb chartered privileges and to weaken, degrade, and overawe the administration of justice; we have to apprehend the establishment of unequal, and consequently, unjust systems of taxation, and all the mischiefs of a crude and mutable legislation. A stable senate, exempted from the influence of universal suffrage, will powerfully check these dangerous propensities, and such a check becomes the more necessary, since this Convention has already determined to withdraw the watchful eye of the judicial department from the passage of laws.

We are destined to become a great manufacturing as well as commercial state. We have already numerous and prosperous factories of one kind or another, and one master capitalist with his one hundred apprentices, and journeymen, and agents, and dependents, will bear down at the polls, an equal number of farmers of small estates in his vicinity, who cannot safely unite for their common defence. Large manufacturing and mechanical

establishments, can act in an instant with the unity and
efficacy of disciplined troops. It is against such combinations, among others, that I think we ought to give to
the freeholders, or those who have interest in land, one
branch of the legislature for their asylum and their comfort. Universal suffrage once granted, is granted forever,
and never can be recalled. There is no retrograde step
in the rear of democracy. However mischievous the precedent may be in its consequences, or however fatal in
its effects, universal suffrage never can be recalled or
checked, but by the strength of the bayonet. We stand,
therefore, this moment, on the brink of fate, on the very
edge of the precipice. If we let go our present hold on the
senate, we commit our proudest hopes and our most
precious interests to the waves.

It ought further to be observed, that the senate is a
court of justice in the last resort. It is the last depository
of public and private rights; of civil and criminal justice.
This gives the subject an awful consideration, and wonderfully increases the importance of securing that house from
the inroads of universal suffrage. Our country freeholders
are exclusively our jurors in the administration of justice,
and there is equal reason that none but those who have
an interest in the soil, should have any concern in the
composition of that court. As long as the senate is safe,
justice is safe, property is safe, and our liberties are
safe. But when the wisdom, the integrity, and the independence of that court is lost, we may be certain that
the freedom and happiness of this state, are fled forever.

I hope, sir, we shall not carry desolation through all
the departments of the fabric erected by our fathers. I
hope we shall not put forward to the world a new constitution, as will meet with the scorn of the wise, and the
tears of the patriot.

A Valedictory

Thomas Jefferson shared Chancellor Kent's fears, except that he believed that dominance by the Northern manufacturing aristocracy posed a greater threat than the urban proletariat, and he proposed States' Rights as a barrier to unwanted change instead of a limitation of the suffrage. His imagery is interesting, because the word "aristocracy" associates the new manufacturing elite with the invasion of America by European privilege. In his public statements, Jefferson was more cautious. In 1805, he had held that his animus against manufacturing was meant to apply "only to the great cities of Europe and not to this country," where American manufacturers were "as much at their ease, as independent and moral as our agricultural inhabitants." In 1817, he had capitulated, publicly at least, to moral American manufacturing by accepting honorary membership in the American Society for the Encouragement of Domestic Manufactures.

The divergence between his public and his private views again illustrates a split in the American psyche with the coming of the Industrial Revolution. Jefferson continued, however, to think of education as being, in the long run, the main cure for America's ills. He died several months after this letter was written.

SOURCE: *The Works of Thomas Jefferson*, edited by Paul Leicester Ford, Vol. XII, pp. 424–28. New York: 1904–5.

To William B. Giles

Monticello, December 26, 1825.
Dear Sir,— I wrote you a letter yesterday, of which you will be free to make what use you please. This will contain matters not intended for the public eye. I see, as

you do, and with the deepest affliction, the rapid strides with which the federal branch of our government is advancing towards the usurpation of all the rights reserved to the States, and the consolidation in itself of all powers, foreign and domestic; and that, too, by constructions which, if legitimate, leave no limits to their power. Take together the decisions of the federal court, the doctrines of the President, and the misconstructions of the constitutional compact acted on by the legislature of the federal branch, and it is but too evident, that the three ruling branches of that department are in combination to strip their colleagues, the State authorities, of the powers reserved by them, and to exercise themselves all functions foreign and domestic. Under the power to regulate commerce, they assume indefinitely that also over agriculture and manufactures, and call it regulation to take the earnings of one of these branches of industry, and that too the most depressed, and put them into the pockets of the other, the most flourishing of all. Under the authority to establish post roads, they claim that of cutting down mountains for the construction of roads, of digging canals, and aided by a little sophistry on the words "general welfare," a right to do, not only the acts to effect that, which are specifically enumerated and permitted, but whatsoever they shall think, or pretend will be for the general welfare. And what is our resource for the preservation of the constitution? Reason and argument? You might as well reason and argue with the marble columns encircling them. The representatives chosen by ourselves? They are joined in the combination, some from incorrect views of government, some from corrupt ones, sufficient voting together to out-number the sound parts; and with majorities only of one, two, or three, bold enough to go forward in defiance. Are we then *to stand to our arms,* with the hot-headed Georgian? No. That must be the last resource, not to be thought of until much longer and greater sufferings. If every infraction of a compact of so many parties is to be resisted at once, as a dissolution of it, none can ever be formed which would last one year. We must have patience and longer endurance then with our brethren while under delusion; give them time for reflection and experience of consequences; keep ourselves in a situation to profit by the chapter of accidents; and separate from our companions only when the sole alternatives left, are the dissolution of our Union with them, or submission to a government without limitation of powers. Between these two evils, when we must make a choice, there can be no hesitation. But in the meanwhile, the States should be watchful to note every material usurpation on their rights; to denounce them as they occur in the most peremptory terms; to protest against them as wrongs to which our present submission shall be considered, not as acknowledgments or precedents of right, but as a temporary yielding to the lesser evil, until their accumulation shall overweigh that of separation. I would go still further, and give to the federal member, by a regular amendment of the constitution, a right to make roads and canals of intercommunication between the States, providing sufficiently against corrupt practices in Congress, (log-rolling, &c.,) by declaring that the federal proportion of each State of the moneys so employed, shall be in works within the State, or elsewhere with its consent, and with a due *salvo* of jurisdiction. This is the course which I think safest and best as yet.

You ask my opinion of the propriety of giving publicity to what is stated in your letter, as having passed between Mr. John Q. Adams and yourself. Of this no one can judge but yourself. It is one of those questions which belong to the forum of feeling. This alone can decide on the degree of confidence implied in the disclosure; whether under no circumstances it was to be communicated to others? It does not seem to be of that character, or at all to wear that aspect. They are historical facts which belong to the present, as well as future times. I doubt whether a single fact, known to the world, will carry as clear conviction to it, of the correctness of our knowledge of the treasonable views of the federal party of that day, as that disclosed by this, the most nefarious and daring attempt to dissever the Union, of which the Hartford convention was a subsequent chapter; and both of these having failed, consolidation becomes the fourth chapter of the next book of their history. But this opens with a vast accession of strength from their younger recruits, who, having nothing in them of the feelings or principles of '76, now look to a single and splendid government of an aristocracy, founded on banking institutions, and moneyed incorporations under the guise and cloak of their favored branches of manufactures, commerce and navigation, riding and ruling over the plundered ploughman and beggared yeomanry. This will be to them a next best blessing to the monarchy of their first aim, and perhaps the surest stepping-stone to it.

I learn with great satisfaction that your school is thriving well, and that you have at its head a truly classical scholar. He is one of three or four whom I can hear of in the State. We were obliged the last year to receive shameful Latinists into the classical school of the University, such as we will certainly refuse as soon as we can get from better schools a sufficiency of those properly instructed to form a class. We must get rid of this Connecticut Latin, of this barbarous confusion of long and short syllables, which renders doubtful whether we are listening to a reader of Cherokee, Shawnee, Iroquois, or what. Our University has been most fortunate in the five professors procured from England. A finer selection could not have been made. Besides their being of a grade of science which has left little superior behind, the correctness of their moral character, their accommodating dispositions, and zeal for the prosperity of the institution, leave us nothing more to wish. I verily believe that as high a degree of education can now be obtained here, as in the country they left. And a finer set of youths I never saw assembled for instruction. They committed some irregularities at first, until they learned the lawful length of their tether; since which it has never been transgressed in the smallest degree. A great proportion of them are severely devoted to study, and I fear not to say that within twelve or fifteen years from this time, a majority of the rulers of our State will have been educated here. They shall carry hence the correct principles of our day, and you may count assuredly that they will exhibit their country in a degree of sound respectability it has never known, either in our days, or those of our fore-fathers. I cannot live to see it. My joy must only be that of anticipation. But that you may see it in full fruition, is the probable consequence of the twenty years I am ahead of you in time, and is the sincere prayer of your affectionate and constant friend.

Document 106

"Woodman, Spare that Tree!"

Some of America's most nostalgic songs and traditions originated in the same period as the steamboat and the factory system. Small children became the sentimental center of the annual Christmas celebration, for which Clement Moore wrote "The Visit of Saint Nicholas." Old-fashioned family life was wistfully evoked in John Howard Payne's "Home Sweet Home," while the passing of the wilderness was lamented in two popular songs, Samuel Woodworth's "The Old Oaken Bucket" and George Morris' "Woodman, Spare that Tree." These musical evocations of the rural past reinforced the mood created by such literary images as Cooper's reconstruction of pioneering life or Irving's tale of Rip Van Winkle (see doc. 107) and by such visual images as the landscapes of Thomas Cole (doc. 62) and Joshua Shaw (doc. 63). Thus, too, images of an idyllic old-time plantation life began to arise, long before the acrimonies which led to the Civil War (doc. 73).

A common theme in all this, as in the conflict of styles and traditions, was the search for a *bridge* between the old and the new (see again docs. 93–103). The following song is introduced by its author, the poet and journalist, George P. Morris (1802–64).

SOURCE: Helen Kendrick Johnson, *Our Familiar Songs and Those Who Made Them*, pp. 25–28. New York: 1881.

Riding out of town a few days since, in company with a friend, who was once the expectant heir of the largest estate in America, but over whose worldly prospects a blight has recently come, he invited me to turn down a little romantic woodland pass, not far from Bloomingdale. "Your object?" inquired I. "Merely to look once more at an old tree planted by my grandfather, near a cottage that was once my father's." "The place is yours, then?" said I. "No, my poor mother sold it,"—and I observed a slight quiver of the lip, at the recollection. "Dear mother!" resumed my companion, "we passed many, many happy days in that old cottage; but it is nothing to me now. Father, mother, sisters, cottage—all are gone!" After a moment's pause he added, "Don't think me foolish. I don't know how it is, I never ride out but I turn down this lane to look at that old tree. I have a thousand recollections about it, and I always greet it as a familiar and well-remembered friend. In the by-gone summer-time it was a friend indeed. Its leaves are all off now, so you won't see it to advantage, for it is a glorious old fellow in summer, but I like it full as well in winter-time." These words were scarcely uttered, when my companion cried out, "There it is!" Near the tree stood an old man, with his coat off, sharpening an axe. He was the occupant of the cottage. "What do you intend doing?" asked my friend, in great anxiety. "What is that to you?" was the blunt reply. "You are not going to cut that tree down, surely?" "Yes, I am, though," said the woodman. "What for?" inquired my companion, almost choked with emotion. "What for? Why, because I think proper to do so. What for? I like that! Well, I'll tell you what for. This tree makes my dwelling unhealthy; it stands too near the house. It renders us liable to fever-and-ague." "Who told you that?" "Dr. S——." "Have you any other reason for wishing it cut down?" "Yes,—I am getting old; the woods are a great way off, and this tree is of some value to me to burn." He was soon convinced, however, that the story about the fever-and-ague was a mere fiction, for there had never been a case of that disease in the neighborhood; and was then asked what the tree was worth for firewood. "Why, when it's down, about ten dollars." "Suppose I make you a present of that amount, will you let it stand?" "Yes." "You are sure of that?" "Positive." "Then give me a bond to that effect." I drew it up, it was witnessed by his daughter, the money was paid, and we left the place with an assurance from the young girl, who looked as smiling and beautiful as a Hebe, that the tree should stand as long as she lived.

Woodman, *Spare that Tree*
Written by George P. Morris, Music by Henry Russell

2ND VERSE

2. That old fa-mil - iar tree,____ Whose glo - ry and_ re - nown, Are spread o'er land and sea,____ And_ wouldst thou hew it down?

con anima

Wood-man, for-bear thy_ stroke!___ Cut

not its earth-bound ties Oh,

spare that a - ged oak,_____ Now_

tow'r ing to the_ skies.

3RD VERSE

3. When but an i - dle boy___ I sought its grate - ful___ shade; In all their gush - ing joy,_____ Here,___ too, my sis - ters played; My mo - ther kissed me__ here;___ My fa - ther pressed my hand, For - give this fool - ish tear,_____ But__ let that old oak___ stand.

4TH VERSE

4. My heart-strings round thee cling,___ Close as thy bark, old__ friend!

Here shall the wild-bird sing, ____ And_
still thy branch - es bend.
Old tree the storm_ shall_ brave, ____ And
wood-man, leave the spot; While
I've a hand_ to save, _____ Thy_
axe shall harm ____ it not.

DOCUMENT 107

(PLATE 55)

The Return of Rip Van Winkle

The retrospective, nostalgic mood of an age of rapid change, one which yearned to return to nature and antiquity, is well conveyed by John Quidor's painting of Rip Van Winkle. Quidor (1801–81) was one of the few people represented in this volume born after 1800. His imagination was well furnished with images to endow the bewilderment of Rip Van Winkle with a vivid, grotesque, traumatic sense of reality as the robust old man tries to orient himself amidst suspicious, hostile strangers in a setting that is strangely familiar yet different. "The technique employed," Daniel Mendelowitz writes in his recent *History of American Art,* "is a painterly one, not the dry and precise style of the engraver or the popular illustrator of the day. Developed by underpainting and glazing, the forms swell up out of a luminous, golden, all-enveloping chiaroscuro. The paint, applied freely and zestfully, infuses the spaces and forms with a baroque animation. The figures move with a diabolic energy far beyond the gentle legends that inspired them."

Comedy and Tragedy

Another robust treatment of the period's sharp contrasts was William Rush's allegorical development of comedy and tragedy, personified with a sprightliness and grace few Americans could emulate. He has not allowed the realistic details of the gowns to obscure the full-bodied forms underneath, which declare themselves not only in feminine sensuality and gesture, but also in vigorous S-curves which rise to beautifully modeled heads. The two figures are counterbalanced by opposing movements of right arm and left arm raised, one holding the mirror of fickle vanity, the other the urn of sorrow's ashes. A similar opposing movement is seen in the positions of the legs. William Rush (1756–1833), a self-taught woodcarver who became the period's most accomplished artist in any medium, was able to bridge the distance between the unself-conscious folk art of the vernacular tradition and the more sophisticated concern of traditional art with the formal problems of sculpture and the human values of personality and character.

Suggested Readings

One of the most useful recent bibliographical guides and the only one which stresses an interdisciplinary approach is Roy P. Basler, *et al.*, *A Guide to the Study of the United States of America: Representative Books Reflecting the Development of American Life and Thought* (Washington: Library of Congress, 1960). For the general reader who wishes to know more about the period 1810–24, an excellent guide is the bibliographical essay in Marcus Cunliffe, *The Nation Takes Shape, 1789–1837* (Chicago: University of Chicago Press, 1959), a brief history which focuses on the emergence of a national character. Other valuable, more detailed histories of the period include Henry Adams, *The Formative Years: A History of the United States During the Administration of Jefferson and Madison,* condensed and edited by Herbert Agar, 2 vols. (Boston: Houghton Mifflin Company, 1947), and the standard modern interpretation by George Dangerfield, *The Era of Good Feelings* (New York: Harcourt, Brace & Company, 1952).

The editor was greatly influenced in his selection and interpretation of documents for this book by two wide-ranging cultural studies: John A. Kouwenhoven, *Made in America: the Arts in Modern Civilization* (Garden City, N.Y.: Doubleday & Company, 1948) and his own *The Quest for Paradise: Europe and the American Moral Imagination* (Urbana: University of Illinois Press, 1961). The latter should be supplemented by Henry Nash Smith, *Virgin Land: The American West as Symbol and Myth* (Cambridge: Harvard University Press, 1950). Also useful for its social and cultural history of the period was Van Wyck Brooks, *The World of Washington Irving*

(New York: E. P. Dutton & Company, 1944). For intellectual history, the editor relied heavily on Merle Curti, *The Growth of American Thought*, second edition (New York: Harper & Brothers, 1951), and Ralph H. Gabriel, *The Course of American Democratic Thought* (New York: Ronald Press, 1940).

It would have been difficult indeed to collect the documents for this volume without the help of a large number of specialized monographic studies of the period, ranging from such subjects as pewter and china to sports. Most of these can be located above in the Basler *Guide*. Among the more valuable to the editor which should be mentioned here were René Brimo, *L'évolution du Goût aux Etats-Unis D'après L'histoire des Collections* (Paris, 1938); William Charvat, *The Origins of American Critical Thought, 1810–1835* (Philadelphia: University of Pennsylvania Press, 1936); Carl W. Condit, *American Building Art; the Nineteenth Century* (New York: Oxford University Press, 1960); John P. Coolidge, *Mill and Mansion, A Study of Architecture and Society in Lowell, Massachusetts, 1820–1865* (New York: Columbia University Press, 1942); James T. Flexner, *American Painting: The Light of Distant Skies, 1760–1835* (New York: Harcourt, Brace & Company, 1954); Louis C. and B. J. Hunter, *Steamboats on the Western Rivers: An Economic and Technological History* (Cambridge: Harvard University Press, 1949); Benjamin T. Spencer, *The Quest for Nationality: An American Literary Campaign* (Syracuse, N.Y.: Syracuse University Press, 1957); and George Rogers Taylor, *The Transportation Revolution, 1815–1860* (New York: Rinehart & Company, 1951).

The full story of the impact of the Industrial Revolution on American life has yet to be written. One of the more useful contributions on the period under study is Jeannette Mirsky and Allan Nevins, *The World of Eli Whitney* (New York: The Macmillan Company, 1952).

Anxieties and tensions of early industrial consciousness are the special subject of Samuel Rezneck, "The Rise and Early Development of Industrial Consciousness in the United States, 1760–1830," *Journal of Economic and Business History*, Vol. IV, pp. 784–811 (1932); the editor's own "The Intellectual Origins and New-Worldliness of American Industry," *The Journal of Economic History*, Vol. XVIII, pp. 1–16 (1958); Leo Marx, "Two Kingdoms of Force," *The Massachusetts Review*, Vol. I, pp. 62–95 (1959); and Marvin Fisher, "The Iconology of Industrialism, 1830–60," *American Quarterly*, Vol. XIII, pp. 347–64 (1961).

A classic treatment of western expansion in the period is Frederick Jackson Turner, *Rise of the New West, 1819–1829* (New York: Harper & Brothers, 1906). Developments in foreign policy are ably reviewed in Samuel Flagg Bemis, *John Quincy Adams and the Foundations of American Foreign Policy* (New York: Alfred A. Knopf, 1949). An interesting recent addition to the period literature on sectionalism is P. J. Staudenraus, *The African Colonization Movement, 1816–1865* (New York: Columbia University Press, 1961). Finally, one should mention foreign views of the United States, for nowhere else can one find the strange mélange of factual observation, oddities, intuitions, and hunches which help to define national character. One of the best critical reviews of such literature for this period, now so little known that it deserves reprinting, is Henry T. Tuckerman, *America and Her Commentators: With a Critical Sketch of Travel in the United States* (New York: Charles Scribner, 1864).

One hesitates to include a printed collection of pictures as a secondary source, but since the originals and the museums or libraries in which they are usually found are not always available, the reader is referred to James Truslow Adams, *et al.*, eds., *Album of American History*, Vol. II (New York: Charles Scribner's Sons, 1945), and to Marshall B. Davidson, *Life in America*, Vol. I (Boston: Houghton Mifflin Company, 1951), both giving a comprehensive visual record of the period. An extensive visual survey based on a collection of color slides assembled by the University of Georgia under a Carnegie grant can be found in William H. Pierson, Jr., and Martha Davidson, eds., *Arts of the United States, A Pictorial Survey* (New York: McGraw-Hill Book Company, 1960).